IMMIGRANTS AGAINST THE STATE

THE WORKING CLASS
IN AMERICAN HISTORY

Editorial Advisors
James R. Barrett, Julie Greene,
William P. Jones, Alice Kessler-Harris,
and Nelson Lichtenstein

*A list of books in the series appears
at the end of this book.*

KENYON ZIMMER

IMMIGRANTS AGAINST THE STATE

YIDDISH AND ITALIAN ANARCHISM IN AMERICA

UNIVERSITY OF ILLINOIS PRESS
Urbana, Chicago, and Springfield

Publication of this book was supported by a grant
from the University of Texas at Arlington.

Library of Congress Control Number: 2015940460

ISBN 978-0-252-03938-6 (hardcover : alk. paper)
ISBN 978-0-252-08092-0 (paperback : alk. paper)
ISBN 978-0-252-09743-0 (e-book)

CONTENTS

ILLUSTRATIONS

Figures

Table

ACKNOWLEDGMENTS

I have been privileged to work with a number of mentors who taught me how to be a writer, scholar, and historian. I am forever in the debt of the late Steven Bach, Ron Cohen, Alejandro de la Fuente, Mark Ferrari, Derek Hutchinson, Jim and Suzanne Jennings, Barry Pateman, David Philips, Miroslava Prazak, Lara Putnam, the late Beth Ryan, Eileen Scully, Carol Symes, Bruce Venarde, and Paul Voice, among others. Donna Gabaccia, Patrick Manning, Richard Oestreicher, and Marcus Rediker deserve special mention for having faith in this project from the beginning.

I also enjoyed the support and camaraderie of my peers at the University of Pittsburgh, including Tania Boster, Roland Clark, Isaac Curtis, Niklas Frykman, Scott Giltner, Bayete Henderson, Mike McCoy, and Lars Peterson. Outside of academia, I discovered a welcoming community of like-minded friends at the Big Idea Bookstore and the Pittsburgh Organizing Group. My colleagues at the University of Texas at Arlington have been generous and supportive, especially Stephanie Cole, Marvin Dulaney, Bob Fairbanks, John Garrigus, and Sarah Rose. Laurie Matheson at the University of Illinois Press has long been a believer in this book.

The research for this project would not have been possible without the aid of the personnel at the various libraries and archives I have frequented. Above all, the interlibrary loan departments at the University of Pittsburgh's Hillman Library and the University of Texas at Arlington Libraries deserve praise for their hard work. In addition, I thank the staff at the Archives of Labor and Urban Affairs at Wayne State University; the Archivio Centrale dello Stato in Rome; the Immigration History Research Center at the University of Minnesota, Minneapolis; the Tamiment Library and Robert F. Wagner Labor Archives at New York University; the YIVO Institute for Jewish Research; the Emma Goldman Papers at the University of California at Berkeley; the American Labor Museum in Haledon, New Jersey; the incomparable International Institute of Social History in Amsterdam; the Joseph A. Labadie Collection at the University of Michigan, Ann Arbor (especially Julie Herrada and the other friendly folks); and the Kate Sharpley Library (where Barry Pateman and Jessica Moran were exceptionally generous and helpful). I also thank Thomas Lang, who tracked me down after discovering my dissertation and shared the invaluable unpublished memoir of his great-aunt, Russia Hughes.

The research for this book was made possible by the financial support of numerous institutions. The University of Pittsburgh kindly funded my research with a C. Y. Hsu Summer Research Fellowship, an Arts and Sciences Summer Fellowship, an Andrew Mellon Predoctoral Fellowship, a Samuel P. Hays Summer Research Grant, and a Lillian B. Lawler Predoctoral Fellowship. I am grateful for special dispensations from the World History Center and Professor Alberta Sbragia of the European Union Center of Excellence and European Studies Center. I also received a grant-in-aid from the Immigration History Research Center and generous startup funds from the Department of History and College of Liberal Arts at the University of Texas at Arlington.

Scholars who generously shared their time, thoughts, sources, and research with me included Bert Altena, Constance Bantman, Marcella Bencivenni, Olivia Cummings, Candace Falk, Mario Gianfrate, Tom Goyens, Bob Helms, Steven Hirsch, Andrew Hoyt, Carl Levy, Michele Presutto, Salvatore Salerno, Kirk Shaffer, David Struthers, Travis Tomchuk, Michael Miller Topp, Davide Turcato, and Anna Torres. Fraser Ottanelli and Davide Turcato commented on chapter drafts, and Jennifer Guglielmo, Barry Pateman, and an anonymous reviewer gave invaluable feedback after reading the entire manuscript. Any errors in the final product are entirely my own.

Nunzio Pernicone, who passed away before this book was completed, also generously commented on the manuscript and shared important sources and insights with me. Audrey Goodfriend, a spirited and generous ninety-one-year-old when I interviewed her at her Berkeley home in 2011, also did not live to see the finished product. This book is dedicated to their memories.

NOTE ON TRANSLITERATION

Transliterations from Yiddish follow YIVO guidelines except in the case of personal names that are included in the catalogs of the Library of Congress and the Yiddish Book Center, which are rendered in the more familiar forms that appear in those records. I have also taken the liberty of capitalizing the titles of foreign-language periodicals according to English practices.

IMMIGRANTS AGAINST THE STATE

INTRODUCTION

In the second half of the nineteenth century, an international revolutionary anarchist movement emerged in opposition to the global expansion of capitalist modes of production, imperialism, and the rise of the modern nation-state. Fusing anticapitalism with antistatism, anarchists rejected nation-states as legitimate sociopolitical units, acceptable guarantors of rights, or viable vehicles for achieving freedom and equality. They instead envisioned a borderless world composed of voluntarily constituted communities, federated regionally and globally, with economies based on libertarian socialist principles.[1] Anarchism was the principal ideology of global radicalism between the collapse of the International Working Men's Association (the First International) in the 1870s and the consolidation of the Communist International, or Comintern (the Third International) in the 1920s. In 1902, an American journalist estimated that anarchism's adherents worldwide totaled one million, and in most parts of the world, those numbers did not peak until the 1910s, 1920s, or 1930s.[2]

In the United States, anarchists outnumbered their Marxist rivals for a much briefer period around the mid-1880s, but their movement nevertheless grew through the first decade of the twentieth century and remained a significant—though largely forgotten—element of the American Left up to the Second World War. American anarchists numbered in the tens of thousands throughout this period, peaking around 1910 at probably more than a hundred thousand. The vast majority of these radicals were immigrants, inextricably linking anarchism and immigration in the American experience and popular imagination.

However, anarchism was not merely a foreign import brought across the Atlantic by unwashed foreigners. In fact, only a small handful of avowed anarchist exiles and labor migrants carried these doctrines with them from Europe. The majority of foreign-born anarchists were not yet anarchists when they arrived in America, a group that included such well-known figures as Alexander Berkman, Emma Goldman, Nicola Sacco, and Bartolomeo Vanzetti. As Berkman put it, "America gave me my second education, the real, rational education of the proletariat, acquired in life, in sorrow and in battle." That education led him to embrace anarchist ideals.[3] The convergence of these two groups—itinerant revolutionaries and immigrant workers—propagated anarchism on U.S. soil. In other words, American conditions rather than European ones produced America's anarchist movement. Furthermore, anarchists' status as immigrants does not indicate that they were peripheral to American labor and political history. To the contrary, by 1880 immigrants and their children comprised the majority of the American industrial working class, and by 1907, foreign-born workers alone accounted for more than half of all employees in mining and manufacturing.[4] And from among such workers, the engine of American industrial capitalism, anarchism drew most of its adherents. By 1910, Italian and Eastern European Jewish immigrants constituted both the largest two groups of foreign-born workers in the United States and the largest two segments of America's anarchist movement.

Immigrants against the State explores the history of anarchism from the perspective of migration history. Utilizing sources in half a dozen languages and from archives on both sides of the Atlantic, it traces the transnational origins and local development of Yiddish and Italian anarchism in America. Two questions are central to this enterprise: How and why did thousands of immigrants become anarchists? And how did their adoption of an anticapitalist, antistatist, anticlerical, and cosmopolitan ideology shape their identities, experiences, and actions in their new home?

This book is, to borrow a phrase from Robin D. G. Kelley, "a social history of politics," focusing on "the worlds from which these radicals came, the worlds in which they lived, and the imaginary worlds they sought to build."[5] As a study of a mobile group of revolutionaries belonging to a global movement, it is also necessarily a transnational history. People, ideas, literature, institutions, and assets entered, traversed, and exited the United States along the myriad connections of anarchists' expanding informal networks. Anarchism was a movement *in* movement. It was also a movement *of* movements, worldwide in scale but composed of overlapping groups and networks loosely demarcated by characteristics such as location, language, and nationality. I therefore alternate between referring to linguistically defined Italian and Yiddish anarchist movements; the geographically defined American, Italian, and Russian anarchist movements with which the Italian- and Yiddish-speaking movements overlapped; and the global anarchist movement of which all were constituent parts. To capture both the local and transnational dynamics of these movements' networks, I anchor my study in three major nodes within anarchism's larger circuits: New York City's Lower East Side; the Italian district of Paterson, New Jersey; and San Francisco's North Beach neighborhood. But I also trace the linkages between these "nodal cities" as well as their connections to other sites of struggle throughout the globe.[6] The result is not a comparative history of Jews and Italians or of anarchism in three cities but an entangled and interethnic history of mutual influences and multilateral connections within specific local contexts. As Kirwin R. Shaffer notes, "Ultimately, one can best understand local and national anarchist organizations by understanding their transnational infusions and vice versa," as activists "constantly adopted global anarchist ideas and adapted them to fit national and subnational realities."[7]

The consolidation of a large-scale, self-avowed anarchist movement in America can be traced to the creation of the International Working People's Association (IWPA) at a congress of "social revolutionaries" (most of them former socialists disillusioned with electoral activity) held in Pittsburgh in 1883. The IWPA's program called for "destruction of the existing class rule, by all means, i.e., by energetic, relentless, revolutionary and international action," and for "establishment of a free society based upon co-operative organization of production" as well as "equal rights for all without distinction of sex or race." Most of the organization's members were Germans, followed by Czech, Scandinavian, and British immigrants; native-born Americans; and a smattering of other nationalities. In 1886, the IWPA's membership reached five thousand, three times that of its main rival on the left, the Socialist Labor Party (SLP).[8] That year, many of its members took part in the nationwide campaign on behalf of the eight-hour workday that culminated in strikes across the country on May 1. Three days later, at a small anarchist-organized rally just off of Chicago's Haymarket Square to protest the killing of locked-out workers by police, an unknown assailant (likely affiliated with the anarchist movement) hurled a homemade bomb at officers attempting to disperse the meeting. The explosion and ensuing gunfire from panicked police—and, according to some sources, members of the crowd—cost the lives of eight policemen and several protesters. At a subsequent trial, eight IWPA members were tried and convicted, on highly suspect evidence, of conspiring with the unknown bomber to commit murder. Four were executed on November 11, 1887, one cheated the gallows by committing suicide in his cell, and three received lengthy prison sentences but were pardoned in 1893.[9]

The executions, however, marked a new beginning for American anarchism rather than its end; as Paul and Karen Avrich note, "By giving the anarchists their first martyrs, the Haymarket executions stimulated the growth of the movement, especially among recently arrived immigrants who were finding their new country indifferent and the authorities undependable."[10] Although the IWPA was decimated in Chicago, elsewhere the organization survived well into the

1890s, while the number of anarchists nationwide grew. Anarchism would be the dominant radical ideology among Jewish immigrants until the mid-1890s, among ethnic Russian and Asian immigrants until the 1920s, and among Spanish, Mexican, and Italian immigrants into the 1930s.

The precise number of anarchists is notoriously difficult to calculate. They did not belong to a political party that issued membership cards or produced election tallies, and few anarchist organizations charged dues or kept rosters. In the absence of such information, the circulation figures for anarchist periodicals provide the best available guide for gauging the size of the movement, including both activists and passive sympathizers, at any given time. It would be difficult to overstate the functional importance of newspapers in the anarchist movement. The printed word created a transnational community of anarchists and transmitted the movement's ideology across space while sustaining collective identities across time. Affiliation with the movement and with particular factions within it often rested on attachments to specific periodicals rather than formal organizations.

Figure 1 shows the combined circulations of all anarchist periodicals published in the United States between 1880 and 1940 for which I have located circulation data, excluding ephemeral publications that survived fewer than four issues. This data must be used cautiously: not all anarchists subscribed to a periodical, while others subscribed to multiple titles; some nonanarchists subscribed to these publications; individual copies were often read by or to multiple individuals; many copies were sent to subscribers abroad; and many readers in the United States in turn subscribed to publications produced overseas. Furthermore, I have found circulation figures for only about a third of all anarchist titles from the period (80 of the 235 I have identified), meaning that the totals shown for any one year are lower than the actual number of copies by a margin of at least several thousand. Nevertheless, nearly all of those publications for which no data exist were small affairs with circulations that probably did not exceed between one and two thousand copies. More important, the data in figure 1 correspond closely with most contemporary and scholarly estimates of the size of the anarchist movement in these years.[11]

However imperfect these numbers may be, they clearly indicate a steady expansion of the movement up to about 1910, followed by a severe decline as a consequence of the collapse of anarchism's German-speaking wing and political repression during and after the First World War. Surprisingly, given that most studies of American anarchism close by 1919, figure 1 also indicates the stabilization and incremental regrowth of the movement between 1920 and 1938. Breaking down this data by language reveals further important details, as shown in figure 2. The Yiddish-speaking anarchist movement was significantly larger than its Italian counterpart from the turn of the century until the First

FIGURE 1. Combined Circulations of American Anarchist Periodicals, 1880–1940.

World War, but the Italian movement flourished in the 1920s and early 1930s. If these figures accurately reflect the number of Italian and Jewish anarchists in the country—and available information for the Italian case indicates that they do—then these groups numbered between twenty and thirty thousand at their respective peaks.[12] Anarchism was therefore not a miniscule sect but a substantial minority political movement within America's largest immigrant communities.

Anarchists were unique among their fellow immigrants in many respects, including their disavowal of attachments to any nation-state. They rejected the political systems of both the United States and their countries of origin, thwarting nationalist projects on both sides of the Atlantic. Geoffrey Ostergaard notes,

> The central negative thrust of anarchism is directed against all the core elements that make up the nation-state: its territoriality with the accompanying notion of frontiers; its sovereignty, implying exclusive jurisdiction over all people and property within those frontiers; its monopolistic control of the major means of physical force by which it upholds that sovereignty, both internally and externally; its system of positive law, which overrides all other law and custom and which implies that rights exist only if sanctioned by the state; and finally—the element that was added last—the idea of the nation as the paramount political community.[13]

This viewpoint had far-reaching consequences for anarchists' relationships with the American government as well as with members of other ethnoracial groups.

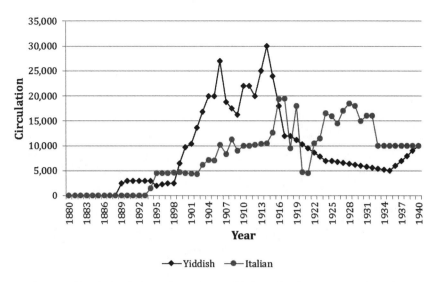

FIGURE 2. Combined Circulations of American Yiddish- and Italian-Language Anarchist Periodicals, 1880–1940.

Anarchist ideology emerged alongside modern nationalist ideologies that called for the creation, preservation, or expansion of independent political states representing allegedly primordial "nations" of people. Exiled Russian radical Mikhail Bakunin, Karl Marx's rival within the First International and in many ways the founding father of the international anarchist movement, honed his critique of nationalism against both the liberal nationalism of the Italian Giuseppe Mazzini, who envisioned an international brotherhood of democratic republics in which every "nation" would have its own state, and the "Prussian despotism" of German imperialism.[14] Bakunin, a former pan-Slavic nationalist, provided the foundation for subsequent anarchist discourses on the topic. For him, rejection of nationalism ("political patriotism") did not mean renouncing affection for the land of one's birth ("the Fatherland"): "The State is not the Fatherland, it is the abstraction, the metaphysical, mystical, political, juridical fiction of the Fatherland. The common people of all countries deeply love their fatherland; but that is a natural, real love. . . . [B]ut political patriotism, love of the State, is not the faithful expression of that fact: it is an expression distorted by means of a false abstraction, always for the benefit of an exploiting minority."[15] Emotional attachment to the geographical place of one's birth, therefore, did not translate into the right or need to exercise sovereign political power over that place through a state.

According to Bakunin, nationality, as distinct from nationalism, is merely "the more or less temporary harmony of different instincts and forces of the nation, spontaneously organized, and not yet divided." Anarchists "reject the rights and frontiers called historic. For us Poland only begins, only truly exists there where the laboring masses are and want to be Polish, it ends where, renouncing all particular links with Poland, the masses wish to establish other national links." Thus, "the spontaneous and free union of the living forces of a nation has nothing in common with their artificial concentration at once mechanistic and forced in the political centralization of the unitary state." Indeed, he concluded, "a nation has never a greater enemy than its own State."[16] In essence, Bakunin and his inheritors recognized early on that nations were "imagined communities" and that alternative voluntary affiliations were possible. Put another way, anarchists saw that no state is in reality a nation-state; the so-called nation-state is an arbitrarily bounded, illegitimate power structure that falsely claims to represent an essentialized and homogeneous "nation" onto which it attempts to impose uniformity and authority from above—it is "an abstraction that destroys living society." Anarchists decoupled the "nation" from the dyad of the nation-state, recognizing, in Maia Ramnath's words, that "the devil's in the hyphen."[17]

Through this antistatist redefinition of nations, anarchists reconstituted themselves as stateless but not necessarily nationless individuals. Anthropologist James C. Scott observes that the "huge literature on state-making, contemporary and historic, pays virtually no attention to its obverse: the history of deliberate and reactive statelessness." The anarchists discussed here belong firmly within this forgotten history of "flight from the state as identity."[18] Once freed from geographical and political definitions, nationality became for them just one manifestation of what Bakunin called the "principle of solidarity"—a natural, fluid structure of affiliations established from the bottom up, not the top down.[19] Alongside or in place of "national" ties, anarchists forged countless transnational, interethnic, and interracial solidarities. In 1919, Emma Goldman, who "never felt particularly Jewish," noted, "community of ideas with us often means more than community of blood."[20]

Anarchists typically categorized their affiliations across national and racial boundaries under the imprecise term *internationalism*. But their internationalist ideal was not a generic, Eurocentric universalism. Rather, their perspective is best understood as an innovation on older ideals of cosmopolitanism that valorized diversity as a positive good.[21] Italian anarchist Gigi Damiani explained, "The equality of the anarchists is not the equality of anatomical characteristics, of cerebral developments one measures, of identical aptitudes and customs, but an equality based on reciprocal respect of the human personality, and which claims for all the same right to life, and to one's own life."[22] As summarized by a contributor to the depression-era anarchist journal *Vanguard*, "We are sympathetic to the cultural aspirations of those folk-groups who wish to guard and enrich their particular culture, language, customs and mores. We have the fullest respect for the healthy personality which is the very essence of human society. We have the same respect for every distinct group which possesses its own individual characteristics. . . . I would call it 'Tolerant Cosmopolitanism.' But we fight nationalism everywhere."[23] In the vocabulary of today's political theorists, these anarchists were "rooted cosmopolitans" with attachments to their native cultures and languages, but they were not "cosmopolitan patriots" who supported their states of origin. Theirs is best described as a kind of radical cosmopolitanism, in the double sense that it both pushed the cosmopolitan ideal to its furthest extremes and sought to actualize that ideal through revolutionary change.[24]

Examining how and to what degree anarchists translated their cosmopolitan beliefs into practice is a central task of this book. Not surprisingly, their efforts were uneven and at times contradictory. Nevertheless, evidence suggests that the demographic and cultural composition of their specific communities, rather than a failure of anarchists to act on their ideals, most often determined the limits of their cosmopolitanism.

In particular, language was often the most significant source of cohesion or the greatest barrier between different ethnoracial groups. The evolution of anarchism was therefore strongly influenced by the languages in which it was articulated. It is no coincidence that the Italian movement was closely linked to its "Latin" French- and Spanish-speaking cousins or that the early Yiddish-speaking movement was closely affiliated with its linguistically related German precursor. Links among divergent linguistic groups were, in turn, largely mediated through English. Not only did most immigrants come to have this language in common, but it, like the anarchist movement itself, derived from both Germanic and Latin roots. Language acquisition was no easy task, however, and many foreign workers failed to master English or did so only after many years. And as long as its constituent parts could not communicate with one another, a fully integrated and multiethnic movement remained out of reach.

Yet these anarchists consistently marshaled support and in some cases risked life and limb for the struggles of peoples whose languages they could not speak— their coworkers and neighbors as well as revolutionary and anticolonial struggles abroad. As Benedict Anderson notes, before the First World War, anarchism "was the main vehicle of global opposition to industrial capitalism, autocracy, latifundism, and imperialism."[25] The movement's dual commitment to national liberation and antistatism defined much of its transnational activity and influenced members' views of everything from Zionism to the First World War.

With regard to transcending America's racial divides, anarchists' record is mixed. Prominent anarchist writers such as Peter Kropotkin, Élisée Reclus, Jean

Grave, Gigi Damiani, and James F. Morton Jr. celebrated the racial diversity as well as the essential unity of humankind, inoculating most of their comrades against racial chauvinism.[26] But anarchists forged few relationships with African Americans, likely as a result of a combination of factors. First, most anarchists' poor command of English severely limited opportunities for meaningful contact. Second, black activism in this period was often organized through churches and focused on attaining federal recognition of civil rights, which clashed with anarchists' antireligious and antigovernment commitments. Third, the anarchist movement had virtually no presence in the Deep South, home to the vast majority of America's black population before the First World War, and in the southern context, anarchists' veneration of the "revolutionary mob" was easily misread as condoning antiblack vigilantism. Finally, many anarchists viewed racism as an ahistorical and illogical "prejudice" rather than a system of structural oppression and therefore underestimated its power and significance.[27] However, a large number of Asian and Mexican immigrants, with whom European immigrants had more contact and common experiences, entered the anarchist fold, especially in the Southwest and along the West Coast.

This regional specificity illustrates how the movement's ideals were articulated and enacted differently within particular local contexts. Yiddish-speaking anarchists in New York were truly "rooted cosmopolitans" whose sphere of activity rarely extended beyond the Jewish ghetto despite their rhetorical commitment to interethnic and interracial solidarity. In Paterson, Italian anarchists fostered interethnic cosmopolitanism, consciously building ties to other working-class immigrant groups. San Francisco's anarchist movement, by contrast, promoted and embodied a multiethnic cosmopolitanism that brought diverse groups together into an increasingly unified whole. Regardless of their differences, the many examples of cosmopolitan practices in each city are a remarkable testament to the possibilities of radical cosmopolitanism as a way of viewing the world and living within it.

The American government, for its part, strove to eradicate the physical and discursive threat that anarchism and its cosmopolitan ideals posed. Anarchists were censored, beaten, arrested, imprisoned, deported, shot, and executed under a variety of pretexts. It would have been rare to find a member of the movement who had *not* experienced some form of government persecution (a fact that some anarchists used to justify violence against political figures and government functionaries). Constrained, under normal conditions, by constitutional protections of free speech and freedom of association, authorities concentrated most of their efforts on taking advantage of the foreign character of the anarchist movement by passing exclusionary immigration and naturalization legislation. Immigration restriction and deportation were the state's ultimate demonstration of territorial authority and of its power to define who did and did not belong to the American "nation."

Building on the precedent set by the Chinese Exclusion Act of 1882, various lawmakers began drafting legislation to define anarchists as an "excludable class" of aliens in the aftermath of the Haymarket bombing. However, the political will to bar immigrants based on political ideology coalesced only following the 1901 assassination of President William McKinley at the hands of novice anarchist Leon Czolgosz. Theodore Roosevelt called for such legislation in his first presidential address, thundering, "Anarchy is a crime against the whole human race; and all mankind should band against the anarchist." In 1903, Congress passed the Anarchist Exclusion Act, which barred aliens from entering the country if they "believe in, advise, advocate, or teach . . . the overthrow by force or violence of the Government of the United States or of all forms of law"; the measure also prohibited entry to anyone who simply "disbelieved in" or was "opposed to all organized government." A 1906 law further barred foreign-born anarchists from becoming naturalized U.S. citizens. But these statutes proved easy to evade and difficult to enforce; between 1903 and 1919, the United States excluded just thirty-eight anarchists and deported less than half that number.[28] The United States also stood aloof from international efforts to coordinate the suppression of anarchism, in part because it had no domestic intelligence agency of its own until Theodore Roosevelt founded the Bureau of Investigation (the precursor to the Federal Bureau of Investigation) in 1908.[29]

Furthermore, anarchist exclusion was based on the faulty assumption that anarchism was a foreign import even though only one of the Haymarket defendants was an anarchist at the time of his immigration, while two were U.S.-born, as was McKinley's assassin. Nevertheless, these laws did deter many internationally prominent anarchists from visiting the country after 1903 and laid the groundwork for the mass deportation of hundreds of radicals during America's first Red Scare.

The Anarchist Exclusion Act, like all immigration restrictions, also produced "a *new legal and political subject*"—the illegal anarchist alien—"whose inclusion within the nation was simultaneously a social reality and a legal impossibility." Internationally, governments were further confounded by the conflict between their desire to expel foreign anarchist revolutionaries and their obligation to tolerate the presence or repatriation of anarchists who were their own citizens or subjects.[30] As a *Washington Post* cartoon depicting a distraught globe holding a menacing anarchist at arms' length commented, "What to Do with Him Is the Problem." Anarchist statelessness was therefore simultaneously imposed from above and self-ascribed from below. Thus Emma Goldman's magazine, *Mother Earth*, responded to the Naturalization Act of 1906 by declaring, "Citizenship has no meaning to [anarchists], since their ideal of human liberty and righ-

FIGURE 3. Clifford Berryman, "What to Do with Him Is the Problem," 1898. Courtesy of the National Archives.

teousness goes beyond the narrow bounds of nationality; it is the international republic of free spirits."[31]

What ultimately proved more damaging to the Italian and Yiddish anarchist movements, however, were racialized immigration restrictions aimed at reducing the overall number of immigrants from Eastern and Southern Europe. Scientific experts, the federal government, and popular opinion categorized these "new immigrants" as belonging to distinct (but nevertheless "white") races that were innately inferior to "Nordics" and "Anglo-Saxons." These views influenced everything from immigrants' treatment at Ellis Island to their employment prospects and wage scales and culminated in discriminatory immigration quotas imposed during the 1920s.[32] The new legislation choked off anarchism's supply of potential new adherents as the American state's growing administrative capacity enabled the government to more effectively—though never completely—control its borders.[33]

The first half of *Immigrants against the State* traces the divergent paths of immigrant radicalization in New York, Paterson, and San Francisco and the distinct forms that anarchism took in each city. Despite local particularities, common factors predisposed these communities' members to radicalism. In each case, migration disrupted Old World cultures and social structures, leading to dramatic declines in traditional authority and religious belief in the New World. Workplace exploitation and racially motivated nativism then contributed to immigrants' disillusionment with the United States. At the same time, a small number of activists and intellectuals within each community translated anarchist ideology into languages and cultural systems familiar to these immigrants, many of whom found that the anarchist critique of capitalist America corresponded with their own experiences and saw in the anarchist program a plausible agenda for bringing about a more just future. Radicalized immigrants then selectively adopted anarchist doctrines and tactics in ways that resonated with their own traditions and worldviews, spawning new cadres of agitators and autodidactic intellectuals in the process. Additional members of each community were subsequently recruited into the movement through the same family, workplace, and community connections that had facilitated their migrations to America. These anarchists then fought against the major institutions exploiting and exercising power over their communities: employers and landlords, clergymen, and local, state, and federal authorities.

The second half of *Immigrants against the State* weaves together the stories of these three cities as they responded to a succession of national and international upheavals. Although this study takes migration to the United States as its starting point, it also follows many of those who remigrated, temporarily or permanently, from the United States. Through such remigrations, the anarchism that took root in America was connected to struggles and adapted to new circumstances abroad. Members of America's anarchist movement were directly linked to and in some cases participated in events such as the Mexican Revolution, the Russian Revolutions of 1905 and 1917, Italy's Biennio Rosso, and the Spanish Civil War. In addition, the international rise of communism, Zionism, and fascism; the repression of the First Red Scare; and the onset of the Great Depression all imposed new challenges. These developments forced anarchists to grapple with fundamental questions of national, racial, and political identity and increasingly circumscribed their sphere of influence. Yet anarchism's persistence is at least as remarkable as its decline. Even as the forces arrayed against them expanded, anarchists busily bridged ethnic, racial, and linguistic divides as they strove to remain relevant and expanded the transnational scope of their activities. The collapse of America's Yiddish and Italian anarchist movements did not occur until the end of the 1930s and resulted less from state repression or rival ideologies than from the tragedy of the Spanish Civil War and the end of mass transatlantic migration. Immigration created anarchists in America, and in its absence, their numbers atrophied.

Immigrants against the State turns much of the conventional wisdom about radicalism and immigration on its head. First, it shows that the anarchist movement in America was not simply transplanted from Europe—and that in some cases, the transfer went in the opposite direction. Second, it unearths an often ignored American leftist tradition that operated outside of formal politics, embraced immigrants of all shades, and made no excuses for authoritarianism. Third, bringing anarchists back into the story fundamentally alters our understandings of such well-worn historical topics as the ups and downs of the Jewish American labor movement, the Paterson silk strike of 1913, California's xenophobic labor unions, the Mexican and Russian Revolutions, and the struggles of American immigrants and workers more generally. Fourth, it demonstrates that immigrants did not inevitably experience political moderation, "Americanization," and incorporation into the political system, nor did they all desire these things. At the same time, the Jews and Italians examined here were not "long-distance nationalists"; they opposed the nation-building projects of republican and Fascist Italy as well as the emerging Zionist movement. As self-proclaimed people "without a country," they defy categorization within existing paradigms of immigration history. Anarchists instead constructed a community that, while rooted in secular ethnic subcultures, was imagined in cosmopolitan and global terms. In short, they constituted immigrants against the state.

CHAPTER 1

"YIDDISH IS MY HOMELAND"
JEWISH ANARCHISTS IN NEW YORK CITY

Between 1880 and 1924, approximately two million Eastern European Jews migrated to the United States. More than half made their homes in New York City, where Yiddish-speaking anarchist and socialist movements emerged from the sweatshops and tenement houses of Manhattan's Lower East Side. Anarchists constituted a "vital minority" within the American Jewish labor movement from its origins in the 1880s until well into the 1920s, and Yiddish anarchism grew to become the largest section of America's anarchist movement by the eve of the First World War. Along the way, anarchists forged a vibrant revolutionary subculture deeply embedded in the larger "cultures of opposition" developed by immigrant Jewish workers and intellectuals.[1]

These radicals carried on a lively debate over the meaning of Jewishness. Many pioneers of the movement began as either quasi-nationalist "Jewish populists" or assimilated "Russified" intellectuals who promoted complete Jewish absorption into cultural majorities. After an early lurch toward the assimilationist position, anarchists redefined Jewish identity as being rooted in the Yiddish language and its cultural productions, encapsulated in the term *yidishkayt*—a Yiddish word literally meaning both "Yiddishness" and "Jewishness." More than an adjective, *yidishkayt* expressed an entire worldview; in making the essential features of peoplehood language and modern secular culture rather than religion, tradition, and homeland, *yidishkayt* was inherently cosmopolitan. In Irving Howe's words, *yidishkayt* "set itself the goal of yoking the provincial to the universal"; equally important, as Karen Brodkin notes, it "did not rest upon invidious comparison for its existential meaning."[2] The anarchist variant of *yidishkayt* rejected both Judaism and Zionism and instead represented an early formulation of Jewish diasporism.

However, Yiddish anarchism's embeddedness in the language and culture of the Jewish working class also enmeshed it in a web of tensions between ethnoracial priorities and universal aspirations. Yiddish became the foundation on which Jewish anarchism was built, but it simultaneously walled off this movement from the world outside the Jewish ghetto. Anarchists who opposed nationalism paradoxically helped foster an insular Jewish culture, illustrating the difficulties inherent in navigating a "rooted cosmopolitanism" that simultaneously exalted Jewish identity and professed a radical cultural pluralism.[3]

In 1897, more than 5.2 million Jews lived in the Russian Empire, the great majority of them restricted to the western region designated the Pale of Settlement. They were the unwanted spoils of the partitioning of the former Polish-Lithuanian Commonwealth at the end of the eighteenth century, and the Russian monarchy alternately attempted to "selectively integrate" and marginalize them. Discriminatory legislation limited Jews' access to education and professional occupations and barred most from residency outside of the Pale as well as from landownership. Czar Alexander II relaxed some of these restrictions in 1861, enabling thousands of young Jews to attend Russian *gymnasia* (advanced secondary schools) and universities. But Alexander's assassination by revolutionaries in 1881 was followed by a wave of pogroms and anti-Semitic legislation, including the expulsion of Jews from Moscow and other major cities and strict new limits on Jewish enrollment in institutions of higher learning.[4]

The forced urbanization of Russian Jewry within the Pale meanwhile created an oversaturated labor market in which Jewish artisans and workshop employees faced increasing competition from non-Jewish workers following the 1861 abolition of serfdom. This economic dislocation, combined with growing anti-Semitism, sparked mass emigration beginning in 1881. By 1914, more than 1.5 million Russian Jews had made their way to the United States, while hundreds of thousands more went to England, Argentina, France, Palestine, Australia, and elsewhere.[5] Most of these migrants had to "steal the border"—that is, illegally cross into Germany, usually with the aid of a paid smuggler, or "agent," to evade anachronistic Russian legislation banning permanent emigration.[6]

Although more than three-quarters of the Jews who arrived in America came from Russia, large numbers also originated in Romania and the Austro-Hungarian Empire, where Jews enjoyed greater legal freedoms but still faced formal and informal anti-Semitism. Romania placed restrictive quotas on Jewish education and employment beginning in 1886, and in 1899 a severe depression and series of pogroms sparked the "Romanian Exodus," proportionately the largest emigration of Jews from any country: nearly 30 percent of Romania's Jewish population emigrated between 1871 and 1914. More than 278,000 Jews also arrived from the Galician region of Austria-Hungary, where market integration, delayed industrialization, and economic discrimination impoverished much of the Jewish populace.[7]

Because artisans and skilled workers were among the most adversely affected by changing economic conditions, and because their skills were likely to be transferable, they accounted for more than 67 percent of those Jews who listed an occupation upon arrival in America between 1899 and 1910. Commercial and professional occupations, meanwhile, were severely underrepresented in the Jewish emigration. A majority of Jews, however, arrived with no experience in factory work, including most women, who comprised 43 percent of Jewish immigrants, as well as the nearly one in four arrivals under the age of fourteen.[8]

A small minority of Jewish immigrants were young men (and a few women) who had attended Russia's *gymnasia* and universities under Alexander II. Though they had few professional prospects in Russia, most emigrated for political reasons. They were strongly influenced by the Haskalah—the "Jewish Enlightenment"—that spread from Germany to Eastern Europe in the Early nineteenth century, inspired by the same universalist and humanist impulses as the eighteenth-century European Enlightenment. Haskalah thinkers hoped to "normalize" Jewish existence through the legal emancipation of Jews and their incorporation into European societies. For most, this process entailed secularization, linguistic and cultural assimilation, and abandonment of "parasitic" economic roles in favor of "productive" occupations like farming and manufacturing. The *inteligentn*, as the leftist Jewish intelligentsia was known, therefore rejected religion, spoke Russian instead of Yiddish, and viewed Jewish culture as anachronistic. Most were sympathetic to or active within the Russian populist, nihilist, or socialist movements, prompting some to flee to avoid arrest.[9] Others, among them future anarchist Isidore Kopeloff, did not wish "to sit and wait for a wedding match with a dowry and then to become middlemen, shopkeepers, or to walk about the streets without purpose—for us worldly, enlightened, socialist-minded youths this was impossible."[10] The largest group of radical *inteligentn* arrived in the wake of the 1881 pogroms, having become convinced that assimilation within anti-Semitic Europe was impossible. Many joined Am Oylom (Eternal People), a movement combining vaguely socialist, nationalist, and populist principles with the aim of remaking Jewish society through emigration to the United States and the formation of collective agricultural communes. Five or six Am Oylom groups with a combined membership of more than a thousand arrived in 1882, but only two founded farms as planned; the rest fell apart, with most members never leaving the vicinity of New York City.[11]

Regardless of class or education in the Old World, "greenhorn" newcomers were overwhelmingly employed as manual or semiskilled laborers. A number of factors concentrated Jewish immigrants in the needle trades: one in three claimed to have previous garment-making experience; the craft unions of the American Federation of Labor (AFL) froze Eastern European Jews out of most skilled occupations; Jewish immigration coincided with a dramatic expansion of American ready-to-wear garment production; and an earlier generation of German and Austrian Jewish entrepreneurs dominated the industry and preferred to hire Jewish workers.[12] These factors also gave rise to the sweatshop system, in which large clothing firms outsourced the sewing of precut material into finished garments to independent contractors, who were paid a predetermined price for the finished product. Contractors therefore underbid each other for jobs and could turn profits only by minimizing labor costs through the creation of a hyperexploitative workplace. Hundreds of these "outside shops" were dispersed throughout Manhattan and Brooklyn, and conditions were uniformly poor and unsanitary. Fifteen- and sixteen-hour workdays were common, and during the busy season, work might continue through the entire night.[13]

Men, women, and children alike labored in sweatshops. But despite a nearly even sex ratio, the workforce was strongly gendered. Unlike Europe, where Jewish women were often household breadwinners, Jewish wives in New York were pressured to conform to American notions of respectability by remaining in the home. In 1905, only 1 percent of married Jewish women held outside employment. Most female garment workers were unmarried young women, a majority of whom worked for wages by age sixteen. Sewing machine operation was generally considered "women's work," while men monopolized better-paying positions such as cutters. Still other jobs, such as buttonhole making and pressing, employed an equal ratio of men and women, but women universally received lower wages.[14]

In addition to the sweatshop, Jewish immigrants rarely escaped the experience of tenement housing. The Lower East Side's tenements were notoriously cramped, overcrowded, dark, poorly ventilated, and unsanitary. The first time anarchist Marie Ganz's mother entered the family's tiny two-room apartment, she cried out in dismay, "So we have crossed half the world for this!" Poet David Edelstadt, who contracted tuberculosis as a result of his poor working and living conditions, proclaimed that tenement houses belonged to "the history of the terrible crimes of man against man."[15]

Immigrants' initial contacts with American political and educational institutions did little to alleviate their disappointment. The corrupt Tammany Hall machine dominated city politics, showing newcomers "another America" that they had never imagined. In school, Jewish children were insulted by Gentile teachers and bullied by peers. Jews enjoyed most of the same legal protections as

"Anglo-Saxons" but still faced pervasive taunts, discrimination, and occasional violent outbursts.[16] Jewish workers quickly discovered, as Edelstadt put it, that "in the free republic / something is only free on paper, / and there the factories are full of slaves, and every boss—a vampire."[17] Sweatshops and tenements were the crucibles in which male needle workers, factory girls, and declassed intellectuals came together to forge Jewish American radicalism.

Romanian Jewish memoirist Marcus Ravage recalled his surprise when he "suddenly realized that everybody I knew was either a socialist or an anarchist."[18] This radicalism was, by and large, American-made. Although a disproportionate number of Jewish immigrants had participated in Eastern European radical circles, a majority of those active in the Jewish American Left prior to 1905 had not.[19] Furthermore, although the two most influential theoreticians of anarchism, Mikhail Bakunin and Peter Kropotkin, were Russians, they spent most of their radical careers in exile, and no exclusively anarchist organizations existed within the Russian Empire until after the turn of the twentieth century.[20] Likewise, Romania and Austrian Galicia were virtually untouched by anarchism. Russian Jewish engineer Leon Moisseiff recalled, "Anarchism as a popular movement was alien to us"; he read anarchists' writings only after coming to America in 1891, "and their principles were to me a new phenomenon." Similarly, though Joseph J. Cohen was active in the socialist movement in Minsk for more than a decade before emigrating in 1903, he never encountered the term *anarchism* before arriving in the United States. Hillel Solotaroff voyaged to America as a member of Am Oylom and then spent four years earning a medical degree before joining the anarchist ranks in 1886. At that time, a comrade noted, "he was already thoroughly 'Americanized.'"[21] The path to a Yiddish anarchist movement, however, began with a Russian detour, German and British interventions, and an American gallows.

The radical Jews who immigrated in the 1880s and 1890s were enamored with the Russian revolutionary milieu. They were especially influenced by writers Peter Lavrov and Nikolay Chernyshevsky, who emphasized both a materialist conception of history in which socialist revolution was inevitable and a subjective view of the role of the individual—and the radical intellectual in particular—in hastening revolutionary change by "going to the people" and preparing them for their historic role.[22] In New York, these migrants still perceived themselves in the Russian mold, and they initially formed Russian-language organizations, the most important of which the Russian Progressive Union, founded in 1886. The group's first undertaking was a fund-raising ball on behalf of Russian revolutionaries that collected $110, which was sent to Peter Lavrov himself. The Russian Progressive Union also functioned as a debating society and clearinghouse for political ideas such as Marxism and, increasingly, anarchism.[23]

This interest in anarchism reflected the growing influence of Jews' German neighbors on the Lower East Side, which before the turn of the century was still known as Kleindeutschland (Little Germany). German radicals predominated within both the Socialist Labor Party and the anarchist International Working People's Association, which had several New York branches. In 1886, a writer for the German anarchist paper *Freiheit* estimated that the city had some twenty-five hundred anarchists.[24] Many Jews were already familiar with the German language, which was relatively easy for Yiddish speakers to learn since both languages are descended from Old High German. As a consequence of this geographic and linguistic proximity, German radicals "served as the midwives of the Jewish labor movement."[25] And no German was more instrumental in this birth than Johann Most, the editor of *Freiheit*. One of the greatest public speakers of his day, Most could, according to Yiddish anarchist Chaim Weinberg, "so mesmerize his listeners that they would at any time go with him should he call them to man the barricades. He could bring the apathetic person to tears with his hypnotizing power." The memoirs of Weinberg's Jewish comrades uniformly note Most's electrifying impact, and Yiddish playwright Leon Kobrin described the German as "the god of almost all the Jewish anarchists in those days."[26] Many Jewish radicals began reading *Freiheit*, while those not literate in the German script had friends read the paper aloud to them.[27]

Developments in England also influenced the emerging Jewish anarchist movement. In London's East End, Jewish immigrants were likewise concentrated in dilapidated housing and sweatshop labor, and in 1884, revolutionary socialist poet Morris Winchevsky founded *Der Poylisher Yidl* (The Little Polish Jew), the world's first radical Yiddish newspaper. Winchevsky replaced it the following year with *Der Arbayter Fraynd* (The Worker's Friend), a publication "open to all radicals," including a growing number of Jews influenced by London's cosmopolitan anarchist movement. By 1887, anarchists comprised a majority within the Arbayter Fraynd Group and had formed their own organization, the Knights of Liberty (Riter fun Frayhayt). London became the "spiritual center" of Jewish anarchism, and most Yiddish anarchist material that circulated in America in the 1880s and 1890s was published there.[28] Many Jewish migrants spent time in England before coming to the United States, and some, like labor poet David Goldstein, joined the anarchist movement while there; in 1889, several of these remigrants founded branches of the Knights of Liberty in New York, Boston, and Philadelphia.[29]

However, the Haymarket trial first instigated organized anarchist activity. According to Edelstadt, with the convictions of the Haymarket martyrs, "a new era started, a new period in the American workers' movement. The illusion, the empty hopes for American freedom of speech and of press got their last deadly blow." The injustice of the trial pushed the twenty-year-old Edelstadt firmly into the anarchist camp, along with future anarchist editor Saul Yanovsky and medical students Michael A. Cohn and Hillel Solotaroff. In Rochester, New York, news of the case attracted seventeen-year-old Emma Goldman to the movement, while half a world away in Saint Petersburg, Russia, sixteen-year-old Alexander Berkman first encountered the word *anarchist* in newspaper coverage of the Chicago trial.[30] On October 9, 1886, in response to the setting of the date for the Haymarket executions, a group of five Jewish workers affiliated with the Russian Progressive Union founded the Pioneers of Liberty (Pionire der Frayhayt), the first Jewish anarchist group in America—and, as London's Knights of Liberty had not yet formed, the first exclusively anarchist Jewish group in the world. The Pioneers affiliated with the International Working People's Association and took as their immediate purpose raising money for their Chicago comrades' appeal. The group organized a fund-raising ball and concert in conjunction with the Russian Progressive Union, collecting one hundred dollars for the doomed cause. The Yiddish anarchist movement, Joseph Cohen later remarked, "was baptized in the blood of the Chicago martyrs."[31]

A number of young *inteligentn* from the Russian Progressive Union subsequently joined the Pioneers of Liberty, which soon boasted an impressive array of speakers and writers including Yanovsky; "sweatshop poets" Edelstadt and Joseph Bovshover; Michael Cohn, Solotaroff, and fellow physician Max Girdzshansky; Solotaroff's former Am Oylom comrades Moyshe Katts and Roman Luis; and activists Isidore Kopeloff, Isidore Prenner, and Berkman, a classmate of Moyshe Katts's from *gymnasium* in Vilnius who joined the group after immigrating in 1888. One of the only female Pioneers was Anna Netter, described by Goldman as an "ardent worker" who "made a name for herself by her untiring activity in the anarchist and labour ranks." However, Netter developed cancer and lived as an invalid until her death in 1920. Another woman close to the group was Katherina Yevzerov, a remarkable female intellectual who had received an extensive religious and university education in Russia before earning a medical degree from New York University in 1893, in the same cohort as Cohn. Yevzerov soon married fellow anarchist doctor Jacob Maryson and distinguished herself as a writer on "the woman question" for the Yiddish radical press.[32] The Pioneers' headquarters was located at 56 Orchard Street, a tenement building in the bustling heart of the Jewish ghetto and the home of Netter and her father, A. Jacob Netter, a former Talmudist scholar and Am Oylom activist turned grocer and "ultra-radical socialist." Their apartment was for several years the "spiritual-intellectual center" of the Lower East Side, an "oasis for the radical element" where socialists, anarchists, and freethinkers read and debated the works of Marx, Bakunin, and Kropotkin.[33]

The *inteligentn* spent their first years in America laboring alongside fellow immigrants. Yanovsky was employed as a dishwasher, sheet-metal worker, cloak maker, cap maker, and shirtmaker, while Edelstadt worked as a buttonhole maker and Bovshover became a furrier. Both Solotaroff and Cohn worked as tailors while earning their degrees, and Berkman, Kopeloff, and Prenner were cigar makers. While some of these activists later became successful doctors, editors, or even businessmen, most retained their radicalism and donated generously to the cause—Cohn in particular used the earnings from his successful medical practice in the Brownsville section of Brooklyn and lucrative real estate investments to bankroll anarchist undertakings and support destitute comrades until his death in 1939.[34] Furthermore, intellectuals' ascent from the working class actually granted them more credibility within it; men of learning were revered in Jewish culture, and since few rabbis or religious scholars emigrated from the Old World, secular radicals often replaced them as community leaders.[35] Anarchist women who became midwives and nurses, like Goldman, also enjoyed an elevated social status in the Jewish community.[36] However, to effectively communicate with their coworkers and neighbors, the *inteligentn* literally had to speak a different language.

Ironically, few founders of Yiddish radicalism actually spoke Yiddish when they arrived in America. Yanovsky's mother had spoken Yiddish at home, but he had to relearn the language in New York, while Katts had to tutor Edelstadt, the father of modern Yiddish poetry, in the language. Berkman likewise "really learned Yiddish in America, through association with my many Yiddish friends and comrades."[37] Nearly all of these intellectuals shared the Haskalah view that the Yiddish "jargon" was a stigma of Jewish otherness and unfit for serious literature, and the early meetings of the Pioneers of Liberty were held in Russian. The German influence was also strong; the group rendered its name in a heavily Germanized Yiddish (Pionire der Frayhayt rather than Pionirn di Frayhayt) and remained for several years little more than an appendage of the German anarchist movement. Its members read *Freiheit*, for which Berkman began working as a compositor, and Most took the young Goldman under his wing, hoping that she would become "the first woman speaker in the German anarchist movement in America."[38]

Some anarchists, Goldman among them, never shook their dislike for "jargon"; Goldman delivered Yiddish lectures throughout her radical career but never became fully fluent in the language and remained on the fringes of the Yiddish-speaking movement, preferring to work in Russian, German, or English.[39] But by 1889, Cohn was already defending Yiddish against critiques from assimilated Jewish socialists: "Our broad literature on socialism will serve as fair proof that we are able to express all we want in our Jewish tongue, or, as you prefer to call it, jargon." The once-Russified intellectuals had been "Yiddishized," and they in turn translated anarchism not only into the Yiddish language but also into a specifically Yiddish idiom and culture.[40]

Once committed to Yiddish, anarchists organized an endless succession of Yiddish-language mass meetings, lectures, and educational groups. Possessing an almost mystical belief in the power of the written word, they distributed an enormous amount of radical literature and created New York's first Jewish self-education associations (*fortbildung-foraynen*), including a special Women's Self-Education Group, indicative of the growing number of women entering the movement through preexisting networks of family, friends, and coworkers.[41] To create their own newspaper, the Pioneers of Liberty recruited anarchist Joseph Jaffa, a writer for London's *Arbayter Fraynd*, to move from England to New York and serve as editor. The new weekly, *Varhayt* (Truth), debuted on February 15, 1889, as the world's first explicitly anarchist publication in the Yiddish language.

Although intended to communicate in "the people's speech," most of *Varhayt*'s articles were written in an affected, Germanized form of Yiddish derisively known as *daytshmerish*, leading one reader to sarcastically complain that he did "not know High German writing." Much of the paper's content, such as a serialized translation of Marx's *Critique of Political Economy*, was also too theoretical for its working-class audience. The exceptions were the popular poems by David Edelstadt and Morris Rosenfeld that graced the front page of nearly every issue, which viscerally articulated the miseries of the Jewish ghetto and exhorted readers to revolt. *Varhayt* reached a circulation of around twenty-five hundred, but its finances were so poor that some of the Pioneers of Liberty used their rent money to keep it afloat and slept in the basement on Suffolk Street where the paper was produced. It folded after just four months.[42]

Undeterred, in late 1889, the Pioneers approached the Jewish sections of the Socialist Labor Party (SLP) to propose collaboration on a nonpartisan radical paper to be overseen by two editors, one anarchist and one socialist. This idea was defeated by a single vote after a tumultuous weeklong conference of representatives from both movements.[43] An independent effort on the part of Dr. Abba Braslavsky, a socialist estranged from the SLP, and anarchist printer Ephraim London, father of future socialist congressman Meyer London, produced *Der Morgenshtern* (The Morningstar). Though officially nonpartisan, *Der Morgenshtern* openly criticized the SLP, and when Braslavsky left the publication, it became a de facto anarchist paper. Then, on January 12, 1890, the Pioneers of Liberty convened a meeting of 215 delegates representing thirty-two Jewish anarchist and workers' groups from the East Coast and Midwest to establish a new publication. Its name, as suggested by Yanovsky, was the *Fraye Arbeter Shtime* (Free Voice of Labor), and *Der Morgenshtern* shut down to make way for it.[44]

The first issue of the *Fraye Arbeter Shtime* appeared on July 4, 1890. Still pursuing a bipartisan vision, the paper included a socialist editor, Braslavsky, as well as an anarchist one, a position that passed from Roman Luis to Hillel Solotaroff and Jacob Maryson and finally to David Edelstadt and Moyshe Katts. Labor lawyer Isaac Hourwich succeeded Braslavsky for a single 1891 issue before the paper became entirely anarchist. Berkman later reminisced,

> We were very poor in funds, but rich in enthusiasm. Our compositors and printer worked more for love than money, and now and then the editor was generously given a quarter to buy a meal. Some of us saved our room rent for the benefit of the paper, and for a long time we slept under the make-up table in the basement where the "office" of our paper was. Often our sleep would be disturbed in the middle of the night by Edelstadt waking us to read a poem he had just composed.[45]

With Edelstadt at the helm, the *Fraye Arbeter Shtime* enjoyed moderate success, reaching a circulation of between two thousand and four thousand copies a week, and the Pioneers of Liberty even considered making it a daily paper.[46]

Anarchist lectures at 56 Orchard Street drew hundreds of workers, while larger events held by the Pioneers at Cooper Union or Union Square could draw thousands. In Philadelphia, too, the Knights of Liberty attracted hundreds of Jews to the cause, and by the early 1890s Yiddish anarchist groups had appeared in Baltimore, Boston, Chicago, Cincinnati, Milwaukee, New Haven, Paterson, Pittsburgh, Providence, and Saint Louis.[47] By all accounts, anarchism was the leading current within the Jewish labor movement in these years.[48]

Of course, not all Jews welcomed the radicals in their midst. New York's conservative *Jewish Times*, for example, proclaimed that these troublemakers "ceased to be Jews when they became anarchists."[49] But Yiddish anarchists had a very different notion of Jewishness and eagerly leveraged the existing cleavages between Jewish workers and Jewish business and religious leaders.

Nathan Goldberg aptly dubbed anarchists' preoccupation with education "the anarchist 'Haskalah.'" Anarchists believed that only a secular, rationalist worldview could produce working-class self-emancipation: according to *Fraye Arbeter Shtime* columnist Thomas Eyges, "To become a radical in those days, one had invariably first to abandon religious belief, to deny the existence of God. Then, as a matter of course, one became convinced of the uselessness of religious ceremonies, and then followed the abandonment of church or synagogue. This was considered necessary in order to leave the mind free to consider life from a materialistic, rather than from a theological, point of view."[50] Religion was not "a private affair," radicals argued, but an objectively counterrevolutionary illusion that poisoned even the most democratic of political systems.[51]

The most notorious form of antireligious activism was the Yom Kippur Ball, a radical tradition that originated in London in 1888 and spread to the United

FIGURE 4. "A Hebrew Anarchist Meeting at Military Hall, in the Bowery," *Harper's Weekly*, August 20, 1892.

States the following year. On the holiest day of the Jewish calendar, while religious Jews fasted and prayed for atonement, anarchists and socialists paraded in the streets and then retired to meeting halls and parks to hear radical speakers, feast, and dance. Fistfights with enraged observant Jews sometimes resulted.[52] From 1890 to 1894, the Pioneers of Liberty also produced thousands of copies of a Rosh Hashanah publication with the Hebrew title *Tefilah zakah* (Prayer of Purity), filled with satirical prayers and revolutionary poetry in Hebrew and Yiddish. Radicals also staged Passover balls, where they read satirical versions of the Haggadah and, according to Ravage, "consumed more forbidden food and drink than was good for us."[53] Other anarchists held secular Passover seders where participants sang revolutionary songs echoing the holiday's theme of emancipation. Radicalism also replaced religiosity on the Jewish Sabbath; Yiddish anarchist groups commonly held their weekly lectures on Friday evenings (the beginning of *shabes*), and some anarchist homes hosted *shabes* dinners where traditional gefilte fish was accompanied by Edelstadt's songs in place of religious blessings.[54]

Anarchists' tongue-in-cheek appropriations of religious forms framed religious orthodoxy and secular radicalism in sharply antagonistic terms, attempting to force Jewish workers to choose between the two—though not always with success.[55] Sometimes this tactic backfired spectacularly; on the night of July 30, 1902, mourners from the funeral of Orthodox chief rabbi Jacob Joseph, whose procession had been attacked by anti-Semitic factory workers and policemen earlier in the day, vented their anger by demolishing the clubrooms of the Pioneers of Liberty after hearing rumors that the anarchists were celebrating the rabbi's death by "eating ham sandwiches, drinking milk, and singing obscene parodies of Hasidic melodies." A number of radicals were badly beaten before being rescued by police.[56] But despite the wrath of the orthodox and opposition from "Uptown" German Jews, these antireligious activities attracted a good number of Lower East Side Jews. Kopeloff's oft-quoted claim that "The war against God . . . played a great part in the decrease of anarchist influence in Jewish life" must be balanced against his observation that "perhaps the Pioneers gained more from the negative publicity" than they lost. New York's inaugural Yom Kippur ball attracted at least two thousand participants, and in 1890, another two thousand people turned out to protest the denial of the Labor Lyceum as the site of that year's ball. Joseph Cohen considered these festivities to have been "a very popular institution among the people," and the period in which they were most visible coincided with the growth of Yiddish anarchism rather than its decline.[57] Because deeply religious Jews were unlikely to join the radical movement, anarchists lost little by alienating them; rather, these events appealed to the mass of Jews already estranged from Judaism. Although the Yom Kippur Ball was gradually replaced by less confrontational "gatherings" and picnics, these events still separated Jewish identity from religious observance and replaced religious bonds with ideological ones.

Nevertheless, these were still principally *Jewish* bonds. Divesting Jewishness of its religious roots therefore became a central anarchist concern. Katts penned the earliest Yiddish anarchist statement on "The Jewish Question," published in *Varhayt* in 1889. He set out to explain "what after all binds together the Jewish people and why the Jews exist [after] so long more or less intact," arguing that Jews were neither a nation (*natsie*), because they lacked a territory and common language, nor a religious group (*religie*), because of the existence of secular Jews such as himself. Rather, they were a people (*folk*), and the basis of their common identity was their shared experience of oppression dating back to "the beginning of their history," an oppression Katts attributed to anti-Semitic ruling classes. In sum, "hate and persecution against them binds Jews together." Moreover, the persistence of anti-Semitism in "civilized" countries such as Germany and the United States demonstrated that the Haskalah strategy of assimilation would be a dead end as long as ruling elites benefited from anti-Jewish prejudice. The objective of the Jewish working class therefore coincided with that of all workers: the overthrow of the capitalist class and its political edifice. "The Jewish question will come to disappear only then," Katts concluded, "when the social question has been solved."[58] One unstated implication of this argument was that Jews would cease to exist as a distinct group with the disappearance of anti-Semitism. The early *Fraye Arbeter Shtime* explicitly embraced this universalizing, assimilationist logic, declaring that the resolution of the "general social question" would create a society "where the designations: Jew, Christian, nation, and faith will disappear." Other Yiddish anarchists did not believe that "the Jewish question" was even worth discussing in a country free of pogroms and anti-Semitic laws; when Katts visited the offices of *Varhayt* to inquire about the response to his articles, Jacob Maryson brusquely responded, "Ach, what? Rubbish! Discover America!"[59]

However, some writers developed an alternative, cosmopolitan conception of Jewishness. Alexander Harkavy, who studied languages in Minsk before coming to New York in 1882 as a member of Am Oylom, continued his linguistic studies in the United States. He also affiliated himself with the Pioneers of Liberty and contributed to the *Fraye Arbeter Shtime* and other anarchist publications. In 1897–98, Harkavy published his own nonpartisan radical paper, *Der Nayer Gayst* (The New Spirit), which carried articles by leading Yiddish anarchists and socialists. One of Harkavy's own contributions playfully combined his linguistic research with his political sympathies by invoking the French anarchist Pierre-Joseph Proudhon; in an article about word borrowing across languages, using the Yiddish word *royb* (robbery) as an example, Harkavy concluded with the comment, "Not for nothing did Proudhon say: *La propriété c'est le vol!* (Property is robbery [*royb*])." In other words, no language is the exclusive property of a particular people, an argument that echoes Proudhon's view that only the product of one's own labor constitutes legitimate private property, while everything else is a collective resource.[60] In an era when language was often the basis for defining "national" groups, this was a nod to a cosmopolitan conception of identity.

Harkavy was an eclectic radical who avoided political labels and "guarded against narrow partiality," participating in both the free thought movement and Hovevei Tsion (Lovers of Zion)—a movement promoting Jewish agricultural settlements in Palestine—as well as anarchist activities.[61] He also produced the world's first English-Yiddish dictionaries and helped establish Yiddish as a legitimate language, "almost single-handedly creat[ing] an intellectual environment conducive to Yiddish in an assimilation-prone society." He further wrote numerous instruction booklets to teach Yiddish-speaking immigrants English, American history, and how to become American citizens.[62] The seeming contradictions between these undertakings only make sense when viewed through a cosmopolitan lens. Harkavy's forays into Jewish colonization movements were responses to the dangers faced by Russian Jewry, and both Am Oylom and Hovevei Tsion were predicated on the idea of Jewish autonomy within host societies rather than establishing a Jewish state. In fact, Harkavy lauded Jews' diasporic status, delivering a series of 1907 lectures before anarchist audiences in which he described Jews as an "international nation" that had, during its time in the diaspora, "created more, accomplished more in all realms of human culture."[63] For Harkavy, Jewish autonomy, culture, and statelessness went hand in hand. His instructional booklets sought not to "Americanize" Jewish immigrants but to equip them to adapt to America and unite with fellow workers while still cultivating their own culture and language. In his view, Yiddish and Yiddish culture formed the basis of Jews' identity as a people. This was a thoroughly anti-essentialist definition of Jewishness; as Harkavy's article on word borrowing attests, languages and cultures are not isolated, impermeable, or unchanging, and his emphasis on bilingualism highlights the possibility of multiple and elective attachments.

B. Rivkin (Barukh Weinrebe), another eclectic anarchist intellectual, later popularized similar ideas. Rivkin arrived in the United States in 1911 after participating in anarchist groups in Geneva and London and soon established himself as one of the great literary critics of his day. He famously argued that modern Yiddish literature functioned as a "spiritual territory for the territory-less Jews," providing a precarious substitute for a physical Jewish homeland. In other words, it created a diasporic imagined community united through the secular written word, as earlier generations of Jews had been united through the "aerial territory" of Judaism.[64] Most Yiddish anarchists eventually adopted similar views. Rather than a nation or a race in need of its own state, they identified Jews as a people (*folk*) defined by *yidishkayt*. In the words of Polish-born anarchist Ahrne Thorne, who edited the *Fraye Arbeter Shtime* in its final two decades, "I have no country of my own, so to speak—I am a citizen of America, I consider myself part of American society—but Yiddish is my homeland.... To anarchists, your identity [is] what you feel, [it means] be true to yourself; if you feel like a Jew, fine, perfect; if you love Yiddish, great, build it."[65]

Having embraced *yidishkayt*, Jewish anarchists also changed their attitude toward the labor movement. Steeped in notions of imminent revolution, "propaganda by the deed," and revolutionary martyrdom, most initially dismissed unions as irrelevant if not downright counterrevolutionary. Michael Cohn later described the Pioneers of Liberty as "impractical, naïve-lyrical dreamers, convinced, that presently the social revolution will come, which will at last bring a new, free world." The group was organized like a revolutionary cell, with a secret "inner membership" of a few dozen individuals who met as an "underground body." Saul Yanovsky described the first Pioneers meeting he attended in the back room of a saloon as having "the appearance of a true conspiracy."[66] What did struggles for a few more cents an hour matter in the face of the impending revolution? These radicals found support for this attitude in German socialist Ferdinand Lassalle's "iron law of wages," which Johann Most popularized within anarchist circles. Lassalle held that labor market competition inevitably drives wages down to subsistence levels, thereby dooming workers' attempts to improve their pay. According to an early issue of the *Fraye Arbeter Shtime*, unions presented a field in which to "spread dissatisfaction, plant the seeds of freedom and equality, to bring unconscious workers to their class consciousness," but were not a space for practical action. To the contrary, many Yiddish radicals believed "the worse the better," hoping that desperate conditions would spark revolt.[67]

But these views contradicted anarchists' own experiences and actions. Both Yanovsky and Edelstadt were fired from jobs after organizing for better conditions, and Berkman felt it was his "duty to stand up for the others in the [cigar] shop."[68] In 1886, during New York's first Jewish cloak makers' strike, young radicals came to the strikers' aid and instructed them on how to go about organizing a union. Soon thereafter, anarchists organized a knee-pants workers' union and a Jewish musicians' union, and Anna Netter was active in several strikes conducted by the Knights of Labor.[69] Anarchists like Moyshe Katts and Roman Luis became prominent union organizers and pressured their comrades to reevaluate their views. Johann Most, too, modified his position, writing a pamphlet in 1890 extolling radical labor unions as having "been given the historic mission to bring into being the complete socialization of production, when the new and free society will come to be built up."[70] He was influenced by revolutionary syndicalism, then being developed in Europe, which resolved the gap between anarchist theory and working-class reality by proposing that militant unions could both defend workers in the short term and act as the instrument of revolution in the long term through workers' direct action and the revolutionary general strike, independent of political parties and the state.

SLP members were eager to supplant the anarchists at the head of the budding Jewish labor movement. In October 1888, they founded the United Hebrew Trades (UHT), a federation of SLP-affiliated unions. Four months later, the Pioneers of Liberty responded by forming its own United Workingmen's Organizations of America, but it was never more than a paper organization, and most of its affiliates subsequently joined the UHT.[71] When three thousand striking cloak makers turned to the UHT for aid in 1890, the federation dispatched charismatic garment worker and socialist Joseph Barondess, who quickly organized the strikers into the Operators' and Cloakmakers' Union. But Barondess also gravitated toward the anarchists, who "had the upper hand" among the cloak makers, and appointed Luis assistant manager of the union while bringing in Emma Goldman and Scottish preacher turned anarchist Thomas Hamilton Garside to agitate on behalf of the strike. Garside was selected to negotiate the union's settlement with employers, but the agreement reached did not include strikers' demands for the expulsion of strikebreakers or the fixing of piecework rates, drawing immediate criticism from the SLP. Cloak makers rejected the proposed settlement and continued the strike on to a complete victory. This debacle severely undermined their support for the anarchists, especially after newspapers revealed that Garside had become a deputy U.S. marshal shortly after the strike. The SLP seized the opportunity to launch a campaign against Barondess and his anarchist allies in the UHT.[72]

This struggle soon involved the *Fraye Arbeter Shtime*'s own typesetters, whose UHT-affiliated union struck after the Pioneers of Liberty fired their foreman, a confrontational SLP member. When the Pioneers hired a new printing crew, UHT leaders condemned the anarchists for employing "scabs," and in September 1891, the federation called on its members to boycott the paper. The boycott created a rift in the Jewish labor movement; the Operators' and Cloakmakers' Union refused to endorse it and withdrew from the UHT, prompting the socialists to form a rival organization, the International Cloakmakers' Union. Anarchists and their supporters, in turn, organized a new alternative to the UHT, the United Trade Unions of New York and Vicinity; its first affiliate was Hebrew Typographical Union No. 317, composed of the *Fraye Arbeter Shtime*'s new typesetters and chartered by the American Federation of Labor (AFL).[73]

The anarchists found a convenient ally in the AFL, which for years had been fighting the SLP's influence in the labor movement, and threw their support behind its conservative United Garment Workers Union. In return, the AFL allegedly helped fund the *Fraye Arbeter Shtime*, which had entered a financial crisis after poor health forced Edelstadt to step down as editor. The anarchists also called a counterboycott of the SLP's Yiddish paper, *Di Arbayter Tsaytung* (The Union Newspaper). Nevertheless, the *Fraye Arbeter Shtime* could not survive both the boycott and the economic downturn of 1893, and it ceased publication in April of the following year, although the United Trade Unions temporarily replaced it with *Di Yunyon Tsaytung* (The Union Newspaper), edited by Barondess and supported by the AFL.[74]

Anarchists again took the lead in an 1893 Cloakmakers' Union strike, during which Emma Goldman organized the union's first women's group and was sentenced to a year in prison for inciting to riot. The struggle between the rival union federations descended into slander and fistfights, and the organizations' membership fell to "between a few dozen and a few hundred." To avoid complete collapse, the rival typographical unions amalgamated and the two cloak makers' unions reunited, but the reorganized cloak makers' union disintegrated in 1896 after a failed strike led by Barondess.[75]

This contest proved disastrous for both the unions and the anarchists, who lost many of their leading figures. A humbled Barondess returned to the socialist fold, and Isidore Prenner and Roman Luis left anarchist ranks in 1892, the latter declaring himself a social democrat. Max Girdzshansky likewise drifted into to the socialist camp, later becoming a "staunch conservative."[76] Edelstadt had grown so ill working in the basement office of the *Fraye Arbeter Shtime* that he had to relocate to the drier climate of Denver, where he succumbed to tuberculosis in October 1892 at the age of just twenty-six. Fellow poet Joseph Bovshover developed a severe mental illness and was permanently institutionalized in 1899.[77]

Yiddish anarchism was also consumed by an internal controversy over revolutionary tactics. On July 23, 1892, Alexander Berkman shot and stabbed steel magnate Henry Clay Frick in Pittsburgh. The failed assassination, plotted with a small group of German and Jewish comrades that included Emma Goldman, was retribution for the deaths of nine workers at the hands of mercenaries hired by Frick to enforce a lockout at the Carnegie Steel Company's mill in Homestead, Pennsylvania. Berkman, who served fourteen years in prison for the act, had expected that killing Frick "would fire the hearts of the disinherited, and inspire them to noble deeds. It would carry to the oppressed the message of the New Day, and prepare them for the approaching social revolution." He also hoped that the attack would "prove a healthy stimulus" to the flagging anarchist movement.[78] This incident represented a quintessential example of "propaganda by the deed," the popular notion within late-nineteenth-century anarchist circles that self-sacrificing acts of violence against members of the ruling class would help spread revolutionary consciousness among the masses and inspire further such actions, ultimately culminating in revolution. Its actual result in this case, however, was to turn popular opinion against the strike, aid the socialists' ascendency within the Jewish unions, and exacerbate a simmering conflict within anarchist ranks.

Discontent with Most's heavy-handedness as titular head of the German anarchist movement and his ill-defined economic theories had given rise to an oppositional current centered on Austrian anarchist Joseph Peukert, who espoused total decentralization of the movement and a communist economic model based on the principle "From each according to ability, to each according to need." These "autonomists" were also alarmed by Most's shift away from propaganda by the deed following the Haymarket Affair. Peukert accused Most of authoritarianism, Most accused Peukert of being a police spy, and polemics flew.[79] In 1891 Most's former protégés, Berkman and Goldman, had joined Peukert's autonomist circle and severed all ties with Most as a consequence of political and personal differences. They were nevertheless shocked and outraged when Most, who for years had called for acts of revolutionary violence and even authored an instructional explosives manual for that purpose, responded to Berkman's attempt by stating, "In a country where we are so poorly represented and so little understood as in America, we simply cannot afford the luxury of assassination." A majority of Yiddish anarchists accepted Most's analysis and even barred Goldman from attending their meetings. For others, however, Berkman's name became "a kind of talisman, a source of enthusiasm and encouragement."[80] By 1895, Yiddish anarchism was marginalized, shrinking, and divided against itself. Its only sign of life was *Di Fraye Gezelshaft* (The Free Society), a thick monthly journal edited by Leon Moisseiff that was too intellectual to reach beyond a limited readership. Such was the situation that greeted Saul Yanovsky upon his return to the United States after a five-year absence.

In 1890, Yanovsky had been invited to London to take over the editorship of the *Arbayter Fraynd*, which under his direction shed its nonpartisan character and became an explicitly anarchist paper. While abroad, Yanovsky honed his skills as a "gifted and cunningly sarcastic writer and editor."[81] He also transitioned from support for propaganda by the deed to sharp criticism of such tactics. The precipitating event was the anarchist bombing of a crowded Barcelona theater in 1893, which killed more than thirty people and provoked a fierce wave of repression. Yanovsky's reversal, however, caused such controversy within the Arbayter Fraynd Group that he was forced to resign as editor.[82] But back in New York he found a more receptive audience for his vision of "constructive" anarchism. Although it took four years of patient work and partisan infighting, particularly against the supporters of the *Fraye Gezelshaft*, a national Jewish anarchist convention convened in Brownsville in 1899 voted in favor of Yanovsky's proposal to revive the *Fraye Arbeter Shtime*.[83] The publication was resurrected in October of that year with Yanovsky as its editor, and over the next twenty years he helped rebuild the Yiddish anarchist movement on a scale that dwarfed its previous incarnation.

The *Fraye Arbeter Shtime*'s reappearance coincided with the explosive growth of the American Yiddish press. As Hutchins Hapgood noted in his 1902 study of the Lower East Side, radical newspapers "largely displaced the rabbi in the position of teacher of the people." Papers were consumed individually and in groups, passed from hand to hand, read aloud, and debated in self-education societies and cafés.[84] Whereas previous anarchist periodicals were filled with dense articles and *daytshmerish*, the new *Fraye Arbeter Shtime* embraced a simpler and less pretentious style that one thankful reader praised as "a plain, flowing Yiddish."[85] Yanovsky adhered to a clear anarchist line in his editorials but opened the pages of the paper to a wide range of radical viewpoints—though contributors could expect trenchant responses from the editor. Yanovsky's trademark sarcasm and unbending will made him difficult on a personal level but earned him thousands of fans as a writer and speaker. The *Fraye Arbeter Shtime* was, in the words of Yanovsky's biographer, his "first and only love," and Joseph Cohen recalled that Yanovsky "singlehandedly had to do all of the hard physical labor that the newspaper required. He was edi-

FIGURE 5. Saul Yanovsky, ca. 1920s. From Saul Yanovsky, *Ershte yorn fun yidishn frayhaytlekhn sotsializm* (New York: Fraye Arbeter Shtime, 1948).

tor, manager, bookkeeper, errand boy and peddler [*pakn-treger*]—all in one."[86] In his first year as editor, the paper's circulation doubled from four thousand to eight thousand, and by 1910 it was printing between fifteen thousand and twenty thousand copies a week, one-third the circulation of the popular Yiddish socialist daily *Forverts* (Forward), edited by Abraham Cahan.[87]

The revived paper promoted gradual change based in day-to-day engagement with cooperatives, education, and labor unions. Yiddish anarchists experimented with numerous worker, consumer, agricultural, and residential cooperative projects intended to free participants from capitalist exploitation. However, they had more success with their educational endeavors, which in addition to self-education circles included the Francisco Ferrer Center, a multiethnic radical venture established on the Lower East Side in early 1911 and relocated to Jewish Harlem the following year. Named for and modeled after the ideas of Catalan anarchist educator Francisco Ferrer i Guàrdia, whose 1909 execution in Barcelona the *Fraye Arbeter Shtime* decried as "the darkest crime of the twentieth century," the Ferrer Center offered evening classes and lectures for adults, as well as a "Modern School" designed to nurture children's individual personal development as well as antiauthoritarian politics.[88] Yanovsky, who had been exposed to syndicalist ideas while in London, also popularized the ideal of the general strike as a nonviolent means of toppling the existing order, albeit after a long period of organization and consciousness-raising.[89] The cataclysmic revolution that had seemed imminent in the 1880s was viewed as an increasingly distant possibility; in the interim, the 1910 annual North American Yiddish anarchist convention resolved, "We recognize the necessity of taking part in all present political, economic and social problems of city and country, and working for their solution in the direction which is the nearest to our goal."[90]

The *Fraye Arbeter Shtime* also firmly renounced propaganda by the deed. Yanovsky distinguished between indiscriminate terrorism, like the Barcelona theater bombing, and "thoroughly anarchist acts" that targeted public figures responsible for violence against the masses, like Berkman's attempt on Frick's life. But even if the latter deeds were justified and ideologically consistent, the real question to be asked was whether they were "worth the trouble." That is, were they an effective method of propaganda that would help make anarchism "a world-celebrated doctrine"? In Yanovsky's eyes, the answer was clearly negative.[91] When Leon Czolgosz shot William McKinley on September 6, 1901, Yanovsky disavowed the action, writing, "The benefits that such an attempt can bring to the propaganda for our ideas are very questionable, the damage however is certain and sure." The damage, in this instance, was a nationwide wave of antiradical hysteria during which dozens of anarchists were arrested, including Johann Most, who was sentenced to a year in prison on the pretense of an inflammatory article that had appeared in *Freiheit*. In addition, on the night of September 16, three days after Yanovsky's words saw print and a day after McKinley succumbed to his wounds, a mob of "Jewish school boys" ransacked the offices of the *Fraye Arbeter Shtime* at 185 Henry Street and chased down and beat Yanovsky.[92] In his 1902 pamphlet *Der olef beys fun anarkhizmus* (The ABCs of Anarchism), Yanovsky reiterated, "Anarchism is not a doctrine of assassination and the anarchists are not murderers." Rather, the foundational principle of anarchism was "peace between men [*menshen*]."[93]

Not all Yiddish anarchists adhered to Yanovsky's views. Revolutionary currents remained, especially among younger radicals. Much of this opposition coalesced around Philadelphia's Radical Library Group, cofounded in 1905 by Joseph J. Cohen, a former rabbinical student turned anarchist. These dissidents made common cause with some of the old guard *inteligentn*, including Solotaroff and Katts, who resented Yanovsky's high-handedness and had, along with Goldman, defended Czolgosz's actions as those of a sincere revolutionary. Jacob Maryson also aligned with the opposition as a consequence of his estrangement from Yanovsky, though Maryson's views were more moderate than even Yanovsky's; in 1906, Maryson began urging anarchists to abandon their "taboos," support political reforms, and participate in electoral politics "to spread decentralizing principles of government and to counteract the manifest tendencies of State Socialism." His wife, Katherina Yevzerov, likewise supported women's suffrage, arguing, "If one cannot introduce socialism in its entirety all at once, one should introduce as many pieces of it as possible." The *Fraye Arbeter Shtime* sharply condemned these "revisionist" ideas, but the young militants opposed to Yanovsky's "despotic" control of the paper defended them.[94] These revolutionaries founded a string of short-lived rival newspapers, but most did not survive their first twelve months, and none lasted more than a few years.

Both the *Fraye Arbeter Shtime*'s success and the opposition against it led to a dramatic increase in the number of anarchist organizations. At least ten new Jewish groups formed in New York City between 1899 and 1914, several of them in the new Jewish communities of Harlem and Brownsville.[95] A number of Jewish anarchists were also involved in the multiethnic circles around the Ferrer Center and Goldman's *Mother Earth*, founded in 1906 after Berkman's release from prison. The following year, Yanovsky launched a daily anarchist publication, *Di Abend Tsaytung* (The Evening Newspaper), to compete with the *Forverts*, but the understaffed experiment lasted only two months. More successful was Yanovsky's revival of *Di Fraye Gezelshaft* as a literary supplement to the *Fraye Arbeter Shtime* in 1910–11, which led to the formation of a network of dozens of Fraye Gezelshaft Clubs across North America. Few American anarchist publications ever approached the *Fraye Arbeter Shtime*'s peak circulation of thirty thousand copies in 1914, which, according to one estimate, translated into as many as 150,000 readers.[96] Anarchism was once again a vital presence in New York's Jewish community.

Romanian Jewish author Konrad Bercovici noted that the Lower East Side anarchists of his youth "believed that people could be educated to a degree that would make every form of constraint superfluous. To achieve that, these anarchists published the best literature, translated the best books from a dozen languages, and organized amateur theatricals, concerts, and lectures. They were saints without knowing it." Through these activities, anarchists played a key role in the creation of a Yiddish public culture that was strongly colored by radical values.[97]

The *Fraye Arbeter Shtime* became an esteemed source of Yiddish poetry, short stories, and literary criticism in addition to radical ideology. Its cantankerous editor developed an unparalleled reputation for discovering literary talent and was an early champion of the modernist Di Yunge and In Zikh schools of Yiddish poetry. Prominent poets whose first published work appeared in the anarchist organ include Mani Leib, A. Glanz-Leyeless, Jacob Glatstein, Leon Feinberg, and Ana Margolin. In his study of the American immigrant press, sociologist Robert E. Park observed that the *Fraye Arbeter Shtime* was "the peculiar organ of the Yiddish intellectual. To be able to say 'I have written for Yanovsky' is a literary passport for a Yiddish writer."[98] Contributors, however, risked Yanovsky's legendary barbed wit if he judged their work substandard; his rejections—published in a special section of the paper to entertain and scandalize readers—ranged from the concise ("Not a spark of talent") to the merciless ("What did you scribble there? It seems to us, that not an editor, but only a doctor can help you, if it is already not too late for the latter").[99]

Anarchist intellectuals such as Yanovsky, Maryson, Yevzerov, Solotaroff, Abraham Frumkin, and B. Rivkin also contributed to a wide range of other Yiddish publications, including the *Forverts*. In addition, when a group of prominent writers formed the Yiddish Writers' Club (Yidisher Literatn Klob) in July 1911 for "the elevation of Yiddish literature in all its forms," they elected the anarchist Solotaroff its first president. Two years later, Maryson oversaw the creation of the Kropotkin Literary Society (Kropotkin Literatur Gezelshaft), which published Yiddish translations of works by European thinkers including Darwin, Marx, Lassalle, and Kropotkin.[100] Anarchist Max M. Maisel, who owned a radical bookstore on Grand Street, ran a small publishing house that translated writers as varied as Shakespeare, Anton Chekhov, Henrik Ibsen, and Margaret Sanger. The *Fraye Arbeter Shtime* also serialized prominent European political works and novels, most of them translated by Yanovsky. Yiddish readers' exposure to both Jewish and non-Jewish writers, therefore, was to a great extent facilitated by anarchists.

But Yiddish theater stood at the center of Jewish immigrant cultural life. Anarchists adored the realist dramas of playwrights such as Jacob Gordin and Sholem Asch, and some anarchists, including Joseph Bovshover and Moyshe Katts, enjoyed modest success writing for the stage. The theater was also one of the primary sources of fund-raising for anarchist causes. Acclaimed Yiddish actor Jacob Adler made his 1899 New York debut as the lead in a production of *The Beggar of Odessa* at the Windsor Theater that raised money to relaunch the *Fraye Arbeter Shtime*, and in December of that year, he performed in a benefit to finance a "legal appeal" for Alexander Berkman. (The money was actually used to fund a failed attempt to tunnel Berkman out of prison.) Eighteen years later, Adler participated in a fund-raiser to prevent Berkman's extradition to California in connection with the Mooney-Billings case (discussed in chapter 5), and joked, "This Berkman has been haunting prisons all his life, and I have been playing benefit performances for him all my life."[101]

Anarchists were also ubiquitous figures in the Lower East Side's bustling café culture. In the 1880s and 1890s, Sachs's Cafe on Rutgers Square was "the headquarters of the East Side radicals, socialists, and anarchists, as well as of the young Yiddish writers and poets." Later, Schmuckler's Cafe at 167 East

Broadway Street became "the mecca of the radicals," attracting "authors, speakers, organizers and radical kibetzers in general," including the staff of the *Fraye Arbeter Shtime*, who for a time worked out of offices on the second floor of the same building.[102]

One institution from which anarchists stood aloof was the *landsmanshaft*, or Jewish mutual benefit society. Thousands of these groups, composed of immigrants from the same town or region, were scattered throughout New York, but radicals considered them parochial and a diversion of workers' funds from more important causes. However, an acceptable alternative presented itself in 1900 when the Workmen's Circle (Arbayter Ring), a secular and nonpartisan socialist mutual aid society founded in 1892, reorganized itself as a federation with branches across North America. The Workmen's Circle provided anarchists with both an organizational structure and access to a large working-class constituency; Morris Nadelman recalled that members of New York's Fraye Arbeter Shtime Group "figured out that by belonging to the Workmen's Circle, which was an official organization, by paying dues and getting benefits, they had more of a chance to exist." Both the Fraye Arbeter Shtime Group and the International Group of New York (which included non-Jewish members) became official branches of the Workmen's Circle, the first of some two dozen anarchist branches to join by the end the of 1920s. Others included Harlem's Ferrer Center Group and the Bronx's Amshol Group, Friends of Arts and Education Group, and Fraye Gezelshaft Group.[103] Additional branches contained strong anarchist constituencies, such as Branch No. 2 in Harlem, which hung Bakunin's portrait inside its headquarters, alongside portraits of Marx and Lassalle. In Rivkin's opinion, the Workmen's Circle and other working-class mutual aid societies "helped to convert the socialistic dream future into a tangible, practical reality."[104]

Anarchists also fostered their own distinct subculture, centered on a variety of invented traditions. These included anarchist picnics, "excursions" to parks or the countryside, *vetcherinkas* (dinner parties), and balls. This last category encompassed several variations, each with its own conventions, including *arestatnbeler* (arrested balls) to raise funds for political prisoners and farcical *boyernbeler* (peasants' balls), in which the attending "peasants" were "arrested" and tried before the presiding "judge" (often Yanovsky himself) for a variety of crimes. "Anarchist justice was then dispensed: fines for kissing a virgin, or for not kissing a virgin; for standing about too quietly, etc. All this was a way of raising money for the cause." A "priest" or "rabbi" also performed "marriage ceremonies" (for a fee), often as punishment for couples caught embracing, kissing, or "spooning." Sought-after young women might "marry" dozens of times in a single night.[105] Such gatherings infused leisure time with radical politics, raised money for anarchist causes, and provided immigrants with a sense of community.

In a movement so invested in Jewishness, however, some members flirted with Jewish nationalism, especially in the face of mounting anti-Semitism. This phenomenon was not yet a problem in the 1890s; unlike their comrades in France, New York's anarchists were little exercised by the Dreyfus Affair, which, they were assured by Peter Kropotkin during his 1897 visit to the city, was primarily a fight "between the Catholics and Monarchists on one side, and Republicans and Liberals on the other." Emma Goldman explained to a reporter, "Of course, the Anarchists are all for Dreyfus. . . . Personally I do not believe Dreyfus is a sympathetic character. What the anarchists did [in France to defend Dreyfus], however, was from a humanitarian point of view—a principle."[106] The impact of the pogrom in the Bessarabian city of Kishinev on April 6 and 7, 1903, which left nearly fifty Jews dead and hundreds injured and maimed, was much greater. In its aftermath, Isidore Kopeloff found, "My entire previous cosmopolitanism, internationalism et cetera vanished with one blow, like a barrel with the bottom suddenly knocked out." A small group of radicals, including Joseph Barondess, Moyshe Katts, and Hillel Solotaroff, convened a rally "where before a packed hall they all declared themselves Jewish nationalists."[107]

The *Fraye Arbeter Shtime* waited nearly three weeks to comment on the pogrom, though it may be no coincidence that it immediately began running two parallel series of articles, one on the fundamentals of anarchism (especially antistatism) and the other a critique of Zionism. When Yanovsky finally addressed events, he condemned the "terrible fantasies" of the Zionists and declared that salvation for Russian Jews would come only with "an end to Tsarism in Russia."[108] Hillel Solotaroff responded with a detailed justification of his position, titled "Serious Questions." Like Katts before him, Solotaroff noted the persistence of anti-Semitism in Europe and pointed out that there were "now even visible signs of Jew-hatred in America." Internationalism and cosmopolitanism had therefore proven ineffective, and, he argued, "The history of the past fifty years is a living testimony, that neither the progress of nations, the light of science, nor even the brotherly ideals of freedom fighters and advocates of social ideals in any way prevented the persecutions or eased the suffering and pain of the Jewish people." For Jews faced with the threat of extermination, therefore, "to preach the internationalist spirit means to preach their own destruction." Their only hope lay in nationalism—"not in religious nationalism, nor in cultural-political nationalism," but in an assertion and defense of Jews' right to an autonomous existence. Nowhere did Solotaroff mention a Jewish state.[109] "Serious Questions" was "soon exciting the entire Jewish radical world." For months thereafter, the *Fraye Arbeter Shtime* burst with articles on "Anarchism and Nationalism," the bulk of them arguing against Solotaroff. For most contributors, the problem was clear: nationalism ultimately meant supporting the creation of a state, and states were inherently oppressive and antithetical to anarchism. One writer asked whether Solotaroff was "an anarchistic nationalist or nationalistic anarchist." The former might condone a nation-state, but the latter never could.[110]

A solution to Solotaroff's dilemma presented itself with the arrival in the United States of Chaim Zhitlowsky in October 1904. An emissary of Russia's Socialist Revolutionary Party, Zhitlowsky undertook an eighteen-month tour during which he promoted what he called "progressive Jewish nationalism." Zhitlowsky's ideas were based on three main tenets: Jews were a nation (*natsion*) defined by a common Yiddish language and culture; Jewish intellectuals had the duty to contribute to and elevate this Yiddish culture; and Jewish survival necessitated autonomous Jewish self-governance in the diaspora as well as in a (socialist) territory of their own—whether in Palestine or elsewhere.[111] Zhitlowsky's views closely approximated those of the "anarcho-nationalists," as their critics called them, and this faction made common cause with Zhitlowsky's "territorialist" movement.[112]

The territorialists and their anarchist opponents shared a cosmopolitan dedication to pluralism and diversity and agreed that Jews constituted a people or nation with a right to an independent existence. Solotaroff and his companions, however, insisted that an autonomous territory was necessary for their self-preservation. This territory would not be a state, they were quick to point out, but rather a federation of self-administered communes formed according to the principle of free association and federated into "one union of all mankind"—the purported goal of all anarchists.[113] Yanovsky countered that any Jewish settlement within an existing state would find itself at the mercy of that state's government, and any truly independent territory carved out of an existing one would need its own state to secure its survival and hence would pledge patriotic loyalty to that state—the opposite of anarchism. He condemned Solotaroff's ideas as "heretical" and maintained that only the complete overthrow of the existing system of capitalism and nation-states could solve "the Jewish question."[114] *Mother Earth* similarly accused territorialists of having "retrogressed from a universal view of things to a philosophy fenced in by boundary lines, from the glorious conception that 'the world is my country' to the conception of exclusiveness," which "means only to lay the foundation for a new persecution that is bound to come sooner or later."[115] As if to confirm this prediction, a distinct anti-Arab chauvinism soon surfaced in Solotaroff's writings; in 1907, he began arguing that the "primitive" culture of "underdeveloped" Palestine would inexorably yield to the "superior" culture of Jewish settlers. As a result, Palestine would "blossom to become an anarchist-communist society" in which Jewish influence would predominate.[116]

This fusion of anarchism and territorialism won over only a small handful of Yiddish anarchists. Before his death in 1921, even Solotaroff seemed to recognize its inherent contradictions; in a speech memorializing the Haymarket executions he reportedly declared, "I still am for a Jewish homeland, because if ever I will be hanged, I would prefer to be hanged by a Jewish hangman."[117] According to Chaim Weinberg, "Comrade Solotaroff's tragedy was that he couldn't go over to the nationalists wholeheartedly. . . . But at the same time, he separated himself more and more from the anarchists, because he felt that they disapproved of his nationalist inclinations." By contrast, Jacob Maryson, who was less invested in territorialism, maintained an active role in anarchist affairs and through his voluminous writings cultivated a reputation as "the Kropotkin of the Jewish anarchist movement."[118] Both Kopeloff and Katts forsook anarchism in favor of Zhitlowsky's Socialist Revolutionary Party and eventually joined the Labor Zionist organization Poale Zion, though Katts remained close to his old comrades and considered himself "the same anarchist as ever."[119] This position was less contradictory than it first appears; Poale Zion leader Ber Borochov described himself as "an anarchist-socialist" working toward a stateless socialist Israel, and in Montreal and other cities, "it was not uncommon for members of the Poale Zion to be active anarchists."[120] Nevertheless, the weekly circulation of the *Fraye Arbeter Shtime* dwarfed that of territorialist publications before the First World War and in 1914 was more than double the size of the membership of all American Zionist organizations combined.[121] Jewish nationalism's moment had not yet arrived.

Yet even antinationalist anarchists were so deeply rooted in the Jewish community and *yidishkayt* that they found it difficult to translate their cosmopolitan ideals into coalitions with non-Jews. Italian migrants, primarily from the agricultural south of the peninsula, began arriving in New York in the same decades and in virtually the same numbers as Eastern European Jews, and the city's first Italian anarchist groups predated the Pioneers of Liberty. By 1914, dozens of Italian anarchist collectives existed throughout the city, including on the Lower East Side, and together they represented an estimated five thousand members and supporters.[122] In 1893, Italian anarchist Francesco Saverio Merlino brought together a scattering of German, Jewish, French, Italian, and native-born American anarchists around the short-lived newspaper *Solidarity*. Individual Jewish anarchists belonged to East Harlem's large Bresci Circle, made up predominantly of Italians, as well as to Brooklyn's Club Avanti, composed primarily of Italian- and Spanish-speaking radicals.[123] Jewish cigar makers also organized alongside their Spanish, Cuban, and Puerto Rican coworkers, among whom anarchism was the dominant political tendency.[124] Such connections, however, were temporary and informal. Italians comprised an increasing number of the city's garment workers, yet the Jewish-dominated garment unions ignored them almost completely until 1910, and the Yiddish anarchists remained aloof from the small number of Italian radicals who joined these organizations.[125]

Interactions with English-speaking radicals were more common. In 1888, members of the Pioneers of Liberty formed the short-lived English-language Alarm Club and Parsons Debating Club, and Emma Goldman's lecture tours and magazine *Mother Earth* reached far beyond the Jewish community. On a more intimate level, four of the most prominent native-born American anarchists married Jewish women: editors John H. Edelman and Harry Kelly were the husbands of sisters Rachel and Mary Krimont; Haymarket riot survivor and editor Jay Fox married Esther Abramowitz (later the wife of Communist leader William Z. Foster); and Ferrer Center cofounder Leonard D. Abbot's spouse was anarchist Rose Yuster. Johann Most, too, had a common-law marriage with Jewish anarchist Helene Minkin, and Italian anarchist men commonly entered into romantic relationships with Jewish women, likely as a result of the uneven sex ratio among Italian immigrants.

Institutional connections were more fleeting. In 1908, Alexander Berkman founded the Anarchist Federation of New York, which embraced Yiddish-, German-, and English-language branches, including the Mother Earth Group.[126] The federation organized demonstrations of New York's unemployed but faced unwanted scrutiny after nineteen-year-old Russian Jewish member Selig Silverstein, who suffered from an incurable heart condition and had been beaten by police at a protest the previous week, attempted to throw a homemade bomb at officers during a demonstration in Union Square on March 28, 1908. The device detonated prematurely, killing a bystander and seriously injuring Silverstein, who died in police custody. Saul Yanovsky denounced Silverstein in the *Fraye Arbeter Shtime*; a friend of the bomber responded by assaulting Yanovsky, who was hospitalized. The editor refused to press charges against his assailant or to tone down his criticisms.[127] The mainstream of the Yiddish movement was thus estranged from this effort to unite local anarchist groups. By 1914, a new International Anarchist Communist Federation existed in New York and included Russian, Spanish, and Italian affiliates but only one small Jewish group, Brownsville's Friends of Art and Education.[128]

The Ferrer Center was another important multiethnic institution with a high level of Jewish participation, but its association with more militant elements likewise brought trouble. During the financial downturn of 1914, a group of English-speaking Jewish, Latvian, and Italian anarchists connected to the center organized a mass movement of the city's unemployed. Its leading figures included Berkman, Marie Ganz, Italian anarcho-syndicalist Carlo Tresca, Irish-American anarchist Charles Plunkett, and twenty-one-year-old Galician Jew Frank Tannenbaum. The anarchists urged laid-off workers to go to uptown restaurants, order food, and "tell them to send the bill to the mayor." Tannenbaum also led marches of the unemployed to the city's churches to demand that they house and feed the needy, eventually leading to his imprisonment for inciting to riot.[129] In the midst of this campaign came news of the Ludlow Massacre in Colorado, where National Guardsmen had attacked an encampment of striking miners and their families, leaving at least twenty-seven men, women, and children dead. Among them were Italian anarchist miner Carlo Costa and his wife and two children.[130] A small group that included Berkman, Plunkett, Irish Canadian anarchist Arthur Caron, and Latvian sailors Carl Hanson and Charles Berg constructed a bomb intended for the Tarrytown home of John D. Rockefeller, who owned the Colorado mine. However, the device detonated in the tenement on Lexington Avenue where it was being assembled, killing Caron, Hanson, and Berg as well as occasional Ferrer Center attendee Marie Chavez. In the aftermath of the explosion, the Ferrer Modern School relocated to rural Stelton, New Jersey, where an anarchist colony formed around it, though the Ferrer Center remained open in New York until 1918.[131] The *Fraye Arbeter Shtime* did its best to distance itself from the Lexington Avenue explosion—and, consequently, the English-speaking militants.[132]

Alliances across racial lines were even more unusual despite the abundant anarchist critiques of American racism. David Edelstadt penned a number of poems about African Americans, whom he called "our dark brothers [*unzer brider shvartsen*]." In "John Brown," he praised the radical abolitionist because, "To black slaves he was the first / to extend a brotherly hand," and to recognize "that people of all races and colors / must and will be free!"[133] When white and black activists formed the National Association for the Advancement of Colored People in 1909, the *Fraye Arbeter Shtime* announced, "With all of our hearts we wish this undertaking great success," and in 1911 the paper printed a Yiddish translation of W. E. B. Du Bois's "The Souls of White Folk," one of the earliest examinations of the social construction of white racial identity, just months after it first appeared in English. That same year, former *Varhayt* editor Joseph Jaffa produced a popular Yiddish translation of the abolitionist novel *Uncle Tom's Cabin*.[134] The *Fraye Arbeter Shtime* also condemned lynchings and American "race hatred," and most Jewish immigrants saw parallels between the treatment of African Americans and their own history of persecution—parallels that became even clearer with the 1915 lynching of American-born Jew Leo Frank. But despite American anti-Semitism and nativist arguments that Jews were an undesirable "Asiatic" race, legally they fell firmly on the white side of the color line. As Irving Howe remarked, black Americans "served, through bitter circumstance, as a kind of buffer for American Jews." Ironically, anarchists' insistence on defining Jews as a *folk* rather than a *rase* helped pave the way for them to eventually identify as unambiguously "white."[135]

Furthermore, New York's Jews had very little contact with African Americans before the First World War. The Lower East Side was a solidly European immigrant enclave, Brownsville and Harlem were still overwhelmingly Jewish neighborhoods, and virtually no African Americans were employed in the garment trades—in 1910, only 2.6 percent of Manhattan's male workforce was black, whereas 24 percent was Jewish.[136] One rare example of interracial collaboration came with black Harlem radical Hubert Harrison's involvement in the Ferrer Center in 1914–15, and for a time Harrison was very close to the city's anarchists, but he then moved on to "race conscious" activism within the growing black community.[137] In sum, Yiddish anarchists' failure to establish lasting relationships with other ethnoracial groups resulted largely from doctrinal differences and linguistic and geographic restraints rather than ideological contradiction.

The greatest failure of Yiddish anarchism was instead its neglect of gender as a category of oppression. As much as one-third to half of the Yiddish movement's members were female, far more than any other segment of American anarchism. Emma Goldman noted, "Jewish meetings are always packed—with men, women, infants, and baby-carriages."[138] Yet few anarchist women were able or allowed to attain much influence, and a clear gendered division of labor existed.

Exceptions of course occurred, with remarkable women such as Goldman, Katherina Yevzerov, Anna Netter, and Chicago's Sarah Edelstadt gaining renown among their comrades as writers and agitators. But Goldman undertook most of her activism in English, as did Rebecca Edelsohn and Marie Ganz, both of whom came to the fore during the unemployment demonstrations of 1914. Men, by contrast, monopolized virtually all public roles within the Yiddish movement, while women performed behind-the-scenes reproductive labor that sustained it. Of the twenty Yiddish anarchist periodicals produced in the United States, for example, not one was edited by a woman.

At the rhetorical and ideological level, anarchists of both sexes insisted that men and women were equals and celebrated female militancy. David Edelstadt's poem "To Working Women" called on them to "Help us to carry the red banner / Forward, through the storm, through dark nights / . . . We fight together, like mighty lions / For freedom, equality, and our ideals!" Marcus Ravage described the attitude in Yiddish radical circles as one in which a "woman was but a human being in petticoats; therefore . . . you need not expect to be looked up to as a superior creature with a whole chain of exploded privileges and immunities. She was in every way your human equal and counterpart, whatever the animal differences between you might be." Dora Keyser, just fourteen years old when she joined the anarchist movement in 1913, likewise later declared, "There was no question of women, because women and men were on the same level. . . . There was no such thing as a separate standard" for women.[139] In this respect, the Yiddish movement was far in advance of its German predecessor, in which women had a marginal presence; when young Emma Goldman asked Johann Most if there were any notable female anarchists in America, he replied, "None at all, only stupids."[140]

Yiddish anarchists' more enlightened attitude was shaped in part by the activism and writings of women such as Goldman and Yevzerov. In 1900, Yevzerov published a series of articles in the *Fraye Gezelshaft*, later printed as the booklet *Di froy in der gezelshaft* (The Woman in Society), that drew on a range of historical and anthropological works, including Lewis Henry Morgan's *Ancient Society* (1877), to emphasize the radically different nature of gender roles across cultures and thus disprove claims of the innate and unchanging nature of those roles. She further argued that women in modern society had shown themselves to be men's equals, and therefore, "one must root a new idea in the minds of both sexes: a woman is a worthy human being [*mensh*], and not a parasite or small child."[141]

Anarchist women also participated in community struggles. For example, during a Jewish rent strike in 1907–8, the Zsherminal Group—which in 1907 published Yevzerov's *Di froy in der gezelshaft*—helped form the Anti–High Rent Socialist League of Harlem.[142] A decade later, Ganz took a leading role in Jewish women's riots against rising food prices.[143] Anarchist men and women alike also took part in movements to unionize Jewish workers and to educate immigrant families about birth control methods.

Saul Yanovsky and the *Fraye Arbeter Shtime*, meanwhile, championed the work of female poets and fiction writers Celia Dropkin, Fradel Stock, Yente Serdatzky, Anna Margolin (who at one point worked as secretary of the paper), and others. Yanovsky was so well known for his encouragement of female poets that after he rejected Jacob Glatstein's first poetry submission, Glatstein began submitting pieces under the name Clara Blum, a subterfuge that was not brought to light until after Yanovsky had published fifteen of "Blum's" poems.[144] Yet in 1915, the *Fraye Arbeter Shtime* printed an article by poet A. Glanz-Leyeless that claimed that women's contribution to Yiddish literature was rooted in innate differences between the sexes. "By nature women are not egotistical," Glanz-Leyeless claimed. "By nature women are bound organically to other lives. Out of her body new life comes. Another kind of knowing exists for her. She has a second dimension and understands nature. She is a mother in the deepest sense of the word." This piece simultaneously recognized the importance of women's writing and reduced womanhood to motherhood, a self-sacrificing role that abrogated the sovereign individual at the center of anarchist politics.[145]

The *Fraye Arbeter Shtime* also carried few political articles by or about anarchist women. Furthermore, unlike their Italian counterparts, Yiddish anarchist women rarely organized independent groups, instead finding support from informal female networks based on kinship, Old World ties, and shared ideology. Few spoke or wrote about the role of women within the anarchist movement, and many appear to have accepted the premise that women and men were treated equally in radical circles: according to Keyser, "There was no feminist special group; the anarchists were all feminists."[146] Others, however, had different experiences. In a rare exposition on the topic from the *Fraye Arbeter Shtime*, Bertha Lieb complained that radical men viewed women as relying entirely on their husbands for their "material existence" and therefore prioritized men's struggles while their wives lived under the "tyranny" of their marital duties.[147] According to former anarchist Lucy Robins Lang, even among radical couples, "The woman keeps house for her man, whether he's a husband or a lover." Young anarchists living together communally also took it for granted that the women would perform such household duties as cooking and cleaning.[148]

Female activism was therefore circumscribed by romantic and domestic relationships. Hapgood observed that radical Jewish women, "so long as they are unmarried, lead lives thoroughly devoted to 'the cause,'" but "afterward become good wives and fruitful mothers, and urge on their husbands and sons to active work in the movement." Keyser, who saw no gender divisions within Yiddish anarchism, nevertheless left the garment shop to raise both her own children and, after the death of her sister, her two nieces.[149] A double standard even existed in how men and women were addressed; second-generation anarchist Audrey Goodfriend noted that of "all the Jewish anarchists that I knew that were my parents' friends, the men were always called by their last name, in Yiddish, and the women would all be called by their first name. . . . For example, it was Karpoff and Ida; Strauss and Pearl; Gomberg and Lisa."[150]

Wives and mothers continued to support the movement—not least by performing the reproductive labor that made men's activities possible—but these contributions were rarely acknowledged or valued.[151] Lang recalled that many anarchist women "went in dread of pregnancy. If she did have a child, the man resented the curtailment of his freedom, while the woman felt that she was bearing too much of the burden." If the couple separated, moreover, the child was invariably left in the care of the mother.[152] Committed activists such as Emma Goldman and union organizer Rose Pesotta were repeatedly forced to break off relationships with men who wanted them to have children and run households.

These realities clashed with anarchists' professed ideals of "free love," which condemned marriage as the legal and economic enslavement of women and extolled the right of any man or woman to enter into or terminate romantic relationships at will for both emotional and sexual fulfillment. The memoirs of Goldman, Lang, and Marie Ganz leave no doubt that this commitment to sexual autonomy nurtured self-assertiveness and independence, but they also demonstrate that jealousy and possessiveness (on the part of men and women alike) posed constant and often insurmountable obstacles. As a result, anarchist "free unions" most often took the form of long-term monogamous heterosexual relationships, many of which eventually resulted in legal marriages.

Try as they might to break free from Jewish tradition and "bourgeois" values, Yiddish anarchists reproduced many of the patriarchal structures they sought to undermine. Nevertheless, the movement's egalitarian ideals, its inclusion of a large proportion of women, and its strident defense of sexual freedom for both men and women still placed it at the forefront of women's liberation in this era. Yiddish anarchism held forth and moved toward a vision of radical equality in all aspects of human life, though it often stumbled along the way.

Most women's activism, like men's, was centered in the workplace, where female anarchists contributed to the radical subculture that helped revive the Jewish labor movement. In 1900, those garment unions that had survived the crises of the 1890s chartered the International Ladies' Garment Workers' Union (ILGWU), the first and most important national needle trades union, with the American Federation of Labor. The ILGWU's advocacy of class struggle and socialism made it unique within the AFL, and anarchists played an active role in the union, albeit as junior partners to the social democratic majority. Like the earlier cloak makers' unions, however, the ILGWU began as an almost entirely male affair, and most Jewish labor organizers dismissed women as "transient" workers destined to leave the workplace after they married. The ILGWU lacked a paid female organizer for its first decade despite the fact that women composed the vast majority of the industry's workforce. Garment union officials even formalized the gender segmentation of the industry by excluding women from the provisions of settlements with employers and institutionalizing higher wages for men.[153] Nevertheless, the *Fraye Arbeter Shtime* supported the unionization of female workers, and rank-and-file anarchist women helped lay the ground for female unionization.

In 1903, Bessie Braut, an "outspoken anarchist" and cap liner, organized her coworkers, including twenty-one-year-old Rose Schneiderman, into a local of the United Hat and Cap Makers' Union. Braut Schneiderman recalled, "wasted no time in giving us the facts of life" regarding unions and class struggle.[154] The newly radicalized Schneiderman, now a socialist, became the first full-time working-class Jewish organizer for the Women's Trade Union League and played a critical role in supporting the 1909 "Uprising of the Twenty Thousand," a general strike of female shirtwaist makers that swelled the ranks of the ILGWU and transformed it into one of the AFL's largest affiliates. The strike definitively demonstrated women's militancy, winning settlements from 339 firms and forcing male unionists to take them seriously.[155] Thereafter, female anarchists were always among the first on the union's picket lines, where they were not afraid to clash with strikebreakers and police; late in life, Sonia Farber recalled with a chuckle how she had fought policemen by kicking them rather than using her fists so that they could not identify who had struck them.[156]

Blouse maker Mary Domsky joined the ILGWU soon after migrating from Russia in 1909 and met her future husband, anarchist bookbinder Jacob Abrams, on a picket line the following year. After being fired for union activity, Domsky took at job at the Triangle Shirtwaist Company Factory in Greenwich Village, one of the few employers that held out against the union in 1909. There she helped organize work stoppages that forced management to recognize a four-person price committee—to which Domsky was elected—that negotiated wage rates. Domsky and the other committee members were just leaving work on the afternoon of March 25, 1911, when a fire broke out on the eighth floor of the building. In the ensuing blaze, 146 of Domsky's coworkers, most of them young Jewish women, were burned alive or leaped to their deaths to escape the flames.[157] The horrific deaths of the Triangle workers—"victims of capital," in the *Fraye Arbeter Shtime*'s words—left a deep impression on an entire generation. For anarchists such as Domsky, "The tragedy steeled us in our later battles for the trade union and libertarian-socialist movements to which we devoted our lives."[158]

Despite the overwhelming importance of women's activism, men monopolized leadership positions within the ILGWU even after women became two-thirds of the union's membership. The meteoric rise of wall-eyed, street-tough anarchist Morris Sigman is emblematic of this disparity. Sigman arrived from Bessarabia in 1903 and became a cloak presser, forming an independent union that affiliated with the SLP's Socialist Trade and Labor Alliance and subsequently with the syndicalist Industrial Workers of the World (IWW). Sigman worked as an organizer for a short-lived IWW local in New York's garment trades, but in 1907 he joined the ILGWU. The following year, he was also elected assistant secretary of the Anarchist Federation of New York. When between fifty thousand and sixty thousand cloak and suit makers struck during 1910's "Great Revolt," Sigman chaired the ILGWU's picket committee and sat on the strike settlement committee, and that same year became a vice president of the union before being elected secretary-treasurer of the ILGWU in 1914.[159] No woman could hope for such rapid advancement within the Jewish labor movement.

When historian and former anarchist Max Nomad arrived in the United States in 1913, he discovered that "anarchism still had a mass following among the Jewish sweatshop workers of New York."[160] Although far more Jewish immigrants supported the Socialist Party of America, cofounded in 1901 by disaffected SLP members affiliated with the *Forverts*, the readership of the *Fraye Arbeter Shtime* still surpassed that of any other American anarchist publication. In the words of lifelong anarchist Israel Ostroff, "Anarchism gave the immigrants a sense of belonging, of family, community, common ideals and aspirations, which we desperately needed." The Yiddish anarchist movement was, in Joseph Cohen's description, "a world unto itself."[161] But this world was an insular one, bounded geographically by the limits of Jewish settlement and linguistically by the use of Yiddish.

From the movement's earliest days, Alexander Harkavy, David Edelstadt, and others urged Jewish workers to learn English—alongside Yiddish—to "unite with the American proletariat and take part in the great struggle for freedom of all workers in America."[162] In 1908, Emma Goldman criticized Jewish anarchists for being "still too Jewish, I fear, to really appreciate the great necessity of a wide-spread agitation in the language of the country they live in."[163] But anarchists' embrace of *yidishkayt* did not contradict their cosmopolitanism. Rather, radical cosmopolitan ideology, suffused in *yidishkayt*, presented an alternative to both Jewish nationalism and Americanization. Though it is true that Yiddish anarchists could forge connections outside of the Jewish ghetto only by participating in English-language efforts, abandoning Yiddish would have destroyed the cultural and institutional base of their movement. The situation presented an insurmountable paradox, but it did not threaten Yiddish anarchism's existence as long as Eastern European Jews continued to flock to America.

CHAPTER 2

I SENZA PATRIA
ITALIAN ANARCHISTS IN PATERSON, NEW JERSEY

Located along the Passaic River just seventeen miles northwest of New York City, Paterson, New Jersey, was America's largest producer of silk by the turn of the twentieth century—as well as a notorious hotbed of anarchism. Italian anarchists were at the forefront of persistent local labor unrest, including the violent 1902 silk strike and famous 1913 general strike conducted by the Industrial Workers of the World (IWW). More infamously, a Paterson anarchist assassinated Italy's King Umberto I in 1900. A year later, the *Outlook* claimed, "Paterson has come to be the center of what is probably the most important Anarchist group in the world," and in 1906, an exasperated Board of Aldermen threatened to bring charges of libel against publications that continued to equate the Silk City with anarchism.[1] Behind the dramatic episodes that so embarrassed city officials stood a dynamic radical subculture rooted in Paterson's Italian population and linked to major transnational revolutionary networks.

The first Italian anarchists arrived in America in the 1870s, fleeing the suppression of the Italian Federation of the First International. An Italian section of the American Federation of the International appeared in New York in 1871 and allied itself with the organization's anarchist-influenced "decentralist faction" but soon disappeared.[2] In 1885, the Gruppo Socialista-Anarchico-Rivoluzionario Italiano "Carlo Cafiero," named for a well-known Italian anarchist, formed and affiliated with the anarchist International Working People's Association. In 1888, it began publishing *L'Anarchico*, the first Italian American radical newspaper, which lasted for less than a year. In 1887, Piedmontese cap makers formed a sister organization, the Circolo Comunista Anarchico Carlo Cafiero, in the Orange Valley section of Orange, New Jersey, about fifteen miles south of Paterson.[3] By the end of 1892, America's growing Italian-speaking anarchist movement had a new publication, New York's *Il Grido degli Oppressi* (Cry of the Oppressed), and groups in at least ten cities in the Northeast and Midwest, including Chicago, Boston, Philadelphia, Pittsburgh, and Paterson.[4]

Paterson's anarchist movement, though profoundly shaped by a small cadre of radical émigrés, emerged from the encounter between immigrant workers and the local silk industry, and Italian anarchists bridged ethnic divisions to contend for hegemony within the local labor movement for more than three decades. To many of the city's immigrants, anarchism was not a far-off utopia but a way of life. As Errico Malatesta wrote in Paterson's anarchist newspaper *La Questione Sociale* (The Social Question), "The subject is not whether we accomplish Anarchy today, tomorrow or within ten centuries, but that we walk toward Anarchy today, tomorrow, and always.... [E]very blow given to the institutions of private property and to the government, every exaltation of the conscience of man, every disruption of the present conditions, every lie unmasked, every part of human activity taken away from the control of authority, every augmentation of the spirit of solidarity and initiative, is a step towards Anarchy."[5]

Italian wool and silk weavers began migrating to neighboring West Hoboken in the 1870s and were first introduced into Paterson's mills as strikebreakers near the end of the decade. But the higher wages available in Paterson, as well as recruitment within Italy by Paterson employers, soon turned that city into a major destination for Northern Italian migrants. According to the U.S. Census, Paterson's Italian-born population grew from just 845 in 1890 to 9,317 in 1910. By the end of that period, 7,000–8,000 Italians were working in the city's silk mills and dye houses—approximately half of that industry's workforce.[6] Unlike the bulk of Italians who came to the United States in these decades, most of these arrivals were skilled workers from Northern Italy. A majority hailed from the wool-producing Piedmontese province of Biella, though a substantial number were Lombardian silk workers from Como.

Northern Italians had long shared a "culture of mobility" rooted in temporary labor migrations to France and Switzerland, and in the late nineteenth century, these migratory circuits expanded to include transatlantic destinations, including Paterson and Buenos Aires.[7] Italy's woolen and silk industries underwent intensive mechanization in the 1870s and 1880s, with water- and steam-powered looms displacing male weavers in favor of cheaper female and child labor, driving wages in Piedmont's wool workshops down by 30 percent between 1891 and 1907.[8] Although Paterson's silk mills were similarly mechanized, they offered employment to both men and women at wages that were more than double those available in Biella. As conditions declined, Piedmont lost 2.1 percent of its population to emigration between 1905 and 1907 alone.[9]

These migrants carried traditions of labor militancy with them. Northern Italian working-class radicalism preceded industrialization, first emerging in the 1860s within mutual aid societies that increasingly performed the functions of labor unions as well as militant workers' organizations called leagues of resistance (*leghe di resistenza*). Biella's weavers soon established "a reputation for militancy and a tradition of collective solidarity."[10] In fact, the strength of the labor movement led Biellese employers to introduce power looms following a major 1877 strike, even though doing so was not yet cost-effective. But mill owners were mistaken if they thought that female workers would prove more tractable than men: women instigated and led general strikes of weavers in Como in 1888 and Biella in 1889.[11] The displacement of male weavers also transformed the patriarchal household in Biella, as income-earning women and children gained greater power and autonomy. A much more rigid gender hierarchy prevailed in Como, where most men dismissed women's role in labor struggles, but during the 1888 strike there, fourteen-year-old Maria Roda-Balzarini was among "the most avid agitators." Significantly, Maria, all three of her sisters, and her father, widower Cesare Roda-Balzarini, were also outspoken anarchists.[12]

Although the early labor movement was strongly influenced by Mazzinian republicanism, in the 1870s and 1880s, anarchism and socialism emerged as competing alternatives. According to Biellese socialist Rinaldo Rigola, "In Biella, as, indeed, throughout Piedmont, the early socialists belonged to the school of so-called communist-anarchists."[13] A key anarchist figure was Alberto Guabello, born in 1874 in the *comune* of Mongrando, a wool-producing center in southwest Biella with some forty-two hundred residents at the turn of the century. As a teenager, Guabello had been a Mazzinian and then a socialist, and he was blacklisted in Biella for distributing strike leaflets. He moved to the nearby city of Turin, where he first encountered anarchist ideas, and after returning to Mongrando in 1891, he formed an anarchist circle, I Figli del Lavoro (The Children of Labor). In 1894, this group opened a "school of anarchy" for weavers' children, though police soon closed it down.[14] Yet Piedmont and Lombardy were never major centers of Italian anarchism, and Italian-French anarchist Charles Malato, who visited Mongrando in 1894, described the anarchists there as "Good comrades, sturdy, refined, [and] confident," but on the fringes of the labor movement.[15] Only a few of the migrants to Paterson, therefore, began their journeys as anarchists.

Nearly all, however, were weavers or dyers. A 1908 survey found that 83.5 percent of Paterson's male northern Italian silk workers and 92 percent of females had worked in textile manufacturing before their arrival. And as in Biella and Como, most family members worked in the mills; more than half of Paterson's

Northern Italian women worked outside of the home—the highest rate of any ethnic group—and nearly a third of Northern Italian households also received income from minors.[16]

Southern Italians, too, began arriving after 1900. At first, they were employed as day laborers by Italian labor contractors (*padroni*) and entered the silk shops only as strikebreakers, but many gradually obtained lower-skilled and lower-paid positions in the industry. Around 20 percent had worked in silk before coming to America and therefore earned wages on par with Northern Italians, but only because their introduction dragged down the northerners' pay—a fact that led Northern Italian weavers to initially resist southerners' employment.[17] Most Southern Italian men, however, worked in Paterson's dye houses as unskilled dyers' helpers. By 1910, Paterson's Italian population was evenly split between northerners and southerners, with more than 90 percent of the men working in silk, along with 45.2 percent of Northern Italian women and 14.5 percent of their southern counterparts.[18]

The structure of Paterson's silk industry introduced new levels of insecurity into these workers' lives. Silk manufacturing suffered rising instability caused by decentralization, changing fashions, seasonal markets, and price fluctuations, causing frequent periods of unemployment, underemployment, and labor conflict. In 1908, just 53.1 percent of Paterson's male Northern Italian silk workers had been employed nine or more months out of the previous year; the corresponding figure for women was 44.4 percent. As one Italian complained, "The occupation of weaver has become the most miserable of all. If one considers that the silk industry is subject to the periodic crises that recur every year and that consequently the weaver is condemned to unemployment for a good third of the year, one can affirm that, on average, the wages of the weaver do not exceed one dollar per day."[19] For Southern Italian dyers, work was arduous and hazardous. According to a contemporary description, "The rooms are constantly filled with steam and the floors are covered with water. The dyers are compelled to work with their hands in strong acids, and must wear wooden shoes weighing about 5 pounds each in order to keep their feet dry. They are subject to rheumatism and colds." Biellese anarchist weaver Vittorio Cravello described the dyers as "really and truly mobs within which the life of the poor worker is not worth a cigarette butt [*cicca*]."[20]

In Biella, silk workers' families owned small plots of land on which they grew food to supplement their earnings and sustain themselves during strikes, but urban New Jersey offered no such relief in lean times. Moreover, British and German weavers in Paterson earned significantly higher wages than Italians, regardless of skill or length of residence, and jealously guarded their privilege against the new arrivals. Northern Italian women did, by dint of their exceptional skill and experience, earn higher pay than any other female weavers except the

English, but their wages were still lower than men's across the board.[21] Whatever advantages Paterson's silk industry held over Italy's were largely offset by labor market competition, accelerating production, irregular employment, and discrimination. In these circumstances, the anarchism that a few Italians brought with them acquired new relevance to their coworkers. The anarchist movement in Paterson therefore expanded during precisely the same period that the movement in Biella and the rest of Italy entered into steep decline as a consequence of government repression and competition from the new Italian Socialist Party.[22]

Anarchism spread through three overlapping circuits within transatlantic migrations. Paterson's first Italian anarchists were weavers who arrived as labor migrants in the 1880s and early 1890s, including a young couple, Firmino Gallo and Ninfa Baronio, both of whom were former members of Mongrando's anarchist group.[23] Once this small cadre had established itself, a parallel process of radical chain migration guided anarchist refugees and exiles to Paterson, which in Biella came to be "considered the Mecca of the anarchists [*libertari*]." For example, when six Biellese anarchists were arrested in September 1898 for possession of anarchist literature, three of them fled to Paterson to evade prosecution, and in 1909, Serafino Grandi also sought refuge in the Silk City to avoid a lawsuit against his short-lived Biellese anarchist paper, *L'Alba*.[24] Piedmontese anarchists in general were an extraordinarily mobile group: out of a sample of two hundred, more than 70 percent emigrated at least once, collectively undertaking more than 280 international migrations—not including frequent (often involuntary) repatriations to Italy. More than half of these migrations were to neighboring France and Switzerland, but one in ten was to the United States, while another 8.4 percent were to Argentina or Brazil.[25]

Alberto Guabello's path from Biella was emblematic of this mobility. Repeatedly arrested in Italy, France, and Switzerland for anarchist activities, he served five months in an Italian prison and two years of *domicilio coatto* (forced confinement) on the Isole Tremiti for his role in an 1894 conspiracy to instigate armed insurrection throughout the Italian peninsula. After his release, Guabello went again to France, where he was detained in April 1898 for violating his earlier expulsion and then returned to Italy. Facing a new sentence of five years *domicilio coatto* if rearrested, he set out for Paterson and "this new continent where the fatal consequences of the reactionary storm that sows mourning in Europe are still not felt." Guabello's journey in turn activated a new migration chain through which his sister and brother, anarchists Adele and Paolo, followed in 1904.[26] Anarchists from Como also came to Paterson to evade persecution. In the aftermath of the 1888 Como strike, Cesare Roda-Balzarini and his anarchist daughters moved first to Milan, where in 1891 Maria was arrested during a strike for singing "seditious songs," and then in May 1893 to New Jersey to escape "the persistent and continuous rigor" of police harassment.[27]

This transatlantic anarchist corridor soon facilitated the migrations of radicals from other regions of Italy as well. In 1897, Tuscan silk weaver and anarchist strike leader Gaetano Bresci came to West Hoboken after serving multiple prison terms for his activities, and in 1901, Giovanni Baracchi, a Milanese bookbinder forced to flee Italy, arrived in Paterson, where fellow anarchists trained him as a weaver.[28] Between 1895 and 1902, moreover, virtually every leading figure of the Italian anarchist movement either visited or moved to Paterson.

Finally, new recruits to the movement—who vastly outnumbered veteran radicals—entered it through the same familial, regional, and occupational networks that brought them to Paterson. Firmino Gallo and Ninfa Baronio were joined by Firmino's brothers, Louie and Andrea, and Ninfa's siblings, Egisto, Abele, and Anetta, all of whom joined the anarchist movement. Antonio Cravello, a socialist weaver who had taken a prominent part in the Biella strikes of 1878 and 1881, transferred to the anarchist camp after coming to Paterson, and in 1895 he was joined by his sister, Ernesta (Ernestina), who soon became a prominent anarchist speaker.[29] Children, too, were incorporated into the movement: Firmino Gallo and Ninfa Baronio's son, William, recalled, "We were raised in an anarchist milieu. We rejected religion and government, even democracy. And we rejected war."[30] William's sister, Lena, married Alberto and Adalgisa Guabello's son, Spartaco, further blurring the lines between political community and kinship network. Among Paterson's Italians, anarchism was a family value.

Local anarchists formed the Gruppo Augusto Spies, named for German-born Haymarket martyr August Spies, around 1890, and between 1892 and 1894, more than 150 residents of Paterson sent donations to New York's *Il Grido degli Oppressi*, making the Silk City that paper's single largest source of funding. By the summer of 1892, the Gruppo Augusto Spies had disbanded and been replaced by the Circolo Studi Sociali (Social Studies Circle), which in 1895 was reconstituted as the Right to Existence Group (Gruppo Diritto all'Esistenza). By the turn of the century, this organization had more than a hundred regular members, and "behind them were many times as many other workers, passive but more or less in sympathy."[31] Nearly all of the Right to Existence Group's founders were Biellese weavers, and as late as 1920, federal agents noted that Paterson's anarchists were "made up mostly of aliens from the north of Italy, commonly known as PIEDMONTESE. . . . Nearly all of the members of the group are engaged in the silk industries in Paterson and are mostly expert weavers."[32] Nevertheless, the group came to include Southern Italians as well, and one of its most active members was not an Italian at all but multilingual Catalan printer Pedro Esteve.

Already a prominent anarchist in Barcelona, Esteve fled to New York in 1892 to avoid arrest. There, he worked on a Spanish-language paper, *El Despertar*, becoming its editor in 1895 and relocating it to Paterson, where he printed it and *La Questione Sociale* on the same press. Esteve cemented his link to the Italian movement by marrying Maria Roda-Balzarini (known within the movement simply as Maria Roda), whom he had first met at an anarchist conference in Milan in 1891. In the description of one reporter, "A more amiable, cultivated, and really scholarly man it would be hard to find anywhere."[33] In addition, according to the Italian consul in New York, Battista Cominetti, a socialist who "converted" to anarchism after migrating from Biella, was also "if not Spanish-born, at least the child of Spaniards."[34] In 1899, Franz Widmar, a Slovenian from Trieste (then part of Austria-Hungary), also joined the Right to Existence Group. Widmar had been active in Trieste's Italian-speaking anarchist circles and was imprisoned and then expelled for articles he had written for *La Questione Sociale*, which circulated widely in the region. In Paterson, he became the paper's business manager and occasional editor.[35] By 1919, authorities reported that the Right to Existence Group included a scattering of "French, German, Dutch, Spanish, Greek, Austrian, and Belgian immigrants."[36]

Some of these members came from preexisting though declining anarchist groups that the Italians encountered in Paterson. In 1871, local French-speaking radicals had founded Section 29 of the First International, which sided with the Bakuninist minority in 1872 and later, after briefly reconciling itself with the Marxist majority, became the anarchist Groupe Socialiste-Révolutionnaire.[37] Although most of the city's two thousand to three thousand French silk workers returned to Europe after 1890, Italian anarchists worked closely with the small number of radicals who remained. Many Italian silk workers had previously sojourned in France for work or, like Alberto Guabello, to escape arrest, and in the 1880s and 1890s, French anarchist literature circulated widely in Biella. Rinaldo Rigola noted that most Biellese workers "knew French as much as Italian," and Northern Italians in Paterson likewise "associated freely with the French, [and] spoke their language."[38] Italian and French anarchists organized joint meetings and social events and led strikes together. Italians also supported Paterson's French-language anarchist newspaper, *Germinal*, named after Émile Zola's radical novel of the same title and published from 1899 to 1902 on the same printing press as *La Questione Sociale* and *El Despertar*.

German anarchists were active in Paterson and nearby cities from 1881 until at least 1902, and their Paterson Group counted eighty members in 1892.[39] Relations between the Germans and Italians, however, were not very close. Language differences bore most of the blame, though factionalism and ethnocentrism played roles as well. Whereas local Germans supported Johann Most's critique of Alexander Berkman's attempt on the life of Henry Clay Frick, the Italians defended

Berkman and complained that their German comrades were "Germans first and then anarchists[, thinking] everything that is not German is not good." However, the two groups did cooperate closely during strikes, and in 1901, they staged a joint May Day celebration featuring a German translation of Pietro Gori's play, *Primo Maggio*, followed by a performance in the original Italian.[40]

Although large numbers of Eastern European Jews did not arrive in Paterson until after the turn of the century, small Yiddish anarchist groups had already emerged there in the 1890s. Among them were the Workingmen's Education Club, the Progressive Women's Society, and the Grupe Frayhayt, which lasted until the 1910s and affiliated with both the Anarchist Federation of New York and the Workmen's Circle. Yiddish anarchists from nearby New York City regularly spoke in Paterson, and Jewish anarchists, including the Grupe Frayhayt's former secretary, Max Goodman, joined the Italians to cofound Paterson's Francisco Ferrer Association and Ferrer Modern School in 1915.[41] *La Questione Sociale* editor Ludovico Caminita, however, charged that Saul Yanovsky of "the so-called anarchist" *Fraye Arbeter Shtime* had downplayed that paper's anarchism following McKinley's assassination to maintain his "no mean salary of 22 dollars per week."[42]

Finally, although Paterson had no significant Spanish community, Esteve kept it closely connected to Spanish-speaking radicals in New York as well as Tampa, Florida, where Esteve, Roda, and Widmar all resided for periods of time. For example, on July 11, 1897, the Italians hosted a *festa* for "the Spanish comrades who came from Brooklyn and New York," and two decades later, an Italian picnic included a "half-dozen Spanish comrades" as well as Mexican anarchist Rafael Romero Palacios.[43] The cross-ethnic solidarity established through shared ideology facilitated the incorporation of multilingual non-Italians into the Italian anarchist movement.

Paterson was also linked to a larger regional movement that encompassed most of New York and New Jersey. Dozens or even hundreds of Italian anarchists traveled by train to attend special events in Paterson or New York City: on one such occasion in November 1900, "several hundred . . . from New York, Brooklyn, Jersey City, Paterson, Hoboken, and West Hoboken and Union Hill" showed up at the Germania Assembly Rooms in the Bowery for a performance of the play *Senza Patria*, only to be turned away at the door by apprehensive police. That same year, the *New York Herald* reported, "anarchy has gained an effectual foothold among the Italian, German, French, Spanish and other foreign residents of Paterson and adjacent cities."[44]

The Right to Existence Group began producing *La Questione Sociale* in July 1895, eight months after *Il Grido degli Oppressi* had folded and twelve months after Italy's imposition of antiradical legislation left that country without a single anarchist publication. Paterson's new paper therefore "fulfilled a fundamental role in the Italian anarchist movement worldwide," garnering readers throughout Europe, the Americas, and North Africa.[45] But however international its scope and readership, *La Questione Sociale* was also intimately concerned with local and national matters. Two decades after its founding, Guabello claimed, "The history of this weekly publication is, you could say, the whole history of the anarchist movement among Italians in this country." Its local influence was especially pronounced: at the turn of the century approximately one-third of its three thousand weekly copies circulated within Paterson, which had an Italian population of just five thousand. This number is all the more impressive in light of Italian immigrants' documented habit of passing copies of newspapers from hand to hand and reading them aloud to acquaintances and family members.[46]

The first issue of *La Questione Sociale* was edited by a collective "whose lack of culture was made up for by good will and ardent faith in their ideal," according to Guabello. Shortly thereafter, Antonio Agresti, a well-known proponent of "propaganda by the deed," arrived from London and was briefly assigned the post of editor. On his heels came renowned anarchist poet, playwright, and lawyer Pietro Gori, who arrived in Paterson in late July 1895 and remained there for three months, briefly taking over editorial responsibilities with the aid of another recent arrival, Tuscan anarchist Edoardo Milano.[47] Gori then embarked on a yearlong coast-to-coast lecture tour, during which he secured support and subscriptions for the paper and organized the brief-lived Federazione Socialista-Anarchica dei Lavoratori Italiani nel Nord-America (Anarchist-Socialist Federation of Italian Workers in North America). Harry Kelly recalled that Gori "had a fine tenor voice, was a poet of merit, played the guitar, and was a highly competent speaker and writer; in short, [he was] one of the most gifted men imaginable, and one of the most capable propagandists I have ever met." Although Agresti, Milano, and Gori had all returned to Europe by the summer of 1896, their brief affiliation with *La Questione Sociale* endowed it with sterling radical credentials. After their departure, editorship of America's only Italian anarchist periodical went, ironically, to Spaniard Pedro Esteve.[48]

Faced with the decline of their movement in Italy, some anarchists appealed for greater anarchist organization and leadership in the labor movement, while others demanded abstention from all official organizations. At the head of the *organizzatori* (organizationists) stood Errico Malatesta, a former pupil of Mikhail Bakunin and the most revered Italian revolutionary of his day. In 1889, Malatesta called for the formation of an "anarchist party"—that is, a well-organized federation of groups dedicated to a mutually agreed upon program and capable of building a mass following.[49] But others saw those who promoted stronger organization as potential apostates who would drag anarchism into the mire of bureaucracy and legalitarianism. These *antiorganizzatori* (anti-organizationists)

FIGURE 6. *Left to right*: Pedro Esteve, Alberto Guabello, and Franz Widmar, *New York Herald*, July 31, 1900.

rejected all formally constituted organizations, even anarchist ones, as inherently authoritarian and stifling of individual initiative. However, they were not individualists, a label they associated with the followers of Max Stirner; instead, they called themselves "anarchist communists" because they believed in free association and the abolition of private property (as did the *organizzatori*, and Malatesta somewhat confusingly also used the "anarchist communist" label on occasion).[50] The struggle between these two camps followed Italians to America.

Unsurprisingly, given the rich organizational life of Northern Italian workers, the majority of Paterson's anarchists agreed with Malatesta. When Francesco Cini, a close comrade of Malatesta's, arrived from London in 1897, he became the new editor of *La Questione Sociale*.[51] After Cini vacated the position a year later, the Right to Existence Group offered it to another of Malatesta's protégés, Giuseppe Ciancabilla, who had been won over from socialism after interviewing Malatesta in 1897. But unbeknownst to Paterson's anarchists, Ciancabilla had, during a brief residence in Paris, gravitated toward anti-organizationist ideas and embraced propaganda by the deed as the only hope for sparking revolutionary uprisings.[52]

When Ciancabilla took charge of *La Questione Sociale*, he therefore wrote against participation in anarchist federations and "sterile" labor unions. He and a small group of supporters argued that the role of anarchists in the labor movement was to propagandize, not organize; according to Ciancabilla, "organization (not free agreement, nor free association, we mean), is absolutely anti-anarchist."[53] Fierce polemics between the *antiorganizzatori* and *organizzatori*, the latter headed by Esteve, filled the paper's pages. In May 1899, Esteve begged Malatesta himself to come rescue *La Questione Sociale*.

Esteve had met Malatesta in Italy in 1891 at the same Italian conference where he first encountered Maria Roda, and the two men became close friends and comrades, touring Spain together later that year in an attempt to organize a series of May Day uprisings. In 1898, Malatesta had been confined to *domicilio coatto* on the island of Lampedusa, but with outside aid, he engineered an elaborate escape and made his way to Tunisia, Malta, and ultimately London, where Esteve wrote to him. He immediately agreed to come to Paterson, which at the time was home to one of only two Italian anarchist periodicals in the world. Malatesta arrived on August 12, 1899, and stayed at Esteve's home. A special meeting of the Gruppo Diritto all'Esistenza voted to replace Ciancabilla with Malatesta by a margin of eighty to three, though editorial decisions were to be made by the group as a whole.[54] The dissenting members—Ciancabilla, Giovanni Della Barile, and Guabello—immediately seceded and founded their own paper, *L'Aurora* (The Dawn), though Guabello soon broke ranks and returned to *La Questione Sociale*.[55] For the next two years, the rival publications battled for leadership of the Italian movement, and Malatesta took his campaign to the road, traveling throughout the eastern United States as well as American-occupied Cuba.

This conflict was rooted in a fundamental disagreement over the mechanics of revolutionary movements. Malatesta and his supporters called themselves "anarchist-socialists" to emphasize their commitment to creating a mass movement based in working-class organizations. Unlike pure syndicalists, who viewed labor unions as sufficient unto themselves for carrying out revolution, socialist-anarchists did not believe that unions were "intended to emancipate the worker, because his slavery depends on causes that cannot be destroyed without revolutionarily transforming the entire constitution of society.... But they can always serve to educate, to morally uplift the working classes and to prepare them, to train them to fight." Moreover, Malatesta observed, "popular movements begin how they can"—that is, the potential results of small-scale struggles are indeterminate, making every strike the possible beginning of a revolutionary upsurge. The *organizzatori* did not oppose violence, which they viewed as an unfortunate necessity in the course of defending the revolution, and proclaimed that the "victorious insurrection is the most effective action for popular emancipation." Individual acts of violence in the absence of popular support, however, they viewed as ineffective and counterproductive.[56] According to Malatesta, "Organization is not a transitory necessity, a question of tactics and opportunity, but it is a necessity inherent to human society, and should be regarded by us as a matter of principle."[57]

Ciancabilla's camp came to the opposite conclusion. "The majority of workers," *L'Aurora* pointed out, "believe that an increase of wages or a reduction of hours of work is the maximum of the claims [a labor union] can achieve," making these organizations poor vehicles for pursuing radical goals.[58] Influenced by a deterministic reading of Kropotkin's writings on mutual aid and evolution as well as by Italian positivism and Marxist historical materialism, the *antiorganizzatori* believed that mass revolution was an inevitable product of historical forces. The compromise of formal organization was therefore unnecessary and would influence the outcome of revolutionary change for the worse. This view conveniently vindicated the increasing isolation of the anarchist movement within Italy but was also based on firsthand experience with conservative American unions and grounded in anarchism's critique of political power.[59] Despite their determinism, however, the *antiorganizzatori* also believed that propaganda by the deed could help spark the revolution—indeed, had they not, their theory would have allowed no historical role for anarchist militants, whom Ciancabilla celebrated as "the aristocracy of the proletariat. The knights of the ideal." Instead, in this view, anarchist violence could spontaneously generate the mass movement that the *organizzatori* hoped consciously to bring into being through patient organization.[60] These disagreements came to a dramatic climax on September 3, 1899, at a debate in a West Hoboken saloon, when a volatile barber and anti-organizationist, Domenico Pazzaglia, drew a pistol and fired at Malatesta, wounding him in the leg. Pazzaglia's own comrades, including Gaetano Bresci, immediately restrained him.[61] Months later, on July 29, 1900, Bresci shot and killed King Umberto I in the Milan suburb of Monza.

Bresci joined a host of anarchist assassins and would-be assassins who struck across Europe in the 1890s. Between 1894 and 1902, Italian anarchists alone killed a president of France, a prime minister of Spain, and the empress of Austria and made unsuccessful attempts on the lives of King Leopold II of Belgium, Italy's prime minister, and Umberto I (before Bresci succeeded).[62] Bresci was motivated by more than just abstract principle, however. In 1898, shortly after his arrival in Paterson, Italian troops opened fire on food protesters in Milan, killing more than one hundred. The following year, Umberto bestowed a commendation on the commander of those troops, General Fiorenzo Bava-Beccaris. As Bresci later testified, "When in Paterson I read of the events in Milan, where they even used cannons, I wept with rage and prepared myself for vengeance. I thought of the king who awarded a prize to those who carried out the massacres, and I became convinced that he deserved death." Bresci was also motivated by his experience of migration. "Besides avenging the victims," he admitted, "I wished to avenge myself, as I was forced, after having lived a very hard life, to emigrate."[63]

Despite Bresci's insistence that he acted alone, and despite his alignment with Ciancabilla's *L'Aurora*, sensationalist news stories attributed the assassination to an international anarchist conspiracy orchestrated by Malatesta and the Right to Existence Group. These rumors were fueled by a Paterson murder-suicide eleven days before Bresci's regicide. Anarchist dye worker Luigi Bianchi, known in Paterson as Sperandio Carbone, shot and killed Weidmann Dye Works foreman Giuseppe Pessina before turning the gun on himself. Two days later, the funeral director preparing Bianchi's body claimed to have found a bizarre suicide note pinned to the anarchist's jacket pocket that detailed how Bianchi had been chosen by a drawing of lots among anarchists to kill the king of Italy but was allowed to choose "a substitute" and settled on the "brute" Pessina. However, the authenticity of the note immediately came into question; police, who had supposedly overlooked the document, were unable to produce the original document, and some versions of the letter published in the press stated that the alleged lottery had occurred across the Atlantic, in Milan.[64] Moreover, Bianchi had personal motives for the murder, none of which were mentioned in the note: Pessina had refused to pay Bianchi for piano lessons the anarchist had given to his children and, more important, had fired Bianchi from the dye works the day before the attack.[65]

Two more anarchists, Paterson barber Nicola Quintavalle and former Paterson resident Antonio Laner, were arrested in Italy as possible accessories because both had traveled on the same ship as Bresci. Likewise, Emma Quazza, a nineteen-year-old Paterson socialist and fellow passenger with whom Bresci had an affair during the journey, was apprehended. But all three were released for lack of evidence. An international manhunt then targeted weaver and former Right to Existence Group treasurer Luigi Granotti, who had departed for Italy a few days before Bresci and was in Monza on the day of the assassination. Granotti, however, evaded capture and secretly returned to America, living undetected until his death in 1949.[66] Although one or more of these individuals may have known of Bresci's intent, no reputable evidence indicates a larger conspiracy.[67]

Nevertheless, Ciancabilla expressed unqualified support for Bresci's act. Somewhat surprisingly, the Right to Existence Group also publicly applauded it. None of its members mourned the loss of a monarch under whom they had personally suffered want and repression, and condemnation of Bresci would have exacerbated the division within the movement. *La Questione Sociale* printed fifteen thousand copies of a special free issue honoring Bresci that included only a passing criticism of propaganda by the deed ("We make propaganda for collective action of the masses," it emphasized).[68] The *organizzatori* appropriated Bresci as a revolutionary martyr, honoring him every July for decades to come, but they used his martyrdom to further their own commitment to organizing a mass movement. In 1901, *La Questione Sociale* reaffirmed its opposition to propaganda by the deed and published Malatesta's response to McKinley's assassination: Malatesta stopped short of condemning Czolgosz but charged that his act had changed nothing "except that the anarchists' position has become a little more difficult."[69]

Even before Umberto's murder, the *organizzatori* were a clear majority in Paterson, and they remained so after Malatesta returned to Europe at the end of 1899 and editorship of *La Questione Sociale* passed to fellow organizationists Widmar and Esteve. *L'Aurora*, for its part, struggled to survive and was forced to relocate, first to a small community of supporters in Yohoghany, Pennsylvania, then after an eight-month hiatus to the mining enclave of Spring Valley, Illinois, before finally folding in 1901, although anti-organizationist sentiments were widespread enough to foil repeated attempts to organize a federation of Italian anarchists in North America. The Italian anarchist movement in Paterson reached its peak between 1897 and 1903, with the formation of five additional groups: the Gruppo Socialista Anarchico "Pensiero ed Azione" ("Thought and Action" Socialist Anarchist Group), Gruppo Veritá (Truth Group), Gruppo i Risorti (The Resurrected Group), Gruppo Emancipazione della Donna (Woman's Emancipation Group), and Gruppo Propaganda Femminile (Woman's Propaganda Group).[70] But the movement was much larger than the official membership of these organizations. Outside of the core of activists who organized meetings, wrote and published literature, arranged and spoke at public events, and agitated in the workplace, the city's anarchists could mobilize between fifteen hundred and twenty-five hundred supporters and sympathizers for major events—a third to half of Paterson's Italian population.[71] In 1900, the *New York Herald* was horrified to discover that "it has come to such a point that anarchist meetings are no longer held behind closed doors in Paterson. Meetings addressed by anarchist leaders are public gatherings in halls connected with various saloons.... There are hundreds of workingmen, regularly attending these meetings.... The meetings are attended, too, by women."[72]

Anarchists were numerous enough to support several local institutions where "ethnicity and radicalism, ... working-class and movement cultures," came together "in the organization and use of leisure time."[73] In Biella, taverns had served as political meeting spaces, and numerous drinking societies (*società vinarie*) doubled as subversive organizations.[74] Italian workers continued this tradition in Paterson, where the back room of Aimone and Bianco's *birreria* at 325 Straight Street, co-owned by anarchist Federico Aimone (or Ajmone), regularly hosted anarchist meetings for many years and at one time housed a small anarchist bookstore. In its early years, *La Questione Sociale* received its mail at the bar's address.[75] Aimone's fellow former weaver and Right to Existence Group member Giovanni Tamaroglio, who came to Paterson from Piedmont in 1895, opened another tavern frequented by radicals. In 1910, however, agents of the Italian consulate noted that they had "reason to believe that the professions of anarchism he continues to make are not sincere but due primarily if not exclusively for reasons of personal financial interest, aimed at maintaining and possibly increasing his customers among the Italians living there and who also profess themselves anarchists"—a business strategy that illustrates the substantial number of local anarchists.[76] In the 1890s, the bar in back of Bartoldi's Hotel at 278 Straight Street, owned by Biellese migrant Bartolomeo Bertoldo Negro, was another center of anarchist activity, and in the 1910s, Tony Ramella's hall and saloon at North Seventh and Temple Streets was "known to be a meeting place of Italian anarchists." According to West Hoboken's police captain, in 1900, the city had "about forty [anarchist] fellows who congregate in various saloons in town here and chiefly at Tivola & Zucca's," while Camillo Tua's saloon served as the meeting place of the L'Aurora Group.[77] For anarchists who experienced upward economic mobility, operating a saloon was a way to remain rooted in the working-class community and provide a space for radical organizing and socializing.

In 1903, Firmino Gallo, who still worked in the mills, opened the Libreria Sociologica (Sociological Bookstore) at 77 Ellison Street; it remained in business until 1920 and served as "a casual meeting place of many anarchists, who purchase there anarchist publications of Italy, France, and the United States." It also functioned as a North American distribution center for anarchist literature; in 1920 federal agents confiscated receipts from the Libreria for orders from twenty-seven states as well as Canada.[78] Italian anarchists also founded a cooperative grocery store on Park Avenue with a meeting space upstairs. William Gallo recalled that the members of this club "met every Saturday and practically every evening. They played cards, had a drink of wine or beer, but not too much liquor. Every Saturday there was a dance, with music played by a little orchestra. . . . Father and Mother, especially Mother, did quite a lot of acting at the club, which had a small stage."[79]

Edoardo Milano formed Paterson's first anarchist mandolin orchestra, La Simpatica, in 1895, and Southern Italian anarchists later founded the orchestra L'Indipendente and the Circolo Corale Figli del Lavoro (Children of Labor Choral Circle). These groups performed at the frequent radical picnics and dances as well as celebrations on such occasions as Primo Maggio (May Day), the anniversary of Umberto's assassination, and the anarchists' secularized version of traditional Italian *feste della frutta* (harvest festivals). As early as 1894, an anarchist "family evening" attracted four hundred Italians, who carried on until four in the morning.[80] Radical dramas and comedies staged by *filodrammatici* (amateur theater groups) were also popular, and Paterson's anarchists formed North America's first *filodrammatica*, La Cosmopolita, in 1895.[81] These events raised money for anarchist causes while allowing families to take part in and consume entertainment infused with radical messages. Politics even extended to wardrobes: women signified their radicalism by adorning their dresses or hats with red ribbons, while anarchist men and occasionally women sported large black Lavalliere neckties known colloquially as "anarchist ties."[82]

These institutions and practices not only sustained the movement but also helped create an "Italian" community out of a fragmented population of Piedmontese, Lombardians, Calabrians, and Sicilians who had little sense of a common identity before emigrating. A clear Piedmontese bias existed within the movement—for example, the meeting space above the cooperative grocery was called the Piedmont Club, and on at least eight occasions between 1899 and 1916, anarchist *filodrammatici* gave performances in the Piedmontese dialect—but this bias was accompanied by a sustained effort to overcome both regional and national divisions. In 1899, *La Questione Sociale* was pleased to announce that a new Circolo Sociale e Filodrammatico (Social and Theater Circle) was "set up by some serious and intelligent youths of Southern Italy together with other of our companions from Piedmont.... We cannot fail to express our satisfaction to note between the Italian elements of Paterson signs of the disappearance of the spirit of parochialism [*campanile*] that always held the children of the various regions of Italy apart and we hope that the example set by the members of this Circle that meets our greatest sympathies has many imitators."[83] Nearly every anarchist office and hangout was located on or near Straight Street, an area originally settled by Northern Italians but largely populated by Southern Italians by 1910, and these institutions remained there despite this demographic shift.[84]

La Questione Sociale likewise helped create an "Italian" cultural identity among its readers. Only between 2.5 and 12 percent of Italians actually spoke the Florentine dialect that became the official language of Italy at the time of national unification in 1870, and most continued to converse in regional dialects, of which there were fifteen main groups, some of them mutually unintelligible. A 1911 study of Paterson's Italians noted that in the 1890s and 1900s, "the Italian language was spoken by few; those of the north . . . spoke their language, and the Southern[ers] keeping by themselves, spoke their different dialects." The Piedmontese "dialect" is in fact its own Romance language, closely related to both French and Catalan (which explains the ease with which Northern Italian, French, and Spanish anarchists collaborated).[85] However, literate Italians as well as many illiterates were also familiar with official Italian, and *La Questione Sociale* was generally written in this language. The Italian-language press was a medium through which migrants from different regions of Italy as well as multilingual individuals from outside the Italian peninsula could communicate, and it was critical for constructing an imagined community of Italian-speaking immigrants.[86]

Consequently, like their Jewish comrades, the Italians focused on adult and child education. At the end of 1899, the Right to Existence Group opened Paterson's only evening school for Italian workers. It offered language and writing lessons as well as classes on "American history, traditions, and social norms." Four years later, anarchists founded the Università Popolare (People's University), which offered free lectures and classes for adults.[87] The Università had transnational roots; socialists in Turin had created the first Università Popolare in 1900, and in May 1901, Italian anarchists in Alexandria, Egypt, had opened another. The Alexandrian group published a report on the project in *La Questione Sociale*, and in November 1901, one of the school's founders, Luigi Galleani, migrated to Paterson to edit *La Questione Sociale*. When Paterson's own Università Popolare opened its doors in February 1903, it was one of the first in the United States.[88] The Università shut down in 1914 but was succeeded by the Circolo di Coltura Operaia (Workers' Culture Circle) in 1915 and the Circolo Instruzione e Diletto Edmondo De Amicis (Edmondo De Amicis Educational and Hobby Circle) in 1916. Paterson's Scuola Moderna Francesco Ferrer (Francisco Ferrer Modern School), which held Sunday classes attended by thirty to eighty children and adolescents, also opened its doors in 1915.[89]

Antonio Rubino, a radical pharmacist who agitated on behalf of the IWW and whom the anarchists referred to as "our friend," directed both the De Amicis Circle and the Ferrer School.[90] From 1908 to 1910, Dr. Rubino also served as the national head of the Order of the Sons of Italy in America (L'Ordine figli d'Italia in America), the country's largest Italian fraternal society. Rubino was forced to resign from this post for reasons that remain obscure, but anarchists and syndicalists dominated the Paterson branch of the Sons of Italy, composed largely of Southern Italians, through at least 1913.[91]

This organization continued Italian workers' strong tradition of mutual aid societies. Already in 1882, the Società di Mutuo Soccorso ed Instruzione fra gli Operai Italiani (Mutual Aid and Educational Society for Italian Workers) existed in Paterson, and Bresci belonged to an Italian "benevolent society" there. In August 1901, the former head of Bresci's organization told the *New York Times*, "There are 5,000 Italians in Paterson, and all of them are more or less Anarchists." Ironically, a month later, *La Questione Sociale* censured two anarchists in nearby Passaic for joining fellow members of their Società di Mutuo Soccorso Cristoforo Columbo in a memorial service for King Umberto.[92] Anarchist Nicola Pirozzi later served as vice president of a mutual aid society in neighboring Dundee Lake (present-day Elmwood Park): according to federal agents, "a large number of the [society's] members are anarchists, all of the remainder are Roman Catholics."[93] Some mutual aid organizations were purely anarchist undertakings, among them the Società di Mutuo Soccorso "l'Aurora," formed in 1906, and in 1920, federal authorities described anarchist brothers

Jacques, Antonio, and Francesco Pitea as "members of the Mutual Aid Society, which is a camouflage for an anarchist group in Paterson."[94]

Of course, not all of Paterson's two dozen Italian mutual aid societies were subversive, and *La Questione Sociale* ridiculed those, like the self-proclaimed "10th Cavalry Regiment of Victor Emanuel's Guard," that were overtly monarchist or nationalist.[95] Moreover, most of these groups, regardless of political orientation, were exclusively male. Italian women, despite their representation in Paterson's workforce, were not encouraged to join anarchist organizations, participate in workers' meetings, lead strikes, or edit newspapers. Instead, they were urged to partake in family-centered events such as dances, picnics, and theatrical performances and to support men's activities. But many were not content in this role.

Female anarchist migrants such as Ninfa Baronio and Maria Roda were few in number but immensely important. By the time Roda arrived in Paterson, she was already an accomplished orator, and she wrote her first piece for *Il Grido degli Oppressi* in 1894, when she was seventeen. That same year, the *New York World* described her as "a black-haired, dark-skinned and black-gowned woman . . . of no uncertain power of speech," and local legend later credited her "with thrashing Paterson's largest, if not most active, policeman."[96] However, most of Paterson's anarchist women were like Ernestina Cravello, who before her emigration had a "good reputation" and was not politically active but who became involved in the anarchist movement as a result of her two brothers' participation. Soon thereafter, in the wake of King Umberto's assassination, American reporters dubbed Cravello the "Queen of the Anarchists," chiefly because her fluency in English temporarily made her the movement's spokesperson to the American press.[97] Regardless of where these women became radicalized, they agreed with Roda's sentiment, as summarized by the *New York Times*, that "women had even more cause than men to complain."[98]

Italian women confronted patriarchy on a daily basis in the home, the workplace, and the anarchist movement. Many anarchist men acted as *padroni di casa* (bosses of the home), and Emma Goldman's dealings with Italian and Spanish anarchists convinced her that "all Latin men still treat their wives, or their daughters, as inferiors and consider them as mere breeding machines as the caveman did."[99] Domestic violence was a pervasive feature of Italian family life on both sides of the Atlantic, and anarchist households were not immune. Nicola Quintavalle, for example, was arrested in West Hoboken for threatening to kill his wife.[100] Men's disregard for female partners took less violent forms as well: when Bresci left on what he knew would be a one-way trip to kill the king of Italy, he left his pregnant Irish American wife ignorant of his plans and with no means of supporting herself or their daughters, and he carried on a romantic affair with a nineteen-year-old during the journey.

FIGURE 7. Ernesta (Ernestina) Cravello, "Queen of the Anarchists," *Evansville Courier*, August 5, 1900.

Three additional factors limited female participation. First, many Italian families subjected unmarried women to stringent surveillance and control outside of the home. Second, Italian women who continued to work after marriage took on domestic duties in addition to workplace ones, making it difficult to find time for other activities. When male weavers reprimanded female coworkers in 1907 for not attending union meetings, the women retorted in *La Questione Sociale* that they were busy washing, cooking, and sewing for their husbands, fathers, and brothers.[101] Finally, as Jennifer Guglielmo notes, the evidence "suggests that women's activism was not only distinct from men's, but also largely invisible or insignificant to them."[102]

Ironically, anarchist men relied heavily on the female labor they valued so little. Performances by *filodrammatici*, in which women were especially active, provided much of the funding for male-run publications like *La Questione Sociale*. Moreover, because Italian women both earned income and managed household finances, many of the voluntary donations listed in these publications under men's names represented, in part, women's labor. Female contributions were sometimes more direct: Baronio helped run Firmino Gallo's Libreria Sociologica, Adalgisa Guabello subsidized much of Alberto Guabello's activism with her earnings as a weaver and did "all the work" running the shop Alberto opened after his retirement from the mills, and Ciancabilla's partner, Ersilia Cavedagni, edited the final issues of *L'Aurora* in Spring Valley after he was arrested for praising Leon Czolgosz.[103] Anarchist women were therefore exasperated by men who viewed them as naturally conservative and intellectually inferior or told them at meetings, "You are a woman, shut up!"[104] Marginalized within their own movement, they organized to advance not only anarchism but also their fight against patriarchy.

Women in Biella began organizing their own mutual aid societies and workers' organizations in the 1870s and, following this model, Roda, Baronio, and Cravello cofounded Paterson's Gruppo Emancipazione della Donna in September 1897. "Men say we are frivolous, that we are weak, that we are incapable of supporting the struggle against this intolerable society, that we cannot understand the ideal of anarchism," wrote Roda on behalf of the organization. "But they are the cause of our weakness, our undeveloped intellects, because they restrict our instruction . . . and ignore us."[105] The group held lectures, contributed articles to the anarchist press, published pamphlets, and formed both the Club Femminile di Musica e di Canto (Women's Music and Song Club) and the Teatro Sociale (Social Theater), which performed dramas about women's self-emancipation that contrasted with radical plays' prevailing depiction of women as victims in need of protection by revolutionary men.[106] Other anarchist *gruppi femminili* (women's groups) soon appeared in West Hoboken, New York, Philadelphia, Chicago, Boston, Barre, San Francisco, and the coal towns of Illinois.[107] These women were interested not in "electoral feminism" but rather in "women's emancipation."[108]

The most immediate form of emancipation they sought was from the bonds of traditional marriage. The *New York Herald* noted that the women who attended Paterson's anarchist meetings, "although in no sense disorderly, fall in readily enough with the anarchist doctrines regarding the looseness of the marriage tie." According to a Catholic Italian journalist, "All of the girls, after a few months, come to abandon the church. Weddings are made into free unions, children are christened . . . in public assemblies, between cups of wine and anarchist songs."[109] In 1920, Gemma Mello, a Piedmontese silk weaver belonging to a small group of anti-organizationists, told federal agents that she believed in neither God ("I have never seen him") nor marriage. When agents pressed her to elaborate, she explained,

A: "I believe in comradeship."
Q: "What do you mean by comradeship?"
A: "Well if I get out of jail I'm going to get a lover
either in this country or Italy."[110]

Men, too, upheld this ideal; in the first issue of *Il Grido degli Oppressi*, editor Francesco Saverio Merlino explained that "Socialist Anarchists want to abolish prostitution within the family and without: to make woman independent from man and man from woman. . . . Socialist Anarchists want man and woman to work, each according to his or her abilities . . . and society as a whole to help parents in the education of their children."[111] Despite the alarm with which outsiders greeted talk of "free love," the ideal "free union" envisioned by the Italians resembled the freely chosen but not formalized monogamy practiced by Yiddish anarchists. These unions were often lifelong, as in the case of Maria Roda and Pedro Esteve or Ninfa Baronio and Firmino Gallo, who had eight and six children together, respectively. William Gallo recalled, "The same was true of all of my aunts and uncles, and none of them ever separated or divorced, none of them."[112]

Most of these relationships reproduced a gendered division of labor. In 1900, Ernestina Cravello was working at the Paragon Mill and, emboldened by her sudden notoriety, broke off a marriage engagement "that she might devote her life to the cause of Anarchy." But two years later, she married fellow anarchist Gaspare Ferro and left the mills to become a mother, eventually raising five children. Baronio also "did not work in the mills but took care of the house and the children."[113] Both *Il Grido degli Oppressi* and *La Questione Sociale* promoted free unions while simultaneously fetishizing women's role as mothers. According to Antonio Agresti, "We think that the one great honor, the greatest triumph for the woman would be to be a mother, to have children: but for society the woman that has children is not a mother until she is united with a man, labeled, branded, stamped, [and] registered like a package for delivery." He asked, "Where is the respect for the will of the woman? Where is the respect for her freedom; where is the respect for her individuality?" That women, emancipated from the authority of a husband, would aspire to motherhood remained beyond question. Another writer sermonized, "If there is in contemporary society a noble, sublime, I might say holy mission; it is certainly the mission of the mother, taken in its true sense"—that is, to instill in her children "the love of humanity" and "love of their own freedom united with respect for the freedom of others."[114] Female writers also took up this argument. According to Ersilia Cavedagni, "The woman is and will always be the educator of the family, that which has and will always have the most direct and the most important influence on the children." By laying claim to "anarchist motherhood," these women placed themselves as integral to the process of sustaining revolutionary ideology through the next generation. This argument reinforced many aspects of the patriarchal order anarchists sought to destroy, but it also highlighted the importance of women's domestic and reproductive labor.[115]

In addition, anarchist women appropriated notions of masculinity and femininity to define their enemies. In 1895, *La Questione Sociale* printed an article—later reproduced as a pamphlet by the Gruppo Emancipazione della Donna—by celebrated Italian feminist Anna Maria Mozzoni, who had ties to both the socialist and anarchist movements. Mozzoni asked her female audience, "And for you, oh woman of the people, what is the *patria*? It is the policeman who comes to take your child to make him a soldier—it is the tax collector who extorts the family tax [*fuocatico*] from your always almost extinct family—. . . it is the law that gives your children as property to your husband and that declares yourself his slave and servant. Of the glories of this *patria*, of its joys, its assets, its favors, not even one reaches you."[116] A few years later, Cravello explained on behalf of the Right to Existence Group, "We approved the killing of Carnot, the President of France. We approved the killing of Canovas, Prime Minister of Spain. We did not approve the killing of Elizabeth, Archduchess of Austria. We do not war on women."[117] Patriarchy and the *patria* were thus linked in anarchist feminist discourse.

In 1902, the Gruppo Emancipazione della Donna thanked the "many good male comrades who have assisted us with great, brotherly encouragement." Among these enlightened men were Esteve, who opened the pages of *La Questione Sociale* to women's writings, and Ciancabilla, whose *L'Aurora* similarly published a number of articles on women's emancipation. However, the Gruppo also observed that "our male comrades have been reluctant to defend us from the angry persecution of many eternal malcontent men who see in our motives nothing but pride, in our actions nothing but mistakes, in our words nothing but orthography, rewarding us with their malice, their jokes, their never-ending arrogance."[118] Some well-intentioned male efforts also went awry. One especially outrageous article in *La Questione Sociale* arguing in favor of women's rights maintained that although the "black race" was "certainly inferior to the White in many respects . . . illustrious men did not hesitate to ask for their equality, and humanity has given them rights," thus proving that equality of rights did not depend on equality of abilities. This argument reinforced the supposed inferiority of both women and African Americans under the pretense of egalitarianism.[119] Women's battle to be treated and regarded as equals was ongoing and never entirely successful. Nevertheless, it added a strong feminist undercurrent to Paterson's radical subculture.

Anarchist men and women alike shared a desire to create a new society fundamentally different from those of the Old World they had left behind and the New World in which they had settled. They found the promises of both Italian and American republicanism hollow and forswore attachments to both. A contributor to the first issue of *La Questione Sociale* recounted how he, "like thousands of others emigrated to this land of America believing it possible to find a living [*un pane*] less bitter and less backbreaking. But alas! Here too I met new disappointments and new abuses, new falsehoods told by the holders of social wealth." He signed with the name Un Cosmopolita (A Cosmopolitan).[120] Even the name of the Right to Existence Group was a protest against American conditions: Ernestina Cravello explained, "We are not treated well. The Americans insult us like dogs. . . . We have the right to live."[121]

Anarchists began to use "Free Country" as an ironic title for news reports detailing violence against immigrants, workers, and African Americans.[122] They sometimes quoted approvingly from "the glorious Declaration of Independence," but only to demonstrate the ways in which America fell short of its principles and to justify the overthrow of government tyranny.[123] With the erosion of its ideals, the United States had become, according to Luigi Galleani, "the grand republic, the fat, Cossack, and bigoted republic of the Morgans, the Rockefellers and the Carnegies, the republic of market fixing, of torment, of lynchings, of the Bible and the gallows."[124]

The "barbaric" treatment of blacks and other minorities provided anarchists with their most damning proof of American declension and hypocrisy. *La Questione Sociale*'s successor publication, *L'Era Nuova*, extolled the virtues of Native Americans, Asians, Africans, Arabs, Jews, and all "the races of color" while declaring, "Since the most ancient times the white race behaved against the other races like a predatory animal." The "systematic destruction of the races of color" by white Europeans and Americans not only betrayed the principles of freedom and equality but also resulted in the "loss of human variety, the beauty of the entire human species, deprived of its very beautiful and powerful branches"—in other words, the loss of cosmopolitanism.[125] In 1916, the anarchists of the Paterson Philosophical Society hosted a lecture by Harlem radical Hubert Harrison with the provocative title, "Shall the Negro Become the Dominating Race?" A public cross burning by local members of the resurgent Ku Klux Klan failed to intimidate either the group or its speaker.[126]

Italians' sensitivity to racism was undoubtedly linked to their experiences as racialized subjects. Although legally defined as "white," they were categorized by scientific and legal authorities as belonging to an inferior racial group variously labeled Mediterranean, Latin, or Alpine. Italians were informally excluded from many occupations and American labor unions and received lower wages than almost any other immigrant group. According to the Italian American anarchist paper *Cronaca Sovversiva* (Subversive Chronicle), in the United States "the Americans and English, the Polish and Slavs, the Germans and French are *whites*; the blacks—there is no possible doubt—are *negroes*. And the Italians? The Italians are no longer black, but they are still not white, they are *Italians*, something between white and black: they are *dagoes* . . . something of a hybrid between a man and a gorilla, an anthropological leftover."[127] Italians were also the only Europeans repeatedly lynched by white mobs in the American South and West.[128]

Yet the act of condemning the "white race" for its crimes against "the races of color" reproduced racial categories, and although the anarchist press lamented Americans' "race hatred" (*odio di razza*) toward Italians, it simultaneously included the Genoese Christopher Columbus—and by logical extension, all Italians—within the ranks of the predatory "white race." Over time, however, Paterson's Italians developed a more nuanced understanding of race. A 1915 contributor to *L'Era Nuova* attacked not just the notion of racial hierarchies but racialization itself, arguing that race is a "historical notion" rather than "a notion of natural science" and that racial categories are based on an "arbitrary conception of race" imposed on conglomerations of "heterogeneous ethnic elements and based initially on intellectual factors: language, religion, custom, law, civilization, etc."[129] This deconstruction prefigured the arguments discrediting scientific racism that would not become generally accepted in academic circles until after the Second World War.

For all of their condemnations of America's economic, political, and racial order, Italian anarchists were not indifferent to the relative advantages that it afforded them. Malatesta noted during his American sojourn, "As bad as conditions may be here in the United States, they are still exceptionally favorable to us, compared to continental Europe: there are more resources than elsewhere, and there is opportunity for an activity that can be expanded slowly, perhaps, but without too much danger of being suddenly interrupted by the government."[130] Italians also enjoyed a higher standard of living in America: a weaver who returned to Biella from Paterson told a Biellese reporter, "Life over there is incomparably better than in Italy; you're paid more, you dress better, even the factory girls wear bonnets." Nevertheless, this migrant had joined Paterson's anarchist movement and declared that she "approved of the anarchy that will save the world."[131] America's benefits did not outweigh its failings.

Italians had the lowest naturalization rate of any European immigrant group, and as late as 1920, two-thirds of New Jersey's Italian-born residents were not citizens. State politics, dominated by a system of boss rule based on graft and patronage, offered little incentive to take part in the democratic process, which in any case was alien to most Italians. In 1911, Paterson had only nine hundred registered Italian voters.[132] Anarchists, of course, saw little value in suffrage and opposed citizenship on ideological grounds; unlike their socialist rivals, they advised fellow immigrants to abstain from naturalization and voting. Nevertheless a few, including Firmino Gallo and printer Beniamino Mazzotta, did become citizens, likely for pragmatic reasons.[133] Franz Widmar, by contrast, recognized that under antianarchist statutes, he could "not be given the paper," but he further informed authorities "he was not an American citizen and had no intention of becoming one." Fellow anarchist Nicola Pironi was more blunt, declaring, "Citizen papers are only good to wipe my ass on."[134]

Resistance to political incorporation did not signify lingering loyalty to the Italian state. Though these radicals remained *Italians* and thought of themselves as such, their sense of *italianità* (Italianness) was cultural and linguistic rather than political. They carried out their activism in Italian or Piedmontese rather than English simply "on the ground that they should only make themselves ridiculous by speaking in an unfamiliar tongue," and as late as 1911, only 23 percent of Southern Italian men and 5 percent of Southern Italian women in the United States could speak English with any fluency.[135] As for the Kingdom of Italy, no term was subjected to as much abuse in Italian American anarchist literature as *la patria*, and anarchists routinely proclaimed themselves to be a people *senza patria* (without a country), an appellation popularized by Gori's play *Senza Patria*, written during his stay in America. An anarchist leaflet distributed in New Jersey in 1907 announced, "In the jumble of all prejudices, hypocrisies and conventionalisms of society, if there is one falsehood that needs to be fought and demolished more than others for the disastrous consequences that it produces, it is certainly the PATRIA."[136] Seven years later, on the eve of the First World War, *L'Era Nuova* declared,

> We anarchists are against the Patria, against all Patrias of the present social order.
>
> The reason we are against the Patria is because in its name injustice, barbarity, inequality, economic exploitation, [and] political lies are perpetuated. . . .
>
> We want to demolish this carnivorous, unjust, Barbarous, fratricidal [*Caina*] Patria, and on the ruins of its rotting carcass we want to plant [the] avenging, sublime and terrible fear of tyrants, the flag of Anarchy.[137]

Cravello explained, "We have a beautiful country in Italy, but we are forced to leave it or die. Thousands of Italians need bread in their own country, where plenty can be produced, but if they ask for it they are thrown into prison." Therefore, *Il Grido degli Oppressi* concluded, "If by *patria* one means the place where one has, at birth, the right to live, in this case *Italy is not the patria of the Italians*."[138]

Many of Italy's first generation of anarchists, including Errico Malatesta and Alberto Guabello, began as Mazzinian republicans but grew disenchanted with Italian unification. Gori explained to his American comrades, "Now, too late, alas! we can understand how all the patriotic declamations of the Italian high class for the 'unification' and the 'independence' of the peninsula tended only (except the disinterested sacrifice of the true martyrs) to the conclusion of a good bargain. After the foreigners were expelled and the bargain closed, the Italian people had to pay a dear and salty bill."[139] Following Bakunin, Italian anarchists instead distinguished between the *paese* or *terra* (one's hometown or native land) and the *patria* (the artificial political state). The decoupling of the Italian "nation" from Italian state allowed for a far more flexible and inclusive definition of *italianità* in which birthplace, descent, geography, and citizenship mattered little, as demonstrated by the inclusion of individuals such as Pedro Esteve and Franz Widmar within the "Italian" movement. Furthermore, anarchists did not regard the Italian nation as a cohesive community with shared interests. "We are not patriots," *La Questione Sociale* emphasized. "The worker, the oppressed, Chinese or Russian or from any land is our brother, just as our enemy is the proprietor, the oppressor, even if born in our own village."[140] By virtue of multilingualism, class solidarity, and cosmopolitanism, individuals could simultaneously belong to one or more "national" movements as well as to a worldwide class of "the oppressed." Thus, in 1919, a single issue of Paterson's anarchist paper *La Jacquerie* referred to those attending an anarchist congress in Florence as "our Italian brothers" and to Emma Goldman, who spoke not a word of Italian, as "our Emma."[141]

During his editorship of *La Questione Sociale*, Malatesta articulated this cosmopolitanism in programmatic terms, calling for "Abolition of borders," "brotherhood between all peoples," and "War on patriotism."[142] Every September, anarchist periodicals and special "antipatriotic" publications railed against Italian American celebrations of XX Settembre, the holiday commemorating Italian unification. In 1895, *La Questione Sociale* admonished, "Workers, on this day on which you talk with rebounding phrases of a *patria* of narrow and petty borders, raise your eyes to the great *patria* of humanity . . . : *the earth*, to the great family of generous hearts: *humanity*." Four years later, Paterson's "Committee against the Celebration of XX Settembre" arranged a lecture by Malatesta at Feist Hall and printed ten thousand circulars condemning the holiday to be distributed in other cities.[143] The uniquely Italian American celebration of Columbus Day, first observed by Italian immigrants in the 1860s, was doubly objectionable as a result of its nationalist and imperialist roots. In 1892, *Il Grido degli Oppressi* denounced Columbus as "a pirate and adventurer . . . indifferent to massacre" and "a man without principles, without any noble purpose, but consumed with the desire to plunder and command" whose subjugation of Native Americans set the stage for "racial prejudices and hatreds" in America and "the martyrdom of the negroes in the South." When this article generated "a sea of protests," the paper reiterated that Columbus was "a great pirate" and enslaver.[144] Over the years, anarchists sporadically disrupted Columbus Day parades in Italian American communities.[145]

They also attacked the Catholic Church. In an 1896 lecture in Paterson, Gori proclaimed that the "war on religion" was of "immense . . . interest to the working class, which has everything to gain with the progress of science and free thought. . . . For free-thinking men, the word *religion* has a certain unpleasant taste; religion and freedom are contradictory terms."[146] Against a church that promoted class cooperation and Americanization, anarchist *mangiapreti* (priest eaters) seized on the figure of Lucifer as the consummate rebel; more than one signed their writings under his name, and an anarchist newspaper published in New York bore the title *La Rivolta degli Angeli* (Revolt of the Angels). Paterson anarchist Ludovico Caminita, who authored a 147-page antireligious tract, even named his son Lucifero (though the boy was mercifully nicknamed Curly, and later went by Ludwig Caminita Jr.).[147]

Italian immigrants were ripe for this anti-Catholic propaganda. The Catholic Church had opposed the incorporation of the Papal States into Italy, making anticlericalism a staple of Italian republicanism, and Italian immigrants had extremely low levels of church attendance.[148] The Piedmontese migrants who settled in Paterson transplanted a strong regional anticlerical tradition with roots in the Mazzinian movement of the 1880s, and few consented to religious services upon their deaths, let alone attended church. Weekly anarchist meetings were invariably scheduled for Sundays, and before 1910, Paterson was home to just a single Italian Catholic church, which faced perennial difficulties collecting adequate funds to pay its mortgage. In 1906, the *New York Sun* noted that Paterson's Italians were "to a great extent irreligious."[149]

Anarchists deliberately sought to fragment the Italian community along ideological and class lines. Catholic priests, the wealthy *prominenti*, and the exploitative *padroni* were all targets of anarchist wrath. Rather than alienating fellow immigrants, the anarchists' antinationalism, anticapitalism, and anticlericalism gained them widespread sympathy, allowing them to stand at the forefront of Paterson's labor movement.

Italians began joining and forming labor unions soon after arriving in the United States. By 1887, more than one-quarter of Paterson's Italians belonged to the Knights of Labor, while many others joined the short-lived Progressive Union of Silk Workers.[150] In May 1892, Italian and French anarchists organized a weavers' strike in one of the city's mills, gaining a one-cent hourly pay increase, and two years later, Italian, German, and English anarchists, joined by Socialist Labor Party leader Daniel De Leon, led a partially successful general strike of silk workers.[151] In 1897, anarchists in West Hoboken formed the Lega di Resistenza Internazionale (International League of Resistance), composed of "various nationality groups that are autonomous," and Paterson's Italian anarchists quickly founded their own affiliate, the Lega di Resistenza fra i Tessitori Italiani (League of Resistance of Italian Weavers). Within seven months, Paterson's League had grown to more than five hundred members, led a string of successful strikes, and arranged to send organizers to silk mills in eastern Pennsylvania. Its leading spirit was Right to Existence Group member Vittorio Cravello, and *La Questione Sociale* acted as the organization's unofficial mouthpiece. The league federated with the United Silk Workers of Hudson County but was expelled in February 1899 and then dissolved.[152] In 1900, several mills fired known anarchists after the killings of Giuseppe Pessina and Umberto I, but a series of shop strikes resulted in the reinstatement of most of those discharged, and over the following months, anarchists led a series of walkouts at some of Paterson's largest mills.[153]

Many of these anarchists came to view labor unions and strikes as central elements of revolutionary change. As early as 1895 Pietro Gori had promoted the revolutionary general strike, the centerpiece of syndicalist ideology, in *La Questione Sociale*, and by 1901 Alberto Guabello, the former insurrectionist, was declaring that the general strike "will be the solution to the social question" and "the onset of the social revolution." Evolving Malatesta's anarchist-socialism into a position closer to anarcho-syndicalism, *La Questione Sociale* now argued: "The Union is a great force, able, not only to achieve momentary advantages, but also to attain, with them, your complete emancipation . . . without begging any help from the capitalists and the authorities who have ever been, and will fatally ever be, the enemies of the working class."[154]

This ideological shift was accelerated by a series of natural and human-caused disasters in 1902. On the night of February 9, fire broke out in a trolley shed and, fueled by sixty-mile-an-hour winds, swiftly consumed the city's business district, including City Hall, several silk shops, and the offices of *La Questione Sociale* at 353 Market Street. As the city struggled to rebuild, a flood inundated its Italian section from February 28 through March 2. Most of Paterson's silk mills and dye houses were destroyed or damaged and suspended operation, leaving thousands of workers temporarily unemployed. *La Questione Sociale* was printed out of makeshift offices in "a building in the rear of a Chinese laundry."[155]

Soon after returning to work in April, a group of Italian dyers' helpers from two dye houses presented a list of demands to the owners. One of the ringleaders was Right to Existence Group member Giovanni Di Nardo, who had been trying to organize his fellow dyers since 1899. After the dyers at Auger and Simon received no response, they walked out, armed themselves with stones and dye sticks, and marched through the streets, calling on fellow dyers to join them and storming dye houses to shut down production. One owner was beaten unconscious and another suffered minor acid burns after being thrown into a dye vat. The following day, police protecting a dye house opened fire and seriously injured a striker. More than three thousand dyers soon joined the strike, and although Italians and Germans predominated, at strike meetings "the proceedings were slow because of the many nationalities represented." In early May, strikers organized themselves into the United Dyers, Helpers, and Finishers of America and elected Di Nardo secretary of its Italian section.[156] The struggle deadlocked, however, after the United Silk Workers of America, which represented many English-speaking weavers, refused to call for a general strike of its members, and employers refused to negotiate with the striking dyers.[157] It fell to the anarchists and their allies to expand the struggle.

La Questione Sociale's new editor, charismatic Piedmontese anarchist Luigi Galleani, spearheaded this effort. Galleani had arrived six months earlier to replace Pedro Esteve at the paper after escaping from *domicilio coatto* and spending time in Tunisia, Malta, and Cairo before making his way to London. According to a spy for the Italian government, Malatesta had dispatched Galleani from London to Paterson "to extend the organizationist propaganda." However, Galleani had already begun to turn away from the ideas of Malatesta and toward the stance of the *antiorganizzatori*. Nevertheless, he did embark for Paterson, where, despite his own views, he worked toward "mitigating and extinguishing the terrible dissidence which the discord . . . between Malatesta and Ciancabilla had left behind." On the eve of the 1902 strike, he even delivered a series of talks to members of the Italian Weavers' Union on "workers' economic organization" and the value of solidarity.[158] After the dyers walked out, Galleani and Vittorio Cravello agitated among the Italian weavers, and French anarchist Michel Dumas ceased publishing *Germinal* in order to participate in the struggle. Galleani also recruited bilingual British anarchist William Mac-Queen and Austrian anarchist Rudolf Grossman from New York to organize the English- and German-speaking weavers. These agitators convened multilingual meetings where they called for weavers to join the strike as well as for the creation of "one big silk union" representing all workers in the industry.[159]

Following one such meeting in the suburb of Haledon on June 18, Galleani led a march of between fifteen hundred and two thousand workers into Paterson. The marchers besieged numerous mills, breaking windows and doors. When police confronted strikers outside of the Hall silk mill, gunfire erupted on both sides, sparking a roving street battle that lasted for several hours. The *New York Times* reported, "Never in its long career of lawless deeds has this city witnessed a sight so remarkable as it saw to-day. A mob ruled it." According to a French observer, "Paterson was in a revolution."[160]

But this revolution was short-lived. The city's firemen were armed and dispatched to aid embattled police, and at least eight strikers and one policeman were shot and hundreds more injured. Galleani received a superficial gunshot wound to the face, while another anarchist, Lora Salvino, had both lungs pierced by a bullet. New Jersey's governor sent infantry and cavalry regiments to restore order, and the strike was officially called off on July 12.[161] Galleani, MacQueen, and Grossman were charged with inciting to riot and malicious mischief, for which Grossman and MacQueen each received five years imprisonment. Both men fled the country, but MacQueen returned to serve his sentence and after three years was deported back to England, where he died in 1908 from tuberculosis contracted while incarcerated.[162] Galleani fled to Canada and then went into hiding among comrades in Barre, Vermont. When he finally returned to Paterson to face trial in 1907, seven sympathetic jurors refused to convict him, resulting in a hung jury.[163]

Galleani also responded to the strike's collapse and the conservatism of the United Silk Workers with a bitter tirade against labor unions in general, arguing that the corruption of their leaders was an inevitable result of "objective causes"—that is, *"the exercise of authority."* He now gave full expression to the doctrines of the *antiorganizzatori* and severed his relationship with *La Questione Sociale*, establishing his own paper in Vermont, *Cronaca Sovversiva*.[164] Most of the strikers, however, came away with very different lessons. Despite the strike's failure, Southern Italian dyers had proven just as militant as their northern counterparts and just as amenable to anarchist leadership. Nine years afterward, a study of Paterson's Italians found that June 18, the anniversary of the riots, "is a day remembered by the dyers, as a day in which they were able to show that patience has its limits, and that a popular furor is above the gun and the sword."[165] The potential for mass working-class action demonstrated in the 1902 strike also pushed the Right to Existence Group to adopt further tactics of revolutionary syndicalism.

As soon as the strike ended, *La Questione Sociale* advised workers to continue their fight on the shop floor by "striking on the job" through direct action. The paper translated a long excerpt from "a pamphlet published years ago by our friends in Europe," although it neglected to name the source: *Boycottage et Sabottage*, a foundational document of the French syndicalist movement written in 1897 by anarchists Émile Pouget and Paul Delesalle. The selection discussed worker sabotage by using the example of the Scottish practice of *ca'canny*, "a short and simple term to designate a new tactic employed by workers instead of the strike": "To work slowly at your leisure," or "bad work for bad pay." The translator, however, omitted the unfamiliar French word *sabotage*, which had not yet entered into common usage in Italy. (In October 1900, when *sabotage* had first appeared in the pages of *La Questione Sociale*, the paper provided an accompanying translation of it as *l'acciabbattamento*, an archaic Italian word literally meaning "bunglement.")[166] Nevertheless, these articles stand out as some the earliest expositions of worker sabotage published in the United States. Combined with their calls for "one big union" and the revolutionary general strike, Paterson's anarchists anticipated what would become the core elements of the Industrial Workers of the World's syndicalist ideology, though sabotage would not be discussed in English-language IWW literature until 1910.[167]

La Questione Sociale, with Esteve again at the helm, was soon filled with articles on syndicalism. In January 1903, anarchists formed the new Unione fra Tessitori e Tessitrici di Lingua Italiana (Union of Italian-Speaking Male and Female Weavers), and many participated in the fifteen strikes conducted by silk workers in 1903 and 1904.[168] In April 1905, *La Questione Sociale* published a translation of the "Industrial Union Manifesto" calling for a convention to meet in Chicago and form a new labor union federation dedicated to "establishing an industrial democracy, wherein there should be no wage slavery, but where the workers will own the tools which they operate, and the products of which they alone will enjoy." Two months later, Joe Corna, an Italian organizer for the

United Mine Workers in Spring Valley and a frequent contributor to *La Questione Sociale*, called on fellow anarchists to attend the upcoming gathering.[169] More than a dozen did so, including Corna and his Spring Valley comrade Antonio Andrà, who together wrote an extensive report on the founding of the Industrial Workers of the World for *La Questione Sociale*.[170] Paterson's anarchists viewed the new organization as the "one big union" for which strikers had called in 1902 and hailed its formation as "almost an anarchist victory." The preamble to the IWW's constitution, a compromise among socialist, syndicalist, anarchist, and industrial unionist factions, declared, "The working class and the employing class have nothing in common. There can be no peace so long as hunger and want are found among millions of working people and the few, who make up the employing class, have all the good things of life. Between these two classes a struggle must go on until all the toilers come together on the political, as well as on the industrial field, and take and hold that which they produce by their labor through an economic organization of the working class, without affiliation with any political party."[171]

Less than three months later, IWW president William O. Sherman and general secretary William E. Trautmann spoke in Paterson at the invitation of the Right to Existence Group, and that November, Alberto Guabello headed a successful strike against the Victoria Silk Company with aid from the IWW. In March 1906, anarchists formed IWW Silk Workers' Union Local 152, which had four branches by the end of the year. The existing anarchist-led weavers' union was incorporated as Local 152's Italian Silk Workers Union, with Guabello as its secretary, while the dyers union created during the 1902 strike joined as the Dyers' Helpers' and Finishers' Union, with Giovanni Di Nardo at its head. Over the next year, the IWW in Paterson conducted twenty-four strikes involving some eight hundred workers.[172] In March 1907, Local 152 launched an organizing drive among dye workers, who "responded . . . in scores." When several IWW members were fired from the Auger and Simon dye house—where the 1902 strike had begun—their fellow workers successfully struck to have them reinstated, and the union grew to one thousand members.[173] That same month Guabello headed a two-week strike at the New Jersey Silk Company that raised wages, and a one-day strike at the Kramer Hat Band Company forced a recalcitrant worker to join the union, while another strike to reinstate discharged IWW members at the Graf Hat Band Company failed.[174]

Men monopolized the leadership of Local 152, and the IWW was steeped in an ideal of "virile syndicalism" that equated working-class militancy with masculinity. However, male syndicalists still needed women's participation in their unions and celebrated female working-class militancy.[175] Women made up a substantial portion of Local 152's membership, and a visiting IWW organizer remarked, "It is very encouraging to see the splendid stand taken by the girls and women in these mills. They grasp the situation and perform their part in a very practical and creditable manner." The organization actively sought to incorporate female workers and, concerned that the women employed as silk winders, quillers, and cloth packers, who made just two to four dollars a week, could not afford monthly dues, successfully petitioned the IWW's General Executive Board to reduce the dues of workers making less than five dollars a week to fifteen cents a month.[176]

In addition to Guabello, the IWW's most active Italian organizer was Ludovico Caminita, a Sicilian typesetter and writer who migrated to the United States with his younger brother in 1902. Born Michele Caminita in 1878, he adopted his brother's name in 1903 after the real Ludovico died, neglected, in a Winnipeg hospital after suffering a broken leg in a rail yard accident. According to Michele/Ludovico, "I use that name as [a] pseudonym in memory of a victim of capitalist greed and evil." Caminita was a socialist when he arrived but quickly became disillusioned with the Italian American socialist movement. After finding work in the print shop of Luigi Galleani's *Cronaca Sovversiva* in Barre, Caminita soon became an anarchist. In 1906, however, he moved into the orbit of the *organizzatori* after a debate with Pedro Esteve. Impressed by Caminita's caustic wit and eloquence, Esteve invited him to Paterson to help edit *La Questione Sociale* and then left the paper in Caminita's hands when Esteve and his family relocated to Tampa later that year.[177] Caminita immediately threw himself into the twin tasks of editing the paper and organizing for the IWW, and transformed *La Questione Sociale* into an unofficial IWW organ, even featuring the union's logo on its masthead and office storefront. Guabello later recalled, "Under the influence of propaganda done by our newspaper, the IWW made rapid progress in Paterson." By September 1907, the union had thirty-five hundred members in the city, including more than twelve hundred weavers and nine hundred dyers' helpers.[178] In May 1908, the IWW's first convention of textile workers met in Paterson, with the local organization supplying ten of twenty-two delegates, including Guabello and Gallo.[179] Shortly thereafter, however, factionalism ripped apart Local 152.

Though most of its members were Italian silk workers who looked to the anarchists for direction, Local 152 also included smaller factions composed of adherents of the syndicalist Federazione Socialista Italiana (Italian Socialist Federation), which had fewer than sixty members in Paterson, and German and Polish Jewish partisans of the Socialist Labor Party (SLP), which had played a major role in founding the IWW.[180] These groups worked side by side within Local 152, but when the IWW's second convention met in Chicago in 1906, former *Germinal* editor Michel Dumas attended as one of three delegates from Paterson and, along with Paterson's Samuel J. French, introduced a motion to strike the words promoting action "on the political field" from the preamble

FIGURE 8. Ludovico Caminita, 1908. Courtesy of the National Archives.

to the IWW's constitution. French noted, "I am casting four votes here for an organization, the active members of which are men absolutely opposed to political action. They are so-called anarchists." Though the proposal was rejected, it marked the beginning of the campaign to eliminate the influence of the SLP within the IWW.[181]

Ludovico Caminita was sent as a delegate to the union's next annual convention where, in halting English, he spoke in support of another motion to remove the "political clause" from the preamble. Citing the European syndicalist model, Caminita claimed "that in France all the working class now stand on the economic field; they do not care for the political field, and they are gaining day by day." Moreover, he argued, "socialist governments are just as bad as the others." Caminita's statements were met with applause as well as with rebuttals from SLP members, and De Leon's lengthy defense of the existing preamble carried the day by a 109–19 vote. Caminita also spoke against a proposal to reinstate the office of union president, abolished the previous year, by invoking an anarchist critique of authority: "If you take a man and put him in a fire he must burn up; you cannot say it is his fault. It is our fault. If we put a man in the office of president, if we give the man power, in one year or two years—I cannot say how long—he will be corrupt. . . . We must show by this organization that people can govern themselves; we must show the ignorant people that without any president that we can live and grow just the same." According to Caminita, the function of the general secretary-treasurer—the highest position within the IWW after 1906—was to be "like a telephone," conveying information, rather than "a chief." On this subject, a majority agreed with the anarchist.[182]

In October 1908, the union's fourth annual convention finally removed the reference to "the political field" from the preamble and ejected De Leon from the organization. SLP members followed their leader out of the IWW and reconvened in Paterson, where they organized what they claimed was the "true" IWW, later known as the "Detroit IWW" after its headquarters were moved to that city. The socialists attempted to transfer Local 152 into their new organization and took out warrants against IWW loyalists who refused to give up the local's property; faithful IWW members, in turn, brought charges of false arrest and perjury, and the police maintained custody of the disputed materials until 1910. This conflict reduced the membership of each organization in Paterson to below three hundred.[183] The anarchists' victory within the national IWW cost them dearly in the city.

To make matters worse, local and federal authorities were in the grip of an antianarchist panic that began in February 1907 after Roberto Cortese, a Paterson judge who had prosecuted Italian organized crime, was killed by a mail bomb. A "Vigilance Committee of Law and Order," mistakenly blaming anarchists for the crime, sent a threatening letter to Caminita warning that "the American citizens will not allow any foreigners to band together to take life and destroy property." In July, Caminita was arrested and questioned regarding articles he had written about the murder.[184] In February 1908, after months of calm, Italian immigrant Giuseppe Alia shot and killed a Denver priest, and a week later, Russian Jewish immigrant Lazarus Averbuch was killed during a scuffle at the home of Chicago's chief of police, who insisted that Averbuch had intended to kill him. The press immediately labeled both men anarchists, although it is not clear that either had any connection to anarchism. On March 28, avowed anarchist Selig Silverstein threw a bomb at police in New York City's Union Square. Overzealous journalists and politicians linked all of these incidents to an imagined nationwide anarchist plot.[185] The mayor of Paterson asked President Theodore Roosevelt to ban *La Questione Sociale* from the mails, and at Roosevelt's urging, postal authorities barred the publication on the flimsy pretense that it did not meet the legal definition of a newspaper as a consequence of occasional irregularities in its publishing schedule. The following month, Roosevelt called for new legislation banning all anarchist material from the mails, and Paterson's mayor pledged to wipe out anarchism in the city and dispatched police to break up meetings of the Right to Existence Group. In May, Caminita was indicted for inciting to riot based on articles that had appeared in the now defunct *La Questione Sociale*.[186]

Caminita had also begun a relationship with a married woman, Amalia Canova (née Fontanella), creating a local scandal. Facing constant harassment, the couple absconded to Philadelphia, where Caminita briefly published his own magazine, *L'Internazionale*, before moving to Pittsburgh, where he worked on Carlo Tresca's *L'Avvenire*. Canova lost custody of her three-year-old daughter and was disowned by her family; in 1917, Caminita was still begging her father to reestablish contact with her.[187] Caminita's departure also opened a rift between him and certain members of the Right to Existence Group—Franz Widmar and Alberto Guabello, in particular—who wrote that the editor had left Paterson "for strictly private reasons of a very personal and intimate nature." In an angry rebuttal, Caminita maintained that he departed to escape arrest, prompting comrades to accuse him of trying to create for himself "a halo of martyrdom and glory that is not yet deserved." Both sides settled their differences with arbitration from a group of "Cleveland comrades," and Caminita later returned to Paterson, but bad blood remained.[188]

The Right to Existence Group launched a new paper, *L'Era Nuova*, edited by Camillo Rosazza Riz and Franz Widmar with the aid of Guabello, and the organization renamed itself the L'Era Nuova Group. This organization included a core of more than thirty members, and a larger community of at least three or four hundred Italian anarchists remained active in Paterson.[189] A number of these radicals set out to revive Local 152.

In late 1908, a group of IWW members began "organizing the workers quietly and establishing committees in all shops to get the feeling of the people to see whether they really wished to make a stand for better conditions or not."[190] The going was slow: in April 1910, a visiting IWW member reported, "The boys in Paterson are still on the firing line, although the condition of the silk industry is so bad that it is almost impossible to do any organizing work at present."[191] These activists still faced direct competition from the Detroit IWW, which gained momentum in Paterson in 1911 and 1912 by leading strikes against an increase of loom assignments from two to four per weaver at several silk shops, including the Doherty Mill, the city's largest.[192] Paterson's Italian weavers "manifested enthusiasm at the outset of the struggle," but after the collapse of an attempted general strike, "The number of adherents to the true organization, the real I.W.W.," grew, while its SLP-backed rival withered.[193]

In March 1912, Local 152 counted five hundred members, and in November it established an Eight-Hour League, in cooperation with the L'Era Nuova Group, to agitate for a reduction in the workday and the abolition of the multiple-loom system.[194] *L'Era Nuova* served as the league's organ and launched a special "Weavers' Page" promoting its goals. Then, on February 1, 1913, weavers at the Doherty Mill walked out in response to the reintroduction of the four-loom system, which they rightly feared would displace workers and drive down wages. They called on the rest of Local 152 "to come and assist them in whatever way we could."[195]

The union responded by forming an executive board composed of fifteen to twenty IWW members and charged it with expanding the strike throughout the silk industry. However, the board acted in a strictly advisory role, deferring all decision making to the strikers themselves. The identities of its members were kept secret, but many must have been the same anarchists who had guided the IWW in Paterson since its formation. IWW leader William (Big Bill) Haywood noted, "The silk workers are fortunate in having Local No. 152 as a nucleus around which to form their organization. This Local was largely composed of seasoned veterans in the labor movement, many of them charter members since 1906."[196] In the three weeks following the Doherty walkout, the executive board arranged a series of mass meetings, brought in national IWW speakers, and organized the Central Strike Committee, composed of two delegates elected from each factory—though in good anarchist fashion, all proposals formulated by this committee were referred back to the rank and file for approval. Participants noted that about half of the strike committee's delegates were dues-paying IWW members, and one of the few whose identity is known was Alberto Guabello.[197] The ultrademocratic structure of the strike was thus in place well before the arrival of visiting IWW organizers and was strongly informed by anarchist principles. The role of the outside speakers often credited with leading the strike—Haywood, Elizabeth Gurley Flynn, Carlo Tresca, and others—was largely limited to keeping up strikers' morale and shielding the leadership of Local 152 from being identified, fired, and blacklisted.[198] As Michel Dumas noted, local anarchists did not speak at the public mass strike meetings, "and yet many were present; they aided the movement of revolt by all means in their power." Margaret Sanger, who came from New York to aid the strike, discovered that "the Italian anarchists had been working among the silk workers for years, sowing the seeds of dissatisfaction and rebellion against their slavery, and when the strike was called this small minority formed the backbone of the strike, which gave to it most of its revolutionary momentum."[199] In the midst of the struggle, *L'Era Nuova* noted that Local 152 had been "in intimate contact in these recent years with the anarchists" and referred to the IWW as "the anarchists' union."[200]

On February 18, the Central Strike Committee called for a general silk strike to begin the following week. Both the strike and Local 152 quickly grew. In the first fourteen weeks of the struggle, twenty-five thousand strikers brought three hundred of Paterson's mills and dye houses to a halt, and the local IWW membership mushroomed to around ten thousand.[201] The weavers' demands were exactly those for which the Eight-Hour League and *L'Era Nuova* had campaigned: a return to the two-loom system for weavers, an eight-hour day (and forty-four hour week) throughout the industry, and wage increases across the board. Dye workers sought greater workplace control through recognition of their shop committees and a minimum apprenticeship age of sixteen.[202]

Anarchists were among the most militant of the strikers, and many were arrested during the conflict. On March 20, Paolo Guabello was part of a group of picketers ordered to disperse, but he "didn't move fast enough and was clubbed to the ground" by police. Ninfa Baronio (referred to by locals as Mrs. Gallo), who was there to escort her fifteen-year-old son home from the picket line, witnessed the attack and, "though weak and thin physically," covered Guabello with her body and was clubbed as well, then "punched on the breast, knocked down, [and had] her head thrown against the wall." The bleeding Guabello and Baronio were hauled away in a police carriage, while young William Gallo ran after it crying out for his mother. The "strikers became very highly incensed" by the attack on Baronio.[203] B. Bertone, an anarchist who had come from Cedar Point, Illinois, to aid the strike, was arrested on May 10 for harassing strikebreakers. Two months later, *L'Era Nuova* reported that the wife of anarchist Ambrogio Pagani had been arrested and sentenced to fifty days imprisonment for insulting a police officer, and Pagani himself had been sentenced to twenty days for trying to intervene. Serafino Grandi, former editor of Biella's *L'Alba*, was also arrested during the strike with longtime Paterson anarchist C. F. Lanfranco.[204]

Although the mob actions and pitched battles of 1902 were absent, Paterson's anarchists were willing to sanction and utilize physical coercion. Violence and property destruction were rare during the first months of the strike, but as the conflict dragged on, assaults against owners, foremen, and strikebreakers as well as vandalism of their homes became "an almost daily occurrence." In addition, a series of small bombs detonated around the city in June. One exploded in Prospect Park, a Dutch suburb that *L'Era Nuova* described as "a den of scabs," slightly damaging the home of some strikebreakers. Though the newspaper declined to assign credit for the bombings, it mused, "If these attacks [*attentati*] sow fear among the traitors and arouse the anger of the police, they find in return the approval of the strikers and keep the hope of victory alive in them." In July, another bomb exploded outside the home of two owners of a dye house, resulting in "much fright and little damage." *L'Era Nuova* advised the victims, "This is only a warning." The same month, anarchist Vittorio Ponderano was arrested as part of a gang that had threatened Henry Doherty Jr., a manager at his father's mill, with a pistol.[205] In total, at least twenty-eight homes suffered broken windows, between six and fourteen bombs were detonated (though reportedly none caused more than five dollars in damage), and fifteen individuals were indicted for assault and battery.[206]

But far more important in sustaining the strike was the widespread community support it enjoyed. "A grocery store, drug store, and restaurant have been opened," one reporter noted, "and arrangements made with a doctor and even a dentist to attend ailing mill hands." The Sons of Italy, which had as many as three thousand local members (five hundred of them strikers), provided one thousand dollars a week to the strike. Rather than evidence of cross-class ethnic solidarity, however, this aid reflected "the domination by the I.W.W." of the local Sons organization. The funds were given with the explicit stipulation that they be distributed to strikers "without distinction of race, religion or nationality," prompting *L'Era Nuova* to boast "that the propaganda of internationalism made for so many years in Paterson by the radicals did not remain without fruit," even within an organization "founded on essentially patriotic and national principles."[207] The freethinking Yiddish anarchists who made up the tiny IWW local on New York's Lower East Side, meanwhile, arranged for a New York bakery to provide free Passover matzo for the three thousand Jewish strikers in Paterson.[208]

The influence of anarchists' cosmopolitan principles was also evident in the strike's multiethnic character. Reporters noted "the absence of race prejudice" among the workers, and unlike Paterson's earlier leagues of resistance or the IWW's 1912 textile strike in Lawrence, Massachusetts, strikers were organized not according ethnicity or language but by shop. Jewish IWW member Sophie Cohen recalled, "When we went to a picnic or mass meeting, we didn't care if someone was a different nationality. The children played together and the people talked together, as well as they could."[209] Silk manufacturers attempted to use patriotism as a wedge between workers and the IWW, declaring March 17 Flag Day and draping their mills with the Stars and Stripes. Local socialists responded by handing out small American flag pins to strikers, who marched under a banner reading, "We wove the flag; we dyed the flag. We live under the flag; but we won't scab under the flag."[210] According to *L'Era Nuova*, however, "the overwhelming majority" of marchers "found [the pins] not to their taste" and wore them only to avoid the negative publicity that would come if they were "trampled by the thousands of feet that . . . beat the pavement of this city of Paterson of so little patriotism." Far more emblematic of the strike, the paper pointed out, were the numerous occasions on which thousands of workers joined together to sing "The Internationale" and "La Marseillaise."[211] When strikers were asked to reenact their struggles in the Paterson Strike Pageant staged at Madison Square Garden two and a half months later, they chose not to re-create the flag march but did sing "The Internationale" and "La Marseillaise" (twice) and included the lyrics in the program so audience members could join in. Appropriately, some of those in attendance also hung a banner bearing the anarchist slogan "No God, No Master" from the upper gallery before an angry socialist member of the IWW tore it down.[212]

Employer intransigence and the entrenched prejudices of British and native-born weavers ultimately broke the strike. The anarchists and the IWW never made significant inroads among Paterson's minority of English-speaking weavers, though not for lack of trying. On July 18, these workers abandoned their fellow strikers and agreed to settle on a shop-by-shop basis, prompting panic among other groups, which scrambled to do the same. The collapse of the strike marked a major defeat for the IWW, and in its aftermath, employers blacklisted some two thousand strikers.[213] Yet the defeat was not crippling.

In May 1914, Local 152 still counted between thirteen hundred and fifteen hundred members in good standing, and another twenty-two hundred whose dues were not current only "due to the fact that this is a time of the year when the silker is really slack." Mill owners also found the blacklist difficult to enforce among hundreds of small establishments and against skilled workers whose labor was necessary. Between 1913 and 1916, the IWW carried out a number of successful shop strikes, regained hundreds of members, built up wage committees in twenty mills, and collaborated with rival unions on a successful drive for a nine-hour workday.[214] When city authorities tried to prevent anarchists and IWW members from speaking in public, a successful free-speech campaign organized by Paterson and New York radicals overturned the ban.[215] Furthermore, most silk mills voluntarily did away with the three- and four-loom system. According to Cohen, "The thing in 1913 that we really acted on and won was the two loom system."[216]

In 1915–16, anarchists founded the Scuola Moderna Francesco Ferrer, Circolo di Coltura Operaia, Circolo Instruzione e Diletto Edmondo De Amicis, as well as the Paterson Philosophical Society, which brought in radical speakers including Emma Goldman, Harry Kelly, Margaret Sanger, and Hubert Harrison. Surveying local anarchist activities in May 1915, Goldman noted, "The most energetic efforts have been made by our friends of *L'Era Nuova* of Paterson."[217] This flurry of activity attests to how deeply embedded anarchism remained within Paterson's immigrant working class.

CHAPTER 3

"ALL FLAGS LOOK ALIKE TO US"

IMMIGRANT ANARCHISTS IN SAN FRANCISCO

The Gold Rush of 1849 transformed San Francisco, only recently acquired from Mexico, into a boomtown, drawing thousands of people from across the globe. The completion of the transcontinental railroad in 1869 allowed a new wave of foreign-born workers from eastern ports of entry to flood the city. By 1890, San Francisco had a population of nearly three hundred thousand, making it the eighth-largest metropolis in the United States, and it more than doubled in size over the next four decades.[1] Anarchist activity in the city likewise grew in these decades, spurred by local conditions as well as the transplantation of East Coast activists such as Giuseppe Ciancabilla and Alexander Berkman and the arrival of radical European and Asian exiles. In 1908, the San Francisco Police Department's captain of detectives estimated that more than five hundred anarchists made their homes there.[2] Together, they comprised the most diverse and cosmopolitan local anarchist movement in the country, and between 1880 and 1940, they published at least nineteen newspapers in seven languages, ranking the Bay Area behind only New York and Chicago in the production of anarchist periodicals.

Anarchism was strongest among San Francisco's Italians, but the city's diversity, mixed neighborhoods, and the Italian community's small size relative to the total population meant that multiethnic alliances were both easy to forge and necessary to sustain radical activity. The result was the emergence of a pan-ethnic "Latin" movement encompassing Italian, French, and Spanish-speaking anarchists and syndicalists. Over time, these radicals formed important links with other groups of revolutionaries, including Asians, Russians, and Eastern European Jews. The networks of the Anarchist Atlantic and the emergent Anarchist Pacific met in San Francisco, directly linking the city to revolutionary and anti-imperialist struggles throughout Europe, Asia, and Latin America. By the First World War, San Francisco's anarchist groups had amalgamated into a loose coalition that extended across virtually the entire ethnoracial spectrum, and the city had become a major nexus of global radicalism that "rivaled Paris in its plentitude of international revolutionaries and progressives of all sorts."[3]

No single ethnic or national group predominated among San Francisco's immigrants, who constituted roughly one-third of the city's population between 1900 and 1930. The largest concentrations were of migrants from Germany, Austria, the British Isles, China, and Scandinavia, who together outnumbered "new immigrants" from Southern and Eastern Europe in the first decades of the century. By 1930, however, Italians had narrowly surpassed all foreign groups except the Irish, though they comprised just 16.1 percent of all non-Asian immigrants. Eastern European Jews, meanwhile, migrated to the West Coast in extremely small numbers: in 1900, San Francisco had only fifteen hundred Russian-born residents, and by 1920, that figure had grown to just fifty-eight hundred, or 3.3 percent of the foreign-born population.[4]

Small groups of German, British, and French immigrants formed branches of the First International in the 1860s and 1870s, but little in the way of an organized anarchist movement existed before the 1890s.[5] The first, inauspicious steps came with eclectic radical editor Burnette Haskell's founding of the Pacific Branch of the International Workmen's Association (IWA) in 1881. Haskell falsely claimed the organization was an official affiliate of the defunct First International and awkwardly attempted to reconcile Marxist and Bakuninist doctrines. The IWA did include a few German anarchists, but when delegates met in Pittsburgh in 1883 to form the International Working People's Association, they emphatically rejected Haskell's proposal to merge with his organization.[6] The IWA is most famous—or infamous—for its virulent campaign against Chinese workers, and four of its German members were arrested in 1885 for plotting to dynamite targets in Chinatown and assassinate city leaders.[7] Although the IWA claimed a membership of six hundred thousand, the real number was likely closer to a couple hundred. Regardless, the organization collapsed after Haskell left San Francisco in 1887.[8] A local German section of the IWPA also existed in the mid-1880s, and it, too, was reportedly involved in anti-Chinese agitation, though it left few traces.[9]

The lone public voice of opposition within the IWA on the Chinese question belonged to Sigismund Danielewicz, a multilingual Polish Jewish immigrant and labor organizer who served as the organization's Italian corresponding secretary and had spent time in Hawaii "vigorously engaged in the labor struggle."[10] In 1889, after the dissolution of the IWA, Danielewicz took over the Bay Area's first anarchist newspaper, *The Beacon*, founded in Dallas by anarchist Ross Winn but soon transferred to San Diego and then San Francisco.[11] Under Danielewicz, *The Beacon* endorsed the IWPA's revolutionary anarchist program and continued to speak out against anti-Chinese prejudice.

Although Danielewicz appears to have known Yiddish—on at least one occasion, *The Beacon* translated a piece by Saul Yanovsky—San Francisco lacked a Yiddish-speaking community or Jewish ghetto, precluding the emergence of a Jewish anarchist movement such as existed in New York.[12] Danielewicz instead participated in English-speaking anarchist circles, which in the Bay Area were dominated by native-born mutualists and individualists who were influenced by Pierre-Joseph Proudhon, Benjamin Tucker, and Max Stirner and who frowned upon *The Beacon*'s advocacy of armed revolution. After the paper shut down in September 1891, it was replaced by a short-lived individualist paper, *L'Enfant Terrible*, and another obscure individualist publication, *Egoism*, sporadically appeared out of Oakland from 1890 to 1897, but its promotion of "intelligent self-interest" over "the delusion of Altruism" earned it just nine California subscribers by 1891.[13] Of far greater importance was the appearance of the revolutionary anarchist communist papers *Secolo Nuovo* and *Free Society*.

Secolo Nuovo (New Century) was the first Italian anarchist newspaper on the West Coast, and its origins reflected the cosmopolitan nature of San Franciscan anarchism. Its publisher was Cesare Crespi, a radical republican journalist who was born near Milan in 1857 and who in the early 1880s absconded to Scotland with his lover, Giuseppina Alberti, a married woman from a "well-established" family. The couple subsequently migrated to New York, where Giuseppina's adolescent son, Enrico (Eugene), joined them; the unorthodox family then settled in San Francisco in 1885. There, Crespi wrote for the local liberal Italian press and founded a weekly paper, *Il Messaggero*.[14] Eugene apprenticed as a sailor at age fourteen but jumped ship in Siberia after his captain shot a crew member and tried to force the youth to help cover up the incident. Eugene soon found work as a sailor with a geodetic survey team on the Yangtze River, and there he met an acquaintance of prominent French anarchist geographer Élisée Reclus. When eighteen-year-old Eugene returned to San Francisco in 1894, he was a committed anarchist. His mother, however, had died while he was abroad, and he subsequently took the maiden name of Crespi's second wife, Sylvia Travaglio, as his own. Crespi helped his foster son establish *Secolo Nuovo*, which Eugene edited.[15]

Bay Area anarchist Cassius V. Cook remembered Eugene Travaglio as "a dashing, graceful vigorous son of Italy, with fine dark eyes and black hair." Under Travaglio's direction, *Secolo Nuovo* was an iconoclastic and militant paper, sharing Ciancabilla's commitment to anarchist communist and antiorganizationist principles. "Anarchy," according to Travaglio, was a "social science" that "propagates the abolition of borders and militarism, human brotherhood, the cessation of all violence and of all exploitation of man by man." Though *Secolo Nuovo* lasted, with some interruptions, for twelve years, it remained an obscure paper with a circulation of no more than eighteen hundred.[16] In 1900, Travaglio launched a more intellectual companion publication, the monthly *La Protesta Humana* (Human Protest).

Unlikely revolutionaries Abe and Mary Isaak, Russian Mennonites who had exchanged Protestant pacifism for anarchism after emigrating to the United States, launched *Free Society* in 1897. The paper was the successor to *The Firebrand*, which the Isaaks had previously helped publish in Portland, Oregon. Michael Cohn and Danielewicz were occasional contributors, as was local multilingual tailor Andrew (Al) Klemencic, a Slovenian born in Trieste, as was Paterson's Franz Widmar. In addition to organizing for the Journeymen Tailor's Union, Klemencic lectured on anarchism, wrote for the English- and French-language anarchist press, and organized Emma Goldman's 1898 Bay Area lecture tour.[17]

A rash of new groups accompanied these publications, including the Italian Anarchist Club, which met every Saturday night at 111 Trenton Street; the San Francisco Freethought Society, in which both Danielewicz and Abe Isaak were active; the International Libertaire Club; and the Liberty Group.[18] Pietro Gori stayed in San Francisco for two months during his 1896 lecture tour and helped local Italians form the Alleanza Socialista-Anarchica (Socialist-Anarchist Alliance), which immediately signed up nearly one hundred members and adopted a Declaration of Principles that read,

> The workers of all countries—despite the declarations of the turgid charlatans of government—are subjected to two forms of tyranny: one economic and one political. . . .
>
> We do not pretend that the social question confines itself within the narrow boundaries of one country [*patria*]—but it embraces all countries . . .—the internationalism of the aims of emancipation must be affirmed on every occasion, and the principle that all workers consider the workers of all other nations as brothers must be upheld, seeking the most high ideals of true civilization, the solidarity of all peoples.[19]

The short-lived federation included at least ten "lady converts," foremost among them Bianca Gaffe, "the best-known lady orator in the Italian colony," who presided over many of Gori's appearances and a few years later attempted to recruit members for New Ideal, a California anarchist colony.[20] By 1897, the Anarchist Headquarters of San Francisco on Folsom Street hosted meetings "in

FIGURE 9. "Mrs. Gaffe Swearing Allegiance to the Anarchist Banner at the Meeting in Washington-Square Hall," *San Francisco Call*, March 16, 1896. Bianca Gaffe is in the upper left; Pietro Gori is in the insert, upper right.

Italian, English, German and French," and two years later, *La Questione Sociale* correspondent Luigi Raveggi founded the Circolo Educativo di Studi Sociali (Educational Social Studies Circle) during a speaking tour.[21]

Yet by 1902, this flurry of anarchist ferment had dissipated and activity was "at a standstill."[22] Klemencic departed in mid-1898 to organize in the Republic of Hawaii and later in Colorado and Oregon. Abe and Mary Isaak relocated *Free Society* to Chicago at the end of 1900, and Travaglio joined Ciancabilla in Spring Valley to help produce *L'Aurora* after *La Protesta Umana* folded in September 1900. Travaglio subsequently joined up with the Isaaks in Chicago and apprenticed as a typesetter for *Free Society*. In the aftermath of McKinley's assassination, police briefly arrested Travaglio, the Isaaks, and several other

Chicago anarchists, while in Spring Valley, authorities rounded up every anarchist they could find—a few hundred in total—including Ciancabilla.[23] *L'Aurora* was forced to close down, and Ciancabilla and Ersilia Cavedagni then joined Travaglio in Chicago, where the trio resurrected *La Protesta Umana* in February 1902. The revived paper continued Ciancabilla's crusade against the *organizzatori*, and its pages were filled with paeans to anarchist assassins such as Gaetano Bresci and Emile Henry.

New stirrings of activity brought *La Protesta Umana* and its editors to San Francisco in early 1903. In addition to the paper's small but loyal following within the Italian community, *La Protesta Umana* received support from a handful of local Spaniards and the new French-speaking Germinal Group, which produced a special French supplement for it. Shortly after the move, however, Ciancabilla and Travaglio had a falling out. Travaglio then partnered with Jewish anarchist Samuel Mintz to produce three issues of *The Petrel*, while *La Protesta Umana* was left in Ciancabilla's hands but folded after the editor's sudden death in late 1904.[24] The Germinal Group then published its own single-issue paper, *L'Effort*, which announced its opposition to "great hollow words, such as God, Religion, Homeland [*Patrie*], Flag, Government, Honor, etc."[25] *Secolo Nuovo* continued to appear, and in March 1905, "Italian, French and Spanish language libertarian groups" staged a benefit play for revolutionaries in Russia.[26]

This growing multiethnic anarchist movement was centered in North Beach, San Francisco's "Latin Quarter," located at the base of Telegraph Hill and demarcated by Jones Street to the west and Broadway to the south, beyond which lay Chinatown. Italians began settling there alongside French, Basque, Spanish, Portuguese, and Mexican immigrants in the 1860s. By the turn of the century, North Beach contained the largest Italian community on the West Coast, but its members were dispersed among the neighborhood's other groups; in 1910, 70 percent of North Beach residents had parents born in countries other than Italy.[27] Another cluster of Italians resided in nearby Oakland, including thirty-six individuals who contributed to the defense fund for Luigi Galleani's 1907 trial in Paterson.[28] Like Paterson, San Francisco had an unusually high proportion of Northern Italian immigrants, but most came from agricultural backgrounds and worked as unskilled farm laborers or self-employed truck farmers, fishermen, bootblacks, and peddlers. Moreover, no single regional group predominated: the four main Italian areas of origin—Genoa and Lucca in the north and Cosenza and Palermo in the south—together supplied less than half of the city's Italian population.[29]

The residents of North Beach appropriated the racial category of "Latin," imposed on them in the American South and West, as a panethnic source of solidarity in the face of "Anglo" prejudice. California labor leaders were convinced that these groups could not be organized and perhaps were not even white, so unions often excluded or segregated "Latin" members. "The results," San Francisco's Italian vice consul reported in 1908, "are that those not belonging to the Unions are unable to practice their trades."[30] In the face of social and economic marginalization, a number of Latin workers turned to anarchism. Crespi noted that when Gori spoke in the city in 1896, his audiences were sympathetic to his ideas after enduring "hardships and endless humiliations" in America.[31]

Further hardships and humiliations came with the Great Earthquake of 1906. The disaster leveled most of the city, including Eugene Travaglio's print shop. In 1907, Travaglio briefly launched a new publication, *La Terra*, out of nearby Stockton, but the experiment did not last and the editor eventually moved to Tacoma, Washington. Back in San Francisco, seven hundred mostly Italian and Greek workers rebuilding the city's streetcar system participated in a strike for a wage increase and eight-hour workday in July 1906, but the native-born members of the Carmen's Union settled independently and taunted the immigrants by singing, "To —— with the —— foreigners." The strike failed, and many participants were fired. Later that summer, a group of Italian laborers walked off a street construction job after a foreman "began to swear at 'the —— dagos,'" and they assembled a protest of three thousand foreign-born workers who marched behind a red flag. The Street Construction Workers' Union, acting on the advice of the San Francisco Labor Council, subsequently had fourteen of the protest leaders arrested for inciting to riot.[32]

A few "Anglo" anarchists, however, collaborated with Latin comrades in 1906 to produce a short-lived newspaper, *The Emancipator*, edited by Germinal Group member Laurent Casas. The paper endorsed the newly formed IWW and included Ludovico Caminita among its contributors. *The Emancipator* also established some of the Bay Area's first links to Mexican radicals and carried several articles denouncing the "Czarism" of Mexico's dictatorial President Porfirio Díaz. The Partido Liberal Mexicano (Mexican Liberal Party), an organization founded in the United States in 1905 by exiled Mexican revolutionaries, made contact with the paper as well as with several other sympathetic American anarchist publications, including *La Terra*.[33] In early 1907, however, *The Emancipator* was absorbed by *The Demonstrator*, a paper published out of the anarchist colony in Home, Washington.

The following year saw the appearance of *Cogito, Ergo Sum*, which featured material in Italian, French, and Spanish. The first issue proudly announced that local "French, Italian and Spanish comrades" had founded a theatrical group, and the paper's lists of financial contributions show that it reached a readership stretching from Los Angeles to Paterson and internationally into Mexico, Puerto Rico, Canada, and France.[34] Its editor, Italian mechanic Carlo Dalboni, had an ideal background for facilitating such connections—he had spent most of the 1890s moving between the multiethnic radical hubs of Trieste, Lugano, Zurich, Paris, and London before landing in San Francisco in 1906. Dalboni was also a proponent of "propaganda by the deed" whom Italian authorities considered "one of the most dangerous anarchists" as well as "very intelligent and very courageous." Like Ciancabilla and Travaglio, he opposed formal organization and labor unions, but his brand of anarchism met with no more success than his predecessors', and *Cogito, Ergo Sum* disappeared after three issues.[35] It was soon followed by the Italian individualist paper *Nihil*, edited by Adolfo Antonelli, a stonemason and Stirner-inspired proponent of violent insurrection who had been ejected from England for his inflammatory writings.[36] *Nihil* continued the anarchists' campaign against the "Mexican despotism" of Díaz, but it, too, failed to gain traction and folded after sixteen months.[37] Nevertheless, these papers contributed to the consolidation of the Latin anarchist movement.

Jaime Vidal, a Spanish anarcho-syndicalist and maritime worker based in New York, edited the Spanish section of *Cogito, Ergo Sum*, and in 1911, San Francisco's growing Spanish anarchist community formed a group with the popular name Germinal. In 1914, Vidal briefly transplanted his publication, *Fuerza Consciente*, to San Francisco, where he helped establish the Libreria Sovversiva Italo-Spagnuola (Radical Italian-Spanish Bookstore) in North Beach.[38] Mexican immigrants made up less than 1 percent of the city's population at the turn of the century, but in 1905, Mexican anarchist Práxedis Guerrero spent several months in San Francisco publishing *Alba Roja* (Red Dawn), which circulated among the city's Spanish dockworkers.[39]

The true institutionalization of Latin radicalism, however, came through the IWW, of which Vidal was an active member. San Francisco's Mixed Local 173 had done little more than set up shop when the 1906 earthquake reduced its members to living out of a shared tent, but in the disaster's aftermath, Latin radicals emerged as the leading force within the organization. In June 1906, hundreds of Italian laborers formed Building Construction Union Local 501, the IWW's first industrial union chapter in California. Local 501 made little headway in an industry controlled by the AFL's powerful Building Trades Council, but in 1906, Mixed Local 363 was established to accommodate the growing number of Italian IWW members.[40]

The union then focused on organizing Latin bakery workers, a segment of the workforce that the AFL had failed to engage. In 1900, the city's German and American bakers' unions had merged and tried to set up a separate local for French and Italian bakers. After Latin members refused to enlist, these unions regarded Latin bakers as a threat. Conditions within the Latin bakeries, meanwhile, remained "a quasi-feudal arrangement in which food and a bed were exchanged for low wages and a seven-day work week."[41] With Italian organizers at the helm, the IWW chartered Bakery Workers' Local 175 in May 1907 with eighty-five members, and a separate branch for French bakers soon followed.[42] Progress then stalled. A strike of around one hundred bakers later that year apparently ended in defeat, and Italian-language Local 363 soon disbanded. Adding insult to injury, in May 1910, two members of Local 173 disappeared with the organization's meager treasury. By the end of that year, fewer than a hundred IWW members remained in the city.[43]

But in May 1911, the local Italian branch of the Socialist Party broke away to join the syndicalist Federazione Socialista Italiana, itself recently absorbed into the IWW, and founded a Latin Branch of Local 173.[44] These Italian syndicalists were soon joined by a small group of French radicals, including anarchist Laurent Casas and French army veteran Basil Saffores. Saffores was a member of a militant French laundry workers' mutual aid society, and by July 1911, he was actively organizing on behalf of the IWW.[45] The Latin Branch opened storefront offices in North Beach and revived the IWW's campaign among bakery workers, establishing a Latin Branch of the Bakery Workers' Industrial Union. By the spring of 1912, Local 173 had to obtain a larger meeting hall to accommodate its growing membership.[46]

Italian anarchists also joined the Latin Branch, including organizer Luigi Parenti. Born in Tuscany in 1887, Parenti was described by Italian authorities as "taciturn in character, educated, intelligent, and cultivated." He had no radical affiliations in Italy but rather had been a Christian Democrat and completed two years of seminary school in Lucca (though some family members thought him an "opportunist" who, "under the religious cloak . . . ate well and received an education"). He then abandoned his religious studies, married, and aided a Lucca streetcar drivers' strike.[47] Migrating to San Francisco in 1910, Parenti rapidly moved to the left, and in 1913 he embarked on a statewide lecture tour on behalf of the IWW, which regarded him as "an enthusiastic, energetic, and convincing speaker." He was soon "recognized as the radical leader" of San Francisco's Italian anarcho-syndicalists, who "found Luigi captivating, charismatic, [and] knowledgeable." Parenti moved among jobs in hotels, restaurants, foundries, factories, and the railroad, organizing wherever he went. The Italian consulate considered him "one of the most dangerous propagandists in the anarchist movement across the United States."[48]

Although the strength of the AFL severely limited the IWW's field of action, its neglect of Latin and unskilled laborers left many workers open to the guidance of organizers such as Saffores and Parenti. The Latin Branch's membership expanded to include employees in the sausage-making, shoemaking, cannery, and fishing industries.[49]

The IWW further headed or supported a number of strikes that were not carried out under its own auspices. For example, when around 150 women in a cannery struck in response to a wage cut at the end of 1912, several members of Local 173's Latin Branch aided them. Cannery worker A. Cappiali joined the strike in sympathy with his female coworkers, and Luigi Parenti recruited IWW members to shore up the women's picket lines and organized meetings on their behalf. Parenti was arrested on charges of inciting to riot and Cappiali was fired, but at least a third of the women had joined the IWW before the strike ended.[50] Similarly, the AFL's Boot and Shoe Workers' Union led a successful 1913 strike at the Frank and Hyman Shoe Company, but a number of its leaders also belonged to the IWW and recruited IWW members to walk the picket lines, and soon "most of the strikers [were] joining the I.W.W."[51] Luigi Parenti's niece, anarchist Carinda (Cari) Piccinini, led a failed walkout at the Petri Italian-American Cigar Company in Oakland.[52] In 1916–17, Basil Saffores played a key role in transforming the Amicale des Ouvriers Blanchisseurs Français de San Francisco (San Francisco Association of French Laundry Workers), of which he was provisional secretary, into an independent syndicalist union, the Syndicat des Ouvriers Blanchisseurs Français de San Francisco, which led a major strike in 1917.[53] That year, IWW and dissident AFL members also formed the Toilers of the World under a charter from the AFL, intending to avoid the growing reaction against the IWW. In July, the Toilers organized a strike of Bay Area cannery workers that was suppressed by federal troops, but strikers in San Jose nevertheless obtained a favorable settlement.[54]

Most of the workers organized by the IWW in the laundries and canneries were women, who often initiated their own struggles that were then supported by the union. However, although male IWW activists made concerted efforts to organize women and supported "general equality and mutual respect in the relations of the sexes," they failed to recruit or foster female organizers and could envision sexual equality only in the context of women becoming independent wage earners. In 1908, San Francisco IWW member Sophie Vasilio proposed a radical alternative: "I believe the married woman of the working class is no parasite or exploiter. She is a social producer. In order to sustain herself, she has to sell her labor power, either in the factory, directly to the capitalist, or at home, indirectly, by serving the wage slave, her husband, thus keeping him in working condition through cooking, washing and general housekeeping. . . . And as an industrial factor in society, I believe the wage slave's wife has got a right to belong to a mixed local." But this proposal, which recognized unwaged housework as an integral form of reproductive labor within capitalism, never gained a serious hearing. Wife and worker remained incompatible roles, leaving the IWW dominated by the ethos of "virile syndicalism."[55]

Some of this male bravado was on display during the IWW's little-known San Francisco free-speech fight of 1911. Members of the Latin Branch began holding Sunday street meetings at the corner of Broadway and Grant Street, primarily as a means to recruit bakery workers. However, the meetings were also near Saints Peter and Paul Italian Catholic Church, and the radical speakers often indulged in antireligious propaganda as well. At one such meeting on August 6, 1911, police responded to complaints from the church and arrested Latin Branch cofounder P. Galeandro and Filippo Perrone, an admirer of Luigi Galleani who had recently arrived in San Francisco after traveling from Vancouver to Tijuana to take part in the Partido Liberal Mexicano's ill-fated invasion there (see chap. 4). Both men were fined ten dollars and released.[56]

The following Sunday, IWW members and anarchists, including Perrone and Fred Rovaldi, also recently returned from Tijuana and the secretary of the Latin Bakers' Union, defied a new police ban on street meetings and addressed a crowd of two hundred listeners. According to the *San Francisco Chronicle*, police arrested all of the organizers after Perrone "spoke disparagingly about the American flag, condemned law and order, denounced all form[s] of government and ended with a tirade against the Pope." The audience then turned violent and forced police to flee with their prisoners to a nearby firehouse, which "thousands of infuriated men besieged" with rocks and bricks until reinforcements arrived. A rioter nearly bit off one officer's thumb, and police took ten individuals into custody and reportedly beat them. Each was held on one thousand dollars bail on charges of refusing to disperse and inciting to riot. "American comrades" stepped in to continue the fight for free speech.[57]

The arrests engendered an outpouring of support from the North Beach community. Two days after the riot, a protest meeting drew a crowd of two thousand, and in the affair's aftermath, the IWW's ranks swelled with "several hundred" new members. The charges against the arrested men were quietly dropped, and thousands turned out for a victory meeting on August 20 to listen to the released radicals.[58] An unusual testament to the number of anarchist sympathizers came from an investigation carried out by the socialist *Oakland World*, which found that North Beach merchants had not pressured police to suppress the Latin Branch's street meetings because they "were pleased with the anarchists since they brought in so much business."[59]

In January 1912, police again arrested speakers from Local 173, prompting a series of illegal outdoor meetings that "led to several minor riots in which policemen and spectators were injured"; immediately thereafter, Oakland Local 174 had its permit for street meetings withdrawn, leading to more clashes between police and IWW supporters.[60] Neither effort, however, prevented the IWW from continuing its open-air meetings or from forming a new Point Richmond local made up of twenty-five Italians. In 1913, members of the Latin Branch also aided an IWW-led strike of three thousand construction workers in Fresno.[61] Small as the official membership of the IWW may have been, its much larger base of support made it difficult to quash.

The anarcho-syndicalists of the IWW never had a monopoly on anarchism in North Beach, but the lines dividing individualists, anti-organizationists, anarchist-socialists, and anarcho-syndicalists were not rigid there. Most Italian anarchists subscribed to multiple publications of different ideological leanings and "socialized across paper lines."[62]

Michele Centrone, a former socialist who embraced individualist anarchism after coming to San Francisco from Apulia in 1903, collaborated on *La Protesta Umana* and *Nihil* but also wrote for Luigi Galleani's *Cronaca Sovversiva*, all the while serving as secretary of Local 95 of the United Brotherhood of Carpenters, a Latin AFL local.[63] Although "a sworn enemy of the I.W.W." who often sparred with Luigi Parenti in the radical press, Centrone "nevertheless extended his solidarity" during the 1911 free-speech fight, during which he was arrested.[64] In 1913, Centrone and other individualists founded the Gruppo Iconoclasti (Iconoclasts Group), many members of which in 1916 helped form the Gruppo Anarchico Volontà (Anarchist Will Group), an association of *antiorganizzatori* with thirty to forty regular members and a meeting hall at 1602 Stockton Street, "optimally located in the heart of the Latin colony." Inside, a visitor noted, "numerous revolutionary booklets, newspapers, etc. are fastened on with clothes pins to a railing midway up the wall and are strung out the entire length of the hall, easily accessible to all who care to read them."[65] Centrone was the local agent for *Cronaca Sovversiva* and distributed between sixty and seventy copies of it each week, but according to the Bureau of Investigation, "Probably most of the members [of the Volontà Group] read the copy of the Cronaca sent to the Gruppo headquarters, and did not subscribe individually." Bay Area readers of the paper therefore numbered around one hundred, possibly more.[66]

The modest-sized Italian anarchist community maintained a lively culture of opposition. Russia Hughes, the daughter of anarcho-syndicalists Cari and Mario Piccinini, recalled that when she was growing up in the 1920s and 1930s, "There were frequent social evenings to raise money for Sacco and Vanzetti, for Mooney and Billings, for 'Vittime Politiche' [Political Prisoners], for the civil war in Spain. These dinners, dance[s] with buffet[s], [and] picnics were attended by the same people, friends with whom to visit, discuss current events, the opera, the theatre—everything except small talk and gossip. That requires a different set of skills altogether."[67] San Francisco lacked the radical tavern culture of Paterson, but some of North Beach's Italian restaurants were owned by anarchists or sympathizers and served as meeting places. Group picnics in parks or on comrades' ranches outside of the city were also common.

As in Paterson, this movement culture rejected both Italian and American nationalism as well as religion. One of the IWW's Latin Branch members sourly complained, "[It is] our *Patria* that has denied us bread, freedom, [and] exis-

FIGURE 10. Anarchist picnic, San Francisco, 1918. Labeled are Elpidio Parenti and his daughters, Carinda (Cari) and Lina Parenti. Courtesy of Thomas Lang.

tence, which forces us to traverse this great and vast *Ocean* called the *Atlantic*, in search of a living [*un tozzo di pane*] less hard; the *Patria* that forces us to leave our parents, our sisters, our friends, our native land [*paese*], yet here in faraway America we are tormented and often hear whispered in the ears of we wretches this *meaningless* word 'Patria.'" Looking toward the revolutionary future, this author warned, "You cops, kings, emperors, governments, patriots, there will be no more land of milk and honey [*la cuccagna*] as in the past. We stand to redeem the *world, humanity*." From the perspective of a global humanity, talk of a *patria* was incomprehensible—literally "ungrammatical" (*sgrammaticata*).[68] As indicated by the 1911 free-speech fight, anticlericalism and atheism were also central to Bay Area anarchist identity. Cari Piccinini was, in the words of her daughter, Russia, "an orthodox atheist," while Russia's father, Mario, instructed her that "when passing the home of the rich, or a government office, or a church, it was important to spit. Then in the event that one has tuberculosis, it could be passed on to the enemy."[69]

Russia's memoirs offer a candid glimpse at gender relations in her anarchist family. Hughes's grandfather, Elpidio Parenti, the estranged brother of Luigi Parenti, was remembered "only for his violent rages, his brutality, his quickness to take out on his family the fury he must have had within him." Elpidio's abuse continued even after Cari's marriage to Mario, leading to an altercation between the two men and Elpidio's eviction from their home. Well into adulthood, Cari "still dreamt of being beaten by her father." Yet Mario was no feminist; Russia recalled, "There was no such thing as equality of the sexes. My free-thinking father used to say he believed in Ladies First, but into the kitchen."[70] American-born Jewish anarchist David Koven, who worked closely with Italian anarchists in New York and San Francisco in the 1930s and 1940s, described the men's attitude as "a product of the 19th century, and few anarchist men . . . treated women as equals." Eugene Travaglio's longtime companion, Esther Hartz, framed this behavior in ethnic terms, recalling that Travaglio "could get his Italian up."[71]

The Volontà Group, like the IWW, was "made up of young men chiefly, though a few women attend its sessions." And, as in Paterson, the women excluded from meaningful roles organized their own *gruppo femminile*, the Group Louise Michel, "a club of Radical Women of every nationality" that met on Friday evenings.[72] Anarchist men and women alike, however, placed great importance on birth control and worked together to disseminate literature on the topic throughout North Beach. On March 10, 1916, local birth control advocate and anarchist Rebekah (Reb) Raney, a contributor to Emma Goldman's *Mother Earth* and Alexander Berkman's *The Blast*, passed out five thousand pamphlets on "preventatives" during a meeting held to protest Goldman's recent arrest for doing the same. The Volontà Group then translated the pamphlet into Italian and printed and distributed twenty thousand copies. Anarchist Joseph Macario was arrested and convicted of dispensing "indecent" material, but his six-month sentence was suspended after a group of influential San Francisco women intervened on his behalf.[73]

Anarchists and IWW members proved far more adept at transcending California's peculiar racial hierarchy than at challenging patriarchy. Nowhere was their multiethnic cosmopolitanism more evident than in their attitude toward California's Asian workers. Chinese migrants—followed by Japanese, Koreans, and Indians—were the "indispensable enemy" against which the state's Anglo-Saxon working class united itself, and California labor unions led the campaign that culminated in the Chinese Exclusion Act of 1882.[74] This law created a void in the unskilled labor market that was quickly filled by a new "Yellow Peril" from Japan, and although the Japanese were never as numerous as the Chinese, the AFL energetically worked to exclude them from both the country and its unions. In 1905, representatives from San Francisco labor groups formed the Japanese and Korean Exclusion League, and in 1910, the San Francisco Labor Council upheld its own ban on Asian membership and asked affiliate unions to withdraw members from any establishment employing Asians.[75] In 1906, the Socialist Party of California passed a resolution calling for the exclusion of Asian immigrants, the same year that the San Francisco School District segregated Japanese schoolchildren into nonwhite schools. The national Socialist

Party passed a similar resolution the following year, when the "Gentlemen's Agreement" between the United States and Japan barred the latter from issuing passports to new emigrants bound for America.[76]

Relations between Asian migrants and the legally "white" but not "Anglo-Saxon" immigrants in neighboring North Beach were unpredictable and unstable but more open to cooperation and solidarity. Some Italians were involved in anti-Chinese agitation, but their own ambiguous position created ruptures in California's racial order. IWW organizer J. H. Walsh highlighted the similar (though by no means equivalent) treatment of Latins, Asians, and African Americans when he noted that the average "American" worker on the West Coast couldn't stand "to think of belonging to an organization that takes in 'Japs,' 'Chinks,' 'Dagoes,' and 'Niggers.'"[77] On rare occasions, articles arguing in favor of Chinese exclusion or disparaging Asian migrants cropped up in English-language anarchist periodicals on the West Coast, though these papers just as often defended the rights of Asian workers and condemned anti-Asian prejudice.[78] Italian-, French-, and Spanish-speaking anarchists, however, demonstrated no such ambivalence. Eugene Travaglio wrote against anti-Chinese "race prejudice" as well as antimiscegenation laws, and in 1908, the Latin anarchists of *Cogito, Ergo Sum* argued that the alleged inferiority of the Japanese resulted not from physical or intellectual shortcomings but from the disadvantages they faced because of "the stupid prejudice [of] 'The difference of the races.'"[79]

The IWW was the sole American labor organization to oppose Asian exclusion and actively recruit Asian members, and anarchist go-betweens were largely responsible for its successes on this front. At the IWW's 1905 founding convention, anarchist and former San Franciscan Al Klemencic, then residing in Colorado, first brought up the issue of Asian workers, stating, "We know we have got Austrians, Chinamen, Japs, and people of all nationalities here in this country. So we have got Frenchmen, Germans and Italians, and we are a cosmopolitan crowd. Now, then, as it is, all lines that were ever established have always been established by men who were a bunch of robbers, thieves and exploiters, and we want to combine ourselves as humanity, as one lot of people, those that are producing the wealth of our oppressors, and we want to have under that banner our brothers and sisters of the world."[80] In 1907, the union's General Executive Board endorsed these sentiments by passing a resolution "protesting vehemently against the Anti-Asiatic agitation" that had swept up even the Socialist Party.[81]

For California's overwhelmingly male Asian immigrants, the revolutionary manhood idealized by IWW activists and writers provided a counterpoint to persistent exclusionist attacks on their masculinity. Testifying before the Congressional Commission on Industrial Relations in 1916, IWW organizer George Speed declared, "While a good many people in the State [of California] object to the Jap and Chinese, I want to say, as far as I am concerned, one man is as good as another to me; I don't care whether he is black, blue, green, or yellow, as long as he acts the man and acts true to his economic interests as a worker." This was a classic example of the IWW's "efforts to disarm race through masculinity"—efforts that fused class and gender in a way that marginalized women within working-class struggles but brought together male workers across ethnoracial lines.[82]

Although the presence of Japanese anarchists on the West Coast was noted as early as 1900, the opportunity for significant anarchist and IWW inroads among Japanese migrants came in November 1905 with the arrival of Shusui Kotoku. A prominent Japanese radical, Kotoku had just finished a prison sentence for opposing the Russo-Japanese War. In 1904, radical American journalist Leopold Fleischmann had met Kotoku in Tokyo and put him in correspondence with Albert Johnson, a sixty-year-old anarchist who in his youth had traveled the world—including China and Japan—as a whaler before settling in San Francisco, where he worked as a ferryman, became president of the Freethought Society, and helped arrange Kotoku's visit.[83] Although already familiar with some anarchist writings and ideas, Kotoku still considered himself a socialist when he came to San Francisco.

He roomed at the home of Rose Fritz, an anarchist obstetrician and friend of Johnson's who had migrated to the Bay Area in the 1880s after studying medicine in Kiev. Dr. Fritz was an unrepentant advocate of propaganda by the deed and "an opponent of discrimination against the Japanese."[84] Portraits of Kropotkin and Bakunin adorned the walls of her guest room, and she supplied Kotoku with further anarchist literature, introduced him to local anarchists, put him in correspondence with Peter Kropotkin, and, he recorded in his diary, "argued strongly for assassinating politicians." Shortly after his arrival, Kotoku was also approached by three IWW members who invited him to speak at a meeting in Oakland and introduced him to the notion of the revolutionary general strike. The great earthquake (which spared Fritz's home) cemented Kotoku's transition to an anarchist position; rather than chaos in its aftermath, he witnessed innumerable acts of mutual aid, and he described the city as being in a state of "Anarchist Communism" or even an "ideal paradise" amid the ruins.[85]

Kotoku merged Fritz's advocacy of propaganda by the deed with the IWW's syndicalism to create the program of the Shakai Kakumeito (Social Revolutionary Party), which he cofounded in Berkeley on June 1, 1906. The party, consisting of more than fifty Japanese radicals described by Kotoku as "clever and devoted libertarians," called on its members to abolish private property and class inequality as well as to "eliminate national and racial prejudice" and "unite with the comrades of the world to carry out a great social revolution."[86] The group founded a bilingual newspaper, *Kakumei* (Revolution), that promoted the violent overthrow of the bourgeoisie and the Japanese emperor while exhorting American workers to unite with Japanese migrants, noting, "Rejection of one nation from your country will not put a stop to the capitalist class taking all and leaving you only what he [*sic*] must in order to keep you alive so that you produce more wealth for them." The paper also promoted the IWW, and members of the Shakai Kakumeito worked with local IWW organizers to translate the union's pamphlets into Japanese.[87]

One writer for *Kakumei* lamented in an open letter to the Socialist Party of America, "So far as I know not a single Socialist paper in this country spoke out plainly on this Japanese question without showing race prejudice.... Do they think that they can stop capitalism by excluding Japanese workers from the land?" The Socialist Party did not respond to this protest, but the anarchist *Emancipator* reprinted the letter in full to "testify our sentiments of fraternity to our Japanese brothers."[88] After Emma Goldman toured California in the spring of 1907, she reported to Kropotkin, "We have quite a Japanese Anarchistic movement on the Coast. I addressed several hundred Japanese, and found them very intelligent and beautiful in Spirit, they are great admirers of yours, great students of everything written on Anarchism."[89]

Although *Kakumei* lasted just three issues, in August 1908, one of its founders, Takeuchi Tetsugoro, helped form the Furesuno Rodo Domeikai (Fresno Labor League), which united two thousand of the region's Japanese grape pickers under a program dedicated to increasing wages, eliminating corrupt labor contractors, and "elevat[ing] the status of workers." Though these were bread-and-butter demands, the league's paper, *Rodo* (Labor), was militantly anarcho-syndicalist and declared the organization's unofficial affiliation with the IWW. In September 1909, the league held a joint rally with the Fresno IWW branch, composed primarily of Mexicans and Italians.[90]

But the Gentlemen's Agreement and unwanted attention from federal authorities placed new pressures on the Japanese radicals, many of whom returned to Japan, and the Fresno Labor League dissolved in 1910. Japanese agricultural workers continued to organize their own labor associations, often in cooperation with Japanese labor contractors, and the IWW hesitated to compete with these organizations. Furthermore, as Chicago anarchist and IWW member T. Takahashi explained, many Japanese "have been so long isolated from the labor movement in this country, that suspicion is still burning in their minds, and it is hard to make him [*sic*] understand that there are white workers who would make comrades of them, who would co-operate and fight with them together."[91] But a small group of Japanese anarchists remained active in the Bay Area, launching a new paper, *Shinsei* (Rising Star), in 1910.[92] The IWW's Fresno branch absorbed many former members of the Fresno Labor League, and in December 1918, the IWW temporarily organized hundreds of Mexican and Japanese orange pickers.[93] Kotoku retuned to Japan less than a month after founding the Shakai Kakumeito in 1906 but remained in contact with American anarchists and IWW members, forging some of the first links of the Anarchist Pacific.

As the supply of Japanese labor declined, California growers turned to migrants from India, who began arriving in large numbers in 1906. These laborers, largely Punjabi Sikhs, were greeted much as earlier Chinese and Japanese migrants had been: they were the victims of mob violence and excluded from the AFL, and in 1907, the Japanese and Korean Exclusion League changed its name to the Asiatic Exclusion League to add Indians to the groups against which it campaigned.[94] Their few allies included anarchists and the IWW.

As early as the 1890s, Danielewicz's *Beacon* had praised the activities of revolutionaries in India, where "there is now growing up a sturdy self reliant race of men, that will in days to come drive the Anglo-Saxon buc[c]aneers from their shores." Nearly two decades later, *Nihil* similarly celebrated the actions of India's anticolonial "anarchists."[95] But the first substantial connections between California radicals and Indian migrants awaited the arrival of Har Dayal in April 1911. A Hindu and anti-imperialist, Dayal had been active in the Indian independence movement in London during his university studies there. He then enrolled at the University of California at Berkeley, rubbing shoulders in the Bay Area with radicals of all stripes, including Irish, Russian, Japanese, Chinese, and Turkish revolutionaries. He soon founded the International Radical Club, a motley assortment of revolutionaries, intellectuals, and eccentrics that met at an Italian restaurant in North Beach.[96] Dayal quickly gravitated to both anarchism and the IWW, becoming secretary of Oakland's IWW Mixed Local 174. In a speech on "The Future of the Labor Movement" delivered to Local 174 in 1912, he condemned patriotism as having been "devised to divide the laborers into their various countries and thus into a false division of society," denounced parliamentary socialism as a dead end, and advocated direct action and the general strike. Finally, he called for "cooperation between the labor movement and the woman's movement. The workers and the women are two enslaved classes and must fight their battles together."[97]

To pursue these goals, Dayal formed the Fraternity of the Red Flag, a multiethnic organization with a declaration of principles that fully displayed his new synthesis of Hindu, anticolonial, anarchist, and syndicalist thought. It called for personal self-improvement; the abolition of private property, religion, and government; the emancipation of women; the "establishment of Universal Brotherhood, and the abolition of patriotism and race-feeling." Claiming to represent members on five continents, the Fraternity pledged to "devote its efforts chiefly to the establishment of Modern Schools, and the promotion of industrial organization and strikes (in cooperation with the I.W.W. and the Syndicalist movements). In Asia and Africa, it will further the movements of progress and revolt in various countries." In 1913, Dayal also opened the Bakunin Institute, an anarchist training center operating out of a small building on six acres of land in nearby Hayward donated by E. Norwood, a "female comrade" from the Fraternity.[98] In 1914, the institute began publishing *Land and Liberty*, edited by Indian-born British anarchist William C. Owen. A former socialist, IWA member, and erstwhile Asian exclusionist, Owen had embraced anarchism in the 1890s and become an unlikely champion of the rights of Asian and Mexican migrants as well as editor of the English-language page of the Partido Liberal Mexicano's paper, *Regeneración*.[99]

The first issue of *Land and Liberty* trumpeted, "Wherever men or women battle for freedom they will find in us a champion, whether that battle is in Mexico or the United States, in Europe or the Orient." Unlike some anarchists, who were skeptical of supporting national independence movements, the paper argued that "the impending struggle in Mexico, Ireland, Egypt, India, [and] everywhere . . . is based on the Anarchist doctrine that the individual is entitled to self-ownership. Because Anarchists cling to this as their fundamental tenet, they sympathize with and do their best to assist national movements of revolt throughout the world."[100] But this brand of anti-imperialism came perilously close to replacing antinationalism with an internationalist celebration of post-colonial nationalisms, a tension also clear in Dayal's activities among his fellow Indian migrants.

At a meeting in Portland, Oregon, in early June 1913, Dayal helped form the anticolonial Pacific Coast Hindi Association, which subsequently became the Ghadar Party, named for its Urdu-language publication, *Ghadar* (Mutiny), edited by Dayal in San Francisco. The organization grew to include seventy-two North American branches and a reported five thousand members, and *Ghadar*'s weekly circulation soared from six thousand to twenty-five thousand copies, with subscribers throughout much of the world. The magazine drew on "a broad range of ideas of nationalist, revolutionary, and anarchist movements to formulate its opposition to British rule."[101] But the Ghadar movement received a severe blow on March 25, 1914, when Dayal and several other leaders were arrested for allegedly violating the Anarchist Exclusion Act of 1903. Freed on one thousand dollars' bail, Dayal fled to Switzerland. The Bakunin Institute and *Land and Liberty* were left in the hands of Owen, who in late 1914 closed the institute and moved the paper to San Francisco.[102] Nevertheless, Ghadar members—most of them Sikh laborers—regularly interacted with members of the Bay Area's multiethnic anarchist movement, and a U.S. immigration official received word that "most of the members of the Hindu nationalist party were also 'IWWs.'" The IWW enrolled Indian agricultural workers in Northern California towns such as Marysville and Wheatland, where some participated in the 1913 IWW-led Wheatland Strike that culminated in a scuffle in which a sheriff's deputy, a district attorney, and two strikers were killed.[103] Despite this incident, the IWW remained the primary union representing California farm-workers for the next decade.

The years following the 1906 earthquake also saw the development of new Jewish and Eastern European anarchist groups. Rose Fritz had been active since the 1880s, and Alexander Horr, a Hungarian-born Jew who migrated to New York in the 1880s and spent three years at the utopian Freeland Colony on Puget Sound, quickly became a prominent figure after his 1907 arrival in San Francisco. Horr arranged many of Emma Goldman's local appearances, became secretary of the jitney bus drivers' union, opened a radical bookstore with socialist William McDevitt, and became "the leading spirit" of the radical Social Science League.[104] Lucy Fox and Bob Robins, Russian Jews formerly active in Chicago and affiliated with *Free Society*, arrived in 1906 and opened the St. Helena Vegetarian Café on Market Street, the city's first vegetarian res-taurant and an important locus of radical activity.[105]

In 1907, Yiddish-speaking anarchists formed their own organization, the Grupe Frayhayt, and anarchists were also active in the Radical Branch (No. 511) of the Workmen's Circle, which had twenty-five members at its founding in 1911.[106] Nevertheless, San Francisco lacked the numbers to support a distinct Yiddish anarchist community. When Fox and Robins moved into a commu-nal house on Telegraph Hill with four other anarchists, all of their roommates were Italians rather than fellow Jews.[107] A growing population of ethnic Russian migrants, however, led to the formation of a Russian-language branch of IWW Mixed Local 173 as well as a large section of the anarcho-syndicalist Union of Russian Workers of the United States and Canada. In addition, in 1909 the lo-cal Yugoslav League of Independent Socialists published the Serbian-language anarcho-syndicalist paper *Volja* (Will), and Oakland police described that city's anarchist movement as consisting "chiefly of Servians [*sic*] and Italians."[108]

In 1915, Alexander Berkman moved to San Francisco to aid in the legal de-fense of anarchists Matthew Schmidt and David Caplan, implicated as acces-sories in the 1910 bombing of the notoriously anti-union *Los Angeles Times*. The bomb, which detonated prematurely and killed twenty people, was part of a desperate campaign of property destruction secretly launched by the ironwork-ers' union in 1906 in the face of a largely successful open-shop movement. In 1910, this struggle was augmented by radical elements of San Francisco's AFL unions, including Schmidt and Caplan, the latter a Russian Jewish grocery store owner whose connection to the labor movement was purely ideological. At trial, Schmidt was sentenced to life imprisonment and Caplan, charged with voluntary manslaughter for helping to obtain dynamite, served seven and a half years.[109]

Berkman, however, remained on the West Coast, viewing San Francisco's strong labor movement as fertile ground for fostering revolutionary class-consciousness.

Fourteen years in a Pennsylvania prison had made Berkman fluent in English, and eight years as editor of *Mother Earth* helped him develop an effective rhetorical style. In January 1916, he began publishing *The Blast*, a "Revolutionary Labor Weekly" that sought "to get the rebels throughout the country in closer touch with each other, to develop a better mutual understanding among them, to crystallize the scattered revolutionary sentiment in some definite active expression, regardless of theoretical differences and varying isms."[110] Berkman had some success at this, attracting English-speaking anarchists such as Eric B. Morton, a Norwegian-born carpenter and AFL organizer who had attempted to tunnel Berkman out of prison in 1900, and young Texas-born cartoonist Robert Minor as well as Tom Mooney, a member of the International Molders Union, and other left-wing socialists. *The Blast* was also in close contact with the Volontà Group, the Union of Russian Workers, the Frayhayt Group, and the Radical Branch of the Workmen's Circle. These organizations frequently held joint events and picnics, one of which was described in *The Blast* as "a truly international gathering, such as can be found only on the Coast: men, women and children of practically every country on the face of the globe fraternized in a truly international spirit."[111] In 1916, the Volontà Group began hosting an "International Meeting" every Thursday evening where speeches were "made in a dozen languages," and on Saturdays it held meetings in both English and Italian.[112]

The Blast's run was almost cut short after the April 1916 issue was barred from the mails for carrying "indecent" articles about Volontà Group's birth control campaign; the postal inspector then used the same loophole in the postal code that had been used to suppress *La Questione Sociale* to strip the paper of its second-class mailing privileges on the grounds that it was not a "newspaper or other periodical publication" as a result of irregularities in its publishing schedule—irregularities caused by the postal service itself.[113] Berkman, however, continued publication and shipped copies of *The Blast* in bulk to comrades outside of the state, who then mailed a few issues at a time out of different post office boxes.[114]

Berkman was also a tireless organizer. He founded the Current Events Club, which held weekly meetings and for a time was "the largest of local anarchistic organizations," and in December 1916 joined with members of the Socialist Party and IWW to form the Jack London Memorial Library and School of Social Science (renamed the People's Institute in 1918).[115] He was also "in touch with Hindu revolutionists and Anarchists of the Hindustan Gadar [*sic*] organization."[116] Ram Chandra, who assumed leadership of the Ghadar Party after Dayal's departure, contributed articles to *Mother Earth* and was close to several affiliates of *The Blast*, among them Ed Gammons, a former Irish nation-

FIGURE 11. Postcard from Luigi Parenti (third from left) to his family, 1916. Archivio Centrale dello Stato, Rome; courtesy of the Ministero per i Beni e le Attività Culturali.

alist who in 1910 migrated to the United States, where he became an anarchist and joined the IWW. Moving to San Francisco in 1914, Gammons joined the Friends of Freedom for India, contributed articles to *The Blast*, and produced English-language literature for the Ghadar Party.[117]

San Francisco's anarchists and anticolonial radicals increasingly acted as a single, multiethnic community within which cosmopolitanism became an everyday practice. The cosmopolitan spirit of this movement was captured at a 1913 New Year's gathering held at IWW Local 173's headquarters, where more than fifteen hundred "men, women and children, representing practically every civilized nation of the world, assembled in the hall and participated in the general jollification that began early in the evening and lasted until the break of day." The walls were "decorated with flags of all nations and on the wall above the speakers' stand were these two mottoes: 'All flags look alike to us,' and 'One Big Union.'"[118]

In 1916, IWW Latin Branch organizer Luigi Parenti came to the attention of both the Italian and American governments when he enclosed a postcard with a letter to his father and sister back in Italy. The card was a photograph of Parenti and seven other armed members of an Italian anarchist shooting club, taken somewhere in the hills of South San Francisco. On the reverse side, Parenti wrote, "I send this present as a token of affection and so that you may see how a group of young subversives *without a 'country'* prepare themselves to freely use arms to be ready for the coming day of the revolution against priests, bosses, and government." Not only did Parenti underline the words *"without a 'country'"* (*"senza 'patria'"*) for emphasis, he also placed the word *patria* within derisive quotation marks. The Italian authorities who discovered the postcard quickly placed Parenti under surveillance through their San Francisco consulate and forwarded a copy of the document to the American Bureau of Investigation, which opened its own file on the anarchist.[119]

Parenti's rejection of nationalism clearly befuddled and frightened government officials. The Bureau of Investigation subjected his postcard to several retranslations of greater and lesser accuracy, apparently seeking to divine some hidden meaning. The Secret Service carried out its own four-month investigation of Parenti and leaked the postcard to the press. The *San Francisco Examiner* neatly completed the work of making Parenti's message intelligible to American eyes by inexplicably mistranslating *senza patria* as "without work," thereby replacing anarchist antinationalism with the stereotype of the unproductive foreigner.[120] But the following year, during a hearing to extradite Parenti to face federal charges in Chicago, the anarchist reasserted his statelessness, declaring, "The I.W.W. is the organization to which I militate—[that] I work in, I am interested in, the United States I have nothing to do with."[121] This attitude was incomprehensible to American authorities but made perfect sense to a member of North Beach's radical cosmopolitan milieu.

CHAPTER 4

"THE WHOLE WORLD IS OUR COUNTRY"
TRANSNATIONAL ANARCHIST ACTIVISM AND THE FIRST WORLD WAR

The chorus of Pietro Gori's popular "Stornelli d'esilio" (Songs of Exile), first printed in an 1898 songbook published in New Jersey by *La Questione Sociale*, proclaims, "The whole world is our country / liberty is our law / and a rebellious thought / is in our hearts."[1] Here, the anarchist experience was stripped to its essentials: mobility, cosmopolitanism, libertarianism, and unceasing rebellion. Gori, the "knight errant of anarchism," was emblematic of these qualities: in addition to his preeminent role in the anarchist movement in Italy and in the formative phase of anarchism in Paterson and San Francisco, he was active in London and especially Argentina, where he was the animating spirit behind the 1901 formation of that country's first national labor confederation, the anarcho-syndicalist Federación Obrera Regional Argentina.[2] As such a biography suggests, attempts to encapsulate the study of anarchism within the fixed boundaries of a particular city or country inevitably miss much of the actual movement. Whereas the preceding chapters examined the transnational roots and local development of anarchism in New York, Paterson, and San Francisco, this chapter turns outward, to these communities' engagement with struggles beyond America's borders.

Anarchism was a transnational movement from its beginnings within the First International. Globally, it was comprised of overlapping networks, loosely defined by region, language, and ideology, which in turn overlapped with a wide variety of other revolutionary causes. Its transnational networks were connected organizationally, through bodies such as the First International; officially, through periodic international anarchist congresses; informationally, through the circulation of periodicals and literature; and informally, through interpersonal and interorganizational contacts. Anarchists belonging to one particular network were typically therefore only one or two removes from any other node within this web of connections.

America's Yiddish and Italian anarchists were committed "internationalists" and cosmopolitans who supported revolutionary and anticolonial struggles throughout the world and gave their support, their meager finances, and at times their lives on behalf of these struggles. If they tended, quite understandably, to prioritize rebellions in their own lands of origin, they were by no means indifferent to more remote events. The anarchist press kept readers informed of revolutionary efforts, labor struggles, and anarchist activities worldwide, all presented side by side on the front page of the *Fraye Arbeter Shtime* or in *La Questione Sociale* and *L'Era Nuova* under the heading "The Social Movement." If the whole world was their country, then revolution anywhere was part of the larger "social movement" within which anarchists situated themselves.

American anarchist groups sent delegates to most of the international anarchist congresses that convened between the collapse of the First International and the beginning of the First World War. These gatherings aimed primarily to foster greater connectivity and coordination between anarchist networks rather than to formulate a "party line." As described by the editors of *La Questione Sociale*, delegates to anarchist congresses "neither make nor prepare laws, but will discuss ideas, and perhaps propose agreements that, in accordance with libertarian principles, will not bind those who do not accept them, until they accept them." Harry Kelly compared these events to "conventions of scientists": "Papers are read at scientific gatherings and discussed at length, but no votes are taken. If the participants see good in the theories and conclusions set forth they are accepted; if not, the listeners disregard them."[3] These meetings were therefore as much about initiating and maintaining informal relationships as they were about coordinating institutional ties.

Five American groups were represented at the 1881 International Social Revolutionary Conference in London, which Boston anarchist Edward Nathan-Ganz also attended as the representative of a Mexican labor federation. In addition, Paterson's French-speaking Groupe Socialiste-Révolutionnaire sent a statement to the proceedings. After much contentious debate, the forty-six assembled delegates officially endorsed "propaganda by deed and insurrectionary action." They also undertook the first of several attempts to create an Anarchist International following the termination of the First International in 1876 and the dissolution of the breakaway Anti-Authoritarian International soon after. The congress announced the creation of a new International Working Men's

Association, dubbed the Black International after the black flag of anarchism.[4] This organization, however, consisted only of a three-person correspondence committee—"an international mailbox," in Nunzio Pernicone's words—and had no real existence outside of America's International Working People's Association, which was intended to be a national affiliate of the larger organization. Although existing anarchist federations in a few other countries also declared their affiliation with the Black International, this gesture meant next to nothing in practical terms, and the correspondence bureau was soon defunct.[5]

Anarchists, who had always considered themselves part of the larger socialist movement, next tried to secure a place within the socialist Second International, founded in 1889. In August 1891, during his time in London, Saul Yanovsky was dispatched as a delegate of the anarchist Berner Street Club to this new International's second congress, in Brussels. But Yanovsky and most other anarchist representatives were excluded from the proceedings and forced to meet separately.[6] Gori returned from the United States to Europe to attend the next congress of the International, held in London in 1896. Gori carried credentials from the Federazione Socialista-Anarchica dei Lavoratori Italiani nel Nord-America, but at the beginning of the congress, anarchists were once and for all expelled from the organization. They again held their own informal congress, where the emerging syndicalist movement was discussed at length.[7]

Between these two meetings, anarchists in the United States set out to organize their own International Anarchist Congress to coincide with the 1893 Chicago World's Fair. Although various circumstances prevented any overseas delegates from attending and Chicago police attempted to prohibit the congress from meeting, it convened in secret and reports were read from anarchists in Paris, London, Amsterdam, and Armenia. Furthermore, the twenty or so "American" delegates in attendance included Austrian, German, Polish, Jewish, Russian, and Spanish immigrants as well as "a mestizo Indian," and the Spanish and Cuban anarchist movements were officially represented by Pedro Esteve, who had arrived in the United States the previous year.[8]

In September 1900, the International Revolutionary Congress was scheduled in Paris, but the assassination of Umberto I less than three months earlier prompted police to suppress the meeting. Delegates representing at least eleven countries nevertheless assembled clandestinely. The American delegation included Michael Cohn and Emma Goldman as well as Dutch-born Boston anarchist Alex K. Snellenberg, while San Francisco's Eric B. Morton, on the run following his unsuccessful attempt to tunnel Alexander Berkman out of prison, attended as a representative of his native Norway.[9] Reports from a number of countries (including no less than ten from the United States, among them Cohn's "History of the Jewish Anarchist Movement in the United States" and a statement from Paterson's Germinal Group) were read and later printed by

Les Temps Nouveaux, and delegates also discussed syndicalism and the general strike.[10] Moreover, "the creation of an official international was agreed on in principle," though no concrete action was taken toward this end.[11]

Goldman again represented the "American" (that is, English-speaking) movement at the more fruitful 1907 International Anarchist Congress in Amsterdam, where German immigrant Max Baginsky represented America's "foreign" anarchists. After much debate, including Errico Malatesta's plea that anarchism not be completely subsumed under syndicalism, the assembled delegates passed resolutions endorsing the revolutionary general strike and urging anarchists to take an active part in syndicalist organizations "without forgetting that anarchist action cannot be entirely contained within the limits of the syndicate." The congress also established a new Anarchist International to be coordinated by a five-person London-based International Bureau with a mandate to "put itself into communication with Anarchists in all countries." The bureau founded an international anarchist bulletin for this purpose, but a lack of funds and international commitment led to the publication's termination in 1910, and this International ceased to exist soon thereafter.[12] In the interim, however, the Anarchist Federation of New York, formed by Berkman in 1908, had affiliated with it, as had the International Federation of Chicago organized the same year.[13] American delegates as well as those from at least thirteen other countries planned to attend another international congress scheduled to meet in London in September 1914, but the event was canceled after war broke out the preceding month.[14]

As this summary indicates, anarchist groups in the United States actively maintained international ties despite the failure to establish an enduring international organization. To the extent that anything resembling an Anarchist International existed in these years, the American movement was an energetic participant, and its publications offered extensive coverage of these congresses and other international developments. The lack of official international coordination should therefore not obscure anarchism's "actual wealth of informal internationalism."[15]

America's immigrant anarchist communities were intimately tied to labor and revolutionary struggles in members' countries of origin and forged links to radical networks spanning both the Atlantic and Pacific Oceans. The Lower East Side's Yiddish anarchists maintained close contact with the revolutionary movement in Russia as well as London's Jewish anarchists, and their reach soon spread. By the first decade of the twentieth century, the geography of Yiddish anarchism extended into Canada, Argentina, France, Germany, Austria-Hungary, Egypt, South Africa, and the Ottoman Empire. Philip Josephs, a Latvian Jewish anarchist radicalized in Glasgow, even founded New Zealand's first anarchist group in 1913.[16] The nodes within this transnational network were connected almost entirely through the circulation of the *Fraye Arbeter Shtime* and London's *Arbayter Fraynd*, both of which carried periodic reports from their far-flung constituents. *Arbayter Fraynd* editor Rudolf Rocker recalled, "There were few movements whose periodical and other literature was so widely spread in different countries as ours. . . . Our movement in London was a hub, from which spokes went out in all directions, to a great number of people, in all countries." Similarly, an American anarchist writer noted that the *Fraye Arbeter Shtime* received "support from an infinite number of groups in the United States, Canada, South America, Russia, France, England and elsewhere."[17]

New York's anarchists also helped introduce anarchism to Eastern Europe. Beginning in the 1890s, Yiddish and Russian anarchist publications from the United States and London were regularly smuggled into the Pale of Settlement, and in the textile center of Bialystok, where Yanovsky had attended school, his pamphlet *Der olef beys fun anarkhizmus* became a local favorite.[18] When Goldman traveled through Kiev in 1920, she even discovered copies of *Mother Earth*, which she "was sure . . . had never been sent to Russia" but had been forwarded to a local anarchist by a brother living in the United States.[19] In the spring of 1903, Jewish revolutionaries in Bialystok broke with the General Jewish Labor Bund and the Russian Social Democratic Labor Party and formed Russia's first self-avowed anarchist group. Originally an exclusively Jewish group with the Yiddish name Der Kamf (The Struggle), the organization soon included Poles and Russians and became known by the Russian equivalent, Borba. The group owed its creation to return migrant Shleme Kaganovich (known as Zeydl), who had joined the Yiddish anarchist movement while in London in 1898–99. Likewise, one of the leading anarchist figures in the nearby town of Krynki was Shmuel Weiner, nicknamed the American as a consequence of his own time abroad.[20] Other anarchist groups composed of Jewish workers and students quickly sprang up in Odessa, Warsaw, and elsewhere.

By 1905, Bialystok was home to a second organization, Chernoe Znamia (Black Flag), comprised mainly of Jewish trade union members. Like most new Russian anarchist groups, Chernoe Znamia advocated armed insurrection, terrorism, and "expropriations."[21] These extremist groups were a product of and contributed to the upsurge of radicalism and violence that culminated in the abortive Russian Revolution of 1905–7. During those years, Russia's anarchist movement counted between five thousand and fifteen thousand followers, with Jews predominating, and was responsible for an estimated one thousand or more deaths in skirmishes, assassinations, and bombings.[22] Early Russian anarchism consequently developed a character fundamentally different from that of the moderate Yiddish anarchism found in New York, but American comrades, with whom the Russians were in direct contact, defended such violence as necessary in the Russian context. In fact, this violence exhilarated America's Russian Jewish radicals, who hastened to aid their comrades or fight alongside them.

"The Russian people have awakened!" trumpeted the *Fraye Arbeter Shtime* in January 1905, and within a month the paper collected five hundred dollars for the Russian anarchist movement.[23] Goldman arranged for Eric B. Morton to smuggle arms to Russia's Socialist Revolutionary Party and worked with Hillel Solotaroff to raise funds for Russian anarchist groups. At the 1907 International Anarchist Congress in Amsterdam, Goldman reported, "Hundreds of thousands of dollars have been sent from America to assist our Russian brothers. . . . Scores of our Jewish comrades have also returned to Russia to aid by word and deed the heroic struggle against Tsardom."[24] Among those travelers to Russia was Benyamin Bahrah, an anarchist radicalized in the United States who was executed in 1906 for attempting to assassinate the governor-general of Lithuania.[25] Victor Rivkind was "well known in the Anarchist centers of Paris and New York," and following his return to Bialystok, he helped establish an illegal anarchist printing press, then traveled to Warsaw and joined an insurgent group, leading to his arrest and execution along with fifteen comrades in 1907. Joseph Spivak, who migrated to New York in 1902, returned to Ukraine in 1905 to join the revolution and the Jewish self-defense movement, then escaped back to America the following year.[26]

The merciless suppression of the 1905 revolution created a new wave of émigrés, including members of Russia's new anarchist movement. Many of these revolutionaries, however, "did not consider Yanovsky and the *Fraye Arbeter Shtime* group to be real anarchists or revolutionists and had a low opinion of them." Odessa-born Kate Wolfson, who migrated to New York in 1907, recalled, "We read the *Fraye Arbeter Shtime*, but we were more in the Russian movement than the Yiddish."[27] Like New York's earliest Jewish anarchists, most of the newcomers believed in insurrectionary violence and preferred to join "Russian" groups. The most important of these organizations was the Union of Russian Workers of the United States and Canada (UORW), an anarchist federation founded in New York in 1908.

The UORW, like the movement in Russia, initially promoted armed warfare against the state and capitalism and considered itself anarchist-communist in orientation. But in 1912, influenced by the IWW and French syndicalism, the organization officially declared itself anarcho-syndicalist, though an insurrectionist wing remained. A new constitution adopted in 1914 drew directly on the IWW's famous preamble while adding a more revolutionary tone:

> Present society is divided into opposite classes, on one side the workers and farmers, submerged in poverty but who have created by their own labor all the

riches of the world; on the other side the rich, who have confiscated all these riches. . . . The struggle between these classes is not finished at the present time, and will end only when the laboring masses, organized as a class, will understand their true interests and will come into possession of the riches of the world through forceful social revolution . . . and at the same time having destroyed all the institutions of sovereignty and government.[28]

By that time, the UORW had seven thousand members throughout North America, and records seized by New York State authorities in 1919 recorded a membership of fifteen thousand.[29]

Although a majority of UORW members were ethnic Russians, Jews were heavily overrepresented in the organization. Conspicuous among them were Maksim Raevsky (real name, L. Fishelev), who became an anarcho-syndicalist in Paris before moving to New York, where he edited the UORW paper *Golos Truda* (Voice of Labor); Khaym (Efim) Yartchuk, a founding member of Bialystok's Chernoe Znamia group who embraced anarcho-syndicalism after emigrating to the United States in 1913; and Daniil Novomirskii (real name, Iakov Kirillovskii), who was the foremost anarcho-syndicalist in Russia before being sent to a Siberian labor camp in 1905 and subsequently escaping to New York, where he contributed to both *Golos Truda* and the *Fraye Arbeter Shtime*.[30] In 1917, prominent Russian-Jewish anarcho-syndicalist Volin (V. M. Eikhenbaum), recently arrived from Paris, also joined the UORW.

San Francisco's UORW section grew to 384 members by 1918, and in 1915 and 1916, two of its members made sensational headlines following shootouts with the police. The first incident occurred on the night of September 11, 1915, when Gregory Chesalkin, alias George Nelson, held off more than fifty officers from within his boardinghouse room. Chesalkin was an ironworker and jitney driver who had robbed a Los Angeles bank with two other men a few weeks earlier, apparently with the goal of sending the money to revolutionaries in Russia. After a seven-hour standoff, he took his own life.[31] On May 26, 1916, another ironworker and UORW member, Vladimir Osokin (aka Philip Ward), was accused of passing counterfeit coins. Osokin, who had made his way to the United States several years earlier after escaping from eight years of imprisonment in Siberia for revolutionary activities, resisted arrest rather than face incarceration, shooting and killing a police sergeant. He then barricaded himself in a boathouse and exchanged gunfire with more than a hundred officers for two hours before dying from multiple wounds. Osokin may well have been engaged in a forgery scheme intended, like Chesalkin's robbery, to fund activities in Russia.[32]

New immigrants from Russia also founded the first American branches of the Anarchist Red Cross, an international organization dedicated to maintaining contact with and providing material aid to anarchists imprisoned under the czar. The Anarchist Red Cross's New York branch soon had "more than a hundred" participants.[33] But these Russian and Jewish radicals were not focused exclusively on events in Europe. The UORW urged its members to join IWW locals wherever possible, and in San Francisco, the organization had strong ties to the IWW as well as the Blast Group, which cosponsored Osokin's funeral along with the Frayhayt Group and Volontà Group.[34] The UORW's "People's Houses" offered free classes to members on everything from English and algebra to Marxism and anarchism. Nor did all new arrivals distance themselves from the Yiddish movement: Anarchist Red Cross cofounder Boris Yelensky, for example, became a partisan of the *Fraye Arbeter Shtime*, later recalling that Yanovsky "had a sharp eye and wit, which opened up many things for me."[35] Ukrainian Jewish shirtwaist maker Rose Pesotta, who migrated to New York in 1913, joined both the UORW and the ILGWU, becoming one of the foremost female Jewish labor organizers of her day. Yiddish writer B. Rivkin was another post-1905 arrival with close ties to the *Fraye Arbeter Shtime*. By 1917, strong links connected Jewish and Russian anarchists in America to their counterparts in Russia.

Likewise, as described by Davide Turcato, the "key traits of Italian anarchist transnationalism" included "its role in times of repression in the homeland, the mobility of militants, the organizational integration of groups, the mutual support and exchange of resources, and the circulation of ideas through the press."[36] Paterson's Italians maintained connections to the labor movement in Biella, even after the Biellese anarchist movement all but disappeared in the second half of the 1890s. Many subscribed to the Socialist *Corriere Biellese* and contributed generously to funds for strikes in their hometowns. In 1909, Paterson anarchists wrote to Biella's short-lived anarchist paper *L'Alba*, "Our heart has throbbed with yours whenever a conflict of some importance took place between capital and labor; and in some important circumstances we have also manifested our solidarity in the only way possible, namely, by sending a few dollars."[37]

Migrants in the United States also read and, more important, sent monetary contributions to anarchist periodicals published in Italy and elsewhere abroad. At times their remittances accounted for more than half of these newspapers' finances.[38] Furthermore, in 1919, an Italian group in Boston, in conjunction with Paterson's Libreria Sociologica, raised funds from 460 donors across North America to purchase the linotype machine used by Rome's anarchist daily *Umanità Nova*, which reached a circulation above forty thousand during its run from 1920 to 1922. American subscriptions to *Umanità Nova* were in turn forwarded through the Libreria Sociologica.[39] Fund-raising campaigns for *vittime politiche* (political prisoners) in Italy were also a permanent fixture of Italian American anarchism.

In addition, notices and letters printed in the more than two hundred Italian anarchist periodicals published worldwide as well as private correspondence between militants gave the global Italian movement coherency even in the absence of formal transnational organizations. So, too, did international travel and migration. A study of two thousand Italian anarchist biographies found that approximately 60 percent of those profiled emigrated abroad at least once for a period of six months or longer. Of the more than 140 in this sample who traveled to the United States, over a third had previously migrated to at least one other destination, and more than 70 percent remigrated—though nearly a third eventually returned to America, most of them permanently.[40] Italian anarchists could be found alongside their Yiddish comrades in North America, Argentina, England, France, and Egypt, and they also established groups in Brazil, Uruguay, Peru, the Balkans, Belgium, Spain, Switzerland, Malta, Tunisia, Algeria, and Australia.[41] In 1906 the Italian ambassador in Cairo complained to his minister of foreign affairs that the number of Italian anarchists in Port Sudan was turning that city into "the African Paterson."[42]

San Francisco's Latin and Eastern European anarchists were also indispensable links in the chain responsible for the appearance of anarchist movements throughout East Asia. In 1916, Hippolyte Havel, the Czech-born editor of New York's anarchist paper, *The Revolt*, wrote in surprise,

> Japanese, Chinese, Hindoo [*sic*] and Egyptian revolutionary papers propagating the same ideas we do are lying on my desk.
>
> The social revolt cannot be confined in the narrow circle of Europe and America. If we cannot bring into our movement the people of the Orient then our cause is lost. Happily our ideas are spreading to a larger extent than some of our pessimists' dream.
>
> THE REVOLT is proud to be in connection with the rebels in the far East. We are proud of the small share we are contributing toward the universal emancipation.[43]

Havel failed to recognize the extent to which this proliferation originated in America.

Returning to Japan from San Francisco as a convinced anarchist in 1906, Shusui Kotoku singlehandedly founded the modern Japanese anarchist movement before being executed in 1911, along with twenty-four others, for participating in a plot to assassinate the emperor.[44] (Emma Goldman led a vigorous but unsuccessful international defense campaign on his behalf.) Iwasa Sakutaro, a cofounder of Berkeley's anarchist Shakai Kakumeito, likewise returned to Japan in 1913 and by the 1920s was a leading figure in that country's growing anarchist movement.[45] In 1910, the publishers of San Francisco's anarchist paper, *Shinsei*, printed Kotoku's translation of Peter Kropotkin's *An Appeal to the Young* to smuggle into Japan, and over the following decade, American-made anarchist and IWW pamphlets "came to Japan by all manner of routes" and were widely read by Japanese radicals.[46]

Kotoku also influenced a group of Chinese students studying in Tokyo who joined with radicalized students returning from Paris in 1911 to form China's first anarchist groups, bringing full circle the transnational transmission of ideology that began with Eugene Travaglio's unplanned journey down the Yangtze River. Anarchism became China's dominant revolutionary tendency through the 1920s, and anarchists helped launch the modern Chinese labor movement.[47] Chinese anarchists subsequently founded the first labor unions in Malaysia, and Vietnamese and Korean students studying in both Japan and China in turn founded anarchist movements in their home countries, using Kotoku's writings as some of their foundational texts.[48] In addition, anarchism, by way of Har Dayal and the California-based Ghadar movement, became an important influence in Indian anticolonialism, influencing everyone from the revolutionary martyr Bhagat Singh to the pacifist Mahatma Gandhi.[49]

Anarchists based in the United States also participated in anticolonial struggles and revolutionary movements far beyond their homelands. However, their support of such causes was neither indiscriminate nor unanimous. In keeping with their antistatist principles, they "sought the grail of an anti-nationalist mode of anti-imperialism"—a goal that they shared with many of the era's national liberation movements but that proved eternally elusive in practice.[50]

Young Mikhail Bakunin was an ardent pan-Slavist and supporter of nationalist movements, but in his later, anarchist years, he balanced anti-imperialism with a refusal to endorse the creation of new nation-states.[51] In 1876, his disciple, Errico Malatesta, unsuccessfully tried to join the Herzegovina Uprising against the Ottoman Empire despite Bakunin's objections. Thereafter, Malatesta was more cautious about intervention in such causes; during his 1882 sojourn in Egypt, he took part in the insurgency against British occupation, but in 1897 he criticized those Italian anarchist "Garibaldini" who joined Crete's struggle against the Ottoman Empire in what amounted to a war on behalf of the Greek monarchy.[52]

Conversely, Kropotkin defended all national independence movements as necessary but insufficient steps toward emancipation. In an 1885 article for the American magazine *The Nineteenth Century*, Kropotkin agreed with Bakunin that "national problems are not identical with the 'people's problems.' . . . [T]he acquisition of political independence still leaves unachieved the economical independence of the labouring and wealth-producing classes." "But," he continued, "both these problems are so closely connected with one another that we are bound to recognise that no serious economical progress can be won, nor is any progressive development possible, until the awakened aspirations for autonomy have been satisfied." In private correspondence, he later elaborated, "It seems to me that the 'purely nationalist character' of national movements is a fiction. There is an economic basis everywhere, or some basis for freedom and respect for the individual."[53] In 1907, during the debates that arose in the aftermath the Kishinev Pogrom, Kropotkin again defended nationalist movements of "oppressed peoples" as laudable and progressive, excepting Zionism, which he argued was an impractical cause that, even if successful, was bound to result in a theocratic state; instead, he insisted, Jews should struggle for cultural autonomy and civil equality wherever they resided in the diaspora.[54] Despite disagreements over whether particular independence struggles merited active support, however, anarchists were united in their conviction that nation-states were incapable of providing the self-determination, freedom, and equality that nationalists sought.

During *La Questione Sociale*'s first year of publication, Italy invaded Eritrea and Ethiopia (Abyssinia), and the Cuban War of Independence broke out. In both cases, the paper unequivocally championed the anticolonial insurgents, declaring, "We know that our *patria* is not the land where we were born, but that, for us, it is the highest concept and no more limited than the entire Universe: we know that we, ourselves, give absolute solidarity to the oppressed of Italy, to those of Abyssinia, of Armenia, as with the glorious insurgents of Cuba and the strong and courageous exiles of faraway Siberia, that, finally, we, without distinction of color, race, language [or] custom, share affection and adoration for all the oppressed of humanity." An Italian circular issued by the "Anarchist Residents in North America" similarly stated, "We applaud the Cubans who want the independence of their island, the Abyssinians fighting to defend their land from foreign invasion—And we all feel morally driven to sympathize with Abyssinia not only for this reason, but also because we see behind the veil of the self-styled civilizing expedition the mark of the exploitation, speculation, [and] rapacity of the capitalists who alone reap the fruit of the battles, of the practices of death, of the blood shed in conquering Abyssinia."[55] Antonio Agresti lamented, "Oh! How much better would they be, the Italian vassals, to direct at Italy itself all of their manias for colonization and civilization." Another writer for *La Questione Sociale* denounced "those who believe the Latin people to be an aristocratic species of mankind," cataloging the horrors of Italian, Spanish, Portuguese, and French imperialism.[56]

Although Italy's ill-fated imperial adventure vexed Italian anarchists, the Cuban conflict was more significant as a consequence of both its proximity and its radicalism. Exiled Cuban nationalist leader José Martí recognized the importance of working-class support as well as the growing influence of Cuban anarchism and incorporated radicals' calls for social justice and economic equality into his political program. Cuban and Spanish anarchists, both on the island and in the United States, in turn overwhelmingly supported the revolt against Spanish rule. Like Kropotkin, they viewed independence as a vital first step toward a libertarian socialist Cuba, which could then serve as a launching pad for revolution elsewhere.[57] Many Italians shared this outlook, and some accompanied the Cuban emigrants who returned with Martí to take up arms. Most were cigar makers in Florida who worked and organized alongside Cubans, though Harry Kelly encountered five young anarchists who "had lately come from Italy; on their way to Cuba to fight for her against Spain."[58]

One vocal dissenter was Pedro Esteve, who had lived in Havana for several months before coming to the United States. Esteve argued that Cuban independence alone would not benefit the Cuban people but would simply replace the Spanish ruling class with a Cuban one. He urged anarchist neutrality in the conflict, and his refusal to support "political revolution" in Cuba led to a split within the group that published El Despertar in New York. This division left the paper in Esteve's hands, enabling him to relocate it to Paterson.[59] La Questione Sociale took an intermediate position, recognizing that the conflict was not "an anarchist revolt" but still hoping that the prominence of the anarchist faction "which gives, today, life, blood, and energy to the fight . . . will not be without influence in the economic and political reconstruction of the island." This influence might then "allow for the Cubans the peaceful evolution towards the abolition of all oppression and all authority."[60]

Nevertheless, all parties applauded the assassination of Spain's prime minister, Antonio Cánovas del Castillo, at the hands of Italian anarchist Michele Angiolillo in 1897. Angiolillo's act was motivated by the Spanish government's bloody repression of both anarchism in Barcelona and the independence movements in Cuba and the Philippines. As Esteve wrote in La Questione Sociale, "A just revenge [vendetta] removed from the world this man who made blood flow so generously in Spain and in the colonies." A reporter visiting the paper's offices in 1900 noted, "Two big medallion busts of Michile Angiolello [sic], the assassin of Minister Canovas of Spain, hang on the walls, and big pictures of him are scattered in various parts of the room." Paterson's Germinal hailed the killing as "an act of justice," and in New York City, a thousand people turned out at Clarendon Hall to celebrate the assassination, with Emma Goldman declaring, "I glory in the death of Cánovas."[61] Ironically, however, the assassination also convinced President William McKinley of Spain's weakness, precipitating American intervention in Cuba and the outbreak of the Spanish-American War. This development placed anarchist backers of Cuban independence in an untenable position, as they could not in good conscience support the openly imperialist motives of the United States. Germinal editor Michel Dumas lamented that "American capitalism" was crushing "Cuba Libre," and the symbolic end of anarchist hopes in Cuba came in 1900, when Malatesta visited Havana and occupying American forces attempted to prevent him from speaking.[62]

American troops also swarmed the Philippines after defeating the Spanish navy in Manila Bay, and their mission to "liberate" the Filipinos soon transformed into a military occupation and brutal counterinsurgency campaign. Anarchist sympathies fell firmly on the side of the Filipinos, whom Goldman described as "those noble rebels who are still defending their independence." *La Questione Sociale*, the *Fraye Arbeter Shtime*, and *Free Society* all condemned the American military and McKinley's "civilizing" mission. According to Yanovsky, if the conflict was about civilization, then "the Filipinos ought to come to civilize America." His paper stood alone within the entire political spectrum of the Yiddish American press; even the Socialist *Forverts* supported the occupation as necessary for modernizing the "savage" Filipinos and incorporating them into the capitalist economy, thereby molding them into proletarians.[63]

Anarchist Al Klemencic, who arrived in Hawaii in the middle of 1898, joined native Hawaiians and Asian laborers there in opposing American annexation of the islands and critiqued American expansionism in *Free Society*, *Germinal*, and France's *Les Temps Nouveaux*. In the following years anarchist periodicals continued to condemn what San Francisco's *L'Effort* called "Yankee imperialism." These same publications were, however, curiously silent on the subject of Puerto Rico, perhaps because Puerto Rican anarchists were themselves profoundly ambivalent regarding the Puerto Rican independence movement. Spanish-speaking anarchists on the mainland, however, "supported the struggle for the independence of Cuba and Puerto Rico."[64]

"What does the liberty of our colonies consist of, anyway?" Emma Goldman asked in 1906. "'Tis merely removing the obstacles in the way of the American capitalists who are eager to press profits from the conquered people." Two years later, she caused a scandal by shaking the hand of a uniformed U.S. Army private and Philippine-American War veteran, William Buwalda, after giving a speech in San Francisco during which she excoriated "patriotism." Buwalda was promptly court-martialed, dishonorably discharged, and sentenced to three years confinement in Alcatraz, though President Theodore Roosevelt issued a pardon, and Buwalda was released after seven months.[65] Buwalda subsequently returned the medal he had earned for service in the Philippines to the secretary of war, accompanied by a letter, published in *Mother Earth*, explaining that the "trinket" "speaks to me . . . of a country laid waste with fire and sword . . . of men, women and children hunted like wild beasts, and all this in the name of Liberty, Humanity, and Civilization. . . . In short, it speaks to me of War—legalized murder, if you will—upon a weak and defenseless people. We have not even the excuse of self-defense." The veteran returned to his hometown of Grand

Rapids, Michigan, an anarchist and arranged Goldman's visit there in 1911.[66] The "outrages committed by the American government in the Philippine Islands" were also a major factor in the disillusionment and radicalization of Leon Czolgosz, in part motivating his assassination of McKinley in 1901.[67]

Anarchists were sometimes less attuned to the struggles of native populations. When the Second Boer War broke out between the British Empire and the Afrikaner colonists of the South African Transvaal Republic and Orange Free State in 1899, both the *Fraye Arbeter Shtime* and Goldman lauded what Goldman called "the brave and marvelously courageous heroes of the Transvaal and the Free State" against Britain's attempt to rob them "of their independence and liberty."[68] Yet while the Boers were technically engaged in an anti-imperialist struggle, American and European anarchists completely disregarded the native Africans who were subjugated and disenfranchised by the Afrikaners, the future architects of South Africa's apartheid regime.

After Italy won control of Libya from the Ottoman Empire in 1912, however, anarchists displayed no such ambiguity. Ludovico Caminita and Firmino Gallo were arrested by Paterson police on charges of inciting hostility against a foreign government—on the basis of a cartoon drawn by Caminita and displayed in the window of Gallo's bookstore. The offending image depicted the king and queen of Italy proudly surveying an endless line of Libyan corpses hanging from gallows. *Regeneración* and *Mother Earth* defiantly reproduced the cartoon in their own pages, and the case was eventually dropped.[69]

Before his 1912 return to Paterson, Caminita had been involved in a major rebellion right on America's doorstep. In November 1910, the anarchist Partido Liberal Mexicano (PLM), in conjunction with other opponents of President Porfirio Díaz's regime, launched an armed uprising in Mexico, marking the beginning of the Mexican Revolution. And in northern Mexico, for the first time in history, revolutionary troops led by anarchists gained control of an expanse of territory where they planned to build a libertarian communist society from which they hoped to spread revolution globally. Furthermore, several hundred foreign anarchists and IWW members joined the PLM's forces in this endeavor.

The PLM, directed by its Organizational Junta in Los Angeles, had strong ties to both the IWW and Italian anarchists. Mexican and Mexican American workers began joining the IWW in 1906, and by 1910 they made up a majority of its membership in California. Most of these Mexican IWW members also belonged to the PLM, which enjoyed a mutually supportive relationship with the union.[70] On April 17, 1910, one of the IWW's major free-speech fights began after a "Mexican socialist" soap box speaker was arrested in Fresno for speaking without a permit. The local IWW organization, which included Mexican, Chinese, Japanese, Russian, and American migratory workers under the leadership of organizer Frank Little, launched a campaign to repeal the ban on street speaking, and IWW members and supporters from across the West—including members of San Francisco's Latin Branch—soon flooded the city and its jails. The union won the fight in March 1911, by which time many of the out-of-town radicals had moved on to the PLM's encampment in Baja California.[71]

Paterson anarchist Vittorio Cravello moved to Los Angeles for work in November 1910, and Caminita and his family joined him shortly thereafter. Caminita began collaborating with PLM members to organize a union for migrant workers, and both Caminita and Cravello agitated on behalf of the Mexican revolutionaries. In May 1911, both men were founding members of the International Committee of the Mexican Liberal Junta, an organization of Italian, American, German, Russian, and Polish PLM supporters.[72] They were also probably involved in planning the PLM's cross-border invasion of Mexicali on January 29, 1911, in which a force consisting of one American IWW member and fewer than twenty PLM partisans departed from the IWW stronghold of Holtville, California, and captured the Mexican city.[73]

This startling victory captivated radicals throughout the Americas and Europe. Support for the PLM came pouring in; the organization's newspaper, *Regeneración*, reported that it was in contact with "Englishmen, Spaniards, Cubans, Americans, Jews and comrades of other races," and donations for its fighters arrived from Argentina, Uruguay, Brazil, France, Italy, and Portugal in addition to the United States.[74] Moreover, on February 5, a band of at least thirty non-Mexican IWW members crossed into Mexicali, where they were soon joined by hundreds of additional foreign volunteers, including Little and IWW songwriter Joe Hill. Most of these newcomers were organized into the PLM's Second Division, an informal foreign legion under the command of Canadian-born IWW member William Stanley.[75] This motley crew included native-born Americans, Englishmen, Spaniards, Russians, Germans, several African Americans, and at least one Chinese immigrant. A handful of French anarchists also crossed the Atlantic to participate. By late February, less than half of the *insurrectos* in Mexicali were Mexican or Mexican American.[76] The revolution had been globalized.

Both the PLM and its anarchist supporters viewed the conflict as the opening phase of a transnational uprising. The Organizational Junta proclaimed the fighting "the first act in the great universal cataclysm which very soon will break upon the scene all over the planet." Victory in northern Mexico, it argued, would establish an autonomous libertarian zone from which revolutionary activity could be launched elsewhere. Therefore, the PLM stressed, "Our cause is your cause."[77] For radicals in the United States, the promise of the revolt spreading north of the Rio Grande was imminent and exhilarating; some of the troops who captured Mexicali wore pins reading, "Los Angeles to be taken in 1912."[78]

Caminita urged, "Comrades around the world, do not forget that the triumph of the social revolution in one nation is the triumph of the coming worldwide social revolution. If today the Mexican is able to expropriate the land owners, the proletariat of the others will not tarry to do the same and to quickly change into reality our persecuted and damned utopia." Cravello was equally euphoric, declaring, "In all the history of our age there has not been a movement of such great importance as that which is taking place in neighboring Mexico."[79]

Yanovsky's journal *Fraye Gezelshaft* compared the situation of the Mexican *campesinos* to that of Jews in Russia and President Díaz to Czar Nicholas II.[80] The English-language IWW press, by contrast, saw the revolution as a chance to emancipate not only Mexicans but also the multiethnic migratory working class of the American West. As the *Industrial Worker* put it, "A rifle on the shoulder of a worker would look better than a bundle of lousy blankets."[81] Indian radicals from the Ghadar Party, meanwhile, planned to raise "a force of Sikh veterans recruited in Oregon and California" to join the troops in Mexicali, but a front-line visit dissuaded the head of the Ghadar "action committee."[82]

Esteve was initially skeptical of the anarchists who flocked to Mexico, fearing "that the same would befall them as befell those who joined the Cuban insurgents for the independence of their land: to die needlessly on the field of battle, or to become petty politicians." But correspondence with PLM leader Ricardo Flores Magón convinced him that a true anarchist revolution was being waged in northern Mexico.[83] Esteve then wrote extensively on behalf of the PLM in *L'Era Nuova* and the Spanish-language *Cultura Obrera*, which he had cofounded after returning to New Jersey following a near lynching at the hands of Tampa vigilantes.[84] *Mother Earth*, the *Fraye Arbeter Shtime*, and initially Luigi Galleani's *Cronaca Sovversiva* all united behind the PLM.

However, a growing number of soldiers of fortune, looters, and "filibusters" hoping to annex the Baja Peninsula to the United States took control of the PLM's Second Division and, against the explicit orders of the Organizational Junta, led its 220–250 members to capture Tijuana on May 9.[85] The Organizational Junta extracted maximum publicity from the victory at Tijuana, but Flores Magón privately wrote to Esteve to request help. "It is imperative," Flores Magón appealed, "for many anarchists from around the world to come to Baja California to support of the expropriation of the land and machinery. . . . In the hands of the libertarians, Baja California could provide sufficient resources to carry the revolution throughout Mexico and even the entire world, because the peninsula is very rich, but sparsely populated." He hoped to form a "special corps of pure libertarians" to educate the politically "unconscious" foreign troops. *Regeneración* invited all "comrades" to come to Baja California and "take possession of the land" under collectivized cultivation. One of the IWW's fighters in Tijuana wrote to the *Industrial Worker*, "We have got a Utopia down here": he urged readers to "take the first train and come down here. Here, there are no bosses and you are FREE."[86]

Responding to these appeals, a group of approximately fifty Italian anarchists crossed the border from San Diego into Tijuana on May 28. Twenty-two came from Vancouver, another six traveled together from Columbus, Kansas; and others hailed from Nevada, Washington, Wisconsin, Pennsylvania, and California. IWW Latin Branch member Fred Rovaldi and individualist Adolfo Antonelli arrived from San Francisco, while B. Bertone, who would later travel to Paterson to aid the 1913 silk strike, came from Los Angeles.[87] The scene that greeted these new arrivals, however, bore little resemblance to the revolution they had envisioned. Tijuana was a small desert gambling town from which most residents had fled ahead of the PLM's arrival, and the summer heat hovered between 95 and 105 degrees. There had been no military engagements since the initial capture of the city, and the insurgents drilled for just half an hour each day, leaving them idle and restless. Neither instructions nor ammunition were forthcoming from the Organizational Junta, which busied itself attempting to recruit volunteers and support without falling afoul of American authorities. The command of the Second Division was also in disarray as various factions vied for control.[88]

These circumstances bewildered and disillusioned most of the Italians. Tensions increased on May 30 when the iconoclastic Adolfo Antonelli, who had long quarreled with the partisans of both *Cronaca Sovversiva* and *L'Era Nuova*, appointed himself head of their division, allegedly declaring that he "was in the field for plunder, not to liberate the Mexican people from slavery." The *galleanisti*, who composed a majority of the Italians, complained that Antonelli had "never seen a topographical map of Mexico nor has he ever, even on a whim, consulted a treatise on the art of war"; furthermore, in their view, he was "not an anarchist." Eight left for the border the following day in "disgust," with many more remaining "only because they did not have the money for the trip back to Los Angeles." Humiliated, Antonelli crossed into San Diego two days later.[89] In less than a week, the "special corps of pure libertarians" had disintegrated without firing a shot. The Italians had arrived at the worst possible moment, and most departed at just the wrong time. The Organizational Junta dispatched a special commission from Los Angeles, including Caminita, that arrived in Tijuana on June 1—the day after the first of the Italians absconded—to reinstate Oakland IWW member Jack Mosby as commander of the Second Division, and two days later—coinciding with Antonelli's departure—a majority of the *insurrectos* voted to accept Mosby's command and expel the filibusters.[90]

With the revolutionary element firmly in control, the Second Division awaited orders to proceed to the regional capital, Ensenada. These orders, however, never arrived. On June 14, authorities arrested the Organizational Junta in Los Angeles for violating American neutrality laws, and Flores Magón was not released on bail until June 23. By that time, the PLM's languishing First Division in Mexicali had surrendered, and on June 22, a force of six hundred federal troops representing the new government of Francisco I. Madero, who had helped launch the revolution, overwhelmed the remaining 230 members of the Second Division at Tijuana in a bloody three-hour battle. Mosby and the surviving foreign volunteers limped back across the border, where most were apprehended by waiting U.S. troops.[91]

Even before these losses, controversy over the Mexican Revolution had erupted in anarchist circles. On June 17, *Cronaca Sovversiva* published an open letter signed by eight Italian volunteers who claimed they had been misled regarding the nature of the revolution and warned fellow anarchists against contributing funds to the PLM.[92] *Cronaca Sovversiva* thereafter waged a vicious campaign against the PLM and its supporters, singling out Caminita, Vittorio Cravello, and *L'Era Nuova* in particular.

The dissidents leveled a number of accusations against the PLM, most of them quite dubious. The most compelling of these was that the glowing reports in *Regeneración* and *L'Era Nuova* had given the false impression that an anarchist revolution was already well under way in Mexico and that Tijuana, "a village of no importance," was of major strategic value. Other grievances were trivial: Italian anarchists in Portsmouth, West Virginia, complained that their offer of "revolutionary assistance of a character which this is not the place to specify"—that is, assassinations or bombings—had been declined. The most serious and least credible accusations were that the Organizational Junta had embezzled funds meant for its troops or was even guilty of filibustering on behalf of American capitalists.[93] The principal claims repeated by critics, however, were that the PLM was not really an anarchist organization and that the struggle in Mexico was not a true "social revolution." As evidence, dissenters pointed to the party's 1906 program, a document that predated the organization's anarchist turn and called for a long list of political reforms. Much was also made of the fact that both *Regeneración* and *L'Era Nuova* referred to nonanarchist Emiliano Zapata as "comrade," and disillusioned volunteer Filippo Perrone even claimed that the PLM planned to install Flores Magón as president of Mexico.[94] Furthermore, according to Galleani, an anarchist revolution was not even possible in Mexico, given its demographics. "If for a population that reaches in all probability fourteen million, *seven million* are pure Indians, four [million] mestizos, two [million] Creoles, half a million Negroes, Zambos [people of mixed African and Native American descent], [and] mulattoes," he argued, "it is clear that for Mexico there is no possibility of a movement with an openly social, revolutionary character, if the most lively, most numerous and most diligent of the population are not interested." In this startlingly Marxian and racist formulation, Galleani claimed that an anarchist revolution could be carried out only by an industrial proletariat, not these preindustrial and therefore "uninterested" racial groups. Another critic agreed that indigenous Mexicans "completely ignore the modern world and can not be the pioneers of a social revolution."[95]

In September 1911, the Organizational Junta responded to charges of "liberalism" by issuing an unambiguously anarchist manifesto declaring war on "the dark trinity" of "Capital, Authority, [and] Clergy."[96] Esteve and Antonelli attacked those disillusioned "adventurers" who during "a 24 hour stay in Tijuana noticed that anarchy does not exist in that place." Esteve chided them that a revolution "is not a day or a few months, but long, very long, and it needs the moral and material support of all the exploited."[97] The PLM's most vocal defender was Caminita, who accused Galleani of "revolutionary masturbation" and in July 1911 began editing a four-page Italian-language supplement to *Regeneración* dedicated almost entirely to combatting *Cronaca Sovversiva*. This debate so consumed the Italian movement that in late 1911 and early 1912, conventions were held in Brooklyn and Boston to discuss "the Mexican question." Predictably, the Brooklyn gathering, convened by supporters of the PLM, found that Mexico was undergoing a true social revolution, while the Boston convention, called by allies of *Cronaca Sovversiva*, came to the opposite conclusion.[98] At the end of 1911, Caminita left Los Angeles to embark on a nationwide lecture tour in support of the PLM and the Mexican Revolution, eventually ending up back in Paterson.[99] In New York, Alexander Berkman also maintained "that the revolution in Mexico is a social revolution," a view shared by *Mother Earth*, *Cultura Obrera*, and the *Fraye Arbeter Shtime*.[100]

These arguments spilled across the Atlantic, where Jean Grave, editor of *Les Temps Nouveaux*, was won over by the dissenters' arguments against the PLM. Kropotkin eventually intervened from London, chiding Grave and "the young Italians and Frenchmen who know 'the revolution' through the books and poems of bourgeois revolutionaries" for not being able to "conceive of 'revolution' other than in the form of fighting on the barricades, or of Garibaldi's triumphant expeditions." These "Garibaldini," he argued, failed to recognize that by expropriating private property, the "peasant movement" in northern Mexico had taken the first essential step toward social revolution.[101] Kropotkin's admonishment persuaded some naysayers, including Grave, to change their stance.

The PLM and its supporters also argued that although events in Mexico were no longer under anarchist direction, a social revolution was still being waged by the forces of Zapata, whom the *Fraye Arbeter Shtime* glowingly described as an "Indian chief"—an inaccurate depiction but an interesting contrast to Galleani's comments.[102] The PLM established contact with Zapata, and in September 1913, a group of fourteen PLM and IWW members set out to join his forces; however, they were arrested at the Texas border after an altercation that left a deputy sheriff and one of their own dead. Vittorio Cravello headed the men's defense campaign from Los Angeles.[103] In September 1914, William C. Owen's *Land and Liberty* reported that it was "in receipt of several letters from men who wish to go to Mexico and fight for Land and Liberty." However, mindful of the previous debacle with foreign recruits, the paper advised "that the Mexicans be left to fight their own battles.... The Mexicans have proved themselves excellent fighters, and foreigners who go into their country, ignorant of its customs and language, are sure to be looked on with suspicion and to be more of a nuisance than they are worth."[104]

That same year, the PLM tried to bring its case to the world stage, demanding that the upcoming International Anarchist Congress scheduled to meet in London issue "a clear-cut declaration that the Mexican peon is right in holding that the economics of liberty can be won only by retaking possession of the land; that he is right in expelling the land monopolist; that you urge the disinherited of all countries to imitate him."[105] But the topic of the Mexican Revolution, like the planned congress, was quickly forgotten in the face of global war.

Following the assassination of Hapsburg heir Archduke Franz Ferdinand by a Serbian nationalist in Sarajevo on June 28, 1914, *L'Era Nuova* declared that the killing "did not have an anarchist character. It was of a nationalist character." Yet the paper saluted the perpetrators and concluded, "The anarchists greet you and are not afraid to express their complete solidarity."[106] This response illustrates the unresolved nature of anarchists' relationship with national liberation movements. Was national independence—and hence the creation of one or more new nation-states—in the Balkans really a cause with which anarchists had "complete solidarity"? Conversely, should anarchists defend already existing independent states threatened by imperialist aggression? And could either of these objectives justify support for a military alliance of imperial capitalist powers? The answers that anarchists formulated to these questions were shaped by earlier debates over anticolonialism and nationalism dating back to the Cuban War of Independence and Kishinev Pogrom.

On the whole, anarchists in the United States and the rest of the world prioritized their commitments to anti-imperialism, antimilitarism, working-class solidarity, and radical cosmopolitanism and refused to support either the Allies or the Central Powers. This stance differentiated the anarchists from the international socialist movement, which shattered when most Socialist Party majorities supported their national war efforts, though the Socialist Party of America and the Bolshevik faction of the Russian Social Democratic Labor Party constituted important exceptions. Nevertheless, a minority of anarchists did back one side or the other in the war. Already by the close of 1914, *Mother Earth* lamented, "Anarchism, as a world-movement, has been devitalized and confused by the war-crisis."[107]

The most startling development was Kropotkin's vigorous support of the Allies, which Goldman called "a staggering blow to our movement."[108] The revered Russian anarchist was enamored with the French revolutionary tradition and believed a German victory would irreparably damage European progress toward freedom and socialism. But his position was also based on his long-standing defense of national liberation struggles. If German subjugation of the nationalities of Central and Western Europe could be prevented only by Germany's military defeat, he argued, then anarchists were morally obliged to aid the Allies. "I consider it the duty of everyone who cherishes the ideals of human progress," he urged, "to do everything in one's power, according to one's capacities, to crush down the invasion of the Germans into Western Europe. . . . The German invasion *must* be repulsed—no matter how difficult this may be."[109] In February 1916, Kropotkin signed the "Manifesto of the Sixteen" along with a number of other pro-Ally anarchists, most of whom, like Grave, were living in embattled France. This document called on anarchists to participate in what its signatories saw as a war of international resistance against German imperialism. "We do not forget that we are internationalists, that we want the union of peoples, and the disappearance of borders," they insisted. "And it is because we want the reconciliation of peoples, including the German people, that we think that they must resist an aggressor who represents the destruction of all our hopes of liberation."[110]

The manifesto found little American support. New York's dwindling Czech paper, *Volnè Listy*, sympathetic to the idea of Czechoslovakian independence, defended it, and Harry Kelly agreed with Kropotkin's stance that any nation had a "duty to repel the invader" but did not press the issue. Kelly later noted that his position was so unpopular that "if the anarchist movement had been an organized one I probably would have been expelled."[111] Owen was more assertive in *Land and Liberty*, writing, "To me it appears absurd to talk of internationalism at this juncture, because military invasion renders the practice of internationalism at once impossible." Owen argued that antiwar anarchists were in fact condoning Germany's invasion of Belgium and therefore denying international solidarity to the Belgian working class, which had a right to self-defense. He also attacked cosmopolitanism—or a simplistic caricature of it—as a dangerous abstraction: "Great as are the worker's wrongs, it is not true that, as a class, he has neither home nor country. It is not true that he has nothing to lose but his chains. It is not true that it makes no difference to him whether he lives under Prussian military rule, as an inhabitant of an annexed and conquered country, or as a citizen of a land that has known how to defend itself."[112] But Owen's position isolated him—some former comrades now regarded him as "an English spy"—and *Land and Liberty* folded in July 1915; the following year, Owen fled to England to avoid arrest in connection with his work on behalf of the PLM.[113]

Within Italy, a small scattering of anarchists promoted Italian intervention against Germany. The interventionists were led by the individualist anarchist Massimo Rocca, who wrote under the name Libero Tancredi, and anarcho-syndicalist Maria Rygier. From 1908 to 1911, Rocca had lived in the United States, where he published the obscure paper *Novatore* (Innovator). Shocked by the denigration of Italian immigrants, Rocca began arguing in favor of "spreading nationalism among the Italian workers, reinforcing their class consciousness with a national consciousness [to] sweep from history this third Italy and create a fourth proletarian Italy." The restoration of Italy's glory became, for him, a prerequisite for internationalism and revolution, and he recast anarchism in ethnoracial terms, arguing that an innate connection existed between "Latin-ness" (*latinità*) and anarchism, in contrast to German authoritarianism, Slavic apathy, and Chinese "immobility." Rocca's newfound nationalism also led him to support Italy's 1911 invasion of Libya.[114] Rygier, by contrast, maintained her opposition to "reactionary patriotism and imperialism," but like Owen, she argued that those pushing for Italy to aid the "Latin peoples" of France and Belgium were the true internationalists, whereas the neutrality of the antimilitarists was a betrayal of internationalism. Antonio Agresti, who had edited some of the first issues of *La Questione Sociale* during his brief sojourn in the United States, was among these interventionists' handful of supporters.[115] Fellow anarchists, however, treated the renegades "with uncommon disdain," and most instead supported a policy of "revolutionary defeatism" in the hopes that a military loss for Italy might spark opposition to the government.[116]

Despite Rocca and Agresti's American connections, they had few supporters in the United States. Edmondo Rossoni, a leading figure in the IWW-affiliated Federazione Socialista Italiana, was a close friend of Rocca's and had been similarly appalled by the treatment of Italian immigrants in America. He, too, concluded that proletarian internationalism would be possible only after Italy earned the respect of foreigners, and in August 1914 declared his support for the Allies and urged Italy to join the war. Rossoni's position reflected that of a growing interventionist faction within Italy's syndicalist movement (though the anarcho-syndicalist majority remained resolutely opposed to war) but was so unpopular among the Federazione Socialista Italiana's membership that Rossoni was assaulted at public events and drummed out of the organization. He returned to Italy in 1916 to volunteer for military service.[117] Domenico Trombetta, a New York tailor and onetime anarchist, was one of the few Federazione members to follow Rossoni's lead.[118]

In stark contrast to the Italian interventionists, before 1917 Jewish-American opinion strongly opposed an Allied—and hence Russian—victory. Russia remained, for Jews, the ultimate embodiment of oppression, and many hoped that a German victory would once and for all depose the hated czar. In 1914, Saul

Yanovsky, while keeping the *Fraye Arbeter Shtime* open to opposing viewpoints, registered his strong disagreement with Kropotkin based on the fact that to support the Allies was to support "Russian despotism."[119] One contributor to the *Fraye Arbeter Shtime* predicted, "No matter how terrible German militarism may be, the Jews of Russia would profit politically, economically and above all spiritually" from its triumph. Some Yiddish anarchists, including Michael Cohn, publicly declared their hopes for a German victory.[120]

The Ghadar movement gave more enthusiastic support to the Germans, hoping that a British defeat would liberate their homeland. After fleeing the United States in 1914, Har Dayal made his way to Germany and joined the Berlin India Committee, a group of Ghadar members working with the aid of the German government to foment a revolt in India. The Germans offered money, arms, and expertise to help undermine their enemy's colonial holdings.[121] Dayal called on his American contacts for aid, asking Alexander Berkman in October 1915, "Can you send some earnest and sincere comrades, men and women, to help our Indian revolutionary party at this juncture? . . . Perhaps you can find them in New York or at Paterson. . . . They should be real fighters, I.W.W.'s or anarchists." Dayal's efforts to recruit Americans failed, however, as did those of the German government, which reportedly sent an agent who "tried to hire anarchists to blow up shipping and start strikes in munitions plants" as America began preparing for war in 1915.[122] But thousands of Ghadar members did return to India from the United States and other countries in 1914–15 to instigate a series of mutinies and uprisings, though the pan-Indian revolution for which they hoped failed to materialize.[123]

Despite these deviations, most American anarchist newspapers, including *L'Era Nuova*, *Cronaca Sovversiva*, *The Blast*, *Mother Earth*, and initially the *Fraye Arbeter Shtime*, refused to endorse either side in the war. Alexander Berkman and Emma Goldman founded the Anti-Militarist League of Greater New York in 1914, and both signed the 1915 anti-militarist "International Anarchist Manifesto on the War," as did Joseph Cohen, Saul Yanovsky, and, despite his personal views, Harry Kelly. The manifesto argued that "the cause of wars, of that which at present stains with blood the plains of Europe, . . . rests solely in the existence of the State, which is the political form of privilege." To support one state's war effort was simply to exacerbate the problem. "The role of the Anarchists in the present tragedy," therefore, was "to continue to proclaim that there is but one war of liberation: that which in all countries is waged by the oppressed against the oppressors, by the exploited against the exploiters," with the goal of "weakening and dissolving the various States" wherever possible.[124]

L'Era Nuova endorsed the manifesto, explaining, "We equally hate Russian tyranny and Teutonic arrogance, Austrian oppression and English treachery, [and] the Republican ferocity of French capitalism as much as that of any constitutional or absolute monarchy."[125] Franz Widmar and Pedro Esteve carried on an extensive debate with Peter Kropotkin in the pages of the paper. Kropotkin reiterated his argument that nationalities had a right to independence and that German imperialism was stripping them of that right. Widmar replied that the "principle of nationality" was flawed because it falsely assumed that the borders of countries such as Belgium and France coincided with divisions between homogeneous nationalities, while Esteve once again cited Cuba as an example in which independence from foreign rule had not substantially improved conditions. Like his Yiddish comrades, Esteve also noted that Russia had more oppressed peasants awaiting emancipation than Belgium did.[126]

When Italy belatedly entered the war in May 1915 and called on its citizens abroad to return and join the army, *L'Era Nuova* urged immigrants not to depart. It published a manifesto by a group in Los Angeles that proclaimed, "We answer that we bastards of the *patria*, forced from an early age to leave our native land [*paese*] and our dearest loved ones, our friends and relatives, to cross huge oceans, to traverse endless continents, among people who do not know and do not understand us, that we, forced to have to wander for a piece of bread under the lash of torturers insensitive to our suffering, we cannot, we will not help this stepmother of a country [*patria matrigna*], from which we never received a single favor." The document concluded with the call, "Down with the fratricidal war! Down with countries [*patrie*]! Long live the International of the people!!"[127] *Cronaca Sovversiva* also published an appeal, "Figli, non tornate!" (Children, Do Not Return!), of which San Francisco's Volontà Group produced fifteen thousand copies.[128]

Throughout the war, *L'Era Nuova* attacked the concepts of nationalism, patriotism, and the *patria*, "a self-serving word used by political candidates and journalists."[129] It condemned interventionists such as Rocca and Rygier as traitors who had committed moral "suicide" and published a satirical epitaph for Rocca that read,

Honor and Pride of Our Patria . . .
He Fell Heroically
Not for Human Liberty
But for Race Hatred
In Defense of the Caesarian Masters
of the Third Italy.[130]

The mention of "Race Hatred" referred to the interventionist argument that the European conflict was a "race war" between Latin and Teutonic peoples, an argument that *L'Era Nuova* patiently eviscerated. No argument for "racial affinity," it pointed out, could be made for the alliance between the French,

Russians, and Japanese. Moreover, the war pitted the Slavs and Poles of Russia against the Slavs and Poles of Austria-Hungary, while the Germanic populations of Switzerland and other countries remained neutral. "Neither race, nor nationality is at stake in this War," the paper maintained, "but [only] capitalist and class interests, commercial and industrial rivalries."[131] When Indian soldiers mutinied against their British commanders in Singapore in 1915, *L'Era Nuova* condemned England's "prejudice of racial superiority" and praised the "so-called inferior races" for "having given this time to the whites, civil and superior, an example of dignity and admirable consistency."[132]

The new International Anarchist Group of San Francisco produced two thousand copies of *The Social Revolution*, a "large and well-illustrated four-page paper" published in English, Italian, French, and German under the motto, "If we must fight, let us fight for the Social Revolution." This group also held mass meetings and Sunday evening conferences at its headquarters on Powell Street. Antimilitarist sentiment ran so strong that one Bay Area anarchist dared to suggest, "Kropotkin should have died before this war. Then he would have been held in grateful remembrance by future working classes."[133]

For the vast majority of anarchists, interventionist endorsements of one imperialist alliance against another in the name of anti-imperialism rang hollow. Nor did most anarchists follow Kropotkin in believing that independent nation-states for oppressed nationalities necessarily represented progress toward a stateless world. Rather, most agreed with a writer for *L'Era Nuova* who declared, "All of you, so-called radicals, who advance illogical and meaningless ruminations (Teutonic danger, Latin race, French liberty) in support of your warmongering theses, you are responsible for a great and dark crime."[134]

Berkman set out to expose the insidious ideas underpinning the growing war fever with a tongue-in-cheek "War Dictionary" published in *The Blast* and including such definitions as

HUMANITY—Treason to government.
LOYAL CITIZEN—Deaf, dumb, and blind.
PATRIOTISM—Hating your neighbor.
SEDITION—The proof of Tyranny.
UN-AMERICAN—Independent opinion.[135]

But by proclaiming themselves members of a treasonous and stateless "humanity" rather than "loyal citizens," anarchists such as Berkman defined themselves as unassimilable and, from the perspective of the U.S. government, intolerable aliens, thereby setting the stage for an irreconcilable conflict between radical cosmopolitanism and state power.

CHAPTER 5

REVOLUTION AND REPRESSION
FROM RED DAWN TO RED SCARE

The First World War and its aftermath fundamentally altered global politics. Empires crumbled, socialist and nationalist revolutions erupted, and tens of millions perished, while in the United States, rising patriotic fervor and wartime demands for "100 percent Americanism" marked immigrant anarchists as doubly dangerous, and Russia's October Revolution amplified antiradical fears a hundredfold. America convulsed with widespread racial violence, its first Red Scare, and a colossal postwar strike wave. In this extraordinary context, the federal government proved willing to suppress radical speech and deport politically undesirable immigrants, efforts that were met with an unprecedented upsurge in anarchist violence, itself both a result and a cause of increasing repression.[1]

Between July 1914 and September 1920, anarchists claimed the lives of fifty-nine largely random victims in the United States, not counting eight anarchists killed when their own explosives detonated prematurely.[2] In Russia and Italy, brief periods of revolutionary euphoria were followed by years of severe repression that virtually annihilated those country's anarchist movements. The transnational circulation of information and individuals intimately linked these experiences of revolution and repression, with major repercussions for American radicalism.

As America's entrance into the war became a virtual certainty, government and private organizations launched a "preparedness" campaign to rally patriotic and martial spirits. On the afternoon of July 22, 1916, while a Preparedness Day

Parade wound through San Francisco's streets, a bomb exploded on a crowded sidewalk along the route, killing ten people and injuring forty. Suspicion immediately fell on the city's radicals, a number of whom were indiscriminately arrested, including IWW Latin Branch members Luigi Parenti and Mario Piccinini.[3] Soon, however, a case was manufactured against Tom and Rena Mooney, Warren Billings, Israel Weinberg, and Edward Nolan. Nolan and Weinberg were anarchists and minor union officials (in the Machinists' and Jitney Bus Drivers' unions, respectively), while Billings and the Mooneys were left-wing Socialists and union militants connected with Alexander Berkman's *The Blast*.[4] These defendants were the first victims of America's developing Red Scare.

The prosecutions started off well, with juries returning guilty verdicts for Tom Mooney and Billings. Police continued to target local anarchists on a variety of pretexts. On August 2, 1916, a group of Italian and French anarchists were arrested for passing out a leaflet protesting the harassment of Bay Area radicals; initially threatened with deportation, the men were eventually sentenced to ninety days' imprisonment for distributing handbills on public streets. On September 19, nine Italians, including Parenti, Michele Centrone, Louis Tori, Giuseppe Scali, and Michele Bombino, were arrested "one after another" at a street corner protest in response to the guilty verdict against Billings; they received prison terms ranging from ten days to three months for "disturbing the peace."[5] On March 3 of the following year, police again arrested Bombino, along with Vincenzo Ferrero and two other members of the Volontà Group, for allegedly passing counterfeit currency; all except Ferrero were sentenced to a year in prison.[6] Police also repeatedly raided the offices of *The Blast*, hoping to connect Berkman to the bombing cases. Knowing that an indictment against him was imminent, Berkman departed for New York and fought off attempts to extradite him back to California. Mooney and Billings were sentenced to death, but the evidence against the other defendants soon began to unravel; Rena Mooney and Weinberg were acquitted, and Nolan was never brought to trial. Mooney's and Billings's sentences were commuted to life imprisonment, and in 1939 both men were acquitted after it was revealed that their convictions had been based on perjured testimony.[7]

The identities of the actual bombers have long been shrouded in mystery. However, in 1919, Luigi Galleani claimed to have "mathematical certitude" that Mooney and Billings were innocent. When questioned by immigration inspectors, he testified that an Italian anarchist had approached him for advice before carrying out the act, but Galleani told the man "he wished not to know of it." When pressed for further information, Galleani insisted "the secret was not his to give."[8] Historian Paul Avrich's posthumously published research, however, identifies the bombing as "an act of antimilitarist protest" carried out by members of the Volontà Group, a conclusion based on information from unnamed sources (likely former members of the Volontà Group itself).[9] Thus, some of the Italians protesting on behalf of Mooney and Billings may have themselves been guilty of the crime.

Regardless, the Mooney-Billings campaign became international as radicals returned to Russia following the February Revolution of 1917. Many of the returnees had been active on behalf of Mooney and Billings, and before anarchist Morris Granberg departed from San Francisco in May 1917, Berkman gave him a document explaining the details of the case for comrades in Russia. Granberg, like dozens of other returning Russians, also visited Mooney and Billings in San Quentin State Prison. Once in Kiev, Granberg passed Berkman's appeal on to a local anarchist group that then distributed copies throughout Russia and organized demonstrations for the men's release. The cause became so popular among the Russians that in the midst of the fighting of the October Revolution, a Red Guard quizzed American Socialist John Reed, "What is the situation in the Mooney case now? Will they extradite Berkman to San Francisco?" In Petrograd, U.S. ambassador David Francis was perplexed by the angry crowds outside of his embassy chanting for the release of "Muni," and over the following months, he received resolutions from Russian anarchist groups warning that if Mooney and Billings were not released, they would hold him personally responsible. President Woodrow Wilson eventually asked California governor William Stephens to commute the death sentences for the sake of U.S. foreign relations, specifically citing Berkman's role in making the defense campaign "world-wide."[10]

Wilson was reelected in 1916 on the slogan "He Kept Us out of War," but he nevertheless brought the United States into the European conflict on April 6, 1917. For Marie Ganz, wartime patriotism was enough to sweep away her youthful anarchism. "I thrilled to the martial spirit around me," Ganz wrote in her apologetic 1919 memoir. "And of a sudden the spirit of national pride awoke in me. The flag bore a new meaning. Oh, America, mighty and just, rallying to save the world! I was proud that I, I too, was an American."[11] For the vast majority of anarchists, however, America's involvement only steeled their opposition to militarism—and at a steep price.

The day after America's declaration of war, police raided the Paterson offices of *L'Era Nuova* and arrested editor Franz Widmar and typographer Giuseppe Marchese on charges of disorderly conduct. Their crime was having printed and distributed a leaflet that called "upon the workingmen to refuse to become 'murderers for Wall Street,' and to resist the attempts of their 'master' to induce them to engage in murder."[12] Eleven days later, Congress passed the Selective Service Act, requiring all male U.S. residents between the ages of twenty-one and thirty (amended to ages eighteen and forty-five in 1918) to register for military conscription. Undeclared aliens—immigrants who had not made formal declarations of their intention to naturalize—were exempt from service but still obligated to register and could face a year in prison if they failed to do so. In response, Emma Goldman and Alexander Berkman worked with a coalition of other radicals to form the No-Conscription League. Its first mass meeting, held at the Harlem River Casino on the day the act was passed, attracted an audience of eight thousand, and another meeting on June 4 brought out fifteen thousand listeners. The League printed one hundred thousand copies of its declaration of principles, which stated, "We oppose conscription because we are internationalists, anti-militarists, and opposed to all wars waged by capitalistic Governments. We will fight for what we choose to fight for; we will never fight simply because we are ordered to fight."[13] Galleani called on readers of *Cronaca Sovversiva* to refuse to register for the draft even if they were ineligible for service, both as a matter of principle and because the law excluding undeclared aliens might change.[14] In Paterson, Italian families with conscription-age men received unsolicited copies of *L'Era Nuova* in their mailboxes, and on June 1, anarchists Gaetano Troiani and Giuseppe Martorelli were arrested while distributing English-language manifestos against the war; four days later, Marchese was again arrested but soon released.[15]

Even before America joined the war, *L'Era Nuova* had condemned military conscription as "the modern slavery," and the pro-Ally *Land and Liberty* similarly warned that a draft would "carry us back directly to chattel slavery." After passage of the Selective Service Act, the Latin Branch of San Francisco's IWW Local 173 placed an anticonscription placard in the window of its headquarters at 403 Broadway Street: "In 1861 Uncle Sam freed the blacks; in 1917 Uncle Sam enslaved the whites"—a doubly unfortunate statement that not only misstated the date of the abolition but also obfuscated the fact that a disproportionate number of African Americans were being drafted. Police and "members of the army provost guard" responded by raiding the IWW's storefront in September, and the four men present, including Parenti, served thirty days for disturbing the peace.[16] Vincenzo Ferrero was arrested "when he inveighed against the draft from a soapbox" and was convicted of vagrancy, a catchall charge commonly used against Bay Area radicals. Jewish anarchist Alexander Horr also served a sixty-day sentence for delivering an antiwar speech on a public sidewalk.[17] In neighboring Oakland, an angry crowd of six hundred soldiers demolished the IWW's headquarters.[18]

Some anarchists obtained false registration cards, while others, including young No-Conscription League members Morris Becker and Louis Kramer, were arrested for failing to register; Kramer declared that he "was a 'citizen of the world' and against the war."[19] A group of Jewish anarchists from Philadelphia left for Canada to avoid registration and ended up participating in the Canadian anticonscription movement while also producing four issues of a Yiddish anti-war paper, *Der Eyntsiker* (The Unique One) in Toronto.[20] Thousands more so-called slackers crossed the border into revolutionary Mexico, including young Lower East Side anarchist writer Itzok Granich, who adopted the name Mike Gold during his stay.[21] Several dozen *galleanisti*, including Nicola Sacco and Bartolomeo Vanzetti, crossed into Monterrey; Vanzetti, who had previously made a declaration of intent to naturalize, was among those eligible for military service. Many of these Italians also anticipated the outbreak of revolution in Italy and believed that it would be easier to return there from Mexico than from the United States.[22] From Paterson, teenagers Spartaco Guabello and William Gallo—both American-born citizens—also fled to Mexico by way of Los Angeles, but when they swam back across the Rio Grande after the war, they were arrested by Texas Rangers and served five months in a Del Rio prison.[23] Alberico Pirani, an Italian anarchist who journeyed from Chicago to Mexico and then Venezuela to evade the draft, later explained his actions in unambiguously cosmopolitan terms: "I'm international. I ain't got no country. When you mention country and religion, wash your mouth. That's the way you kill millions of people, for God and country and flag."[24]

Other anarchists registered as required but were nevertheless victimized by overzealous authorities. IWW Latin Branch member Louis Tori was shocked to receive a summons to report for induction into the military despite the fact that he was an undeclared alien; the order was issued on the dubious grounds that he "had made no claim for exemption" at the time of registration. Tori was about to flee to Tijuana with a false passport and allegedly materials for manufacturing explosives when federal agents arrested him for draft evasion.[25] Philip Grosser, a Jewish anarchist born in Boston in 1890, was conscripted in August 1917 and refused to serve, but contrary to established procedure, he was tried in a military court rather than a criminal one on the premise that he had become a member of the armed forces the moment he was drafted. Grosser was summarily sentenced to thirty years hard labor, though he was released at the end of 1920 following a public campaign by anarchists and civil libertarians.[26]

In June 1917, the new Espionage Act made it a federal crime "to cause or attempt to cause insubordination, disloyalty, mutiny, refusal of duty, in the military or naval forces of the United States, or to willfully obstruct the recruiting or enlistment service of the United States," punishable by up to twenty years in prison and a ten-thousand-dollar fine. The consequences were immediate: the day after the law went into effect, police arrested Goldman and Berkman for their role in the No-Conscription League.[27] The Espionage Act also required foreign-language newspapers to supply translations of all articles to the Post Office, which received the authority to declare unmailable any material it deemed in violation of the statute. Anarchist publications across the country, including *L'Era Nuova*, *Cronaca Sovversiva*, *The Blast*, *Regeneración*, and *Mother Earth* were banned from the mails, while others, like Carlo Tresca's *L'Avvenire*, folded as a consequence of the cost of supplying translations.

Nevertheless, many of these papers continued publication and arranged alternative means of distribution. *L'Era Nuova* began shipping issues in bulk to local volunteer distributors, but this system lasted only until October 1917, when the paper shut down.[28] The L'Era Nuova Group then issued a one-off paper, *Nuovi Tempi* (New Times), in March 1918, followed a year later by *Il Bollettino de L'Era Nuova* (The New Era Bulletin), which ran for five issues. This publication, in turn, was replaced by the illegal paper *La Jacquerie*, which was sent to former subscribers of *L'Era Nuova* in bundles transported by train to New York and other nearby cities to be mailed out from scattered letter boxes.[29] Copies of *Cronaca Sovversiva* were delivered by motorcycle in some areas and arrived in Paterson in bulk bundles addressed to "B. Emilio" (Gemma Mello) care of a local grocery store, to be distributed locally. After the paper finally shut down it was, like *L'Era Nuova*, replaced by a succession of short-lived new titles, including *Cronache Rosse* (Red Chronicles), *L'Anarchia* (Anarchy), *Il Diritto* (The Right), and *Il Refrattario* (The Refractory One).[30] The *Mother Earth Bulletin* replaced *Mother Earth*, and in April 1918, Carlo Tresca took over an existing radical publication, *Il Martello* (The Hammer). Anarchists turned out to be much better guardians of freedom of the press than did the American government.

The *Fraye Arbeter Shtime*, though still the largest-circulating anarchist periodical in the country, had an easier time. An earlier intervention by both liberal and conservative Jews on behalf of the Socialist *Forverts* after it was briefly banned for antiwar articles, probably discouraged action against the *Fraye Arbeter Shtime*.[31] But more important, Saul Yanovsky belatedly came out in support of the Allies. The central pillar of Yanovsky's opposition to the war collapsed with the abdication of the czar following the February Revolution, and the editor was soon arguing that a victory for the Western democracies was far more desirable for Europe than was German rule. An undercover Bureau of Investigation agent who shadowed Yanovsky during a 1918 visit to Pittsburgh reported that the anarchist's speeches were "decidedly pro-war, and he urged all young men to join the army and fight the Germans." Although Yanovsky "was heckled by the audience . . . he succeeded in holding his own on the pro-war question." In print, he also praised Wilson's Fourteen Points as the most pragmatic way to ensure a lasting postwar peace.[32] Yanovsky's reversal reflected a general shift in the attitude of American Jews toward the war, especially after the British government issued the November 1917 Balfour Declaration, expressing the intention to create "a national home for the Jewish people" in Palestine, a cause that Yanovsky continued to vigorously oppose.[33] Nevertheless, scattered issues of the *Fraye Arbeter Shtime* were still deemed unmailable under the Espionage Act.[34]

Anger over Yanovsky's stance engendered a new wave of oppositional Yiddish groups that coalesced around underground newspapers like East Harlem's

Der Shturem (The Storm), published in 1917–18 by a group that included Triangle Fire survivor Mary Domsky and her husband, Jacob Abrams; the young firebrand Mollie Steimer; and sisters Ethel and Rose Bernstein. *Der Shturem* condemned the "hypocritical leaders of the Jewish workers" and lamented, "Our self-conscious Jewish workmen have not only lost their heads in the war rumble, why they simply are out of their minds."[35] In Toronto, *Der Eyntsiker* likewise dedicated most of its efforts to "denouncing Yanovsky."[36] These papers, illegal from the start, were hand delivered to subscribers or distributed at random.

The Ghadar movement's alliance with Germany became a major liability once America entered the war. The sensationalized "Hindu Conspiracy" trials, which began in San Francisco in November 1917, revealed that in 1915 a German agent had tried to ship 275 tons of munitions to anti-British colonial subjects out of Washington state, in violation of American neutrality laws. Seventeen Indians, nine Germans, and nine Americans were convicted, and a Ghadar member shot Ram Chandra dead in the courtroom after Chandra was shown to have misappropriated funds for personal use. By 1919, the exiled Har Dayal had turned against the Germans, disavowed anarchism and violent revolution, and made peace with the British Empire.[37] In the aftermath of these scandals, a California Bureau of Investigation agent arranged a meeting between the British Secret Service and disillusioned Irish anarchist Ed Gammons, who had recently fallen out of favor with Ghadar leaders and agreed to become a paid informant for the British government he had previously despised.[38]

The Department of Justice had much bigger targets in mind, however. The IWW, now with an estimated one hundred thousand members, led several strikes in industries deemed integral to the war effort and was a constant thorn in the side of American business and law enforcement. On September 5, 1917, federal and local authorities raided IWW headquarters throughout the country. In Paterson, agents "took practically everything but the furniture, the chairs and the desk," including membership lists. Federal agents then began visiting individuals' homes; "some of the members got scared" and dropped out of the union.[39] The day of the raids, the government also handed down indictments under the Espionage Act for 166 prominent IWW members, including Luigi Parenti. Of the 101 who ultimately stood trial in federal court in Chicago, all were found guilty and received sentences of up to twenty years in prison; Parenti was sentenced to five years and a thirty-thousand-dollar fine. From the time of his extradition to Chicago until June 1919, Parenti was also refused permission to see or communicate with his wife and three daughters, one of whom was born while he was incarcerated.[40] He eventually accepted a deal whereby his sentence was commuted on the condition that he and his family voluntarily repatriate to Italy at their own expense. They arrived there in August 1922, just two months before Mussolini's March on Rome.

While repression was battering anarchism in America, revolution in Russia was revitalizing it. In March 1917 (February, by the Russian calendar), a popular uprising overthrew the czar and established a new government composed of liberals and Socialists. American radicals of all stripes rejoiced, especially Russians and Russian Jews. Many anarchists, however, were dismissive of the provisional government. Berkman wrote that it "feels like any other government. It wants to strengthen its position and to perpetuate itself in power. . . . But they will have to reckon with the Russian people." *L'Era Nuova* similarly worried that Russia was experiencing a "political" revolution that had only created a new state to carry on the war in place of the old.[41] The provisional government, however, inadvertently precipitated its own demise by issuing a blanket amnesty for all political crimes and funding the repatriation of revolutionary émigrés.

At least 8,421 Russians and "Hebrews," including an estimated 600 anarchists, left the United States in 1917, nearly all bound for Russia. More than 12,000 Russian-born migrants followed over the next three years. By one estimate, the Union of Russian Workers "lost half its membership" to this return migration.[42] These repatriations were coordinated by regional committees consisting of representatives from the UORW, the Russian Federation of the Socialist Party, and other radical groups, who had taken over Russian consular offices. In New York and Pittsburgh, these committees were firmly under anarchist control.[43] The entire editorial staff of the UORW paper *Golos Truda*, with their printing press in tow, departed via Vancouver on the same boat as Leon Trotsky, while the members of Brownsville's Broyt un Frayhayt (Bread and Freedom) Group likewise returned en masse with their press.[44]

These returned anarchists had a profound impact on both the Russian Revolution and later anarchists' critiques of it. An analysis of nearly six hundred anarchists active during the revolution found that one in ten were émigrés who had returned from extended time abroad, mostly in the United States or Western Europe.[45] Ukrainian Jew Morris Nadelman recalled, "When the Revolution broke out, all the immigrants in Germany and the United States came back to Russia as revolutionists. Through them, I learned, more or less, the philosophy of different groups"—and became an anarchist.[46] Numerous American visitors noted encounters with Russian anarchists and syndicalists they had known in the United States: Robert Minor, who traveled to Russia in 1918, wrote, "I ran across these American-Russians everywhere, and every one of them who has been here [in America] got his political education here." Returning radicals were welcomed with open arms, especially members of the Anarchist Red Cross who met the former prisoners with whom they had corresponded.[47] The anarchist movement in Russia, largely under the guidance of returned migrants from America, mushroomed from a mere two hundred members at the beginning of 1917 to an estimated ten thousand the following year.[48]

In July 1917, UORW organizers arrived in Petrograd and founded the Union of Anarcho-Syndicalist Propaganda and reestablished *Golos Truda*. The paper called for a renewed revolution that would "be anti-statist in its methods of struggle, Syndicalist in its economic content and federalist in its political tasks." *Golos Truda*'s circulation quickly reached twenty-five thousand and "at various moments . . . rivaled Lenin's *Pravda* in influence."[49] Its program found strong support among several unions and within the blossoming factory committee movement, which sought to establish worker control of Russia's industries. Returned Anarchist Red Cross member Boris Yelensky helped the workers of his native Novorossiysk, a major port city on the Black Sea, organize control of their workplaces along anarchist lines, while in the Donets Basin, returnees organized a reported twenty-five thousand to thirty thousand miners under the IWW's program. In July 1917, the IWW's General Executive Board approved a request to send the Cyrillic type from the union's defunct Russian-language newspaper to repatriates in Vladivostok "to be used in starting a Russian I.W.W. paper there."[50]

Anarchists also swelled the ranks of the Red Guards and workers' militias and occupied key positions in the Red Army well into 1918. In the civil war that raged from 1917 to 1922, anarchists led partisan forces against the counterrevolutionary White Army (and at times the Red Army) in Ukraine, Tambov, and Siberia.[51] Jewish anarchist Maxim Chernyak led one such band in the Donets Basin. A former member of Bialystok's Chernoe Znamia Group, Chernyak fled to the United States after the 1905 revolution and was involved in anarchist groups in Chicago and Brooklyn before his return. Yelensky recalled visiting Kharkov in 1918 and noticing

> one man who was draped with weapons from head to foot and who hurled commands to the partisans. He looked so familiar that I was certain I had met him previously. . . . I had to peer through his long beard for a moment before I recognized him as Max Chernyak, the barber from Chicago.
>
> I could scarcely believe my eyes. In Chicago he had not been particularly active in the movement. He was the father of two children and frequently attended our affairs together with his family. None of us could have dreamed that he possessed the capacity to lead a partisan band and wage battles against well-organized units of the White Army. I asked him how all this had come about and he replied simply that in revolutionary times, all kinds of miracles occur.[52]

Jews such as Yelensky and Chernyak predominated among the returned anarchists, and during the revolution, the proportion of Jews within the Russian anarchist movement stood at more than 25 percent.[53] However, the same conditions that contributed to anarchism's phenomenal growth—the failure of the provisional government to stabilize the economy or pull out of the war—fostered far greater support for the Bolsheviks, who quickly moved to consolidate their control.

The Bolshevik-led October Revolution toppled the ineffective provisional government and proclaimed "All Power to the Soviets"—the democratically elected councils of workers, peasants, and soldiers that had sprung up across Russia. This turn of events fired anarchists' imaginations as not even the Mexican Revolution had. Swept up in the enthusiasm of the moment and delighted by the libertarian turn in the rhetoric of Lenin, the Bolshevik leader who called for "the 'smashing' of the present-day state machine," many believed the revolution was taking an anarchist turn.[54] A number of anarchists had also met Leon Trotsky during his brief stay in New York prior to the revolution, lecturing before Jewish anarchist groups and attending classes at the Ferrer Center. The *Fraye Arbeter Shtime* hailed "Our Trotsky" as a hero, and Emma Goldman reported that the anarchists returning to Russia "left this country with the determination to help the Bolsheviki."[55] In a bizarre turn of events, anarchists hoping to hasten the destruction of the state eagerly aided the establishment of a Marxist dictatorship.

Three American anarchist returnees belonged to the Petrograd Soviet's Military-Revolutionary Committee, which under Trotsky's leadership engineered the overthrow of the provisional government: UORW activists Bill Shatoff and Efim Yartchuk as well as I. S. Bleikhman, who had become an anarchist in the United States before returning to Russia several years earlier. Both Bleikhman and Yartchuk had been instrumental in the earlier uprising against the provisional government known as the July Days, and in October, Shatoff helped command the storming of the Winter Palace.[56]

The Bolsheviks, however, reserved all power for themselves in the name of the Russian proletariat. Some anarchists embraced the Leninist version of Marxism, while other "Soviet anarchists" endorsed the dictatorship of the proletariat, or an ostensibly syndicalist "dictatorship of labor," as a necessary transitional step on the road to anarchism. Still others were wary of Bolshevik authoritarianism but felt cooperation was necessary until the forces arrayed against the revolution were defeated.[57] In 1922, the renamed Russian Communist Party counted some 432 former anarchists in its ranks.[58]

Among the returnees who joined the party was Daniil Novomirskii, who became an official of the newly formed Communist International. However, in 1921 Novomirskii returned his party card out of disgust with Lenin's New Economic Policy and the suppression of anarchist critics of the regime. Novomirskii was briefly imprisoned and emerged "a frightened and broken man," working on scientific research and no longer engaging in politics. He explained to a friend, "I'm no longer young and I have my wife to think of. . . . Under the Czar we believed that the Revolution would bring universal freedom. The Revolution came. What are we to cling to now that the princess of our dreams has turned into an ogress?"[59] Shatoff also served in a number of official roles, including chief of police of Petrograd and supervisor of the construction of the Turkestan-Siberia Railway, all the while insisting to old comrades that he remained an ideological anarchist.[60] Former *Golos Truda* editor Maksim Raevsky acquired a "nonpolitical" clerical position in the new government and withdrew from the anarchist movement.[61]

Fragmentary and contradictory news about events in Russia reached America, allowing most radicals to believe those stories that corresponded with their own aspirations. The L'Era Nuova Group, *Cronaca Sovversiva*, and Carlo Tresca's *Il Martello* all hailed the new Communist regime, and *Il Martello* even printed a long excerpt from the *Communist Manifesto* and lauded the "dictatorship of the proletariat."[62] During the first years of the revolution, it was not unusual for Italian and Yiddish anarchists to consider themselves "Bolsheviks" or to take out membership in one of the two American communist parties founded in 1919. When asked that year by Bureau of Investigation agents if he opposed all governments, Paterson anarchist Serafino Grandi replied, "I believe in a government of the workers, for example, the one in Russia." Authorities also noted that Firmino Gallo's Libreria Sociologica was well stocked with American communist publications, and a search of Gallo's home in 1920 turned up a "receipt of payment of dues to the communist party."[63] This ideological fuzziness extended in the other direction as well: in 1919, San Francisco's Communist Party hall proudly displayed Emma Goldman's portrait alongside those of Lenin and Trotsky.[64]

A number of anarchists volunteered for the "American Red Guard," organized by New York Socialists in February 1918, in hopes of fighting in Russia. On March 2, New York's Francisco Ferrer Association cabled Trotsky, "Ferrer Association is with you to the death. Are forming Red Guards to help you defend the Revolution." Among these volunteers was draft dodger Mike Gold, who had gravitated toward communism during his time in Mexico. The L'Era Nuova Group also called on comrades to join the Red Guard because "the cause of the *Bolshewiki* [*sic*] is the cause of all workers."[65] The U.S. government, however, refused to permit the group to leave for Russia. Elpidio Parenti was so impatient to take part in the revolution that he purchased a small boat, named it *Russia*, and set sail out of San Francisco Bay—only to capsize in the open ocean, where he was pulled from the water by passing fishermen. It was perhaps a small consolation that his granddaughter, born in 1920, was also named Russia.[66]

One of the few anarchists to not share in the enthusiasm for the October Revolution was Saul Yanovsky. He condemned the Bolshevik seizure of power, insisting that any dictatorship was "not anarchistic" and "not kosher," and described Lenin as a deceitful Mephistopheles who would not live up to his libertarian rhetoric. Watching the stampede of Jewish radicals returning to Soviet Russia, Yanovsky lamented, "I have raised a generation of idiots."[67] In the *Fraye Arbeter Shtime,* Yanovsky warned, "The Russian czar used terror against all who were his opponents, and the Bolsheviks now use this exact same medium of all despots." But Yanovsky's credibility among anarchists had plummeted following his reversal on the war, and the circulation of the *Fraye Arbeter Shtime* dropped to twelve thousand by 1919, less than half of its prewar height.[68] After two decades as editor, Yanovsky was forced to resign his post. The *Fraye Arbeter Shtime*'s publication committee appointed Jacob Maryson as Yanovsky's replacement, but Maryson was also skeptical of the Russian Communist Party and was discharged a few months later after refusing to print a pro-communist article by Michael Cohn. Beginning in late July 1920, the paper was edited by Communists Haim Kantorovitch and Mosheh Kats (not to be confused with former anarchist Moyshe Katts), briefly losing its anarchist identity.[69]

Even anarchists ambivalent toward the Soviet regime came to its defense when the United States dispatched thousands of troops to Russia as part of the Allies' failed campaign to aid anti-Communist forces. Radicals saw this as a flagrant attempt to roll back the revolutionary gains of the Russian people, and in August, several members of the group that published New York's *Der Shturem* and its successor, *Frayhayt,* were arrested for distributing a circular urging workers to stage a general strike against American intervention. Anarchist Jacob Schwartz died in police custody, allegedly as a result of police beatings, and his comrades Mollie Steimer, Hyman Lachowsky, Samuel Lipman, and Jacob Abrams were convicted of violating the Sedition Act and sentenced to between fifteen and twenty years apiece.[70]

In the rising hysteria fueled by the Russian Revolution, California radicals were blamed for all manner of misdeeds. When a bomb exploded outside the Sacramento home of Governor Stephens on December 17, 1917, police immediately charged fifty-three local IWW members in connection with the crime and then arrested forty more radicals in San Francisco, including Basil Saffores and Michele Centrone. All charges were dropped, however, after no evidence linking any of the men to the bombing was discovered.[71] In February 1918, Saffores was again arrested, this time in connection with the mysterious deaths of a few hundred sheep in South San Francisco. Despite the fact that federal officials were "sure the poison plot was planned and carried out through I.W.W. agencies," Saffores was released following the revelation that the animals had died after their owner fed them spoiled beans.[72]

More serious were the more than fifty indictments of California IWW members handed down on February 8, 1918, for violation of the Espionage and Selective Service Acts. Saffores was again a target, as was his fellow Latin Branch member Louis Tori. Five of those charged died in a prison, two turned state's evidence, and the remaining forty-six faced trial in Sacramento. Most, including Tori, were convinced that they would not receive a fair trial and engaged in a "silent defense," refusing to obtain council or speak during the proceedings. All were found guilty and received sentences ranging from one to ten years.[73] Saffores and two others, however, undertook an active defense and received lighter sentences: Saffores served just two months. Bitter feelings within the IWW resulted, and in 1919, the three were expelled. Saffores petitioned unsuccessfully for readmittance, and at the end of that year, facing a deportation warrant as an alien anarchist, he jumped bail and disappeared.[74] On June 12, 1918, police raided the new headquarters of San Francisco's Latin Branch at 1614 Stockton Street and charged the three Frenchmen and seven Italians present with vagrancy.[75]

In May 1918, a new Sedition Act greatly expanded the government's ability to police speech, making it a crime to "utter, print, write, or publish any disloyal, profane, scurrilous, or abusive language about the form of government of the United States, or the Constitution of the United States, or the uniform of the Army or Navy of the United States, or any language intended to . . . encourage resistance to the United States, or to promote the cause of its enemies."[76] More important, revisions to the Anarchist Exclusion Act in February 1917 and October 1918 addressed that legislation's main deficiencies by allowing the deportation of immigrants who came to hold anarchist doctrines after their arrival—first within a window of five years, and after 1918 at any time following their immigration. The revised law also allowed naturalized anarchists to be stripped of their American citizenship. Thereafter, deportation was legally mandated for any foreign-born anarchist (or other individual who advocated "the overthrow by force or violence of the Government of the United States," "the unlawful damage, injury, or destruction of property," or "sabotage"), regardless of their citizenship status or length of residence.[77] Berkman and Goldman, who were among the first to fall victim to these new statutes, noted the stunning precedent they set: "Henceforth the naturalized citizen may be disenfranchised, on one pretext or another, and deported because of his or her social views and opinions."[78]

Application of these expanded powers, however, was sporadic and not always successful. On May 15, 1918, Michele Centrone was once again arrested, this time as an alien anarchist, and held for deportation on Angel Island. (Ironically, as this occurred before the second revision of the Anarchist Exclusion Act, Centrone was not technically eligible for deportation because he had resided in the United States for longer than five years. It is likely that Centrone did not fully understand the law and that local immigration officials either ignored it or were themselves unclear about its application.) The anarchist posted two thousand dollars bail but then waited a year and a half for his case to move forward. The mounting interest on his bail bond, meanwhile, became insupportable, forcing Centrone to surrender himself to authorities at Angel Island. At wit's end, he wrote to the secretary of labor, the commissioner of immigration, and Attorney General A. Mitchell Palmer asking them to move forward with his deportation. In February 1920, he finally appealed to anti-immigrant and antiradical congressman Albert Johnson: "As you are one of the Congressman [*sic*] who wish to rid this Country of the Reds, I take the liberty to turn my plea to you with the request that you bring my case to a conclusion." With Johnson's intervention, Centrone's deportation finally proceeded.[79] When his friend Giuseppe Scali showed up to post a new bail so that Centrone could settle his affairs before leaving, authorities arrested Scali on the spot as an alien anarchist, but he, too, had to eventually appeal to antiradical officials to expedite his own deportation.[80]

In Paterson, police arrested Firmino Gallo and Ninfa Baronio on September 11, 1918, for posting antiwar flyers. Although Baronio "admitted . . . that she was an anarchist and that she did not believe in war," only Gallo was charged with violating the Espionage Act. He was released two months later because of a hung jury.[81] Alberto Guabello, Serafino Grandi, and Pietro Baldisserotto were arrested on September 28 and held for deportation as alien anarchists, but their warrants were canceled the following year for lack of evidence. In the wake of these arrests, local anarchists decided to defer "overt activities until the peace treaty is ratified, which will terminate the criminal war legislation which they fear will be applied to them."[82] However, what Goldman and Berkman called "the Frankenstein of intolerance and suppression cultivated by the war campaign" only expanded after the war.[83] Perhaps the ominous date of 1918's Armistice Day should have given the anarchists pause: November 11, the thirty-first anniversary of the Haymarket executions.

On January 23, 1919, police raided Jack London Memorial Hall in San Francisco and arrested all those present. In April, California passed a stringent Criminal Syndicalism Law, modeled on Idaho's 1917 criminal syndicalism legislation, which had specifically been designed to outlaw membership in the IWW. (By 1920, eighteen other states had followed Idaho's lead.) May, June, and July saw a series of police raids on the homes and meeting halls of IWW members in San Francisco and Oakland, with dozens of arrests for either criminal syndicalism or vagrancy. In total, at least 531 Californians were charged with criminal syndicalism between 1919 and 1924, resulting in 164 convictions and 128 prison sentences ranging from one to fourteen years.[84] In 1921, San Francisco's chief of police simply ordered his officers to stop all IWW meetings and arrest all known IWW members on sight, and union members began holding meetings on the lower decks of ferryboats crossing the bay to avoid raids.[85]

In New York, several former members of the Der Shturem and Frayhayt Groups, including Mollie Steimer, who was out on bail, began issuing a new underground publication, *The Anarchist Soviet Bulletin*. Hippolyte Havel, UORW member Arthur Katzes, and Shmuel Marcus, one of the anarchists who had fled to Canada during the war, joined them in this endeavor. Marcus edited the first issue of the *Bulletin*, which appeared in April 1919 and claimed to represent a nationwide revolutionary organization with an unwieldy name, American Anarchist Federated Commune Soviets. Enthralled with the Russian Revolution, the paper condemned American intervention and called on workers to arm themselves, organize "anarchist soviets"—many of which, it alleged, already existed throughout the country—and initiate a revolutionary general strike to topple the U.S. government.[86] Although much of what appeared in the *Anarchist Soviet Bulletin* was little more than fantasy, it was more than enough to alarm the authorities, who immediately set out to suppress the seditious paper.

But rather than relying on the postal system, the *Bulletin*'s publishers distributed it clandestinely through the UORW and other anarchist groups. They also threw copies out of windows and off of rooftops in New York's Garment District and stuffed them into mailboxes in working-class neighborhoods. On April 15, Shmuel Marcus traveled to Paterson to distribute the paper but was arrested after a police officer demanded to see the contents of his suitcase, which contained twenty-five hundred copies of the first issue. Local and federal authorities interrogated Marcus in the Passaic County Jail, demanding to know the location of the *Bulletin*'s printing press. Throughout, the anarchist claimed that his name was "Robert Parsons," that he was a Canadian citizen born in Montreal, and that he did not know where the paper was printed. (In fact, Marcus was born to Orthodox Jewish parents in Dorohoi, Romania, in 1893 and had migrated with his family to Philadelphia in 1907, later joining the Radical Library Group and becoming one of its most militant members.)[87] On May 1 "Parsons" was transferred to Ellis Island to await deportation to Canada, but two weeks later, he posted one thousand dollars bail and returned to the task of editing the *Bulletin*. In the following months, unidentified persons paid the unsuspecting children of prominent Paterson citizens—including those of a rabbi, a silk manager, and a black minister—to hand out copies of the *Bulletin* on the sidewalk.[88] Back in New York, several anarchists, including Steimer, Ethel Bernstein, and Katzes, were caught distributing the paper, but the *Bulletin* continued to appear, much to the government's chagrin.[89]

Nationwide, however, attention shifted to a sensational series of bombings in the spring and summer of 1919. At the end of April, explosive devices were mailed to the homes of twenty-nine individuals, all in some way affiliated with the suppression of radicalism. The bombs were meant to simultaneously strike their targets on May Day, but only one functioned correctly, and it maimed a maid rather than its intended victim; most were discovered before reaching their destinations. These failed attempts were followed by the coordinated bombings of several homes on the night of June 2, with explosions occurring in Boston, New York, Paterson, Philadelphia, Pittsburgh, Cleveland, and Washington, D.C., including one that demolished the home of Attorney General Palmer. Again, however, none of the targets were killed or seriously injured, and the man who placed the bomb at Palmer's residence was blown apart when the device exploded prematurely. The bombings were carried out by a group of Luigi Galleani's followers who first formulated the plot in response to Galleani's arrest in the summer of 1917 while they were in Mexico to avoid the draft.[90] For these uncompromising revolutionaries, antiradical repression left no alternative but violent retaliation. Copies of a circular, "Plain Words," strewn at each bombing site expressed the immigrant revolutionaries' pent-up rage: "We have been dreaming of freedom, we have talked of liberty, we have aspired to a better world, and you jailed us, you clubbed us, you deported us, you murdered us. . . . There will have to be bloodshed; we will not dodge; there will have to be murder: we will kill, because it is necessary; there will have to be destruction; we will destroy to rid the world of your tyrannical institutions."[91]

The attacks sparked a massive wave of government retaliation. Believing them linked to an international anarchist-Bolshevik conspiracy, Palmer, the Bureau of Investigation, and the Bureau of Immigration formulated a plan to arrest and deport alien radicals en masse. They began on November 7, 1919, with coordinated raids on the UORW. New York City police arrested 162 men and women at the UORW's headquarters on Fifth Avenue and savagely beat many of those detained. Among them was Ethel Bernstein, recently out on bail, who reported, "It was wholesale clubbing. . . . [B]lood was everywhere, blood of our comrades! Such a scene I have never witnessed before."[92] Authorities invoked New York State's criminal anarchy statute, which had been on the books since 1902 but had never been used and which made it a crime to advocate, disseminate material advocating, or belong to a group that advocated the doctrine that "organized government" should be "overthrown by force or violence . . . or by any unlawful means." The law imposed punishments of up to ten years' imprisonment and five thousand dollar fines. Five individuals were indicted for criminal anarchy; two were convicted, while the other three were deported as alien anarchists.[93] After the raid, cautious UORW members stored most of the organization's literature in the offices of the *Fraye Arbeter Shtime*, just ahead of new police raids on seventy-three of the state's radical centers, during which roughly a thousand arrests occurred. The Bureau of Immigration issued deportation warrants for all of those apprehended who were foreign-born, and thirty-five others were charged with criminal anarchy.[94]

Over the course of 1919–20, thousands of deportation warrants were supplied for suspected alien radicals. Galleani and eight of his Italian comrades were deported in June 1919, but the high point of the deportation campaign came with the sailing of the USS *Buford* on December 21, 1919. Onboard were Emma Goldman and Alexander Berkman, the prize catches of the Bureau of Investigation's rising star J. Edgar Hoover, along with 247 other Russian-born radicals. Most were members of the UORW, including Ethel Bernstein and Arthur Katzes. Another group of anarchists deported in February 1921 drafted a bitter parting statement, lamenting, "We came to this country years ago, thinking it was a country which offered free asylum to the oppressed of all nations. Upon arriving the only thing we found, however, was the 'chance' of toiling from 10 to 16 hours a day at a wage hardly enough to keep us alive."[95] In November of that year, Jacob Abrams, Mollie Steimer, Hyman Lachowsky, and Samuel Lipman were also deported after losing a landmark free-speech Supreme Court case; Abrams's wife, Mary, accompanied them.[96]

The *galleanisti* struck back on September 16, 1920, when a powerful bomb carried in a horse-drawn cart exploded on Wall Street, killing more than thirty people. The deadly attack was likely a response to the indictments of anarchists Nicola Sacco and Bartolomeo Vanzetti on charges of allegedly participating in a robbery and murder in South Braintree, Massachusetts. The bomber was almost certainly anarchist Mario Buda, who subsequently fled to Italy.[97] However, the American public had grown weary of the Red Scare and, unlike earlier outrages, the Wall Street bombing did not provoke a new wave of repression.[98] The bombing campaign did, however, deal a near fatal blow to the anarchist movement in Paterson.

One of the June 2, 1919, explosions occurred at the Paterson home of Harry Klotz, president of the Suanhna Silk Company, a member of the Paterson Manufacturers' Association's executive board, and an outspoken opponent of silk weavers' prevailing forty-four-hour week. The bomb "tore a hole large enough for a good sized man to climb through" in the building's foundation and did "considerable damage" to an adjacent structure. Klotz and his family were on vacation at the time, though another family occupying the second floor of the home was left shaken. The previous winter, an IWW-led strike at the Suanhna Mill had resulted in the discharge of two L'Era Nuova Group members, and the Bureau of Investigation immediately seized on the apparent—yet false—connection between the bombing and this group, which Hoover placed at the top of the Bureau's target list.[99]

Special agent Frank R. Stone oversaw the Paterson investigation and hired Joseph Define, an Italian American sergeant in the army's Military Intelligence Division, as an undercover operative. Define introduced himself to Paterson's

FIGURE 12. "An Outing of Members of the L'Era Nuova Group Held at Haledon N.J.,"
ca. 1919. Circled and numbered (*left to right*): (1) Pietro Baldeserotto, (2) Alberto
Guabello, (3) Umberto Croce, (4) Paolo Guabello, (5) Serafino Grandi, (6) L. Cauceglio,
(7) Franz Widmar, (8) "An unknown member of the 'En Sorte,'" (9) Taldi Coppo,
(10) John Ferraro. Courtesy of the National Archives.

radicals as "Joseph Termini," an anarchist born in Algeria to a Sicilian father.
Within less than a month, Define had infiltrated both the Francisco Ferrer Association and the L'Era Nuova Group. According to Ludovico Caminita, at
meetings "Termini" "always entered first, swept, cleaned, tended the stove, and
was always the last to leave." He also advocated for "energetic action"—that is,
violence—and although "nobody agreed with him . . . nobody realized that Joe
Termini had to be an agent provocateur in the pay of the police." Furthermore,
Termini gained the trust of Firmino Gallo and Ninfa Baronio, who took him
into their home and began to apprentice him as a silk weaver.[100]

After months of investigation, bureau agents and dozens of volunteers from
the American Legion descended on Paterson on the night of February 14, 1920,
with J. Edgar Hoover tagging along on his first federal raid. Agents arrested
twenty-nine local anarchists, including Caminita, Gallo, Beniamino Mazzotta,
Franz Widmar, Serafino Grandi, Pietro Baldisserotto, and Alberto and Paulo
Guabello. Define was also arrested to maintain his cover but was allowed to
"escape" and then disappeared from Paterson. When Baronio showed up at

the jail with cigarettes for both her husband and their lodger, she was shocked when the incredulous guard exclaimed, "Joe Termini? But he's a spy for the federal agents!"[101] Mazzotta, who was a naturalized citizen and denied being an anarchist, was released the day after the arrests, followed by several others, but Caminita and the remainder were held on bails of between five thousand and ten thousand dollars each and transferred to Ellis Island to await deportation. A surprising scene unfolded as the prisoners were transported to the train station: as Caminita described it, "Along the way the sidewalks were crowded with people who hailed us waving hats and handkerchiefs. A policeman said to a federal agent: 'You see? We told you that public opinion is with them. You wanted to put on this spectacle because you do not know the place.'"[102]

The Bureau of Investigation fixed its attention on Caminita. It had discovered that he was the anonymous editor of *La Jacquerie* through pure chance: in June 1919, former subscribers to *L'Era Nuova* received letters informing them that *La Jacquerie* would be appearing as "another paper better than L'Era Nuova" and instructing them, "Hide it and do not be caught by the police. If some one asks you who sends it to you, answer and say you do not know." All funds and correspondence were to be directed to "L. M. Caminita, 12 Planten Ave., Paterson, N.J." But one subscriber failed to take proper precautions, and a copy of the letter was found "in the street" in Guelph, Ontario, and turned in to Canadian authorities, who forwarded it to the Department of Justice.[103] During his interrogation, Caminita initially denied editing *La Jacquerie* but—after being punched and slapped, according to his later account—he not only admitted to producing the paper but also took responsibility for the entirety of its contents, falsely claiming, "I have no contributors. They cannot write. I wrote all of the articles myself." He further declared that he had received no financial support for the publication from anyone and that it only had "about 300" subscribers, around one-tenth the actual number. Caminita told the truth, however, when he denied any knowledge of the June bombings, stating, "I don't believe in terrorism"; he speculated that the attacks constituted a "frame-up."[104]

At immigration hearings the following month, however, Caminita retracted his previous admissions in an effort to avoid deportation. He denied having written for or edited *La Jacquerie* and sought to ingratiate himself to his interrogators by claiming that the classes he taught at Paterson's Ferrer School instructed immigrants "to be good citizens of this country," which had "one of the best governments in the world." Caminita also received false information through his wife—probably planted by the authorities—to the effect that the other Paterson anarchists, all of whom had been released except for Paolo Guabello, had agreed to testify against him in exchange for their freedom.[105] Federal agents further claimed that they discovered Caminita's editorial role because he was named as such in Carlo Tresca's *Il Martello* and the Socialist paper *La*

Folla, both of which he had attacked in the pages of *La Jacquerie*, rather than because of the letter handed over by Canadian authorities.[106]

On March 8, 1920, Hoover "informally" interviewed Caminita. The anarchist was impressed by "the young lawyer," describing him as "extremely intelligent, very clever, [and] diplomatic." For his part, Hoover proved a shrewd interrogator. Although he quickly realized that Caminita had no firsthand knowledge of the bombings, he exploited the editor's feuds with both the *galleanisti* and his fellow Paterson anarchists. "By working upon Caminetta's [*sic*] feelings," he reported to Bureau of Investigation director William J. Flynn, "I was able to point out that by assisting the Government in this matter he was also helping his own group in Paterson, N.J., for he claims that his group is not a terroristic organization." More important, Hoover discovered that Caminita "has a boy about ten years of age in whom he has centered his affection," and "by playing on Caminetta's [*sic*] emotions" and threatening to separate him from his wife and son, Hoover extracted "much information." Having been arrested as a consequence of the rash actions of the *galleanisti* and believing himself betrayed by his closest comrades, Caminita succumbed to Hoover's manipulations and named several individuals he considered likely perpetrators of the bombings, including Filippo Caci, a member of Paterson's small anti-organizationist group, Gli Insorti (The Insurgents).[107]

The Bureau of Investigation retained Caminita as a resource by using the threat of deportation as leverage and obtaining temporary postponements of his deportation warrant when he cooperated. An agent overseeing the case admitted to Hoover, "It would of course be very disastrous to the best interests of the government if Caminita should be deported," but the pretense of this imminent expulsion was maintained for more than four years. "Above me hung the sword of Damocles," Caminita later lamented.[108] Although released from Ellis Island on bond in May 1920, he was rearrested in September 1921 and again in January 1922, and each time Hoover "held several interviews with him," eventually convincing Caminita to write a damaging exposé of the Italian American Left for publication in a mainstream American newspaper. Caminita, however, took the opportunity to pen a tirade against Carlo Tresca and Italian American Socialist leaders—but did not mention his Paterson comrades or even the *galleanisti*. Moreover, Caminita apparently never finished the memoir; instead, he wrote and published an Italian-language account of his arrest and time at Ellis Island.[109]

But in May 1920, Tresca began warning fellow anarchists and IWW members that Caminita had supplied information to the authorities, and the editor's second arrest and release revived these accusations. Debate over Caminita's possible cooperation with police raged in the Italian anarchist press on both sides of the Atlantic, and an anarchist committee formed to investigate the charges concluded that although there was no evidence that Caminita had been employed as a spy, he was nevertheless "a very dangerous element in the labor movement in general." *L'Adunata dei Refrattari* (The Cry of the Refractories), the unofficial successor to Galleani's *Cronaca Sovversiva*, similarly doubted that Caminita was a spy but declared that he was "a dangerous element" and no longer "worthy" of belonging to the radical movement.[110] Finally, in July 1922, *Il Martello* published excerpts from Caminita's statements to the Bureau of Investigation that Tresca had obtained, allegedly through a Department of Justice stenographer who was friends with Tresca's lover, IWW organizer Elizabeth Gurley Flynn.[111]

Caminita's betrayal was viewed as especially egregious because many believed him to be responsible for the arrests of the *galleanisti* Roberto Elia and Andrea Salsedo, who were held informally at the Bureau of Investigation's New York offices for several months until Salsedo either jumped or was pushed from a fourteenth-floor window after both men supplied information about their comrades. Two days later, authorities arrested Sacco and Vanzetti.[112] Caminita was thus accused of precipitating the chain of events leading to Sacco and Vanzetti's convictions and death sentences. However, Elia's arrest occurred on February 25, 1920, two weeks before Hoover first interrogated Caminita. In fact, on the night of the Paterson raids, printer Beniamino Mazzotta had suggested to authorities that Elia might have printed the "Plain Words" circular found at the scenes of the 1919 bombings.[113] Nevertheless, Caminita became a pariah in radical circles. And the L'Era Nuova Group, the Libreria Sociologica, the Francisco Ferrer Modern School, and the local IWW organization all permanently dissolved in the wake of the federal raids and revelations about Caminita.

The Bureau of Investigation's campaign to eliminate anarchism soon encountered resistance from within the federal government as well as from the anarchists themselves. The downfall of Caminita and the deportations of Berkman, Goldman, Galleani, and hundreds of others highlighted foreign-born anarchists' vulnerability to state repression and exclusionary immigration statutes. But deportation involved an unwieldy bureaucratic process and relied on the cooperation of the Department of Labor, which oversaw immigration enforcement before 1940. All deportation warrants had to be personally signed by the secretary of labor or an assistant secretary of labor after reviewing evidence furnished by district immigration inspectors.[114] In the early days of the Red Scare, immigration officials worked hand in hand with the Department of Justice, issuing blanket deportation warrants on the slightest evidence provided—or promised. But plans for additional mass deportations following the *Buford* soon collapsed.

In March 1920, liberal assistant secretary of labor Louis F. Post became acting head of the Department of Labor. Increasingly uncomfortable with the suppression of civil liberties, Post began subjecting political deportation cases to

TABLE 1. Deportations under the Anarchist Exclusion Act, 1918–1929

1918	1919	1920	1921	1922	1923	1924	1925	1926	1927	1928	1929
2	37	314	446	64	13	81	22	4	9	1	1

Note: These numbers do not include radicals deported under other provisions of immigration law.
Source: Jane Perry Clark, *Deportation of Aliens from the United States to Europe* (New York: Columbia University Press, 1931), 225 n. 1.

close review, dismissing most for lack of evidence and outraging the Department of Justice in the process.[115] In many cases, including those of the Paterson anarchists, Post canceled warrants even when sufficient evidence of anarchist beliefs existed. Of the more than 6,300 deportation warrants issued under the Anarchist Exclusion Act in 1919–20, fewer than 1,000 were executed and only about 350 of them were for actual anarchists or UORW members: most of the deportees were Socialists or Communists.[116]

Thus, the vast majority of foreign-born anarchists remained at liberty. They did so only partially as a result of interbureau hostility. Although the denaturalization of foreign-born anarchists was legally sanctioned and upheld by federal courts, it involved a complicated process that rendered it nearly impossible and was rarely invoked.[117] Firmino Gallo, Beniamino Mazzotta, and other individuals who had obtained American citizenship were therefore effectively shielded from deportation. So, too, was Carlo Tresca for the simple reason that authorities were unable to ascertain his citizenship status.[118] Exclusionary laws also had exceptions: immigrant women who married U.S. citizens automatically received citizenship even if they fell within an excludable class. Emma Goldman, for example, had lost her citizenship in 1909 only because the government claimed that her estranged husband, Jacob Kershner, had fraudulently obtained his own.[119] Otherwise, she, too, would have been unremovable.

Even unnaturalized alien anarchists, the government found, could not always be deported. On November 18, 1919, the Bureau of Immigration issued a warrant of deportation for the return of "Robert Parson (or Parsons)"—Shmuel Marcus—to Canada. British authorities, however, informed the Bureau of Investigation that the Canadian address supplied by "Parsons" was false, and there was no record of his presence in Canada before 1917.[120] "Parsons" jumped his bail and continued to secretly edit the *Anarchist Soviet Bulletin*. But when workers in England threatened a general strike in the event of Allied intervention in the Polish-Soviet War in August 1920, Marcus mistook this movement for an impending revolution and surreptitiously traveled to London for three months before clandestinely returning to New York by way of Canada.[121] The following month, the Bureau of Investigation finally caught up with him as he exited the

New York Public Library. Marcus was returned to Ellis Island, interrogated for twenty-four straight hours, stripped naked, and beaten, but he refused to divulge the location of his group's secret printing establishment.[122] He also continued to insist that his name was Parsons and that he was a Canadian citizen. Bureau agents incorrectly guessed he was "a Russian subject," but even if that had been true, the United States had no diplomatic relations with the new Soviet government, and the Russians had begun refusing entry to anarchist deportees. After six months, Marcus was again released on bond.[123] Ignorant of both Marcus's real name and place of birth, the government suddenly found its own borders working against it. As a de facto man without a country, Marcus could not be expelled since no other country was obligated or willing to receive him.

Even those who were deported did not always stay away. Jewish anarchist Jack Isaacson was ordered to report for deportation but instead fled to Canada, then returned secretly and lived under his wife's maiden name, Denenberg, for the rest of his life.[124] Filippo Perrone, a veteran of the Mexican Revolution and San Francisco free-speech fight, was deported in early 1922, but covertly returned to New York in 1926 and remained in the United States under the name Vincenzo Lentini until the end of the Second World War.[125] After Mussolini came to power, Michele Centrone also attempted to return to the United States, emigrating from Italy to Mexico and then making his way to New Orleans, but he was apprehended and again deported.[126]

Ironically, at the same time the government was having trouble expelling foreign-born radicals, it was unable to hold onto those it wished to incarcerate—the perpetrators of the 1919 bombings. In the months following the raid on the L'Era Nuova Group, members of Paterson's anti-organizationist Gli Insorti began to disappear: among those who stowed away on ships to Italy were Filippo Caci and Ruggero Bacchini, the men suspected by both Caminita and the Bureau of Investigation of planting the Paterson bomb.[127] Not a single individual ever faced trial for the 1919 bombings. The territorial boundaries of the United States again hampered the government's efforts because the state's authority ended at the borders across which anarchists so frequently moved.

By the close of 1921, postal authorities had ceased pulling radical periodicals from the mails and restored second-class mailing privileges. Joseph Cohen reported to Max Nettlau, "The censorship is not strict here now. We are preaching Anarchism openly."[128] Over the next three years, all remaining prisoners held under the Espionage and Sedition Acts were released. Just as this uneasy peace was reached in the United States, however, anarchists found themselves facing new crises in Russia and Italy.

As the Russian Communist Party consolidated its hold on power, its relationship with the anarchists deteriorated. The soviets, trade unions, and factory committees in which anarchists placed so much hope were transformed into appendages of centralized Communist power, and workers' control gave way to "one-man management" and militaristic "iron discipline" in the workplace.[129] Then, in April 1918, the Cheka (All-Russian Extraordinary Commission for Combating Counterrevolution and Sabotage) raided anarchist groups in Moscow and Petrograd, encountering armed resistance in several locations. More than fifty deaths and five hundred arrests resulted. Afterward, many anarchists fled to Ukraine, where Communist authority had yet to solidify. There they flocked to the Nabat (Alarm) Confederation of Anarchist Organizations as well as to anarchist Nestor Makhno's peasant army, which had established an autonomous region of several hundred square miles in which it founded libertarian "free soviets."[130] The Makhnovists' Cultural and Educational Section was soon filled with returnees from America, including Jewish anarchists Volin, Aron Baron, Elena Keller, Joseph Goodman, and Leah and Joseph Gutman. Rachel Hurwitz, formerly of Philadelphia, worked as a nurse's aide in Makhno's army, and Maxim Chernyak became head of the Kontrrazvedka, Makhno's counterintelligence service.[131]

Their participation is an important counterpoint to the charge, originating with the Soviet government, that Makhno was an anti-Semite and pogromist. Although it is certain that some Makhnovists did engage in pogroms, Makhno himself "did all in his power to counteract anti-Semitic tendencies among his followers" and dealt harshly with those responsible for violence against Jews, usually having them summarily executed.[132] Russian Jewish anarchist Mark Mratchny, who was sent on behalf of the Nabat Confederation to edit the Makhnovists' newspaper, testified that Makhno "was in no way at all a *pogromshchik*," although in private correspondence he complained of widespread anti-Semitism among Makhno's soldiers.[133] In 1924, Saul Yanovsky used the pages of the *Fraye Arbayter Shtime* to accuse Makhno of committing pogroms, but on the occasion of Makhno's death seven years later, Yanovsky publicly recanted: "I cannot forgive myself that I could so misjudge a man merely on the basis of calumny by his bitter enemies."[134]

Regardless, Makhno's army was hardly a safe haven. It was engaged in a protracted struggle against the White Army and Ukrainian nationalists, alternately fighting alongside and against the Red Army. Finally, in November 1920, the Red Army betrayed a treaty with the Makhnovists, routed their forces, and arrested their supporters, marking the end of major anarchist activity. Symbolically, on February 8, 1921, Peter Kropotkin, who had also returned to Russia after the February Revolution, died at the age of seventy-eight. In his final letter abroad he had warned, "We are learning to know in Russia how *not* to introduce communism." A number of anarchists imprisoned in Moscow were granted permission to join the twenty thousand mourners at Kropotkin's funeral, the last legal anarchist demonstration under the Communist regime. Emma Goldman spoke at the graveside.[135] Yet many, including Goldman and Berkman, did not become convinced that there was no longer hope for the revolution until the bloody March 1921 suppression of the Kronstadt "free soviet," which had called for the restoration of civil liberties and democratic soviets in the place of one-party rule.[136]

In the aftermath of Kronstadt, the Communist Party banned internal factions and ordered renewed raids on anarchist groups. A few months later, Russia expelled several leading anarchists, including Volin, Efim Yartchuk, and Grigorii Petrovich Maksimov, who were joined in European exile by Goldman and Berkman. In 1923, Mollie Steimer and her partner, returned Russian Jewish anarchist Senya Fleshin, were likewise deported, and Jacob and Mary Abrams briefly joined them in Paris in 1925 before going into exile in Mexico.[137] In 1923, thirty-five anarchists were also included in the initial group of political prisoners sent to the island of Solovetsky, the first outpost of the Gulag Archipelago. By 1924, anarchists abroad could document at least 300 anarchists in Russian prisons or work camps, 181 who had been deported or exiled, and scores who had been executed or died in prison. Boris Yelensky, who became secretary of the resurrected Anarchist Red Cross after returning to the United States in 1923, estimated that 90 percent of the anarchists who had returned from America eventually met their deaths at the hands of the Soviet state under Lenin or Stalin.[138] Among them were Daniil Novomirskii, Samuel Lipman, Efim Yartchuk (who returned to Russia in 1925), and Bill Shatoff, while Ethel Bernstein spent ten years in a Soviet labor camp.

Disturbing reports of these events trickled into the United States. "As time went on," Harry Kelly recalled, "word came from some of our comrades overseas that the new Soviet nation was not the workers' paradise that it had been pictured in the early elated reports from Petrograd and Moscow. Letters from the disillusioned were read aloud at some of our meetings."[139] At the beginning of 1919, one writer noted that "a considerable number of Anarchists do not agree with the Bolsheviki in Russia." Two months later, *Il Bollettino de l'Era Nuova* urged its readers to "aid the Bolsheviks in all that truly serves the emancipation of the proletariat" but followed with a warning that the Bolsheviks made use of "a government, of an authority that, however different in form from capitalist governments and authority, will be a substantial obstacle to all additional progress."[140] Russian-speaking anarchists, who had access to copies of Petrograd's *Golos Truda*, were firmer in their rejection of bolshevism. During a conference of Russian radicals convened in New York to establish the Soviet of Workers' Deputies of the United States and Canada, controversy erupted when anarchist delegates refused to endorse the Bolshevik regime. Some Marxist delegates walked out in disgust, and others labeled the dissenters "Anarcho-Mensheviks" and "counterrevolutionists." This prompted a reprimand from the Comintern, which, ironically, demanded cooperation with the anarchists.[141]

In February 1919, Robert Minor, who had arrived in Russia on the eve of the April 1918 raids against the anarchists, published the first in a series of articles in the *New York Evening World* and *Butte Daily Bulletin*. Minor painted a picture of a popular revolution in which "workmen had taken the factories, and the peasants the land," and "anarchistic syndicalism was practically controlling the industries of Russia." Then the Bolsheviks had taken power, legalized what had already occurred, and turned against the anarchists, who became "the strongest opponents Lenin now has."[142] The first issue of the *Anarchist Soviet Bulletin* defended Minor against his critics, and the publication later explained that the Communists had "no faith in the workers' intelligence and capacity to run things himself [*sic*]"; therefore "Bolshevism stands for *new slavery—Centralized Government*," whereas "Anarchism stands for Decentralization—for *real freedom*."[143] *Il Martello*, however, dismissed Minor as an "intellectual" writing for the "reactionary" press and continued to support the Soviet regime until 1921.[144]

Nevertheless, in 1920, the trickle of critical anarchist writings became a deluge. Rudolf Rocker's essay, "Soviet System or Dictatorship?," first serialized in the *Fraye Arbeter Shtime*, praised soviets as model revolutionary bodies, in contrast to a revolutionary dictatorship, which Rocker labeled "Jacobin" and "wholly bourgeois and as such, has nothing to do with socialism." The following month, Luigi Galleani, having reestablished *Cronaca Sovversiva* in Turin after his deportation from the United States, condemned Lenin in a series of articles and sent four thousand copies of each issue of the resurrected paper back to the United States.[145] Kropotkin's final warnings were also reprinted in American papers.[146]

In addition, between 1922 and 1924, Berkman and Goldman wrote several influential critiques of the Communist dictatorship, and Berkman compiled a valuable collection of firsthand accounts from Russian political prisoners, published as a book by a committee of American radicals and liberals headed by American Civil Liberties Union cofounder Roger Baldwin.[147] Most of these publications were bankrolled by one thousand dollars wired to Berkman in Berlin by Michael Cohn, who wrote to his old friend in May 1922, "I am busy lecturing against Bolshevism. You know, I presume, that I was a hog-headed Bolsh[evik] for the first 2, 3 years following the Soviet Revolution. But the Vetcheka's recent activities, the requisitions in the villages of Russia, the Kronstadt uprising and also the recent face about of the Bol. Regime itself, made my position untenable."[148]

Only a small number of American anarchists became and remained full-fledged Communists. To the shock of his former comrades, one of them was

Minor, an early anti-Communist who announced his conversion to Leninism in late 1920 after reading *The State and Revolution*.[149] In response, between stays at Ellis Island, Shmuel Marcus used the pseudonym Fred S. Graham to pen a seventy-page pamphlet that made liberal use of quotations from Minor's previous critiques of the Bolsheviks to counter his more recent arguments. In January 1921, Marcus also relaunched the *Anarchist Soviet Bulletin* under the new title *Free Society*, noting that the word *soviet* had become too closely associated with the Communist regime and that the soviets themselves "had become nothing but . . . tools in the hands of the Communist (Bolshevik) Party."[150] The half-imaginary American Anarchist Federated Commune Soviets was similarly rechristened the Anarchist Communist Groups of the United States and Canada, and its members coauthored a manifesto on the Russian Revolution condemning the Bolsheviks for "*leaving the masses* and establishing themselves into a *Centralized Dictatorial Government over the masses*," when the "duty of every sincere Revolutionist was to *remain among and with the masses*, always trying to show them the right way."[151] In 1921, the *Fraye Arbeter Shtime*'s publication committee also discharged that newspaper's Communist editors and recruited Philadelphia's Joseph Cohen to turn it back into an explicitly anarchist publication.

Anarchist analyses of the Russian Revolution agreed on several key points. First, the popular insurrection of February 1917 and the numerous forms of self-organization that followed, from soviets and factory committees to militias and partisan armies, corroborated anarchists' faith in the capacity of ordinary people to collectively overthrow their oppressors and restructure society from below. "The Russian masses," Alexander Berkman reflected, "were not too 'backward' to abolish the Tsar, to defeat the Provisional Government, to destroy capitalism and the wage system, to turn the land over to the peasantry and the industries to the workers." However, "disastrous results were inevitable" from the moment the Bolsheviks seized power. "Not that they are insincere men, or that their intentions are evil," Emma Goldman insisted; rather, the "principles and methods of Bolshevism," aimed at seizing and consolidating state power, inexorably determined the course of events. "The very means they have employed," argued Goldman, "have destroyed the realisation of their end." A dictatorship of any minority party—especially one faced with civil war and foreign intervention—would necessarily resort to unilateral decrees and terror, thereby becoming a "dictatorship *over* the proletariat."[152]

Anarchists were also the first of many left-wing critics to label the economic structure of the Soviet Union "state capitalism." By this they did not mean that the economy was capitalist in the traditional sense—as it largely lacked markets and competition—but rather that under state ownership, the relations between workers, employers, and the means of production remained exploitative, and "inherent social antagonisms" (that is, class conflict) persisted. Anarchists further viewed the reforms reinstating limited private enterprise under Lenin's New Economic Policy as a synthesis of traditional and state capitalism that "made the proletarian 'dictator' a common, every-day wage slave, like his brother in countries unblessed with Socialist dictatorship."[153]

These critiques were rooted in anarchism's theory of class, which differed from Marxists' strictly economic definition. In the anarchist view, political power exercised through a monopoly over the means of coercion was analogous to ownership of the means of production. Russian Jewish anarchist Abba Gordin later explicitly compared the two: "A ruler is an owner. He owns a certain Public force, a public energy. He uses and, very often, almost always, abuses it."[154] In other words, anarchists perceived two overlapping forms of class division, one economic and the other political. A "workers' state" was therefore a contradiction in terms, as state functionaries and political leaders constituted a separate class with its own interests—the consolidation and perpetuation of its own political and economic power. This was, in essence, the same objection that some anarchists had leveled against statist national liberation struggles. Paradoxically, therefore, the Russian Revolution substantiated anarchist doctrines. In 1922, the first issue of *L'Adunata dei Refrattari* flatly stated this contradiction: "Our hopes of a worldwide revolution fell, reconfirming us, with a practical demonstration, in our theoretical affirmations."[155]

In Italy, another attempted revolt yielded significantly different results. Many anarchists deported or fleeing from the United States arrived there just in time for the upheaval known as the Biennio Rosso (Two Red Years) of 1919–20. Mass protests against Italy's postwar economic crisis expanded into factory takeovers that spawned a network of factory councils and armed Red Guards, bringing the country to the brink of revolution. Italy's anarchist movement, Socialist Party, and labor unions all grew tremendously, and anarchists played a major role in the factory occupations, especially in the industrial center of Turin. At the same time, Benito Mussolini's Fascist movement made common cause with Italian capitalists and targeted radicals and working-class institutions with extralegal violence, leading to two years of virtual civil war on the streets of Italian cities.[156] In May 1921, Sicilian anarchist Paolo Schicchi wrote to his comrade Joe Russo of Oakland, California, "We are fighting the *Fascisti*. We have been the only ones fighting them with success. Help us. I need above all a good gun and an excellent pistol."[157]

Following Mussolini's ascension to power in 1922, the reaction was swift and fierce. The new regime imprisoned tens of thousands of radicals and anti-Fascists and placed another 160,000 under surveillance, while Fascist *squadristi* continued to engage in street violence. Historian Carl Levy writes, "Between 1921 and 1926 the anarchist rank and file were driven out of the factories and forced into poverty and exile. The anarchists probably suffered greater violence in proportion to their numbers than other political opponents of fascism."[158] Turin's *Cronaca Sovversiva* was shut down in October 1920, and Rome's *Umanità Nova* was closed at the end of 1922. In November of that year, Luigi Galleani was sentenced to the first of several prison sentences; he remained the subject of surveillance and harassment until his death from a heart attack in 1931. Paterson bombing suspect Ruggero Bacchini was involved in numerous clashes with Fascists in his native Lazio, where he suffered a gunshot wound and received a short prison sentence. In 1927, he was charged with murder and fled to France.[159]

A few former anarchists, however, were incorporated into the new Fascist government. In its early years, Italian fascism encompassed a wide spectrum of tendencies and included a number of former syndicalists and a much smaller group of former anarchists who had, like the erstwhile Socialist Mussolini, embraced interventionism during the First World War. Among them were former emigrants Edmondo Rossoni and Massimo Rocca, who briefly became the regime's leading economic theorist. However, in 1924, he was expelled from the Fascist Party as a result of differences with Mussolini, and two years later, Fascist violence forced him to flee to Paris, where, despite his estrangement from the Italian government, he acted as an informant for its secret police.[160] Other beleaguered anarchists "gave in and swore allegiance to the regime."[161]

One such individual was former IWW organizer Luigi Parenti. After returning to Italy with his family, Parenti participated in anarchist activities and continued to subscribe to banned Italian American publications such as *Il Martello* and the IWW's *Il Proletario*. In 1926 he attended a convention of the outlawed Unione Sindacale Italiana. In 1928, however, he traveled to Rome to meet with Edmondo Rossoni, whom Parenti had known in America through the IWW, and began working on behalf of state-controlled Fascist labor unions and as a correspondent for a Fascist paper in Livorno. Parenti's relatives in San Francisco permanently cut all ties with him, and in 1929, Italian authorities reported that he "demonstrates obedience to the directives of the Regime." Yet early the following year, the same authorities discovered that Parenti was still secretly receiving copies of *Il Martello* shipped from the United States. In 1932, he again reportedly displayed "ideas in full agreement with the directives of the Regime." These oddly contradictory reports suggest that for at least some time, Parenti publicly played the part of a dutiful Fascist citizen while secretly maintaining his anarchist ideals.[162]

In the United States, a few anarchist interventionists joined the Fascist cause. Wartime Italian nationalism served as "a sort of halfway house on the road to fascism for radicals who had become disenchanted with working-class empathy across ethnic lines," including former anarcho-syndicalist Umberto Menicucci, who sat on the directorate of the first Italian American Fascist club, formed in New York in 1921. Edmondo Rossoni's former collaborator, Domenico Trombetta, edited the notorious Fascist paper *Il Grido della Stirpe* (The Cry of the Race) and sat on the Central Council of the Fascist League of North America, and former anarchist and Federazione Socialista Italiana member Filippo Bocchini of Philadelphia founded the Fascist Party of Pennsylvania in 1934.[163] For the rest of the Italian anarchist movement, however, the fight against fascism became an all-consuming cause.

The geopolitical consequences of the First World War proved disastrous for anarchism across much of Europe and the United States. Wartime patriotism, state repression, and the emergence of potent new political ideologies completely uprooted the anarchism of some radicals. Yet the majority stayed the course. As Hippolyte Havel noted in 1918, "The authorities may deport a few poor devils, but never anarchism."[164]

Though few recognized it at the time, the most damaging American postwar development came in the form of the Immigration Act of 1924. The First World War interrupted more than three decades of mass migration from Southern and Eastern Europe, but the 250,000 Italians who arrived between 1920 and 1924 suggested that earlier patterns would resume. Before they could, however, a convergence of nativist, eugenicist, and antiradical influences coalesced in the most sweeping immigration restrictions in American history. In addition to banning virtually all migration from Asia and Africa, the act severely limited the number of Southern and Eastern European migrants who could enter the United States each year.[165] Although fear of foreign anarchists and Bolsheviks played a secondary role in crafting this legislation, the law inadvertently struck at the very root of the domestic anarchist movement and its global connections: transnational working-class mobility. These controls were neither total nor immediate—they went fully into effect only in 1928—but the consequences for America's Yiddish and Italian anarchist movements were inevitable: cut off from a significant influx of potential new recruits, they would wither away. Yet this process would take more than a decade, during which time anarchists struggled to keep alive their cosmopolitan vision.

CHAPTER 6

"NO RIGHT TO EXIST ANYWHERE ON THIS EARTH"
ANARCHISM IN CRISIS

In January 1925, ILGWU organizer and anarchist Anna Sosnovsky noted "a general revival amongst the Comrades." By 1933, one anarchist newspaper counted seventy-five anarchist groups across the country, and a U.S. military intelligence agent reported "a keen revival of activities among the anarchists" on the East Coast. At the end of this period of recovery, anarchist sources could enumerate "some one hundred groups throughout the country actually functioning."[1] This persistence and modest resurgence is reflected in available circulation figures from the era, which show that from 1925 to 1940 the American anarchist press retained approximately half to three-quarters of its prewar readership. The spread of multiethnic, English-speaking "international groups" led to the unprecedented growth of the English-language anarchist press, while Italian-language anarchist periodicals maintained a higher combined circulation between 1925 and 1933 than at any time prior (see figures 1 and 2).

The Italian movement's revitalization resulted in part from the arrival of anti-Fascist exiles, including anarcho-syndicalist leader Armando Borghi and his companion, poet Virgilia D'Andrea, both of whom lectured across the country. Despite his anarchism, Borghi obtained a visa, while D'Andrea gained entry by legally marrying a comrade in Brooklyn who was a naturalized American citizen. Others came secretly and illegally, including Raffaele Schiavina, who had been deported with Luigi Galleani in 1919, participated in armed resistance to fascism in Turin, emigrated to France in 1923, and clandestinely returned to New York in 1928. There, under the assumed name Max Sartin, he became editor of *L'Adunata dei Refrattari*. Ottavio Volpin and Giovanni Vattuone escaped by joining the Italian navy and then jumping ship in New York.[2] The peripatetic Enrico Arrigoni (aka Frank Brand or Branch), by contrast, paid a ship captain to smuggle him and two comrades from Cuba to New Orleans in 1924. In 1928, after time abroad, Arrigoni obtained a visa to reenter the United States using a false Colombian birth certificate he had purchased in Havana, which he also used in 1936 when he became a naturalized citizen.[3] Dozens or even hundreds of additional, lesser-known anarchists clandestinely entered the United States during Mussolini's rule, defying tightening restrictions on both Italian emigration and American immigration.

Long-standing cross-border connections with Canada and Mexico facilitated such crossings. Joining the Mexican Revolution, evading conscription, and routine travel to attend radical events or organize workers across America's borders created networks and established routes that were later used by foreign anarchists with real passports, counterfeit or borrowed ones, or none at all. For example, World War I "slacker" Alberico Pirani purchased a fake passport in Venezuela that he used to reenter the United States in 1919, and he later loaned the forged document to both Armando Borghi and Enrico Arrigoni for travel abroad. Italian anarchist and IWW organizer Romolo Bobba, husband of Elizabeth Gurley Flynn's sister, Bina, smuggled individuals across the Canadian border hidden in the rumble seat of his automobile.[4]

Grigorii Petrovich Maksimov, a leading Russian anarcho-syndicalist who was imprisoned and then expelled by the Bolsheviks, made his way to Canada in 1925 with the aid of an affidavit of support he bribed a Canadian farmer to supply. He was then smuggled by boat across Lake Erie and into Detroit by a comrade. He later wrote detailed instructions to a friend and fellow exile, former Nabat Confederation member Mark Mratchny, who followed the same path into the country in 1928.[5] Even as security was tightening along America's northern border, it largely targeted Asians; for many anarchists, therefore, "the border acted more as an inconvenience to be worked around than an impenetrable barrier."[6] However, as Maksimov warned Mratchny, the more heavily patrolled U.S.-Mexico border was no longer a dependable point of entry. Enrico Arrigoni, for one, was arrested and deported in 1922 after wading across the Rio Grande in his first attempt to enter the United States.[7] Although the American state was increasing its capacity to regulate immigration and passed legislation that ended mass transatlantic migration, thousands of determined individuals with adequate funds or connections still illegally crossed its borders each year, including anarchists.[8]

Nevertheless, anarchism was becoming increasingly isolated during what Joseph Cohen called the movement's "defensive" era.[9] Communism, fascism, and Zionism all outflanked libertarian socialism among America's immigrants, and for several years, the public face of the anarchist movement was reduced to the struggle to save the lives of Sacco and Vanzetti—a struggle that forced anarchists into unhappy alliances with Communist and liberal allies.[10] Even in San Francisco, where the movement's cosmopolitan practices reached their apex, anarchists exerted little influence on local events. The climatic and tragic peak of transnational anarchist activism came with the Spanish Civil War of 1936–39, in which Spain's anarchists faced impossible odds in their battle against fascism. The defeat in Spain also constituted a devastating loss for the American anarchist movement.

The anti-Communist imperative imposed on anarchists by their analyses of the Soviet Union propelled them into major conflicts within the labor movement, and at an enormous cost. The Industrial Workers of the World collapsed following the Red Scare and a disastrous 1924 split between "decentralists," supported by many anarchists, and "centralists," supported by the Communist Party: the organization had between twelve thousand and seventeen thousand members in 1925 and only between three thousand and eight thousand five years later.[11] By that time, IWW influence among the immigrant workers of Paterson and North Beach was a distant memory. This left the International Ladies' Garment Workers as the anarchist movement's last major union foothold.

The small but influential Yiddish anarchist cadre within the ILGWU included a number of veteran unionists who had moved up the union's hierarchy by the 1920s. These included Bernard Shane and Louis Levy, successive managers of Cloakmakers' Union Local 1; Joseph Schneider, Mendel (Max) Bluestein, and Leibush Frumkin, all members of the executive board of Dressmakers' Union Local 22; Nicholas Kirtzman, head of Local 9; and Morris Sigman, who moved up from ILGWU secretary-treasurer to general manager of the Joint Board of the Cloakmakers' Union and in 1920 to first vice president of the union. Israel Feinberg, who became general manager of the Joint Board of the Cloakmakers' Union after Sigman, as well as an ILGWU executive board member and vice president, had been an anarchist in London before migrating to New York in 1912, and although he strayed from the movement (in 1916 and 1920, he campaigned for Socialist congressman Meyer London), he maintained close anarchist ties.[12]

These figures were joined by a younger generation of rank-and-file militants, including Rose Pesotta, Anna Sosnovsky, Rose Mirsky, Sara Rothman, Clara Larsen, Isidore Wisotsky, Israel Ostroff, and Simon Farber. Moreover, when Saul Yanovsky was forced to step down as editor of the *Fraye Arbeter Shtime* in 1919, he immediately found a position editing the ILGWU's new newspaper, *Justice*, and its Yiddish-language edition, *Gerekhtikayt*, thanks to Morris Sigman's recommendation. Yanovsky received almost total editorial freedom, and according to one scholar, under his direction these publications became "among the liveliest and best edited labor papers of America."[13]

In 1917, a group of female dressmakers within Local 25, inspired by the Russian Revolution, formed a Current Events Committee that criticized the union's social democratic leadership as too conservative. The committee soon dissolved, but these sentiments remained, and in 1919, radical rank-and-file women formed the Workers' Council to advocate the creation of shop delegate leagues, modeled on Russian soviets, to replace the ILGWU's leadership structure. The shop delegate movement attracted Communist, left-wing Socialist, syndicalist, and anarchist members as well as support from the *Fraye Arbeter Shtime*. But in 1921, the shop delegate leagues affiliated with the Trade Union Educational League, which in 1922 joined the Soviet-controlled Red International of Labor Unions. Most non-Communist members promptly withdrew, and in the words of journalist Benjamin Stolberg, the anarchists, "who had played a leading role in the opposition movement from the beginning, at last realized that the Communists had captured the whole left flank" of the union.[14]

The Socialist leadership of the ILGWU, still stinging from the Communists' unpleasant split from the Socialist Party in 1919, acted decisively against this growing threat by ruling that the leagues violated the union's constitution. However, this action did little more than engender sympathy for the radicals and further tarnish the administration's reputation. At a special February 1923 convention, Morris Sigman, who was affiliated with neither party and respected by the rank and file, was elected president of the ILGWU. But his selection came with an unofficial mandate from both his anarchist comrades and his Socialist Party backers to quash Communist influence, and he lost little time in this regard. Sigman ruled that the shop delegate leagues constituted dual unions, and he ejected several Communists from the union or deprived them of the right to hold office, while dissolving or reorganizing Communist-controlled locals.[15] Moreover, at the union's 1924 convention, Pesotta—whose lover and fellow anarchist Theodore Kushnarev had been deported on the *Buford* and briefly imprisoned by the Bolsheviks—introduced a motion demanding the release of all political prisoners in the Soviet Union, which passed by a vote of 222 to 25. Thereafter, in the revealing words of anarchist Isidore Wisotsky, "The Russian Revolution was fought out on the streets of New York and in meeting Halls."[16]

Yanovsky continued to criticize the Soviet Union from his post as editor of *Justice* and *Gerekhtikayt* and declared that the Communists of the ILGWU's self-described "Left" faction (anarchists invariably placed contemptuous quotation marks around the term) were a "cancer, that is devouring the innards of the union" and had to be removed "with a strong, fast hand."[17] An ad hoc Anarchist Group of the ILGWU published its own newspaper, *Der Yunyon Arbayter* (The Union Worker), from December 1925 to July 1927, with former

FIGURE 13. Morris Sigman (*center, with glasses*) and Fiorello LaGuardia (*left*), ca. 1924. Courtesy of the Kheel Center for Labor-Management Documentation and Archives, M. P. Catherwood Library, Cornell University.

shop delegate movement leader Simon Farber serving as editor. The Anarchist Group also convened conferences, often featuring Sigman, to make its case against the Communists to union members, but these gatherings were poorly attended and marred by disruptions and scuffles with their opponents.[18] *Der Yunyon Arbayter* criticized both the "'Left' demagogues" of the "communist clique" and the Socialist officials of the "Right machine," but its anticommunism placed it in de facto coalition with the Socialists.[19]

A few anarchists refused to support such an alliance. Sosnovsky accused both factions in the ILGWU's "civil war" of "seeking nothing but control," while Simon Farber's brother-in-law, Abraham Blecher, insisted that "we, as anarchists, cannot align ourselves with the officials." Isidore Farbiash, by contrast, sided with the Communist faction because he "thought they were more effective and also I liked their slogan of a maximum of two years for all union officers," but he abandoned it in 1926 after becoming disillusioned with its tactics and motives.[20] Meanwhile, the small number of Italian anarchists in the union, as well as Carlo Tresca and other outside commentators, admired the Communists' militancy and supported their demands for greater rank-and-file representation. A majority within the union's two all-Italian locals, however, stood with Luigi Antonini, president of Local 89, in support of Sigman. Even Antonini, however, butted heads with Yanovsky by refusing to take an uncompromising stand against all of the Communists' demands.[21]

Sigman, the unlikely anarchist president, found his own loyalties divided among the majority of union members who supported the Communists' program, the Yiddish anarchist movement to which he felt himself beholden, and the social democrats whose support was critical to maintaining his position. One anonymous union member later noted that Sigman "didn't have his own power."[22] Urged on by his anarchist and Socialist allies, he had resorted to startlingly authoritarian tactics against the Communists. But in 1925, under pressure from the powerful *Forverts* to bring the conflict to an end, Sigman negotiated a truce that allowed expelled Communists back into the union. The night before Sigman announced the agreement, a delegation of four anarchists, including Simon Farber, stayed up arguing with him for hours. Farber later recalled, "We were all in tears. Sigman pleading, 'I agree fully with you. I am aware of the danger lurking in the peace settlement; but what can I do? The *Forward* is threatening to cut off my support. Besides I do not want people to accuse me later of being the cause of the ruin of the ILGWU.'"[23] Israel Feinberg resigned from the Joint Board and General Executive Board to protest the settlement, and Yanovsky likewise resigned rather than condone the concessions to "the worst enemies of the union."[24]

This uneasy peace ultimately was undermined by resistance from Socialist union officials such as David Dubinsky as well as by Sigman's refusal to accept the Communists' demand that he endorse the formation of an American labor party. The breach fully reopened after Communist organizers led a disastrous 1926 strike of New York cloak makers, and Sigman once again suspended Communist members. By 1928, the union's civil war had decimated its treasury and membership and left "several dead and hundreds injured and maimed."[25] Sigman was reelected ILGWU president in 1928 but resigned after the General Executive Board divided locals he had previously amalgamated on an industrial union model, reversing what he viewed as one of the few constructive accomplishments of his administration.[26] He left New York and died on his Iowa farm in 1931. The Communists seceded and founded an ill-fated dual union, leaving the ILGWU's leadership in the hands of the increasingly moderate social democrats.

A handful of anarchists remained significant figures in the union. Farber became editor of *Gerekhtikayt* in 1929, Feinberg was placed in charge of the ILGWU's Pacific Coast District in 1932, and Pesotta was elected a union vice president in 1934. In 1930, the anarchist Dressmakers Trade Union Circle pressured the union to appoint its first Spanish and Greek organizers, and the following year, Max Bluestein, manager of Local 22, negotiated the reentry of followers of the dissident former Communist Jay Lovestone into the ILGWU. The Lovestonites joined with the anarchists to form a strong "Progressive" bloc within the union, but this coalition was little more than a loyal opposition. As a critical anarchist journal noted in 1935, "Because [the anarchists] did not take an independent position and swung their influence to the corrupt officialdom [of the ILGWU], they unwittingly became a support for the machine politicians."[27] Moreover, even as anarchist women took on prominent roles in the anti-Communist struggle, their defense of the union's male leadership against the majority of its predominantly female membership further entrenched the gendered division of power.[28] Yet little choice existed. In the postwar political realignment of the Left and labor movement, anarchism had been pushed to the margins.

The broader Yiddish anarchist movement was likewise in a state of crisis. Radical Jews, including a small number of former anarchists such as Mike Gold, flocked to the Communist Party in the 1920s and 1930s, comprising an estimated half of its membership.[29] American anti-Semitism also reached its peak in the interwar years and, coupled with increasing persecution of European Jewry and the promise of the Balfour Declaration, contributed to a dramatic rise in support for Zionism. The growth of both of these movements came in part at the expense of anarchism, especially as they attracted politically active Jews who might otherwise have joined anarchist ranks. Demographics presented another challenge. The tight-knit working-class immigrant community in which Yiddish anarchism was based was coming apart both geographically and socially. By 1920, only 40 percent of New York City's Jews lived in Manhattan, as opportunity and economic mobility carried increasing numbers to better housing available in Brooklyn and other outlying boroughs. By 1930, another 160,000 Jews had left the Lower East Side.[30] (Ironically, anarchist engineer Leon Moisseiff was indirectly responsible for facilitating these departures, having designed the Manhattan Bridge, across which much of this exodus flowed.) The generational divide between Jewish immigrants and their American-born, English-speaking children further undermined the cultural foundations of Yiddish radicalism, as English newspapers, motion pictures, radio, and other forms of mass consumer culture replaced the Yiddish theater and radical press.

The Union of Russian Workers, which renamed itself the Union of Russian Toilers in 1922, was virtually wiped out as a consequence of return migration and the Red Scare, and by the mid-1920s, the *Fraye Arbeter Shtime*'s circulation had slipped to between seven thousand and ten thousand, a third of its prewar peak.[31] The minority of insurrectionist Jewish anarchists clustered around the "eight or ten secret groups" that constituted the Anarchist Communist Groups of the United States and Canada and the Russian Federation of Anarchist Communists of the United States and Canada, which in 1923 unsuccessfully attempted to secure Nestor Makhno's passage to the United States and bemoaned the fact that "today the influence of anarchistic ideas on Jewish life is completely dead. The movement is demoralized and altogether broken."[32]

The task of salvaging the diminishing movement fell to the *Fraye Arbeter Shtime*'s new editor, Joseph Cohen. Though a reserved and emotionally distant man, what Cohen lacked in charisma he made up for in tenacity: his friend and mentor Voltairine de Cleyre described him as "undaunted, indefatigable, and—yes, inscrutable." In 1921, Cohen oversaw the formation of the Jewish Anarchist Federation of America and Canada, which had twenty-five chapters at its founding and guaranteed the *Fraye Arbeter Shtime* a stable base of financial and organizational support.[33] The federation maintained a high level of activity, and in the early 1920s, members in New York opened a Free Workers' Center on Second Avenue that "always buzzed with activity" such as lectures, meetings, and dances and featured a vegetarian diner run by Cohen's wife, Ida.[34]

Under Cohen, the anarchism of the *Fraye Arbeter Shtime* became even more moderate. According to his friend Harry Kelly, by 1924, Cohen had "practically given up the idea of revolution and from all accounts he seems pretty pessimistic over things."[35] The Jewish Anarchist Federation officially condemned violence and adopted a gradualist, reformist approach, which Shmuel Marcus dismissed as "*Marxian*" and "revisionism."[36] Both factions tried to expand their bases beyond Yiddish-speaking immigrants. Marcus had already abandoned the Yiddish movement to his opponents in order to address "the necessity for the creation of an English-speaking Anarchist movement in the United States," concentrating his energies on the *Anarchist Soviet Bulletin* and *Free Society*.[37] In 1922, Cohen proposed introducing an English-language page into the *Fraye Arbeter Shtime*, explaining, "I want the children of our Jewish readers to get acquainted with the libertarian ideas and movements." Another decade passed before a four-page English supplement, *The Voice of Youth*, finally appeared, but American-born readers found it "old-fashioned and outdated," and it was discontinued after the Post Office ruled that it constituted a separate publication requiring additional postage.[38]

Both the Jewish Anarchist Federation and the Anarchist Communist Groups of the United States and Canada sent delegates to the International Anarchist Congress held in Berlin from December 25, 1921 to February 2, 1922, the first such gathering since 1907. Harry Kelly, an American-born Gentile married to a Jewish anarchist, represented the Jewish Anarchist Federation; he arrived late but delivered "a detailed account" of the state of the American labor movement. The assembled delegates unanimously condemned the Soviet "dictatorship of the proletariat," and over the objections of the Anarchist Communist Groups and other insurrectionists, a majority passed a resolution calling for anarchist participation in the formation of a Syndicalist International scheduled to occur in Berlin in December 1922.[39] There, anarchists took the lead in founding the syndicalist International Working Men's Association, but because the IWW decided not to take part, the new organization had no American affiliate.[40]

The need to expand beyond the Yiddish milieu intermittently reconciled members of the two Jewish factions. The newly formed International Group of New York, a coalition of Jews, Italians, Spaniards, native-born Americans, and a smattering of others, included Pesotta and Marcus, and in 1924 it launched its own paper, *The Road to Freedom*. But Marcus's intransigent views put him "on the fringe always alone." Disgusted that the new publication was being "corrupted" by working "hand in hand" with partisans of the *Fraye Arbeter Shtime*, he left the group in 1925.[41] Marcus then retreated for a time to the multiethnic anarchist colony in rural Stelton, New Jersey, home to a number of moderate Jewish anarchists. There, his longtime desire to work the land was made more challenging by his refusal to exploit or harm animals—the fiery revolutionist who called for armed revolution against the ruling class was a strict vegan who wore rubber boots instead of leather shoes, plowed the soil at Stelton by hand instead of using the draft horses, and painstakingly removed potato bugs from the field and released them into the woods (prompting his friend, anarchist archivist Agnes Inglis, to inquire, "Can potato bugs live in the woods, without potatoes?").[42] Such actions were indicative of Marcus's refusal to compromise: according to Joseph Cohen, "nature endowed him with a measure of obstinacy, *chutzpah*, and a hot revolutionary temperament."[43] During his time at Stelton, Marcus gravitated toward the similarly intransigent adherents of *L'Adunata dei Refrattari*, to which he began contributing occasional articles.

Another factor that bridged factional and linguistic divides was the campaign to save the lives of Sacco and Vanzetti, which become a global crusade uniting radicals, liberals, and labor movements.[44] Most of Marcus's articles for *L'Adunata dei Refrattari* were English-language appeals on behalf of the condemned anarchists, while *Fraye Arbeter Shtime* supporter Michael Cohn poured his own time and money into the cause, even authoring two pamphlets about the case and publishing them at his own expense. A few weeks before his execution on August 23, 1927, Vanzetti scrawled a short note of thanks to Cohn in broken English: "I feel to like and love you who call me brother and correct my agony. All my heart is in this few words."[45] The state-sponsored killings of Sacco and Vanzetti were heartbreaking for the anarchists, who had labored for a nearly a decade to prevent this outcome.

Coalitions across factional lines rarely lasted, however. The heterogeneity of the International Group of New York led to constant infighting, and *The*

Road to Freedom remained financially insolvent. In 1928, contributor Joseph Spivak complained of "the lack of interest in the English propaganda and the lack of the proper methods of organization," claiming, "There are enough active anarchists in this country to build one of the strongest movements" if only the insularity of the ethnic groups had not prevented their unification. At an anarchist conference convened by the International Group later that year, Hippolyte Havel also lamented the lack of an "American" anarchist movement, noting that instead there existed "a Spanish Anarchist movement, Italian Anarchist movement, a Jewish Anarchist movement etc." Kelly somberly observed that as a consequence of the recent immigration restrictions, "within the next 25 years, 95% of the present language papers will have disappeared because . . . there will be no one to read the foreign language papers. The movement must be in the English language which will be the language of the future." But others had no faith that the "American type" would adopt anarchist ideas, pointing out that many of the "foreign comrades" were not literate in English.[46]

Although Kelly's prediction was sound, it did not address the fact that Yiddish and Italian anarchism were deeply embedded in specific ethnic and linguistic communities and therefore could not be transformed into component parts of a generic, English-speaking "American" movement. Doing so would have destroyed the bedrock on which American anarchism rested. Caught in this contradiction, *The Road to Freedom* folded in 1932. A series of "English Propaganda Conferences" conducted by the International Group over the following year established a new weekly paper, *Freedom*, edited by an unlikely trio consisting of Kelly, former IWW organizer Manuel Rey y García (aka Louis Raymond), and Austrian dentist and anarchist Moritz Jagendorf. But *Freedom* collapsed after seventeen months because of chronic financial difficulties and because, Kelly admitted, it "did not reach an American audience."[47]

Italian anarchists had much more pressing concerns than future demographics. Admiration, sympathy, and support for Mussolini had become ubiquitous within Italian American communities by the end of the 1920s. Although only an estimated 5 percent of America's Italian-born population could be counted as "out-and-out" Fascists, the influential *prominenti* rallied behind fascism for their own benefit, and the vast majority of Italian workers were thrilled by Mussolini's mission to make Italy a great power. By contrast, just one in ten Italian Americans are believed to have held anti-Fascist convictions.[48] Respect for Mussolini also ran high in certain sections of the American government, which collaborated with the Fascist regime to attempt to deport anti-Fascist radicals back to Italy, where they could be imprisoned.[49]

The epicenter of Italian American fascism and its opposition was New York City, where in 1923, Carlo Tresca was the driving force behind the formation of the Anti-Fascist Alliance of North America (AFANA), a United Front effort composed of anarchists, syndicalists, Socialists, Communists, and the Italian sections of the garment workers' unions. Tresca and his comrades maintained unusually good relations with Italian Communists, viewing them as important allies in this struggle. However, the AFANA's social democratic and garment union majority left the organization in 1926 in response to growing Communist influence as well as the contemporaneous struggle occurring within the ILGWU. These dissidents formed their own short-lived Anti-Fascist League for the Freedom of Italy, but Tresca and his allies remained with the AFANA until 1932, when Tresca finally found the Communists' "zig-zag politics" intolerable.[50]

The *galleanisti* of *L'Adunata dei Refrattari* refused to cooperate with either Communists or Tresca, whom they considered a Soviet sympathizer and a charlatan. The notion of a United Front with Communists against fascism was absurd, they argued, because "all the characteristics, practices, and tendencies" of Soviet communism and Italian fascism were identical. "It will not be because one or the other dictatorship killed or imprisoned or deported or burned a few more or a few less that we will favor the Fascist or the Bolshevik dictatorship with more sympathy." It was incomprehensible to aid the agents of Soviet totalitarianism in the name of combating Fascist totalitarianism.[51] This rejection was made easier by the fact that Italian anarchists far outnumbered Italian Communists in America; the Italian Federation of the Communist Party never exceeded one thousand members.[52]

The anarchists sustained their battle against Mussolini's supporters however they could—with invectives, humor, fists, bricks, baseball bats, stilettos, pistols, or explosives, as the situation demanded.[53] In Italy, at least five anarchists made attempts on Mussolini's life or were arrested while preparing to carry out such deeds between 1926 and 1933, and most of these would-be assassins received aid from America. In 1929, Italian anarchists in the United States and France hatched an unrealized plan to kill the dictator while he visited Milan, and in April 1931, Emidio Recchioni, a London anarchist and delicatessen owner, placed a call in *L'Adunata dei Refrattari* to raise funds "for our war"—that is, to finance Mussolini's assassination. Recchioni himself donated a thousand dollars to the cause, and within several months *L'Adunata* had collected another ten thousand dollars.[54] This money funded Brooklyn anarchist Michele Schirru, a naturalized American citizen, who journeyed to Rome to kill the dictator but was betrayed and arrested before taking action and executed by firing squad. In 1933, Mussolini's agents discovered another plot involving Pittsburgh-based anarchist Vincenzo Capuana, though Capuana was tried and convicted only of entering Italy using a false passport.[55]

Paterson's anarchists were fully committed to the anti-Fascist campaign. In 1924, a year before his death, Pedro Esteve cofounded Brooklyn's anti-Fascist paper *Umanità Nova*. An unofficial successor to the suppressed Roman anarchist publication of the same name, the paper declared its intent to engage in "all of those actions, without exception, tending to repay to the greatest criminals in recorded history, tit for tat [*pan per focaccia*]."[56] Esteve also wrote for Tresca's *Il Martello*, which had numerous subscribers in Paterson. That city's Circolo Educativo Sociale (Social Education Circle), formed by anarchists following the suppression of the Francisco Ferrer Association, raised funds for both *Umanità Nova* and *Il Martello* and published its own anti-Fascist pamphlets. In 1923, members of the Circolo organized the Anti-Fascist League of Paterson, with Alberto Guabello at its head. In 1926, this group became a branch of the Anti-Fascist Alliance of North America. The league was largely made up of veteran anarchists and IWW members, including Paolo Guabello, Firmino Gallo, Eligio Strobino, and Pietro Baldisserotto, all now in their forties and fifties. An affiliate also formed in neighboring Haledon, and the two groups founded the Anti-Fascist Federation of New Jersey.[57]

In 1924, the Anti-Fascist League of Paterson launched its own publication, *La Scopa* (The Broom), with offices located in the old storefront of the Francisco Ferrer Association. Former anarchist printer Beniamino Mazzotta, "a clever, terrible punster," and former Ferrer Association member Francesco Pitea, a poet who wrote under the name Libero Arsenio, served as its editors.[58] *La Scopa* was a unique publication that used humor as its weapon of choice against fascism; its cartoons, satirical poems and songs, and sarcastic editorials exposed the hypocrisy and criminality of the Italian regime and its local supporters. Included among the latter were Paterson's Italian Chamber of Commerce and the Italian consul, Matteo Ricco, whose office was just two blocks from *La Scopa*'s. The paper was partially funded by Alberto and Adalgisa Guabello, who by 1926 had retired from the silk mills and opened a "Stationery, Ice-Cream & Cigar Store" two doors down from *La Scopa*'s headquarters. Both the paper and the Anti-Fascist League also received support from the Associated Silk Workers, an independent union founded in 1919 by a local coalition of Italian anarchists, German syndicalists, Jewish Socialists, Labor Zionists, and Communists that led a successful 1924 strike of five thousand weavers against the multiple-loom system.[59]

Alberto Guabello, like Tresca, urged his comrades to prioritize practical action and broad coalitions over ideological purity, and in March 1926, he and twenty other prominent Italian American radicals and labor leaders signed a public declaration renouncing their Italian citizenship.[60] The Anti-Fascist League favored a United Front with Communists and other anti-Fascists and remained affiliated with the AFANA after the 1926 split. However, conflict between the Communist and anti-Communist elements within the Associated Silk Workers could not be contained, and in the midst of a failed 1928 strike for the eight-hour day, twenty-two Communist Party members who had gained control of the strike committee were expelled, prompting the Communist faction to withdraw and form an ineffectual dual union.[61]

Nevertheless, the Anti-Fascist League met with remarkable success. Although the national Sons of Italy had aligned itself with Mussolini in 1922 and New Jersey was honeycombed with Fascist organizations—including groups in Camden, Garfield (where the local Sons of Italy lodge was named for Mussolini), Hackensack, Hoboken, Jersey City, Montclair, Nutley, Orange, Trenton, West Hoboken, and West New York—none appeared in Paterson or Haledon.[62] Members of the Anti-Fascist League were on hand to quash any pro-Fascist manifestations at Paterson's 1926 Columbus Day celebration but were happy to discover that "either fear, or prudence, or sense," prevented any from materializing. In May of the following year, a contributor to *La Scopa* wrote, "We note with pleasure that Paterson Fascism has evaporated." That December a *festa* held by the Anti-Fascist League of Haledon sold 504 admission tickets. Moreover, Haledon's police commissioner was none other than the son of Firmino Gallo and Ninfa Baronio, former Ferrer Association member and draft dodger William Gallo, who aided local anarchists when they were arrested during clashes with area Fascists.[63]

Such confrontations could turn deadly. In May 1926, Giovanni Faiddi, an anarchist in the neighboring city of Elizabeth, was gunned down after "a discussion" with a local Fascist leader named Castranova. And although Paterson's *organizzatori* did not indulge in bomb making, they did support the plots of their comrades in Europe. Alberto Guabello forwarded "large sums of money" to Italian anti-Fascists in France as well as to Emidio Recchioni's fund for Mussolini's assassination. Another Biellese anarchist, Vittorio Blotto, reportedly raised money for the cause in Somerville, New Jersey, by illegally producing alcohol and counterfeit American currency.[64]

La Scopa, however, struggled financially and closed in 1928, though the Anti-Fascist League persevered. That same year, Firmino Gallo was invited to Chicago to help edit the new anti-Fascist anarchist publication *Germinal*, but an injury that put him on crutches deterred him from making the move. Four years later, the Circolo Educativo Sociale was reconstituted as the Independent Social Club, which subsequently became the Dover Club. Under the guise of this Italian cultural society, anarchists continued their anti-Fascist agitation and attached the organization to the Mazzini Society, formed in New York in late 1939 by Italian anti-Fascist exiles.[65]

Shunned by his former comrades, still under threat of deportation, and in dire need of income to support his family, former anarchist editor Ludovico Caminita found employment working for the conservative *New York World* and *New York Herald* as well as for the pro-Fascist papers *Il Corriere d'America* and

Il Bollettino della Sera. In 1923, the anarchist paper *La Difesa* sneered, "Caminita has become a Fascist. When a dead body begins to roll downhill it has to hit bottom." The Italian consul in Paterson likewise reported that Caminita's former comrades "hate him for the substantial changes" to his politics but later surmised, "Much of this change of ideas was due to a sentence of deportation issued for Caminita."[66] In 1929, Caminita relocated his family to Scranton, Pennsylvania, where he took over the editorship of *Il Minatore* (The Miner), a local labor paper that reconciled "defending the rights of workers, nationalistic pride, and proclamations of loyalty to the regime of Rome." It even lionized members of the Fascist government and defended the passage of Italy's anti-Semitic Racial Laws in 1938. Yet in 1940, Caminita was forced to close down *Il Minatore* because his increasing divergence from the Fascist party line had caused Italian American advertisers to withdraw.[67] His last major undertaking was a celebratory 1943 biography of Amedeo Obici, the Italian entrepreneur who founded Planters Nut and Chocolate Company in Pennsylvania in 1906. On its surface, the book signaled the successful Americanization of a once-radical immigrant. But Caminita also lauded Obici's religious nonbelief, his antiracism, and his friendships with Socialists—hardly mainstream American values of the era. Moreover, the book's back page proudly listed "Other Works by Ludovico Caminita," including all of the anarchist tracts published during his Paterson days.[68] Despite his public proclamations to the contrary, traces of Caminita's radicalism remained.

In San Francisco, the Red Scare had smashed the vibrant Latin IWW movement, and a vigorous open-shop campaign launched in 1921 reduced union enrollment citywide by nearly a third within three years. But the 1920s were also years of economic opportunity, rising wages, and greater social acceptance for Bay Area Italians, who by 1930 numbered more than twenty-seven thousand, and the Great Depression affected the Italian community less than other local immigrant groups.[69] One sign of Italians' improving fortunes was the 1931 election of San Francisco mayor Angelo Rossi, the son of a Genoese gold rusher. Rossi, like most of the *prominenti*, was an outspoken Mussolini enthusiast. So was the editor of the city's largest Italian paper, *L'Italia*, which in 1936 purchased the liberal *La Voce del Popolo* to silence its criticisms of fascism. Even if fascism in North Beach was only, as one historian claims, "a confused bid for respect," it was nevertheless wildly popular.[70] But anarchists stood at the heart of what opposition did exist.

The Bay Area's Italian anarchist community grew in the 1920s as a consequence of resettlement from the East Coast as well as the arrival of new anti-Fascist exiles and included some three hundred individuals by 1930. It remained informally divided between those, like the former members of the Gruppo Anarchico Volontà, who were adherents of *L'Adunata dei Refrattari*, and the smaller group of anarcho-syndicalists aligned with Carlo Tresca's *Il Martello*. However, members of each faction "read both newspapers, attended all money raising events, [and] supported common causes." The exceptions were Angelo Luca and Mario Piccinini, the de facto leaders of each faction, who refused to speak to one another even when Luca's only son, Mark, married Piccinini's only daughter, Russia, in 1939.[71]

Both groups collaborated in hosting lectures by such prominent opponents of fascism as Armando Borghi, Virgilia D'Andrea, and Socialist intellectual Gaetano Salvemini and in collecting funds for Italian political prisoners. Anarchists also cooperated with liberals and Socialists in anti-Fascist ventures such as California's Associazione Libero Pensiero (Free Thought Association), headed by Los Angeles sociology professor Constantino Panunzio. Though Italian authorities described the association's membership as "absolutely minimal," it helped support San Francisco's remaining liberal anti-Fascist paper, *Il Corriere del Popolo*, to which many anarchists contributed and subscribed.[72] But the anarchists brooked no compromise with Communists, who made little headway in North Beach. In early 1928, Italian anarchists and the Radical Branch of the Workmen's Circle formed the Committee for the Relief of Political Prisoners in Russia, which raised funds for comrades incarcerated in the Soviet Union and set out to expose "the hypocrisy and tyrannical dictatorship of the Russian Communist party."[73]

If the fallout from the 1916 Preparedness Day Bombing made San Francisco's *galleanisti* more circumspect about resorting to dynamite, it did not dissuade them altogether. Late on the night of July 30, 1927, a pipe bomb prematurely exploded on the passenger side of Angelo Luca's automobile as it drove down Balboa Street, shattering windows for blocks around and launching Luca and his passenger, anarchist Dominick Caffodio, from the vehicle. Caffodio died instantly and Luca, who suffered severe burns and two broken legs, one of which had to be amputated, was arrested. Police identified the explosive device as "almost an exact replica" of two bombs detonated at the Hall of Justice over the previous two years, likely in protest of the persecution of Sacco and Vanzetti. The device that exploded in Luca's car, however, was intended for the local embodiment of Mussolini's regime, the Italian consulate. Yet police were unable to disprove the elaborate alibi invented by Luca, an insurance salesman, that Caffodio was merely "an insurance prospect" with whom he had been meeting and, unbeknownst to Luca, was carrying the bomb in his satchel. All charges against Luca were eventually dropped.[74] After his recovery, Luca continued to carry on anarchist activities, but his injuries meant that he had to be financially supported by his wife, Jessey Dorr, a painter and renegade daughter of a prominent San Francisco family.[75]

In August 1927, another former Volontà Group member, Vincenzo Ferrero, launched *L'Emancipazione* (Emancipation), "a small monthly publication to agitate and debate local problems specifically and those of the Pacific coast in general." The new paper was in many ways a West Coast supplement to *L'Adunata dei Refrattari*, yet it attracted readers and contributors from across the country and as far away as Argentina, Switzerland, and Belgium. By 1931, *L'Emancipazione* was printing three thousand copies of each issue and had more than two thousand subscribers.[76] The new Emancipazione Group also recruited dozens of members from throughout the Bay Area and Central California.[77] It attracted both old-timers such as former *Nihil* editor Adolfo Antonelli and members of a new generation of anti-Fascists. The second group included Domenico Sallitto, a twenty-eight-year-old laborer and former choirboy who was radicalized by a university professor in his native Sicily and arrived in New York in 1920 as a Socialist and a refugee from Fascist violence. Sallitto began reading anarchist publications, joined the International Group of New York, and campaigned on behalf of Sacco and Vanzetti before relocating to Oakland and joining the Emancipazione Group in 1930.[78] Raffaele De Rango and Mercedes Valeria, a Calabrian individualist anarchist couple, had been among those to call for Italian intervention in the First World War, but this stance did not propel them toward fascism; instead, they emigrated to Chicago in 1920, and their home became the headquarters of an anti-Fascist group; by 1928, they were living in Oakland and helping to produce *L'Emancipazione*.[79]

Accordingly, *L'Emancipazione* was militantly anti-Fascist. It praised every attempt on Mussolini's life and chronicled the ongoing repression of anti-Fascists in Italy and elsewhere in Europe. Among those on whom it reported was deported anarchist Michele Centrone, who was an occasional contributor. The paper also campaigned against *L'Italia* and other local sources of support for Mussolini, and on December 2, 1929, police arrested Vincenzo Ferrero and a comrade for trying to disrupt a Fascist demonstration in Berkeley. In 1932, the Italian consulate in San Francisco declared Ferrero "without a doubt the worst and most dangerous element among many anarchists residing in this district."[80]

Male anarchists such as Ferrero continued to overshadow Valeria and other women in the movement (and its historical record), but the impact of Aurora Alleva, a Philadelphia-born second-generation anarchist who moved to Oakland at the end of the 1930s, was substantial. At Alleva's lectures, Russia Hughes recalled, there "was no talk of feminism; the subjects were economics and justice. Yet, the fact that an effective young woman speaker could capture and hold the attention of the male comrades in itself was a statement." Alleva "represented some of our needs and aspirations simply by her presence." But she remained "one of the few independent feminist women in the anarchist movement."[81]

By contrast, the Emancipazione Group energetically built on the Bay Area's earlier multiethnic coalitions, declaring its goal to be "overcoming all race hatred for the solidarity of all peoples, [and] the destruction of all borders: to inaugurate the true and sincere pact of human solidarity."[82] The Red Scare had dispersed most local anarchist groups, and in the aftermath of the Hindu Conspiracy Trials and the Russian Revolution, the remnants of the Ghadar movement turned increasingly to communism. Longtime anarchist Alexander Horr had joined the Socialist Party and ran as its gubernatorial candidate. However, the Radical Branch of the Workmen's Circle grew to some thirty-nine members by 1925, and the following year it spawned an Anarchist Branch (No. 693) that affiliated with the Jewish Anarchist Federation.[83] More ephemeral organizations appeared and disappeared throughout the 1920s, and a May Day 1926 picnic outside of the city brought together "Italian, Jewish, French and some German speaking comrades. . . . Men, women and children—young and old; dark, brown and blonde; big black eyes—and blue and gray."[84] In September 1927, Italian and Jewish anarchists cosponsored a bilingual conference on "Fascism and Class Struggle" in Stockton, and when Los Angeles anarchist Joseph Spivak visited San Francisco later that year, he found active Italian, Russian, Jewish, and Chinese groups.[85]

The belated addition of Chinese immigrants is especially noteworthy. In May 1919, "a zealous group of idealists," composed of twenty-nine young Chinese anarcho-syndicalists, founded the Sanfanshi Gongyi Tongmeng Zonghui (Unionists' Guild of San Francisco). The guild organized and led several strikes of Chinese garment workers, then expanded its scope to include agricultural workers. It soon enrolled around one thousand members and changed its name to the Meizhou Gongyi Tongmeng Zonghui (Unionists' Guild of America).[86] The union's officers included Chen Shuyao, who had founded an anarchist newspaper in Vancouver before fleeing to San Francisco to avoid police harassment, and Cai Xian, who embraced anarchism after migrating to San Francisco in 1909 as a university student; he then abandoned his family name in favor of the pseudonym Liu Zhongshi, which his non-Chinese comrades corrupted into Jonesie and later Red Jones.[87] The Unionists' Guild lasted until around 1927, by which time Shuyao, Zhongshi, and others had founded Pingshe (The Equality Society), an overseas branch of a similarly named Shanghai anarchist group. In 1926, the Equality Society, which had only about a dozen regular members, launched the journal *Pingdeng* (Equality), which printed around two thousand copies, which were sent "to China and all over the United States."[88]

In October 1927, the Emancipazione Group resolved to bring together the various segments of the movement. It invited members of all local anarchist groups to a large picnic where, according to *L'Emancipazione*'s description of the event, "they ate, they sang, they debated. Laughter and voices mingled in the air. The Spanish, Russian, Yiddish, French, Chinese and Italian, instead of the Discord of Babel, seemed to harmonize together. And English of course, but perhaps it is useful to note that it was only spoken by the undesirables of this country [that is, immigrants] and that there was no trace of natives?"[89] At a formal meeting on December 3, representatives from Italian, Russian, Polish, Yiddish, and Chinese organizations established the International Group of San Francisco. Within a month, "some French-language comrades" and a "Mexican group in Berkeley" had also joined.[90]

The Russian anarchists' reading room at 2787 Folsom Street became the International Group's "Club Rooms," open to the public six evenings a week and hosting monthly "comraderies" featuring spaghetti, concerts, and dancing. The remarkable cosmopolitan atmosphere of the organization can be glimpsed in the program for an April 1933 fund-raiser that featured a "three-act play in the Russian language," a "piano solo by Macario Jr.," a "Recitation by S. Menico [Domenico Sallitto]," "Songs in German and English by Eleanor Eyre, accompanied by Louise Gerboth," and a "Popular Balalaika Orchestra."[91] Such boundary crossings were personal as well as political: Chinese member Eddie Wong and Polish Jewish member Bella Friedman married after meeting in the International Group.[92]

The Italians and a small number of like-minded Jewish anarchists dominated the International Group. The most vocal Jewish member was Sam Cohen, a tailor described by Ferrero as "the traveling salesman of anarchism, a hobo with a purpose," who constantly locked horns with local members of the Communist Party as well as the Jewish Anarchist Federation, and considered *Fraye Arbeter Shtime* editor Joseph Cohen "a disgrace to our movement."[93] This majority butted heads with the Russian and Polish affiliates, many of them former members of the Union of Russian Workers, as well as with the Chinese and Mexican contingents, all of which were syndicalist in orientation. The anti-organizationist element blocked a proposal to make the International Group an official federation with a central committee of delegates from each affiliated group; instead, according to Ferrero, "Each national group had its own members but attended picnics and lectures together and worked together in common causes." These joint efforts included the production of *L'Emancipazione* and its successor, *Man!*. Even though many Pingshe members were unable to write in English, some, including the accomplished Chinese American artists Suey B. Wong and David Chun, contributed striking woodcut illustrations to these periodicals.[94] Domenico Sallitto recalled, "One of the best pictures of Jonesie was at a lecture by Armando Borghi. Jonesie came before everyone else, set up the chairs, listened attentively to Borghi's lecture—never understanding a word—then put away all the chairs and was the last to leave."[95] However imperfectly realized, this was radical cosmopolitanism in action.

This reciprocal solidarity proved invaluable. In March 1928, the U.S. government refused to extend Armando Borghi's visa and initiated deportation proceedings against him, forcing him underground; the same month, Liu Zhongshi and Chen Shuyao were arrested while handing out English-language leaflets produced by the International Group and protesting Borghi's deportation. The men's apartment, which doubled as the offices of *Pingdeng*, was raided, and deportation proceedings were initiated against the pair as alien anarchists. Their comrades of the International Group, however, secured their bail and publicized their case in *L'Emancipazione*, and the deportation warrants were canceled after false documents were procured showing that they had been born in the United States.[96] Zhongshi and Shuyao, like thousands of other illegal Chinese aliens, had become "paper sons" of America and thereby gained citizenship, safeguarding themselves against deportation.[97]

Eighteen months later, the stock market crashed, precipitating an unprecedented economic crisis. But while the Great Depression caused many Americans to question capitalism for the first time, anarchism played no significant role in the major upheavals of the era: the struggles of the Unemployed Councils, the industrial unionism of the Congress of Industrial Organizations, the politically and culturally influential Popular Front, and the creation of the multiethnic New Deal coalition.[98] These movements' commitment to state-centered solutions to workers' problems and to the self-conscious "Americanization" of the working class and its political commitments made them anathema to the anarchists, and the prominent role of the Communist Party in many of these efforts only made them more unpalatable.

The depression presented anarchists with an unenviable choice between economic necessity and ideological purity, confining most to the roles of incredulous observers, ineffectual critics, or at best conflicted participants. Few disagreed with Raffaele Schiavina's view that the New Deal represented "an enormous conscription of public wealth to repair the abysmal cracks made into the private fortunes of the basic capitalistic institutions of the nation," thereby perpetuating the economic system that the anarchists opposed.[99] Nevertheless, in 1932 Chicago's multiethnic Free Society Group admitted, "We don't know whether it is right or wrong for anarchists to demand a certain amount of money or food from the government, but we do know that the unemployed must eat, that their children must have food and shelter." Some of this group's members participated in Communist-organized demonstrations at Chicago's City Hall to demand relief, though others strenuously objected, and by 1935, this United Front was "ancient history." Yet a number of anarchists survived by finding employment in New Deal programs. Harry Kelly confided to Max Nettlau, "They are compelled to do it or starve. I tell you I know hundreds of radicals all working on one project or another." An inveterate founder of anarchist colonies, Kelly was invited to take a job organizing subsistence homesteading in the South, but the offer was soon retracted as a consequence of Kelly's radical reputation.[100] In San Francisco, third-generation anarchist Russia Hughes took a job with the U.S. Housing Authority, but across the country, second-generation anarchist Audrey Goodfriend, having recently earned a mathematics degree from New York's Hunter College, refused "to go work for the State" as most of her classmates had.[101]

The crisis took a heavy toll on the Yiddish movement. Ironically, some radicals lost substantial amounts of money in the crash; Michael Cohn, who had for decades subsidized much of the American anarchist movement, was left heavily in debt (though not bankrupt), and Joseph Cohen reportedly "lost his shirt."[102] By 1930, the Jewish Anarchist Federation counted just thirteen branches and four hundred paid-up members, and the *Fraye Arbeter Shtime* was "in dire distress, living from hand to mouth," and thousands of dollars in debt.[103] In 1933, Cohen resigned as editor amid accusations by some critics that he was too moderate and others that he was too soft on communism. He left New York to pursue his longtime dream of establishing a self-sufficient anarchist colony, founding the Sunrise Co-Operative Farm and Community in Alicia, Michigan. Like most such enterprises, it was wrought with factionalism and unable to sustain itself; the experiment collapsed, and at the end of 1936 the land was sold to the federal government's Resettlement Administration.[104] The Jewish Anarchist Federation temporarily replaced Cohen with a committee of elected editors that included Michael Cohn, Leibush Frumkin, Dr. J. Globus, Abe Grosner, and Saul Yanovsky. However, Cohn confided to friends, Yanovsky was "getting old and more cynical. He curses and cusses privately and openly everything and everybody" and could not tolerate the arrangement, "cussing and abusing everybody who dares to differ with him." In late 1934, Mark Mratchny, the illegal Russian Jewish refugee, was appointed the *Fraye Arbeter Shtime*'s sole editor. By that time, the paper's circulation had dropped to five thousand.[105] Abe Bluestein, son of longtime Jewish anarchists and ILGWU activists Mendel and Esther Bluestein, vented that the movement was "stagnant, stagnating, submerged, impotent, weak, ineffectual [and] confined in its leadership (speakers, writers etc.) to a few old comrades who have devoted their lives to the Cause, and very ably at that, but comrades, nevertheless, who are OLD, who no longer possess the vitality, the strength and the energy to carry on as they once did."[106]

Bluestein belonged to a new generation of young New York anarchists, most of them American-born children of Jewish and Italian immigrant radicals, who began to organize autonomously from the older movement. In 1927, Sara and Elizabeth Goodman, twin daughters of a Jewish anarchist couple, founded the Rising Youth Group, made up of "young people who work in the shops." The group published its own paper, *Rising Youth*, which criticized the moderate anarchism and insularity of the *Fraye Arbeter Shtime*. Both the publication and the group folded when the Goodman sisters departed in 1929, but former members immediately formed the equally short-lived Militant Anarchist Youth, followed by the Friends of Freedom, which in 1932 became the more enduring Vanguard Group.[107]

The Vanguard Group, together with its youth affiliate (known alternately as the Rebel Youth and the Vanguard Juniors), grew to include some sixty regular members, including a group of second-generation Yiddish anarchist girls in the Bronx called Di Yunge Odler (The Young Eagles). By 1938, affiliated groups had formed in Youngstown, Pennsylvania; Canton, Ohio; Philadelphia; Boston; Brooklyn; and Stelton, New Jersey.[108] Many Vanguard members had prominent Yiddish anarchist parents, including Clara Freedman, daughter of Jewish Anarchist Federation secretary and *Fraye Arbeter Shtime* manager Samuel Freedman; Audrey Goodfriend, daughter of Jewish Anarchist Federation members Morris and Gussie Goodfriend; Roman Weinrebe, son of Yiddish writer B. Rivkin; and Abe Bluestein. But many, including Bluestein, spoke "poor Yiddish."[109] Other members included Eddie and Bella Wong, formerly of the International Group of San Francisco; young Russian Jewish immigrants Sam Dolgoff and Jack Frager; Polish Jewish sisters Ruth and Zina Dickstein; and Glenn Carrington, a gay black activist, journalist, and photographer who wrote and spoke on "the Negro question" under the name George Creighton. The intellectual mentor of the Vanguard Group was Mark Schmidt, a thirtysomething Russian Jew who had returned to Russia during the 1917 revolution and come back to America an anarchist, though with strong Marxist leanings.

The group published the journal *Vanguard*, with some interruptions, from 1932 until 1939. It criticized older anarchists for being "cooped up within the confines of little national colonies" and advocated anarcho-syndicalism, but only in the form of the moribund IWW; it rejected mainstream labor unions—including the ILGWU and the Congress of Industrial Organizations—as hopelessly bureaucratic and undemocratic. When members of the ILGWU's "Progressive" bloc approached the Vanguard Group to recruit organizers, they were rebuffed on the grounds that the union was "not revolutionary."[110]

For young American-born anarchists, the Vanguard Group provided a social and political space outside of the seemingly anachronistic world of immigrant radicalism; Audrey Goodfriend described it as having the feeling of "a teenage revolutionary commune."[111] The group did, however, forge strong ties with Carlo Tresca, and when *Vanguard* temporarily ceased publication in 1934, Tresca created a temporary English-language page in *Il Martello* that was edited by Vanguard members. The following year, the Vanguard Group transferred its headquarters to 94 Fifth Avenue, the same building that housed *Il Martello*.[112] Nevertheless, the group's energetic work did not have the desired results: a substantial English-speaking anarchist movement failed to materialize, and *Vanguard*'s circulation peaked at just three thousand, no more than previous English-language anarchist periodicals.[113] The most successful experiment in English-language movement building instead occurred across the country, in California.

Members of the International Group of San Francisco used English as an unofficial lingua franca, but its members published *L'Emancipazione*, *Pingdeng*, and other foreign-language papers that not all comrades could read. After some trepidation, therefore, in October 1932 *L'Emancipazione* announced that it would discontinue and would be replaced by a new periodical "using the language of the land."[114] In a move that linked the anarchist movements of New York, Paterson, and San Francisco, Vincenzo Ferrero recruited Shmuel Marcus to edit the new paper.

Marcus, now using the pseudonym Marcus Graham, launched a high-profile cross-country lecture tour in late 1931 and finished his trek in San Francisco, where he immediately accepted the International Group's invitation. The first issue of *Man!*, its name taken from Greek sophist philosopher Protagoras's declaration that "Man is the measure of all things," appeared in January 1933. Despite his abrasive personality, Marcus was well chosen: he was an experienced editor and, in the description of one reporter, "unusually well educated, remarkably well read, and an apparent deep thinker. With it all, he carries a conviction of sincerity." His politics also aligned so closely with those of the Emancipazione Group that some critics described the new publication as "an Italian paper with English vocabulary" despite its Romanian Jewish editor.[115] Nevertheless, under Marcus, the paper became the finest and most popular English-language anarchist publication of the era. In 1935, he confided to Agnes Inglis that *Man!* reached "the largest reading circle that any libertarian publication may perhaps ever had."[116]

Man! championed revolutionary self-activity while condemning the rising worldwide tide of statism whether in the form of fascism, Stalinism, or the welfare state. It did not, however, advocate any program of action beyond spontaneous individual and mass rebellion. Marcus and the adherents of Luigi Galleani believed that labor unions functioned as "a protective barrier against any spontaneous revolutionary action that may arise from among the exploited toilers," and Marcus denounced anarchist union organizers—including Rose Pesotta of the ILGWU, with whom he had clashed in the International Group of New York—for participating in the "fascist scheme" of the National Recovery Act and holding paid union positions.[117] The International Group's Polish, Russian, and Chinese anarcho-syndicalists did not share this view. When Pesotta visited San Francisco in 1934, members of Pingshe, with whom she had corresponded as secretary of

New York's International Group, introduced her to a group of female Chinese garment workers, establishing the ILGWU's first contacts in San Francisco's Chinatown. This connection paved the way for a groundbreaking ILGWU-led Chinese garment strike four years later, which Pingshe actively supported but *Man!* ignored.[118] The paper praised San Francisco's 1934 general strike but condemned the "deceitful mis-leaders" of the unions involved, who called off the strike after four days and advised workers to submit to arbitration, for "selling out" their members and averting a potentially revolutionary situation.[119]

All members of the International Group, however, were united in their strident rejection of racism. The group embraced Chinese, Mexican, and other nonwhite members, and Marcus, an aspiring poet, championed the writers of the Harlem Renaissance. In 1929, he had published *An Anthology of Revolutionary Poetry*, which included works by Countee Cullen (who helped publish the book), Paul Laurence Dunbar, Fenton Johnson, Georgia Douglas Johnson, James Weldon Johnson, Claude McKay, and Langston Hughes, whom Marcus had known in New York. As editor of *Man!*, Marcus also defended the nine black teenagers being tried for rape in Scottsboro, Alabama; condemned "the mistreatment and shameful degradation that the Negro of the South is forced to undergo"; and celebrated black political militancy.[120] However, *Man!* never discussed or reached out to the Bay Area's own small black population, whose political activism centered on legal rights and the ballot.

Man!'s appearance also coincided with Adolf Hitler's rise to power in Germany, which the paper lost no time in attacking. One Jewish contributor proclaimed, "The ideal of Anarchism should be to unite all isolated peoples in one solidified humanity. . . . Only in this manner can we expect to extirpate the silly egotism which every Nordic idiot carries in his manly chest. And only in this order of society can we ever think of eradicating the racial animosity which every national 'banner' brings upon our stricken world." Former *Fraye Arbeter Shtime* coeditor Dr. J. Globus contributed an article that deconstructed "the racial myth," explaining, "Race, or more correctly racism, [is] the mystification and exaggeration of the simple fact, that people differ somewhat in the pigment content of their skins or in other small ways." In another piece, Raffaele Schiavina inverted popular racial tropes of savagery and civilization, insisting, "The respect of man for man, no matter his descent, is the first requirement of civilization."[121]

Although *Man!* did not openly advocate violence, it warmly approved of the actions of those who practiced it, including Marinus van der Lubbe, who was accused of burning down the German Reichstag in February 1933. The paper defended this act "as a signal for the German working class to rise against the bloody dictatorship of the Nazis" and argued that by disowning Van der Lubbe, Germany's Communists and Socialists had abandoned a true revolutionist,

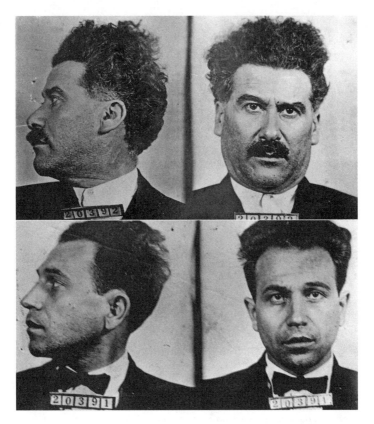

FIGURE 14. Vincenzo Ferrero (*top*) and Domenico Sallitto (*bottom*), 1934. Archivio Centrale dello Stato, Rome; courtesy of the Ministero per i Beni e le Attività Culturali.

dampened opposition to the Nazis, and created the conditions for their own repression. In March 1934, Marcus even debated the topic with representatives from the San Francisco branches of the Communist and Socialist Parties at the San Francisco Labor College.[122] Sallitto chaired the debate, leading an undercover immigration inspector in the audience to take out a warrant for Sallitto's deportation as an alien anarchist.

Domenico Sallitto and Vincenzo Ferrero lived at 1000 Jefferson Avenue in Oakland, on the premises of a small Italian restaurant they ran together. The offices of *Man!* also rented space on the mezzanine level of the building. When immigration inspectors raided the address on the night of April 11, 1934, therefore, they arrested both Sallitto and Ferrero after discovering issues of *L'Emancipazione* and *Man!* in Ferrero's room. The pair were held at Angel Island for deportation. Within days, foreign-born subscribers to *Man!* throughout the country were also visited and threatened by agents of the Bureau of Investigation, who "evidently ... obtained the mailing list from the local Post Office."[123] San Francisco's Italian consul informed immigration officials that it was "very much interested in the deportation" of the two outspoken anti-Fascists, and Italy "would be only too glad" to issue passports for their repatriation.[124]

Italian anarchists in New York spearheaded a nationwide defense campaign on Ferrero and Sallitto's behalf, with aid from the ILGWU, the American Civil Liberties Union, and the Communist-organized American Committee for Protection of Foreign Born. One hundred prominent progressives signed their names to a letter of protest that was delivered to secretary of labor Frances Perkins, including Countee Cullen, John Dewey, W. E. B. Du Bois, Max Eastman, Arthur Garfield Hays, Granville Hicks, Langston Hughes, Sinclair Lewis, Dorothy Parker, Upton Sinclair, Ida B. Tarbell, Norman Thomas, and Mary Heaton Vorse.[125] Meanwhile, the anarchists utilized their own transnational networks to develop a contingency plan; in May 1935, "trusted sources" informed Italy's Ministero dell'Interno that anarchists in Geneva had made arrangements to smuggle Ferrero and Sallitto into France via Spain should the need arise.[126]

L'Adunata dei Refrattari portrayed the pair as "two victims of persecution instituted by the New Deal." When a small group from the Ferrero-Sallitto Defense Conference crashed a dinner attended by Secretary Perkins in New York, therefore, they were surprised when she privately advised, "As far as Sallitto is concerned, we have no proof that he is an anarchist, so he will be released and his bail returned. As for Ferrero, we have ample proof that he is an anarchist—he was the editor of an anarchist paper, and so on. My advice is to have him disappear, and we will not look for him. You will lose a thousand dollars [in bail], but it can't be helped."[127] As promised, in January 1938, the Immigration and Naturalization Service (INS) ruled that insufficient evidence existed that Sallitto belonged to an excludable class and canceled his warrant, and he returned to California in the company of Aurora Alleva, who had served as secretary of the Ferrero-Sallitto Defense Conference. The annual convention of California's Daughters of the American Revolution responded by passing a petition urging that action be taken against Perkins for her unwillingness to deport illegal aliens, including "the cancellation of a warrant of deportation of Vincent [*sic*] Sallitto, self-admitted anarchist dedicated to the overthrow of our government."[128]

Ferrero's attorneys convinced Democratic congressman and immigrant rights advocate Emanuel Celler to introduce a House resolution calling for the cancellation of the deportation warrant against their client and granting him "permanent residence as a political refugee." The House Committee on Immigration and Naturalization heard arguments on the bill in February and March 1938 but declined to make a recommendation, and the bill never reached the congressional floor. During his testimony before the committee, however, Ferrero outlined a cosmopolitan vision of citizenship based on voluntary affiliation and mutual respect: "I am under the impression," he declared, "that a man when he is living peacefully and successfully in the community where he is residing, when he respects every other one and is respected, and he tries to help others as much as possible, and he has no request to be helped, but if the help is coming he is grateful, I think that is indeed citizenship of the place where he is living." When pressed on the subject he simply insisted, "I am a citizen without papers."[129] Having exhausted every legal and legislative avenue his attorneys could devise, Ferrero took Perkins' advice and disappeared; months later the Defense Conference announced that he had "fled from the United States, and is now a refugee in another country." In fact, Ferrero secretly crossed into Canada but not long thereafter smuggled himself back across the border, settling first in Detroit and then returning to the Bay Area under the moniker John the Cook. Comrades in California kept his identity secret and supported him until his death in 1985, at the age of one hundred.[130]

In March 1936, in the midst of the Ferrero-Sallitto case, emboldened immigration inspectors also ordered Shmuel Marcus (Marcus Graham) to report for deportation under his 1919 warrant. Marcus complied but was released after several weeks when officials once again found it impossible to proceed without having established his country of origin. During his incarceration, *Man!* continued to appear, secretly edited by Aurora Alleva and Domenico Sallitto. Marcus then relocated the paper to Los Angeles, where INS agents arrested him again in October 1937. He was released on bail, and a new Marcus Graham Freedom of the Press Committee took up his defense.[131]

His case attracted a wide range of artists and writers, including many who had campaigned for Ferrero and Sallitto and before them Sacco and Vanzetti. A number had been involved with or included in Marcus's *Anthology of Revolutionary Poetry*, including Alice Stone Blackwell, Countee Cullen, and Edna St. Vincent Millay (who in 1935 had purchased a subscription to *Man!* and copies of all its back issues). Supporters also formed branches of the defense committee in France and Spain. The American Civil Liberties Union, which considered the case one of "the chief issues of national importance pending in the courts," took the lead in Marcus's defense.[132]

The INS employed a new strategy and subpoenaed Marcus to appear in District Court to "produce his birth certificate and his passports for entry into the United States" and answer questions put to him by an immigration inspector "touching on his birthplace, his entry into the United States, his citizenship and his right to be and remain in the United States." Marcus reported as ordered, refused to answer any questions, and was charged with contempt of court. At his contempt hearing, Marcus seized the opportunity to indict the entire legal system: "By letting its order of yesterday stand and sentencing me today, this court substantiates as correct the position of the anarchists toward the government as an administrative organ not serving the interests of, but against the people, not of truth, not of justice but of rank injustice," he declared. "Marcus Graham" was then sentenced to six months in the Orange County Jail, "where," a reporter noted, "mysteriously, the jailers apparently had the problem all solved by listing Graham's birth-place, correctly or incorrectly, as Canada." The immigration officers present at court, meanwhile, fumed in "helpless fury" at their inability to "make Graham tell where he came from."[133]

Marcus was released on bond pending appeal, and in October, the Ninth Circuit Court of Appeals referred the case back to the lower court. Marcus again refused to comply with the court's instructions, was again ruled in contempt, and again posted bail pending appeal.[134] When the new appeal was heard in June 1940, the anarchist's "sphinx-like attitude" continued to stymie officials. After the case was once more referred back to the lower court and the contempt charges were once more appealed, the Ninth Circuit Court ruled against Marcus and he was forced to serve the six-month sentence.[135] Nonetheless, his resistance had finally broken the will of the INS, which declined to revive the case against him. By refusing to reveal his birthplace (or even his name), Shmuel Marcus became functionally stateless, thus living up to *Man!*'s claim that the editor was "a man without a country—and truly so, since the entire world is the only country he recognizes as his, and also that of every human being."[136]

In the 1930s, both *Man!* and the *Fraye Arbeter Shtime* were in contact with Jewish anarchists in Palestine, the first of whom arrived there as refugees from the 1905 Russian Revolution. Many were involved in the communal kibbutz movement, which was deeply influenced by anarchist ideas. However, these anarchist settlers opposed Zionist designs on the region because, as one reported, "We didn't lose our faith that there is a possibility of mutual understanding with the Arabs, and secondly because we are against the Jewish State."[137] Likewise, in America "the mood among the comrades was very strongly anti-Zionist and anti-national."[138] When Palestinian Arabs rose up against British forces and Jewish settlers in 1936, the response of Jewish anarchists abroad was ambivalent, with some blaming all parties involved, others condemning Zionism, and still others defending the settlers.[139] In this context, Abba Gordin and Rudolf Rocker, two more anarchists without a country, developed sophisticated but antagonistic analyses of cultural belonging and nationalism.

Gordin, a Russian Jew and former "Soviet anarchist," was an eccentric radical who, with his brother Velvel (Wolf), had transitioned from Zionism to anarchism in 1907. The brothers wrote prolifically on anarchism in Russian and in

1917 formed the Union of the Oppressed Five, an anarchist organization dedicated to the emancipation of workers, women, youth, oppressed nationalities, and the individual. In 1920, Moscow munitions workers twice elected Abba to the Moscow Soviet, but each time the Bolsheviks invalidated the results. He subsequently cofounded the Universalists, an anarchist faction that supported the "dictatorship of the proletariat" and that Alexander Berkman considered "worse than crazy." However, the Universalists turned against the Soviet regime following the Kronstadt massacre and were broken up by the Cheka.[140] In 1924, Abba Gordin fled to the United States, where he mastered English while simultaneously reconnecting with his Yiddish background.

The First World War, the failure of the Russian anarchists, and the rise of fascism had left Gordin disillusioned with working-class revolution. In his New York anarchist paper, *The Clarion*, published from 1932 to 1934, he declared "the class-theory to be impotent in its opposition to the national theory and its economo-political practice. The nation as a social aggregate is stronger, more cohesive than the class-unit. Its roots are deeper. It is grounded in biology, racial elements being involved, and psychology in its concrete form of a national tongue, and that is why unlike the class, it has managed to create its political expression, the NATIONAL IMPERIALISTIC STATE." Rather than viewing nations and races as social constructs, as so many of his fellow anarchists did, Gordin believed that "there is absolutely no escape from the clutches of race or nation. It will never unloose its hold upon the individual. There is no voluntarily entering it and no voluntarily quitting it." The only thing stronger than this bond was "the wedge of the Individual, the EGOIST, an entity more solidified, more centripetal than even the tribe, nation, class or caste, and surely more monolithic and homogeneous than the class."[141] Gordin therefore melded his anarchist philosophy of "interindividualism" with Jewish religious tradition. In a rather transparent effort to leverage national, racial, and religious identity to anarchist ends, he presented a selective reading of traditional Jewish religious law as a fundamentally antistatist and anarchistic doctrine. In 1936, Gordin founded the Jewish Ethical Culture Society (Yidish-Etishe Kultur-Gezelshaft), dedicated primarily to publishing the extraordinary number of books that Gordin produced on this theme.[142] Although Gordin's work was also printed in the *Fraye Arbeter Shtime*, where it sparked heated debate, he remained "a one-man movement" with few supporters.[143] Fellow anarchists simply could not accept this attempt to fuse nationalism, religion, and anarchism.

Rocker's writings were far more influential, and his biography is an exceptional example of the possibilities afforded by radical cosmopolitanism. A German Gentile who first encountered Jewish anarchists in Paris in 1893, Rocker immersed himself in the Yiddish anarchist movement of London's East End after moving there in 1895. He taught himself Yiddish, began contributing articles to the *Arbayter Fraynd*, and became that paper's editor in 1898 after Saul Yanovsky's return to America. By the turn of the century, Rocker had established himself on both sides of the Atlantic as one of the leading intellectuals of Yiddish anarchism—an anarchist "rabbi" to some—and a leader of the Jewish labor movement in London's East End. Rocker was a thoroughly Yiddish anarchist, though not a Jewish one.[144] The German Empire stripped Rocker of his citizenship in 1901, although he was not aware of this fact until he was deported from England as an "enemy alien" during the First World War. The "stateless repatriate" then had his citizenship reinstated by the Weimer Republic, became the foremost figure within the interwar German anarcho-syndicalist movement, and played a central role in the formation of the anarcho-syndicalist International Working Men's Association in 1922.[145] Rocker also began work on a monumental study of nationalism, but the Nazi crackdown on radicalism following the Reichstag Fire sent him and his partner, Ukrainian Jewish anarchist Milly Witcop, on the run. The manuscript of Rocker's book, *Nationalism and Culture*, was the only possession he carried with him as they fled the country.

Rocker and Witcop's arrival in New York on September 2, 1933, was arranged and financed by Michael Cohn. But the couple's legal status remained precarious, as they had to apply to extend their residence permits every six months. Matters improved in 1935 after Rose Pesotta convinced ILGWU president David Dubinsky to intervene on their behalf, and it was rumored in anarchist circles that Eleanor Roosevelt personally interceded to ensure that their visas were renewed.[146] Rocker, who had lectured throughout North America in 1925 and 1930, was welcomed back with open arms by the faltering Yiddish movement and immediately offered the editorship of the *Fraye Arbeter Shtime*. But he declined the offer, preferring instead to focus on public lectures and revising *Nationalism and Culture*, which was translated into English and published in 1937.

The book was at once a sweeping reinterpretation of the history of Western Civilization and a sustained critique of the idea that the modern nation—as opposed to a "people" or "culture"—is a natural or primordial entity. "A people is the natural result of social union, a mutual association of men brought about by a certain similarity of external conditions of living, a common language, and special characteristics due to climate and geographic environment," he argued. In contrast, nations—or "state peoples"—are "the artificial result of the struggle for political power, just as nationalism has never been anything but the political religion of the modern state." Therefore, "The nation is not the cause, but the result, of the state. It is the state which creates the nation, not the nation the state."[147] Although Rocker used the term *nation* differently than Bakunin had (Rocker's *people* or *culture* was equivalent to Bakunin's *nation*), he agreed with the Russian that nationalism originated in the secularization of religious belief and its transference from church to state. The worship of the state evident in fascism and communism, Rocker contended, was simply the culmination of this shift. He then proceeded to systematically refute the arguments put forth by modern nationalists—particularly those in Germany—that defined nations, and hence nation-states, on the basis of language, culture, or race. Echoing Alexander Harkavy's earlier forays into anarchist lexicography, he detailed the ways in which "no language is the purely national product of a particular people, nor even of a particular nation," because "every language is an organism in constant flux" that absorbs all kinds of "foreign" elements. Similarly, cultures are constantly evolving and mutually transformative, and there "is no culture of any sort of which it could be asserted that it arose altogether independently and without outside influences."[148]

Perhaps the most important portion of *Nationalism and Culture* was its chapter on scientific racism, in which Rocker charted the genealogy of modern racial thought and debunked its claims of biologically distinct races and racial hierarchies. In his conclusion to this section, Rocker foresaw the horrendous potential inherent in Nazi ideology: "He who thinks that he sees in all political and social antagonisms merely blood-determined manifestations of race, denies all conciliatory influence of ideas, all community of ethical feeling, and must at every crisis take refuge in brute force. . . . This delusion is not only a permanent danger to the peaceful relations of peoples with one another, it kills all sympathy within a people and flows logically into a state of the most brutal barbarism."[149] Rocker's book was an instant sensation within anarchist circles and met with some critical acclaim but was largely ignored by the public and scholars.

The first attempt to translate *Nationalism and Culture* into English was undertaken by Alexander Berkman, yet another man without a country, but Berkman eventually found the task too difficult and was replaced. Exiled from both the United States and Russia and scraping by thanks to freelance translation work and the generosity of comrades like Michael Cohn, Berkman was hounded by European authorities. Living precariously and at times illegally in France, he wrote to his American comrades, "My case certainly illustrates most strikingly the brutality and stupidity of government. The situation is actually such that I have no right to exist anywhere on this earth. . . . The only thing that remains is to get off the earth, but the earth being round, that is also not practical."[150] However, depressed and suffering from a painful prostate condition, Berkman eventually found a way to orchestrate his departure from the earthly realm: he shot himself on June 28, 1936. Less than three weeks later, the Spanish Civil War began, and with it came perhaps the greatest accomplishments of twentieth-century anarchism.

By the mid-1930s, Spain was the only European country still home to a mass anarchist movement. This was organized within the million-member anarcho-syndicalist Confederación Nacional del Trabajo (National Confederation of Labor, or CNT) and the militant Federación Anarquista Ibérica (Iberian Anarchist Federation, or FAI), known collectively as the CNT-FAI, as well as an anarchist youth federation and the anarchist feminist Mujeres Libres (Free Women).[151] Anarchism and other radical movements flourished under the Second Spanish Republic, established in 1931 after years of dictatorship, and elections in 1936 narrowly brought to power a Popular Front government of Socialists, Republicans, and Communists with the tacit support of many anarchists. In response, a right-wing coalition of monarchists, Fascists, and Catholic conservatives within the military calling themselves Nationalists, launched a July 1936 uprising to overthrow the new regime. The coup, however, was defeated in Madrid, Barcelona, and most of southern and eastern Spain by an unlikely alliance of loyal soldiers, police, and armed workers headed by anarchists and socialists. Thus began a protracted civil war in which the Nationalists, under the leadership of Francisco Franco, received aid from Fascist Italy, Nazi Germany, and Portugal, while Western powers imposed an embargo against both sides in the name of neutrality. In the ensuing power vacuum left by the equivocal governments of Madrid and semi-autonomous Catalonia and the flight or forcible removal of many factory owners and large landowners, members of anarchist and Socialist unions took over the majority of Spain's industry and collectivized more than half the agricultural land in Popular Front territory. Within a week of the uprising, key factories and public utilities were operating under workers' control, and a full-fledged social revolution was under way in many areas.[152]

New York's *Vanguard* exclaimed, "The dream of Bakunin is no longer utopian, no longer a myth; it is a living reality in Spain." According to *L'Adunata dei Refrattari*, "Spain today confirms the observations of our predecessors, and confirms these in an area that in past experiences was never even approached: the social-economic area, offering suggestive examples of practical anarchist realizations."[153] More than sixty years later, Clara Freedman Solomon of the Vanguard Group recalled, "The inspiration of the revolution was tremendous. Here was anarchism in practice on a large scale, a true people's revolution. And anarchism *worked* in the factories and farms."[154] Fate seemed to have given the anarchists another chance at making their revolution, and this opportunity offered far more promising prospects than had existed in Mexico or Russia.

Yet the Spanish situation was more complicated than most American anarchists realized. The balance of power within Popular Front Spain was precarious and volatile, with each faction distrustful of the others and no one group securely in control. Economic conditions were also less than ideal. In some cases, armed anarchists had forcibly coerced peasants into joining agrarian collectives, and within some collectivized factories, divisions developed between union militants and apolitical workers. In addition, the harsh circumstances of an economy in the midst of a depression and civil war was made worse by the Western embargo severely limiting these enterprises' potential. German anarcho-syndicalist Helmut Rüdiger, like earlier critics of the Partido Liberal Mexicano, subsequently complained that the "propaganda of the first months was allowed to portray an exaggerated optimism, and account was not taken of how complicated was the problem in both social and military terms. . . . All of this made the foreign comrades think that the Social Revolution had already advanced much more than was really true."[155]

Nevertheless, the extent of bottom-up collectivization and armed resistance was extraordinary, and anarchists in the United States dedicated themselves to aiding the CNT-FAI. An unprecedented collaborative effort brought together nearly every major American anarchist and syndicalist organization under the umbrella of the United Libertarian Organizations (ULO), which included the Jewish Anarchist Federation, Vanguard Group, Il Martello Group, Cultura Proletaria Group, Union of Russian Toilers, International Group of New York, and the General Recruiting Union and Marine Transport Workers' Union of what remained of the IWW. Isaac Radinowsky of the *Fraye Arbeter Shtime* served as treasurer. Only the anti-organizationists of *L'Adunata dei Refrattari* and *Man!* were conspicuously absent (though San Francisco's International Group did contribute funds). The ULO founded a semimonthly newspaper, *Spanish Revolution*, edited by a committee that included former *Road to Freedom* editor W. S. Van Valkenburgh and members of the Vanguard Group. The paper quickly reached a circulation of seven thousand, making it one of the most popular English-language anarchist papers in American history.[156] The pages of its fellow anarchist publications were also filled with news and commentary about Spain, and during the war, the circulation of the American anarchist press nearly doubled, as did that of the *Fraye Arbeter Shtime*.

The bulk of the anarchists' efforts focused on funneling money and supplies to Spanish comrades. In the midst of the depression, American workers contributed tens of thousands of dollars to the CNT-FAI. Paterson's Anti-Fascist League and new Gruppo Libertario organized a series of events to publicize the struggle and raised hundreds of dollars, and an anarchist *festa* in San Francisco in November 1936 gathered $247.15.[157] *L'Adunata dei Refrattari*, though suffering from a $1,000 deficit in its own finances, collected more than $7,500 for Spain during the first six months of the war, and by August 1937, the ULO had sent another $7,200 to the CNT. The Detroit International Libertarian Committee against Fascism and Chicago's Free Society Group each raised around

$9,000, and the Spanish anarchists' Comité de Defensa y de Auxilio al Pueblo Español (Committee for Defense and Aid to the Spanish People) sent more than $11,400 between January and September 1937.[158]

The CNT appointed Spanish anarchist Maximiliano Olay, who had migrated to the United States via Cuba in 1917, as its one-man "Permanent Delegation of the CNT in North America." Olay and his wife Anna, a Jewish anarchist, relocated to New York from Chicago and established the Spanish Labor Press Bureau, a newswire service dedicated to publicizing the activities of the CNT-FAI.[159] Italian sailor Bruno Bonturi, known as Bruno l'Americano because of the several years he had previously spent in the United States, was living in Spain when the war broke out and traveled to New York in late 1936 or early 1937 to purchase arms for the CNT's militias. He made contact with the Vanguard Group, but the embargo meant that his mission "turned out to be a plan in futility." Bonturi returned to Spain, smuggling only a small quantity of weapons purchased by members of the Vanguard Group.[160] Carlo Tresca also reportedly acquired munitions and "had people coming over on the ships from France and other places" to smuggle them into Spain, while members of the anarchist colony at Stelton established a fund to purchase an airplane for the CNT in memory of fallen Spanish anarchist Buenaventura Durruti, though it is unclear whether the effort succeeded.[161] But whatever shipments of arms American anarchists engineered, they were miniscule. With foreign comrades unable to provide the necessary support, the CNT-FAI and the rest of the Popular Front turned to the Soviet Union, which covertly began sending arms in October 1936.

Around two thousand foreign anarchists, among them at least 100–150 from the United States, journeyed to fight alongside their Spanish comrades.[162] An unknown number of Spanish emigrants also returned. *L'Adunata de Refrattari* declared, "To those without a county we say: your place is alongside the Spanish people, who fight for a society of equals." Because America's anti-anarchist laws could bar foreign-born volunteers from reentering the country, a group of Italian anarchists later explained, "the men of action made their way to Spain in silence, by their own means or with the aid of comrades. Their names are not always famous and they could not make themselves known without also exposing themselves to reprisals."[163] Among them were L'Emancipazione Group member Vigna Antonio Casassa, a Torinese miner who immigrated to San Francisco in 1920 and served in the Garibaldi Battalion of the Communist-organized International Brigades. Enrico (Henry) Albertini of Paterson also joined the International Brigades, while Domenico Rosati, a veteran of the Biennio Rosso who also resided in Paterson, served in the Italian section of the CNT's Ascaso Column, and Pietro Cerruti, a weaver who had formerly lived in Clifton, New Jersey, and been affiliated with *L'Era Nuova*, was wounded while serving in an unknown unit.[164]

From Stelton, Anna Sosnovsky wrote to Rose Pesotta, "There is quite a movement, comrades are leaving in great numbers, especially Italians and Spanish. I would not mind being among them, however."[165] Most anarchists had to find their way to Spain individually or in small groups, a task made more difficult by a government ban on travel to Spain enacted in January 1937. Furthermore, in September 1936, the CNT-FAI explicitly asked foreign anarchists not to come to Spain, explaining that its forces lacked weapons, not soldiers, and asking comrades abroad to instead raise funds for arms and work to end the embargo.[166] Nevertheless, Vanguard Group member Esther Dolgoff recalled, "Many did go and never came back."[167]

One of the first foreign casualties in Spain was Michele Centrone, the twice-deported Bay Area anarchist, who was living illegally in Paris when the war broke out and was part of the first contingent of Italian volunteers to cross the border into Spain and join the Ascaso Column. He was killed in action on August 28, 1936, at the Battle of Monte Pelato, months before the first International Brigades arrived, at the age of fifty-seven.[168] Centrone's friends and comrades in America mourned him as a martyr to the anarchist cause. A fellow member of the Ascaso Column informed *L'Adunata dei Refrattari* that Centrone had died "not for the liberation of his *patria*—a name empty of meaning, which raises no enthusiasm in the heart of the bastard of all nations: but for the liberation of himself, his brothers, his children and grandchildren from the tyranny of the policeman and the *padrone*; not for the conquest of power, which he neither knows nor wants to exercise: but for bread and freedom, for security and justice, for well-being and progress." Centrone, a radical cosmopolitan, "would have felt offended by those who said that they had gone to fight and die for the prestige of the *patria*—of the 'true' Italy—and for its glorious, but moldering, traditions. He went to Spain to fight for the Social Revolution: for a liberty without shackles, for a justice that does not admit privilege, for a *patria* with neither borders nor bastards."[169]

Not all American anarchists in Spain took up arms. David Koven recalled that several Jewish anarchist women he knew in New York "took themselves to Spain when the anti-Fascist struggle broke out in 1936 and worked as nurses in the field hospitals set up by the revolutionary forces." These women were in fact addressing a much more critical shortage in the Popular Front's forces than the foreign combatants were.[170] Abe Bluestein and his partner, Selma Cohen, traveled to Barcelona after Bluestein was elected as a delegate to an international anarchist congress scheduled to be held in revolutionary Barcelona in 1937. On the basis of a letter of recommendation from *Fraye Arbeter Shtime* editor Mark Mratchny, who had met the acting head of the CNT's Foreign Information Bureau, German anarcho-syndicalist Augustin Souchy, when he visited Russia in 1920, Bluestein and Cohen were recruited to take over the bureau's

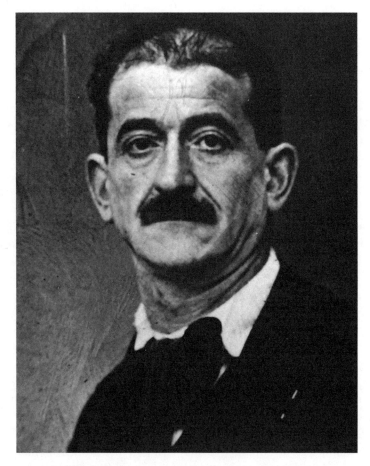

FIGURE 15. Michele Centrone, 1930s. Archivio Centrale dello Stato, Rome; courtesy of the Ministero per i Beni e le Attività Culturali.

English-language desk. The couple wrote reports of events in Spain and produced radio broadcasts for the CNT-FAI. They also toured the collectivized farms of Aragon, about which Bluestein wrote for the *Fraye Arbeter Shtime* and other anarchist papers, and their office became an unofficial welcome center for English-speaking foreigners.[171]

Enrico Arrigoni initially tried to join the American section of the International Brigades—the famed Abraham Lincoln Brigade (actually a battalion)—but "smelled the stink of totalitarian communism under their democratic cover" and changed his mind. He instead set out for Spain on his own as a correspondent for *L'Adunata dei Refrattari* and *Cultura Proletaria* and a delegate to the upcoming anarchist congress.[172] Vanguard Group member Ruth Dickstein, who was Arrigoni's girlfriend, and her sister, Zina, later joined Arrigoni in Barcelona "to be a part of this struggle."[173]

Rudolf Rocker and Rose Pesotta also hoped to see the Spanish Revolution firsthand, but Emma Goldman convinced Rocker that he would be of greater benefit agitating abroad, and ILGWU president David Dubinsky forbade Pesotta from making the trip. Carlo Tresca was similarly anxious to get to Spain but was unable to obtain a passport to travel abroad.[174] However, Goldman herself, still recovering from Berkman's suicide, made her way to from France to Spain, where she reported on the situation for the anarchist press and was asked by the Jewish Anarchist Federation to be its representative at the upcoming Barcelona congress.[175] But she soon found herself embroiled in debates over the actions of her Spanish comrades.

At the end of September 1936, the CNT-FAI made the momentous and controversial decision to participate in the coalition government of Catalonia, and in November it likewise entered the national Popular Front government in Madrid. The CNT-FAI's leaders justified this unprecedented compromise of anarchist principles on the grounds that the anarchists were not strong enough to fight against both Franco and the various parties of the Popular Front and that they did not want to allow the government free rein to use state power against the ongoing popular revolution. Thus, in the name of preserving anti-Fascist unity and the revolutionary gains of the Spanish workers, several anarchist militants awkwardly accepted government posts.[176]

Although Goldman, with the experience of the Russian Revolution very much in mind, warned that the "villainous gang" of Communists in the Popular Front would attempt to "sabotage" the revolution if given the chance, she staunchly defended the anarchists' collaboration with political parties as a necessity imposed by the war. "People in a burning house cannot stop to consider theories," she wrote. "They must use the best methods at hand to save themselves from being burned alive."[177] Rocker likewise viewed collaboration as an unfortunate necessity but warned that the Soviet Union, through its growing influence in Spain, would seek to terminate the social revolution in an attempt to appease Western democracies so that they might intervene and undermine the threat that Fascism posed to the USSR.[178] The CNT-FAI's political collaboration caused many American anarchists to waver in their rejection of Popular Front strategies, and most hesitated to criticize their Spanish comrades. Even *Man!*, usually eager to condemn every perceived deviation from anarchist principles, demurred for several months. *L'Adunata dei Refrattari* was less restrained, declaring somewhat defensively, "To say that the participation of the anarchists in the anti-Fascist government of Spain is a violation of the principles of anarchism, is neither an insult nor a crime against the heroic defenders of Madrid or the valiant fighters of the Aragon front, it is a simple statement of fact."[179]

In an undated letter to Pesotta, probably from early 1937, Sosnovsky wrote, "The situation of our movement in Spain is not in the best of shape, [and] a secret call has been issued for comrades to come over and help them in the anticipated fight with the Marxists after the fascists are defeated."[180] The source of this "secret call" is unclear, though it almost certainly did not come from any official CNT-FAI source. More likely, it originated with Italian volunteers already in Spain who were uncomfortable with the direction events were taking. Regardless, the Communists moved first, confirming anarchists' worst fears. On May 3, 1937, Barcelona's Communist chief of police dispatched officers to evict CNT members from the city's Telephone Exchange as part of an ongoing effort by the anarchists' ostensible allies to dislodge the CNT from strategic positions. The Telephone Exchange had been retaken from Nationalist soldiers after a bloody battle during the first days of the war and had subsequently been run by anarchist and Socialist union members. The Catalan government had legally recognized the enterprise's collectivization, and the workers therefore saw the raid as an outrage and resisted with force. The conflict quickly spilled out into street fighting throughout the city, pitting anarchists and members of the anti-Stalinist Partido Obrero de Unifación Marxista (Workers' Party of Marxist Unification, or POUM) against Catalan police and Communist soldiers. By the time CNT-FAI leaders negotiated a cease-fire several days later, the "May Days" had left at least four hundred people dead, one thousand wounded, and thousands imprisoned.[181]

Bluestein and Cohen, who had arrived in Barcelona on April 30, were caught in the fighting on the way to their first day of work at the CNT's Foreign Information Bureau and watched in horror as anarchists were shot down in the street. With the aid of Enrico Arrigoni, whom they knew from the Vanguard Group, they made their way to the CNT-FAI's headquarters by pretending to be lost foreigners when they encountered armed Communists and by identifying themselves as comrades when they encountered anarchists. The pair remained holed up in the Casa CNT-FAI throughout the conflict, giving nightly radio broadcasts about events outside while hiding in a closet to avoid sniper fire.[182] Arrigoni, for his part, wrote a wrenching firsthand account of the fighting for *Cultura Proletaria*.[183]

The Catalonian government viewed the fighting as a threat to the government's ability to sustain its struggle against the Nationalists and fraudulently claimed that the May Days were an attempt by the POUM and its anarchist allies to seize power. Communists went further, accusing the POUM and the "uncontrollables" among the anarchists of being Fascist agents.[184] The POUM was outlawed, the CNT was forced out of the governments of Barcelona and Madrid, and a wave of armed repression forcibly dissolved many collectivized enterprises, destroying all hopes of sustaining the social revolution. The scheduled international anarchist congress was canceled, and many dispirited foreign anarchists left Spain.[185] Those who remained risked reprisals at the hands of the Spanish government or the Communists' secret police, who viewed any expression of dissent as the divisive work of Fascist spies. Arrigoni was arrested for "public disorder" in October 1937 when he accosted police after finding them firing on members of the CNT they were attempting to evict from a building. He was held without charges for two months until his American comrades, with the aid of Goldman, convinced the U.S. consul to intervene based on Arrigoni's (fraudulently obtained) U.S. citizenship.[186] Following the May Days, Tresca lamented, "Ah! Anarchists still must undergo much torment before finding a '*patria*.'"[187]

To anarchists abroad, the Spanish conflict had suddenly transformed from an epic battle between anarcho-syndicalist revolution and fascism into a desperate struggle for survival against the twin evils of fascism and communism (entirely overlooking the equally anti-anarchist Republicans and Catalan nationalists). Many anarchist observers drew parallels with the fate of the Russian Revolution. Arrigoni gloomily concluded from his Spanish prison cell, "As in Russia, the Communist counterrevolution is marching."[188] According to *Man!*, "Our Anarchist comrades in Spain have so quickly forgotten what happened to the anarchist peasantry of Ukrainia [*sic*] as well as to the entire Anarchist movement in Russia"; consequently, "the bloody massacre of Kronstadt has been repeated in Barcelona." *L'Adunata dei Refrattari* agreed that "the analogy between the ferocious repression of Kronstadt in 1921 and the bestial repression of Barcelona in 1937 is incontestable."[189] Seen through the lens of Russia, history was tragically repeating itself, confirming in the minds of many anarchists that communism was at least as great a foe as fascism. *Spanish Revolution* declared, "The line between Franco and Spanish Stalinists is rapidly being obliterated," and Tresca, who now turned fully against his erstwhile Communist allies, concluded, "Fascism and bolshevism—it will seem strange to the ignorant, easy prey for illusions, [who] simply look on the surface of things and events without further investigation—are not two parallel lines, but converging ones. . . . They are twins."[190]

Bluestein returned to New York in early 1938 and with the aid of Cohen and the Dickstein sisters founded a new anarchist newspaper, *Challenge*, that criticized the CNT-FAI's choices and took a vehemently anti-Communist stance. Echoes of the factional violence he had witnessed in Barcelona followed him home, as on at least two occasions Communist Party members assaulted anarchists selling copies of the paper.[191] Communist disruptions at the street corner meetings of the ULO became so violent that the group appealed privately and publicly for the formation of a "defense body" to protect speakers from "the fascist tactics of Communist Party hoodlums." Tresca received a special request to dispatch "some of the boys over there" so that the skills they had honed fighting Italian American Fascists could be turned on Communist aggressors. Sam Dolgoff recalled that one of the organizers, amputee W. S. Van Valkenburgh, "would attach his wooden leg and assail the Communists with his crutches" when they tried to rush the speakers' platform.[192] Elsewhere, street-tough IWW members armed with sticks and pipes concealed in rolled-up newspapers or handkerchiefs guarded anarchist events against Communist interference.[193]

Tensions also grew within anarchist ranks. Mark Schmidt of the Vanguard Group was a proponent of the Popular Front and remained so even after the May Days. He clashed with members of his own group as well as with the ULO and was divested of some of his editorial duties for *Spanish Revolution*.[194] Critics of the CNT-FAI became more vocal, with *Man!* and *L'Adunata dei Refrattari* pitting themselves against *Vanguard*, the *Fraye Arbeter Shtime*, *Cultura Proletaria*, and *Spanish Revolution*, which continued to argue that no realistic alternative to collaboration existed for the CNT-FAI, a position espoused by a majority of the CNT's members.[195] As Arrigoni put it, "To believe that the anarchists by themselves could defeat the fascism of four nations—of Spain, Italy, Germany, and Portugal—and at the same time fight against the counterrevolution represented by the anti-anarchist coalition of all [Popular Front] parties—from the communists to the bourgeois parties—is to greatly overestimate our forces."[196]

By this point, however, such debates were purely academic: the Spanish anarchist movement had been crippled, and Franco's forces were inexorably advancing. With anarchist morale collapsing along with the Spanish front, donations for Spain dropped off sharply. Suddenly struggling for financial solvency, *Spanish Revolution* limped on until May 1938 and then shut down.

Between the May Days and Franco's final victory in early 1939, anarchism in America collapsed as a mass movement. The demise of *Spanish Revolution* was followed in quick succession by the expiration of *Challenge*, *Vanguard*, and three additional anarchist papers. Furthermore, when *Man!* editor Shmuel Marcus finally secured his freedom in 1940, he discovered that, having gone through nine printers over the previous seven years, he could not find an establishment willing to print the paper and had to suspend publication.[197] America was left with its fewest anarchist periodicals since before the formation of the IWPA in 1883. Though the *Fraye Arbeter Shtime* weathered the storm, editor Mark Mratchny did not. The fall of Spain, he recalled, "was a crushing disappointment to me. I had also become disappointed with my work. I felt like a rabbi in an empty synagogue. So I resigned from the *Fraye Arbeter Shtime* and from the anarchist movement."[198] Reeling from what George Woodcock describes as "the last, greatest defeat of the historical anarchist movement" and already suffering from the profound effects of immigration restriction and political marginalization, droves of demoralized radicals dropped out of active participation in anarchist activities.[199]

Moreover, few of those who had fought in Spain were able to return. Most, including Bruno l'Americano, were not American citizens and were therefore excluded from reentry as alien anarchists.[200] Some Italian veterans of the conflict, however, were smuggled into the United States by comrades in Canada.[201] Those who remained in Spain until the end of the war ended up in French refugee camps, which were transformed into concentration camps after Germany occupied France in 1940. The Vichy regime interned former Paterson anarchist Domenico Rosati and onetime *L'Adunata dei Refrattari* editor Ilario Margarita, along with at least five other Italian American anarchists. Some were transferred to Nazi camps in Eastern Europe, including *L'Adunata dei Refrattari* partisan Armando Rodriguez. Rodriguez survived until the Red Army liberated his camp, but when his rescuers escorted the survivors back to Soviet territory, he had to flee or risk being sent to the Gulag as an anarchist; with little chance of being allowed back into the United States, he made his way to Italy.[202] Shunned by the United States, European fascism, and Soviet communism alike, Rodriguez's plight was emblematic of the fate of anarchism in the era of the Second World War and its Cold War aftermath.

CONCLUSION
"THE WHOLE WORLD IS TURNED INTO A FRIGHTFUL FORTRESS"

The Second World War presented the remnants of the anarchist movement with another seemingly impossible choice between ideology and necessity. Fascism represented all the anarchists abhorred, and its destruction of the once powerful anarchist movements of Southern and Central Europe only heightened their hatred of it. But anarchists bore no love for British and French colonialism or the U.S. government and were sworn enemies of the Soviet Union. Furthermore, as the Allies battled fascism in Europe but left Franco's Spain untouched, the war in the Pacific was steeped in brutality and racism (on both sides), and Franklin Roosevelt authorized the mass internment of 110,000 Japanese Americans for the duration of the war. The destruction of Europe's Jews, which Zionists and territorialists had long feared, commenced with ferocious efficiency under the Nazis. In such circumstances, no consistent anarchist position existed. Nor did the Cold War that followed leave room for anarchist politics in a world sharply divided between the Soviet-centered "Left" and anticommunist "Right."

The world wars and descent of the Iron Curtain also signaled the apex of a global transition to vastly restricted and intensely monitored migration in which states laid claim to a "monopoly of the legitimate means of movement."[1] As early as August 1938, Emma Goldman commented, "More and more the whole world is turned into a frightful fortress from which one can neither get out [n]or to which one can get in." To secure her own tenuous place within this fortress of nation-states, Goldman had in 1925 accepted anarchist miner

James Colton's offer to marry her and thus give her British citizenship, which allowed her to settle in Canada, as close as she could get to the United States, which had become her home.[2]

World War II and the Cold War also starkly illustrated the triumph of nationalism and Americanization. After the United States entered the war, the vast majority of Italian Americans abruptly embraced Americanism, decoupling their *italianità* from identification with fascism and the Italian state.[3] Many anti-Fascists had likewise linked their politics to "American" values or to the redemption of their home countries, spawning a doctrine of "anti-Fascist nationalism." During the war, most radicals ceased pursuing the transformation of American society, abandoned their previous commitment to antimilitarism, and threw their support behind the Allies.[4] Anarchists' antinational cosmopolitanism appeared completely irrelevant as the world was consumed in yet another global conflict between patriots fighting on behalf of competing fatherlands, empires, and "races."

The result was a deeply fractured response. Yiddish anarchists in both America and Europe overwhelmingly supported the Allied war against Nazism. Rudolf Rocker, although forced to register with the American government as an "enemy alien" (despite the fact that the Nazis had again stripped him of his German citizenship), firmly backed the Allies, prompting charges of betrayal from Shmuel Marcus and London's Freedom Group.[5] Rose Pesotta had served on the board of the Keep America Out of War Congress, but after Pearl Harbor, she supported the war effort and quit her position within the ILGWU to work sewing uniforms for the armed forces.[6] And in one of the most unusual honors ever bestowed on an anarchist by the government against which he had agitated, the United States in 1944 launched the *Morris Sigman*, a Liberty Ship named for the former president of the ILGWU.

The second-generation anarchists affiliated with the defunct Vanguard Group split between those who deemed antifascism imperative—and in some cases joined the military or merchant marines—and those who adopted a pacifist position. The latter group published the journal *Why?* from 1942 to 1947, and several of its male members went to prison for resisting conscription. Italian anarchists split largely along existing factional lines, with the anarcho-syndicalists associated with Paterson's Dover Club and Carlo Tresca's *Il Martello* offering conditional support to the Allies in the name of antifascism and the intransigents of *L'Adunata dei Refrattari* opposing the war.[7] In San Francisco, anarchist couple Cari and Mario Piccinini supported the Allies, but their daughter, Russia, and her husband, Mark Luca, involved themselves in antiwar groups and worked with a Quaker organization to aid Japanese internees. They eventually moved to the internment camp at Granada, Colorado, where Mark was employed as a teacher; according to Russia, "We protested the government[']s suppression of an American racial minority in the only way we knew how: we joined the evacuees." Other Bay Area anarchists aided local conscientious objectors.[8]

The war and its aftermath were particularly devastating for Yiddish anarchism. The movement had lost some of its leading lights even before America entered the conflict. In 1939, Saul Yanovsky, a lifelong smoker, died from lung cancer, and fellow former Pioneers of Liberty member Michael Cohn succumbed to a heart attack. A year later, Goldman passed away in Toronto. They were spared from the horrific spectacle of the Holocaust, in which around half of the world's speakers of Yiddish were murdered. Among the casualties were members of Jewish anarchist groups throughout Nazi-occupied Europe, including twenty belonging to the small anarchist circle in the Lodz Ghetto. Yet when Pesotta visited that devastated city in 1946 on behalf of relief efforts organized by the ILGWU, a member of that group greeted her waving a copy of the *Fraye Arbeter Shtime* and introduced Pesotta to the handful of other survivors. "Curiously enough," she reported, "none of them asked for help for themselves, or for visas, but all they wanted was moral support, literature, a printing press and a linotype machine in Polish."[9] Having survived the worst slaughter in history, a few idealists in the remnants of a Nazi ghetto tapped into a transnational network for help in disseminating their vision of a new world based on humanity's potential to cooperate for the common good. There is perhaps no greater testament to the enduring power of such a vision or to the crucial role that publications such as the *Fraye Arbeter Shtime* played in sustaining the global connections of those who believed in that vision.

The enormity of the Holocaust also shattered most Jewish anarchists' opposition to Zionism, especially once the state of Israel was made a reality. Herman Frank, a Jewish anarchist from Bialystok who studied in Berlin before coming to the United States in 1922, replaced Mark Mratchny as editor of the *Fraye Arbeter Shtime* and criticized the "new type of Zionist-Anarchist ideology" that pervaded the movement as being "even more vague and more involved in internal contradiction than the pristine cosmopolitan faith preached by the founders of the Jewish Anarchist movement."[10] But he was removed in 1951 due to his anti-Zionism and died of a heart attack the following year. Rocker also denounced anarchist support for Israel, writing to Boris Yelensky in 1949, "Most Jewish anarchists, blinded by its promises, had forgotten the lessons of history, and naively believed that the new state would become an exception to the atrociousness of others." Joseph Cohen, too, was discouraged by this Zionist turn and after visiting Israel in 1949 settled in Paris, where he briefly edited the anarchist paper *Der Frayer Gedank* (Free Thought) before returning to New York, where he passed away in 1953.[11] Nevertheless, most surviving Yiddish anarchists accepted Israel as at the very least an unfortunate necessity, and many lauded the kibbutz movement as an essentially anarchist enterprise that could act as a counterweight to Israeli statism—a position that Rocker dismissed as wishful thinking and that ultimately proved to be so.[12]

Postwar Polish Jewish refugees formed Tel Aviv's first anarchist group in the late 1940s, and in 1958, seventy-one-year-old Abba Gordin migrated to Israel, where he founded the bilingual Hebrew-Yiddish anarchist journal *Problemot/ Problemen*. Most Israeli anarchists reconciled themselves with the "anarcho-Zionist" position, sometimes by invoking earlier anarchist arguments in favor of anticolonial and national independence struggles. Visiting American anarchists Sam and Esther Dolgoff were told by Israeli comrades in the mid-1970s, "Israel must be defended. . . . [T]he unilateral dismantling of the Israeli state would not at all be anarchistic. It would, on the contrary, only reinforce the immense power of the Arab states and actually expedite their plans for the conquest of Israel."[13]

This tacit surrender of one of anarchism's core principles was also influenced by the phenomena of mass denaturalization, changing national borders, and restricted exit and entry policies that were a particular burden for European Jews. Hannah Arendt explored the impossible dilemma faced by Europe's "displaced persons" in her seminal book, *The Origins of Totalitarianism*, in which she observed that statelessness had become "the newest mass phenomenon in contemporary history," creating millions of persecuted refugees whose lack of citizenship stripped them of a "right to have rights."[14] This nightmare of statelessness was a far cry from the cosmopolitan working class "without a country" that the anarchists had celebrated—and embodied.

On the one hand, this confirms that the anarchists, with their hopes for a stateless world, were egregiously out of step with the major political developments of twentieth century. Their refusal to make peace with capitalism, communism, or "Americanism" rendered them anachronisms, especially as many "Third World" anticolonial movements, many of which previously owed much to anarchist influence, turned to communism or authoritarian leaders for salvation. As long as the Cold War persisted, anarchism was widely regarded—even by some anarchists—as irrelevant. Many within the movement tried to navigate the razor's edge between compromise and contradiction, usually by passively supporting the Western democracies against Soviet totalitarianism. The *Fraye Arbeter Shtime* adhered to this position, prompting Joseph Cohen to condemn its "cold war mentality" and accuse comrades of acting as "the right wing of the State Department." In 1969, former Communist Melech Epstein sarcastically observed that the *Fraye Arbeter Shtime* had become "as anarchistic as the *New York Times* and, in foreign policy, less liberal."[15]

The Cold War so fundamentally altered the political landscape that immigration authorities even made exceptions to the Anarchist Exclusion Act in the case of Cuban anarchist refugees, who fled after the Castro regime began cracking down on its erstwhile revolutionary allies.[16] But anarchists never constituted part of the machinery of McCarthyism. Nor did they contribute to the creation of Cold War anticommunism, which developed quite independently of anarchist influence. Anarchists did not support government repression of Communist Party members and none served as informants for anticommunist congressional committees—though at least one, Italian watchmaker Giordano Bruch, was deported in 1953 after appearing before such a body. Anarchist anticommunism was an alternative to, not a forerunner of, McCarthyism.[17] It was, however, an alternative that was ignored. Anarchism had virtually no impact on the postwar generation of left-wing anti-Stalinists, most of whom were instead drawn to the Trotskyist opposition or Cold War liberalism or embarked on the long journey to conservatism.

However, anarchists' refusal to abandon their goal of a cosmopolitan and libertarian socialist society—even if many came to believe its achievement was far off and made all manner of compromises they viewed as necessary in the interim—may vindicate them in historical hindsight. Their critique of democratic republics' inability to resolve class conflict, their warnings about the dangers of nationalism and socialist dictatorship, and their predictions of inevitable conflict between Zionists and Palestinians all proved substantially correct. As early as 1948, Lucy Robins Lang, who had long since strayed from her anarchist roots, reflected, "It is easy to say that Anarchist ideals are impractical, but as I look back and think of friends of mine who have lived by those ideals for half a century, I am not so sure. I have seen ideologies come and go, and I have seen the enthusiastic advocates of some of these ideologies end either in disillusionment or in betrayal of their principles. In a world in which totalitarianism flourishes, I know of no more worthy ideal than the respect for the individual that is the foundation of Anarchism."[18] This respect for the individual and corresponding defense of diversity as a positive good in itself formed the core of anarchists' cosmopolitan thought and practice.

Yiddish anarchists had the most difficulty bringing these ideals to realization as a consequence of the insular nature of New York's Jewish community and the immense countervailing pressures exerted in the face of anti-Semitism. Yiddish-speaking radicals were also hamstrung by the lack of language loyalty among second-generation Jewish immigrants. The fusion of *yidishkayt* and anarchism that had made the movement relevant and influential became its Achilles' heel. In 1938, Goldman observed that her Jewish comrades "have done nothing to acquaint their children with the ideas for which they were willing to sacrifice so much. The irony of it is that the younger generation have drifted away and certainly never acquire the Yiddish, consequently they do [not] know what is going on."[19]

Yiddish anarchism persisted for another four decades but did so as a shrinking movement of elderly radicals whose activities were limited almost entirely to reading and raising funds for the *Fraye Arbeter Shtime*. In 1977, that paper's circulation had shrunk to just seventeen hundred, and it ceased publication. At the time of its closing it was the longest-running Yiddish newspaper in the world. All subscriptions were transferred to Tel Aviv's *Problemot/Problemen*, but that paper folded in December 1989. A single issue of an Israeli paper, *Fraye Shtime*—a clear homage to New York's trailblazing periodical—appeared in September 1991, the last publication of its kind.[20]

Dictating his memoirs in the 1960s, Isidore Wisotsky lamented that there were "no 'inheritors'" of Yiddish anarchism.[21] Yet some anarchists did pass their ideology on to their children, even if those children abandoned the language and culture of their parents. New York's Vanguard Group and its successors, the pacifist Why? Group and Resistance Group and the anarcho-syndicalist Libertarian League, kept the embers of anarchism alive, and a new generation of American-born radicals, including New Left icons Paul Goodman and David Dellinger, received much of their political education within these organizations.[22]

Italians in Paterson more easily absorbed radicals of other nationalities into their movement and had much more success in forging ties with other immigrant workers. They also kept fascism within their community at bay for many years. Some of their children participated in the anarchist movement through the Francisco Ferrer Association and other institutions, but by the end of the Second World War, almost no trace of the movement remained. Already in 1914, a witness for the Commission on Industrial Relations noted that in Paterson, "those [Italians] that are born here and speak English you can hardly detect any more. They just simply grow up like the rest does."[23] Many anarchists' children and grandchildren repressed the memory of anarchism within their families and community. What was arguably the most influential local anarchist movement in America was therefore almost completely eradicated from Paterson's public consciousness.[24]

Radicals in San Francisco came closest to creating a truly multiethnic, cosmopolitan anarchist movement that was a significant force among Latin, Asian, and Russian immigrants. However, the anarchists' modest numbers limited their influence, particularly as the city's Italians flocked behind the Fascist banner in the 1920s and 1930s. Like their comrades elsewhere, many also failed to pass their beliefs on to the next generation. According to Domenico Sallitto, Italian anarchists "couldn't communicate well with their children. There was a language barrier and a cultural barrier."[25] Repression also played a role, driving influential anarchists such as Vincenzo Ferrero underground and Shmuel

Marcus into a semiclandestine existence following his release from prison in 1940. But Bay Area anarchists did embrace English-language activism through publications such as Berkman's *Blast* and Marcus's *Man!* that provided much of the movement's lasting impact. Adoption of English also allowed old-timers to attend meetings of the Libertarian Circle, founded after World War II by anarchist poet Kenneth Rexroth. This group met in the Workmen's Circle hall and brought together aging immigrant anarchists, a small group of transplanted former Vanguard Group members, and young "Beatniks" for whom Rexroth served as a political mentor, including poets Gary Snyder and Lawrence Ferlinghetti.[26] In 1953, Ferlinghetti cofounded the iconic City Lights Bookstore, an institution with strong links to San Francisco's Latin anarchist past. Ferlinghetti's business partner was Peter Martin, the illegitimate son of Carlo Tresca and Bina Flynn and the stepson of anarchist Romolo Bobba, and the store was located in the heart of North Beach, where it catered to surviving members of the anarchist community. Ferlinghetti later recalled, "The garbage men on the truck would roar up to the bookstore and run in and get their Italian anarchist newspapers."[27]

Beat poets such as Ferlinghetti, Snyder, and New York's Diane Di Prima (whose grandfather, Domenico Mallozzi, was a member of Tresca's circle) as well as American-born activists Dellinger and Goodman transmitted anarchist ideas to the New Left of the 1960s. The intimate connection between migration and anarchism was by then a relic of the prewar past. But the earlier immigrant generation's refusal to accommodate nationalism, communism, or Cold War anticommunism kept the anarchist tradition largely free from these movements' poisonous legacies and subsequently made it attractive to some 1960s radicals as well as an even larger section of the late-twentieth- and early twenty-first-century anticorporate globalization and Occupy Wall Street movements.

Though these later movements had no more success than their predecessors in bringing about systemic revolutionary change, they have perhaps nudged events in such a direction, answering Errico Malatesta's call to "walk toward anarchy today, tomorrow, and always." Therefore, insofar as anarchists contributed to expanding freedom in their own day, and insofar as their legacy and influence continue to do so, they may be judged as successful. Moreover, some of the institutions that they helped to build, including labor unions like the ILGWU—the descendant of which today constitutes part of UNITE-HERE, one of America's largest unions—are still fighting on behalf of immigrants and workers, and a new generation of immigrant activists seeking dignity and rights regardless of citizenship has in recent years reclaimed May Day.

Furthermore—and perhaps most important—the anarchists themselves stand as a remarkable historical example of an antiauthoritarian and cosmopolitan collective whose identities, modes of organization, and solidarities transcended race and nation. If such ideas seemed hopelessly utopian in the middle of the twentieth century, they seem less so in our own age of globalization, transnational social movements, and intercultural connectivity. With scholarship on the history of American immigration and labor increasingly preoccupied with the seemingly inescapable influence of nationalism and racism, it is all the more imperative to take note of those who stood against the tide. Today's world is "a frightful fortress" only because it has been made so, and the anarchists' dream of a *patria* without borders still stands as a tantalizing alternative.

NOTES

Abbreviations

AdR	*L'Adunata dei Refrattari*
Berkman Papers	Alexander Berkman Papers, International Institute of Social History, Amsterdam
BS	Bureau Section Files, Records of the Federal Bureau of Investigation, Record Group 65, National Archives and Records Administration, College Park, Maryland
CPC	Casellario Politico Centrale, Archivio Centrale dello Stato, Rome
CS	*Cronaca Sovversiva*
EN	*L'Era Nuova*
FAS	*Fraye Arbeter Shtime*
GdO	*Il Grido degli Oppressi*
IISH	International Institute of Social History, Amsterdam
IUB	*Industrial Union Bulletin*
IW	*Industrial Worker*
Labadie Collection	Joseph A. Labadie Collection, Special Collections Library, University of Michigan, Ann Arbor
Nettlau Papers	Max Nettlau Papers, International Institute of Social History, Amsterdam
NYH	*New York Herald*
NYT	*New York Times*
OG	Old German Files, Records of the Federal Bureau of Investigation, Record Group 65, National Archives and Records Administration, College Park, Maryland
QS	*La Questione Sociale*
SFC	*San Francisco Chronicle*
TN	*Les Temps Nouveaux*

Introduction

1. *Libertarian socialism* refers to a range of economic systems based on collective (but not state) ownership of the means of production, including those referred to by anarchists as mutualism, collectivism, and communism. See Knowles, *Political Economy from Below*; Shannon, Nocella, and Asimakopoulos, *Accumulation of Freedom*.

2. Hobsbawm, *Age of Extremes*, 74; Goodwin, "What Anarchy Is," 599. Useful overviews include Woodcock, *Anarchism*; Marshall, *Demanding the Impossible*; Schmidt and van der Walt, *Black Flame*; Hirsch and van der Walt, *Anarchism and Syndicalism*.

3. Berkman, Bauer, and Nold, *Prison Blossoms*, 20.

4. Gutman and Berlin, "Class Composition"; Collomp and Debouzy, "European Migrants," 340.

5. Kelley, *Hammer and Hoe*, xi.

6. I borrow this term from Khuri-Makdisi, *Eastern Mediterranean*.

7. Kirwin R. Shaffer, *Black Flag Boricuas*, 2, 7.

8. Avrich, *Haymarket*, 75, 83–85; Nelson, *Beyond the Martyrs*; Goyens, *Beer and Revolution*, 108; Hillquit, *History*, 238.

9. Avrich, *Haymarket*; James R. Green, *Death in the Haymarket*. For a provocative but flawed reassessment of the bombing, see Messer-Kruse, *Haymarket*.

10. Avrich and Avrich, *Sasha and Emma*, 22.

11. Zimmer, "American Anarchist Periodicals"; Avrich, *American Anarchist*, xviii; Marsh, *Anarchist Women*, 10; Koenig, "American Anarchism," 18.

12. "Manet Immota Fides: Italian Anarchism in the United States," n.d., IISH; D'Attilio, "Adunata dei Refrattari," 4.

13. Ostergaard, "Resisting the Nation-State," 172.

14. Bakunin, *Political Philosophy*, 175.

15. Ibid., 324.

16. Mikhail Bakunin, "The Political Theology of Mazzini and the International," trans. Sarah E. Holmes, *Liberty*, April 23, 1887; Cahm, "Bakunin," 43, 36.

17. Bakunin, *Basic Bakunin*, 176; Anderson, *Imagined Communities*; Ramnath, *Decolonizing Anarchism*, 23.

18. Scott, *Art of Not Being Governed*, x, 176.

19. Forman, *Nationalism*, 37–38.

20. Goldman and Berkman, *Nowhere at Home*, 8.

21. See Hollinger, *Postethnic America*; Sznaider, *Jewish Memory*.

22. Damiani, *Razzismo e anarchismo*, 29. All translations are the author's unless otherwise noted.

23. *Vanguard*, August–September 1936.

24. Cheah and Robbins, *Cosmopolitics*; Levy, "Anarchism and Cosmopolitanism."

25. Anderson, *Under Three Flags*, 54.

26. See, for example, *Free Society*, October 23, 1898; Fleming, *Geography of Freedom*, 181–85; Grave, *Moribund Society*, 102–11; Damiani, *Razzismo e anarchismo*; Morton, *Curse of Race Prejudice*.

27. Ferguson, *Emma Goldman*, 220–21, 238; Hill, *Men, Mobs, and Law*, 107; Koenig, "American Anarchism," 134.

28. Hong, "Origin of American Legislation"; *NYT*, December 4, 1901; Preston, *Aliens and Dissenters*, 32–33.

29. Richard Bach Jensen, "United States."

30. Ngai, *Impossible Subjects*, 4; Richard Bach Jensen, *Battle against Anarchist Terrorism*.

31. *ME*, July 1906.

32. Jacobson, *Whiteness of a Different Color*; Roediger, *Working toward Whiteness*; Thomas A. Guglielmo, *White on Arrival*; Brodkin, *How Jews Became White Folks*; Eric L. Goldstein, *Price of Whiteness*.

33. Skowronek, *Building a New American State*; Torpey, *Invention of the Passport*; Lee, *At America's Gates*; Ngai, *Impossible Subjects*; St. John, *Line in the Sand*; Chang, *Pacific Connections*.

Chapter 1. "Yiddish Is My Homeland"

1. Howe, *World of Our Fathers*, 105; Kosak, *Cultures of Opposition*.

2. Howe, *World of Our Fathers*, 643; Brodkin, *How Jews Became White Folks*, 186.

3. On this paradox, see Michels, *Fire in Their Hearts*.

4. Baron, *Russian Jew*, 39–64; Nathans, *Beyond the Pale*.

5. Mendelsohn, *Class Struggle*, 4–15; Kuznets, "Immigration of Russian Jews"; Joseph, *Jewish Immigration*; Kobrin, *Jewish Bialystok*.

6. U.S. Immigration Commission, *Reports*, 4:251–59; Nadell, "From Shtetl to Border."

7. Joseph, *Jewish Immigration*, 39, 73–80, 93, 106–8; Kissman, "Immigration of Rumanian Jews"; Mahler, "Economic Background."

8. Kuznets, "Immigration of Russian Jews," 105, 122; Kosak, *Cultures of Opposition*, 62–63; Lederhendler, *Jewish Immigrants and American Capitalism*, 30–37; Joseph, *Jewish Immigration*, 128, 154, 179.

9. Haberer, *Jews and Revolution*; Nathans, *Beyond the Pale*, chaps. 6–7; Mendelsohn, "Russian Roots"; Cassedy, *To the Other Shore*; Michels, *Fire in Their Hearts*, chap. 1.

10. Kopeloff, *Amol in Amerike*, 7. Many sources give Kopeloff's first name as Israel; see, however, Reisen, *Leksikon*, s.v. Kopelef I.

11. Menes, "*Am Oylom* Movement"; Mendelsohn, *Class Struggle*, 152–55.

12. Kessner, *Golden Door*, 37; Rischin, *Promised City*, 231; Glenn, *Daughters of the Shtetl*, 24; Lederhendler, *Jewish Immigrants and American Capitalism*, 48.

13. Levine, *Women's Garment Workers*, chaps. 3–4; Soyer, "Cockroach Capitalists."

14. Glenn, *Daughters of the Shtetl*, 66–89, 106–31; Kessner, *Golden Door*, 76; Nancy L. Green, "Women and Immigrants."

15. Ganz, *Rebels*, 4; "Tenement hayzer," in Bialostotsky, *David Edelshtat gedenk-bukh*, 233.

16. Wisotsky, "Such a Life," 21; Dinnerstein, *Antisemitism in America*, chaps. 3–4.

17. "Natur un mensh," *Varhayt*, March 29, 1889.

18. Ravage, *American in the Making*, 106.

19. Haberer, *Jews and Revolution*; Sorin, *Prophetic Minority*, 46; Michels, *Fire in Their Hearts*, 3–5.

20. Venturi, *Roots of Revolution*; Avrich, *Russian Anarchists*.

21. Moisseiff, "M. Katts," 39–40; Joseph J. Cohen, *Yidish-anarkhistishe bavegung*, 142–43; Yanovsky, "Genose H. Zolotarov," 28.

22. Mendelsohn, "Russian Roots"; Cassedy, *To the Other Shore*.

23. Michels, *Fire in Their Hearts*, 37; Kopeloff, *Amol in Amerike*, 191–92.

24. Goyens, *Beer and Revolution*, 147.

25. Michels, *Fire in Their Hearts*, 43.

26. Weinberg, *Forty Years*, 7, 9, 154. See also Benequit, *Durkhgelebt un durkhgetrakht*, 59; Goldman, *Living*, 6; Kopeloff, *Amol in Amerike*, 106.

27. Goldman, *Living*, 9; Benequit, *Durkhgelebt un durkhgetrakht*, 52–55; Weinberg, *Forty Years*, 153.

28. Tcherikower, *Early Jewish Labor Movement*, chap. 11; Fishman, *Jewish Radicals*, 138–59; Frank, "Anarkho-sotsialistishe ideyen," 262.

29. *Varhayt*, February 22, March 8, 1889; Benequit, *Durkhgelebt un durkhgetrakht*, 107; Weinberg, *Forty Years*, 19.

30. *FAS*, May 15, 1891; Yanovsky, *Ershte yorn*, 89–100; Avrich and Avrich, *Sasha and Emma*, 22–23, 124.

31. *TN*, supplément littéraire, no. 29, 1900; *Varhayt*, March 1, 1889; N. Goldberg, "Pionire der frayhayt," 305; Joseph J. Cohen, *Yidish-anarkhistishe bavegung*, 44. The founding members of the Pioneers of Liberty were Faltsblat, H. Kaplansky, D. Strashunsky, M. Yudelevitsh, and L. Bernshtayn, who served as the organization's first secretary.

32. Goldman, *Living*, 54–55, 672; Reisen, *Leksikon*, s.v. Merison Katerine; Cassedy, *Building the Future*, 194. Emma Goldman does not appear to have been a member of the group; see Goldman, *Living*, 75.

33. Cohn, "In Neters keler"; Goldman, *Living*, 55.

34. On Cohn, see Frumkin, *In friling fun idishn sotsializm*, 263–80.

35. Sanders, *Downtown Jews*, 53; Glenn, *Daughters of the Shtetl*, 139–43; Michels, *Fire in Their Hearts*, 10–15.

36. Ewen, *Immigrant Women*, 130–35.

37. Maryson, "Der ershter period," 31; Gordin, *Sh. Yanovsky*, 129; Katts, "Zayn geshtalt," 178–79; Kitz, *Poetics of Anarchy*, 42; Alexander Berkman to Zalman Reisen, February 1931, folder 65, Berkman Papers.

38. Gordin, *Sh. Yanovsky*, 125; Goldman, *Living*, 47.

39. Falk, Pateman, and Moran, *Emma Goldman*, 1:46, 430, 2:193.

40. Michels, *Fire in Their Hearts*, 63.

41. *Varhayt*, March 1, 1889; Maryson, "Der ershter period," 31; Glenn, *Daughters of the Shtetl*, 194–97.

42. *Varhayt*, March 19, May 3, 1889; Schulman, "'Varhayt,'" 197–98; Kopeloff, "M. Katts's tetigkayt," 22–23.

43. Michels, *Fire in Their Hearts*, 95–96; Tcherikower, *Early Jewish Labor Movement*, 240–45.

44. Burgin, *Geshikhte*, 180–83. The Yiddish spelling of the *Fraye Arbeter Shtime*'s title changed over time as the language became more standardized; I use the transliteration from the final version throughout this volume.

45. Maryson, "Der ershter period," 32–33; Alexander Berkman, "Stray Thoughts (on the Occasion of the 25th Anniversary of the F.A.S.)," 1924, folder 191, Berkman Papers.

46. Kitz, *Poetics of Anarchy*, 68.

47. Joseph J. Cohen, *Yidish-anarkhistishe bavegung*, 56; Benequit, *Durkhgelebt un durkhgetrakht*, 107; N. Goldberg, "Pionire der frayhayt," 312–14.

48. Abraham Rosenberg, *Klokmakher*, 22; Tcherikower, *Early Jewish Labor Movement*, 208; Burgin, *Geshikhte*, 311.

49. Quoted in Margolis, "Tempest in Three Teapots," 154.

50. N. Goldberg, "Pionire der frayhayt," 307; Eyges, *Beyond the Horizon*, 75.

51. *Fraye Gezelshaft*, April 1900; *FAS*, September 20, 1901.

52. Tcherikower, *Early Jewish Labor Movement*, 253–60; Margolis, "Tempest in Three Teapots"; Goldman, *Living*, 365.

53. Ravage, *American in the Making*, 107.

54. Shuldiner, *Of Moses and Marx*, 133–34; Lang, *Tomorrow Is Beautiful*, 30.

55. Polland, "'May a Freethinker Help a Pious Man?'"

56. Blumenson, "Culture on Rutgers Square," 74.

57. Kopeloff, *Amol in Amerike*, 275, 237; Tcherikower, *Early Jewish Labor Movement*, 263–64; Joseph J. Cohen, *Yidish-anarkhistishe bavegung*, 70; Margolis, "Tempest in Three Teapots."

58. "Di yudenfrage," *Varhayt*, February 15–March 22, 1889.

59. *FAS*, September 19, 1890; Maryson, "Ershter period," 30–31.

60. *Der Nayer Gayst*, October 1897, 19–20.

61. Frumkin, *In friling fun idishn sotsializm*, 193–94.

62. Dovid Katz, "Alexander Harkavy."

63. Frumkin, *In friling fun idishn sotsializm*, 194–96.

64. Bordo-Rivkin, *B. Rivkin*, 13–29; Rivkin, "Distinguishing Characteristics," 95–96. See also Rivkin, *Grunt-tendentsn*.

65. Thorne interview.

66. Cohn, "In Neters keler," 183; Yanovsky, "Genose H. Zolotarov," 28; Yanovsky, *Ershte yorn*, 84.

67. *FAS*, December 25, 1890; Barondes, "Zikhroynes fun amol," 35–36.

68. Yanovsky, *Ershte yorn*, 51–58; Kitz, *Poetics of Anarchy*, 31; Goldman, *Living*, 54.

69. Abraham Rosenberg, *Klokmakher*, 8, 22; Tcherikower, *Early Jewish Labor Movement*, 239, 290–91; Goldman, *Living*, 26.

70. Goyens, *Beer and Revolution*, 100; Johann Most, *Unsere Stellung in der Arbeiterbewegung* (New York: Müller, 1890), Yiddish translation in *FAS*, October 20, 1899.

71. Schappes, "Political Origins."

72. Abraham Rosenberg, *Klokmakher*, 23–24, 29–30; Goldman, *Living*, 54–56; Burgin, *Geshikhte*, 335–38; Levine, *Women's Garment Workers*, 51–54; Weinberg, *Forty Years*, 165–66 n. 35.

73. Abraham Rosenberg, *Klokmakher*, 49–54, 61; Levine, *Women's Garment Workers*, 59–63, 72; Joseph J. Cohen, *Yidish-anarkhistishe bavegung*, 63–64; Burgin, *Geshikhte*, 331–35.

74. Abraham Rosenberg, *Klokmakher*, 61, 64; Burgin, *Geshikhte*, 331–35; Levine, *Women's Garment Workers*, 73–75; Sanders, *Downtown Jews*, 162–63.

75. Avrich and Avrich, *Sasha and Emma*, 112–15; Epstein, *Jewish Labor*, 1:210; Levine, *Women's Garment Workers*, 76–83.

76. Burgin, *Geshikhte*, 329–30; Weinberg, *Forty Years*, 169 n. 54; Avrich, *Anarchist Portraits*, 184–85; Benequit, *Durkhgelebt un durkhgetrakht*, 71.

77. Marmor, *Yosef Bovshover*, 64–70.

78. Berkman, *Prison Memoirs*, 7; Berkman, Bauer, and Nold, *Prison Blossoms*, 86.

79. Carlson, *Anarchism in Germany*, chap. 8–11; Goyens, *Beer and Revolution*, 124–42; Avrich and Avrich, *Sasha and Emma*, 44–46, 89.

80. Goldman, *Living*, 74–75, 106; Avrich and Avrich, *Sasha and Emma*, 46–48, 87–91; Most quoted in Falk, Pateman, and Moran, *Emma Goldman*, 1:119–20 n. 1; Joseph J. Cohen, *Yidish-anarkhistishe bavegung*, 194.

81. Fishman, *Jewish Radicals*, 197–201; Frank, "Anarchism and the Jews," 280.

82. Yanovsky, *Ershte yorn*, 204–10; Gordin, *Sh. Yanovsky*, 193–201.

83. Joseph J. Cohen, *Yidish-anarkhistishe bavegung*, 104–5.

84. Hapgood, *Spirit of the Ghetto*, 177; Michels, *Fire in Their Hearts*, 113–15.

85. *FAS*, October 13, 1899.

86. Gordin, *Sh. Yanovsky*, 315; Joseph J. Cohen, *Yidish-anarkhistishe bavegung*, 116.

87. Gordin, *Sh. Yanovsky*, 249, 314; *N. W. Ayer and Son's American Newspaper Annual and Directory*, 1910.

88. *FAS*, May 29, 1909; Avrich, *Modern School*.

89. Yanovsky, *Ershte yorn*, 262–65; Fishman, *Jewish Radicals*, 197–201; Gordin, *Sh. Yanovsky*, 153–54, 182.

90. Quoted in Epstein, *Jewish Labor*, 1:218.

91. *FAS*, November 8, 1901.

92. Ibid., September 13, 20, 1901; Fine, "Anarchism and the Assassination"; Gordin, *Sh. Yanovsky*, 258–59.

93. Yanovsky, *Der olef beys fun anarkhizmus*, 3.

94. Goldman, *Living*, 37; Maryson, *Teorie un praktik fun anarkhizm*, 60–62; Cassedy, *Building the Future*, 198; Joseph J. Cohen, *Yidish-anarkhistishe bavegung*, 136, 193, 259–60, 265.

95. Joseph J. Cohen, *Yidish-anarkhistishe bavegung*, 445; Avrich, *Anarchist Portraits*, 190–91, 293 n. 61. These new groups were the Anarchist Red Cross, the Anarkhie Group, the Broyt un Frayhayt Group, the Frayhayt Group, the Friends of Art and Education, the International Group, the Jewish Self-Education Group, the Solidarity Group, and the Zsherminal Group.

96. *NYT*, June 5, 1977.

97. Bercovici, *It's the Gypsy in Me*, 50; Michels, *Fire in Their Hearts*, 61.

98. Park, *Immigrant Press*, 100.

99. *FAS*, November 20, 1909, September 17, 1910.

100. Michels, *Fire in Their Hearts*, 148–49.

101. Hapgood, *Spirit of the Ghetto*, 141; *FAS*, December 8, 1899; Lang, *Tomorrow Is Beautiful*, 116–17.

102. Goldman, *Living*, 5; Eyges, *Beyond the Horizon*, 127–28.

103. Soyer, *Jewish Immigrant Associations*, 84–85, 69; Nadelman quoted in Shuldiner, *Of Moses and Marx*, 64; Avrich, *Anarchist Portraits*, 190.

104. Gurock, *When Harlem Was Jewish*, 61–62; Kliger, *Jewish Hometown Associations*, 56.

105. Howe, *World of Our Fathers*, 211; *The Agitator*, January 1, 1912.

106. *Man!*, March 1935; Falk, Pateman, and Moran, *Emma Goldman*, 1:369. In 1894, French artillery captain Alfred Dreyfus was sentenced to life imprisonment for allegedly passing military secrets to Germany. However, evidence soon emerged that Dreyfus was innocent and had been framed by the military for another man's crime due to his Jewish ancestry, and many French and Jewish anarchists took up his cause. He was finally exonerated in 1906.

107. Kopeloff, *Amol in Amerike*, 458; Barondes, "Zikhroynes fun amol," 38.

108. "Anarkhizmus" and A. G., "Di kulturele un politishe tsionisten," *FAS*, April 11-May 16, 1903; "Der blut-pad in Kisheniav," *FAS*, May 2, 1903.

109. *FAS*, May 23, 30, 1903.

110. Frank, "Anarkho-sotsialistishe ideyen," 286; *FAS*, June 6-August 15, 1903.

111. Michels, *Fire in Their Hearts*, 128–29.

112. Zhitlowsky, "Dr. Hillel Zolotarov," 14 n; Michels, *Fire in Their Hearts*, 140, 146–47.

113. Solotaroff, *Geklibene shriften*, 3:307; Zhitlowsky, "Dr. Hillel Zolotarov"; Graur, "Anarcho-Nationalism," 14–16.

114. Gordin, *Sh. Yanovsky*, 279–80, 305–13.

115. *ME*, March 1906.

116. Solotaroff, *Geklibene shriften*, 3:320–30; Graur, "Anarcho-Nationalism," 14–16; Frank, "Anarkho-sotsialistishe ideyen," 289.

117. Thorne interview.

118. Weinberg, *Forty Years*, 112; Frank, "Anarchism and the Jews," 284.

119. Kopeloff, "M. Katts's tetigkayt," 27–29; Weinberg, *Forty Years*, 111.

120. Borochov, "Two Currents," 151; Margolis, "Tempest in Three Teapots," 152.

121. Michels, *Fire in Their Hearts*, 146–47; Urofsky, *American Zionism*, 104.

122. Jennifer Guglielmo, *Living the Revolution*, 142–43; Bencivenni, "'Fired by the Ideal.'"

123. Tunney, *Throttled!*, 40; Gabaccia, *Militants and Migrants*, 139–41.

124. Vega, *Memoirs*, 115.

125. Zappia, "Unionism and the Italian American Worker"; Jennifer Guglielmo, *Living the Revolution*, chap. 6.

126. *ME*, January, February 8, 1908; Goyens, *Beer and Revolution*, 199–201.

127. Avrich and Avrich, *Sasha and Emma*, 201–3; Wisotsky, "Such a Life," 76. On Silverstein's illness, see Liber, *Doctor's Apprenticeship*, 364.

128. *ME*, February 1914.

129. Ibid., April 1914; Ganz, *Rebels*, 126–54 (quote on 126); Avrich, *Modern School*, 199–211.

130. On Costa, see Tresca, *Autobiography*, 235.

131. Avrich, *Anarchist Voices*, 218; Avrich, *Modern School*, 215–35.

132. See, for example, *FAS*, July 11, October 17, 1914.

133. Eric L. Goldstein, *Price of Whiteness*, 75, 80; Bialostotsky, *David Edelshtat gedenkbukh*, 367–68.

134. *FAS*, May 29, 1909; W. E. B. Du Bois, "A veh geshrey fun a shvartsen," *FAS*, March 4, 11, 1911; Stowe, *Onkel Tom's kebin*.

135. Howe, *World of Our Fathers*, 631; Eric L. Goldstein, *Price of Whiteness*.

136. Gurock, *When Harlem Was Jewish*; Pritchett; Eric L. Goldstein, *Price of Whiteness*, 75–76; Lederhendler, *Jewish Immigrants and American Capitalism*, 80–84.

137. Perry, *Hubert Harrison*, 234–36.

138. Ferguson, *Emma Goldman*, 268; *ME*, March 1908.

139. Bialostotsky, *David Edelshtat gedenk-bukh*, 321–22; Ravage, *American in the Making*, 108; Goyens, *Beer and Revolution*, 155–58; Keyser interview.

140. Goldman, *Living*, 34.

141. Yevzerov, *Froy in der gezelshaft*, 19.

142. Gurock, *When Harlem Was Jewish*, 72. Gurock garbles the transliteration of *Zsherminal* (the Yiddish spelling of "Germinal") as "Charmigal."

143. Ganz, *Rebels*, 246–60; Ewen, *Immigrant Women*, 177–83.

144. Pratt, "Culture and Radical Politics," 76–85; Hadda, *Yankev Glatshteyn*, 13–14.

145. *FAS*, October 30, 1915; Pratt, "Culture and Radical Politics," 77.

146. Keyser interview.

147. *FAS*, December 8, 1899.

148. Lang, *Tomorrow Is Beautiful*, 43; Goldman, *Living*, 81; Weinberg, *Forty Years*, 65.

149. Hapgood, *Spirit of the Ghetto*, 190; Keyser interview.

150. Goodfriend interview.

151. Karen Rosenberg, "Cult of Self-Sacrifice," 190.

152. Lang, *Tomorrow Is Beautiful*, 33.

153. Levine, *Women's Garment Workers*, 54; Glenn, *Daughters of the Shtetl*, 117–18, 227–38.

154. Schneiderman and Goldthwaite, *All for One*, 48–49.

155. Levine, *Women's Garment Workers*, chap. 21; Seller, "Uprising of the Twenty Thousand."

156. Farber interviewed in Fischler and Sucher, *Free Voice of Labor*.

157. Spivak, "Lebnsveg fun Yankev Eybrams," 11–12; Domsky-Abrams, "My Reminiscences."

158. *FAS*, April 1, 1911; Domsky-Abrams, "My Reminiscences."

159. Levine, *Women's Garment Workers*, 124–25, 187–88, 593; Alexander Berkman to Tillie Sigman, August 25, 1931, folder 58, Berkman Papers.

160. Nomad, *Dreamers*, 153.

161. Avrich, *Anarchist Voices*, 350; Joseph J. Cohen, *Yidish-anarkhistishe bavegung*, 100.

162. Quoted in Kitz, *Poetics of Anarchy*, 67.

163. *ME*, December 1908.

Chapter 2. *I Senza Patria*

1. Nichols, "Anarchists in America," 860; *NYT*, June 20, 1906.

2. Cerrito, "Sull'emigrazione anarchica italiana"; Bernstein, *First International*, 122.

3. Creagh, *Anarchisme*, 1005; Bettini, *Bibliografia*, 2:290; Ostuni, *Diaspora politica*, 28.

4. *GdO*, June 5, November 10, 1892.

5. Errico Malatesta, "Verso l'anarchia," *QS*, December 9, 1899, translated in Malatesta, *Method of Freedom*, 299–302.

6. Starr, *Italians of New Jersey*, 62; Altarelli, "History and Present Conditions," 3; U.S. Immigration Commission, *Reports*, 11:17–19.

7. Sione, "Industrial Work, Militancy, and Migrations"; Ramella, "Across the Ocean"; Baily, *Immigrants*, 1–9.

8. Ramella, *Terra e telai*; Bull, "Lombard Silk Spinners"; Davis, "Socialism and the Working Classes," 207.

9. U.S. Immigration Commission, *Reports*, 11:37–38, 4:172, 175.

10. Berta, "Formazione del movimento"; Davis, "Socialism and the Working Classes," 206.

11. Nascimbene, *Movimento operaio*, 351–63; Berta, "Formazione del movimento," 306–8; Ramella, *Terra e telai*, 242–74.

12. Bessone, *Uomini tempi*, 71; Bull, "Lombard Silk Spinners"; Cesare Roda-Balzarini file and Maria Roda-Balzarini file, box 4368, CPC.

13. Bessone, *Uomini tempi*; Rigola, *Rinaldo Rigola*, 96.

14. Rigazio, "Alberto Guabello," 180; De Maria, "Anarchici italiani"; Bessone, *Uomini tempi*, 194–95.

15. Malato, *Joyeusetés de l'exil*, 113.

16. U.S. Immigration Commission, *Reports*, 11:34, 46–48.

17. Altarelli, "History and Present Conditions," 2–3; Sione, "Industrial Work, Militancy, and Migrations," 130, 147, 150.

18. Altarelli, "History and Present Conditions," 3–4; U.S. Immigration Commission, *Reports*, 11:35–36, 46.

19. Scranton, "Exceedingly Irregular Business"; U.S. Immigration Commission, *Reports*, 11:53–54; *QS*, March 25, 1905.

20. Koettgen, "Making Silk," 554; *CS*, May 18, 1907.

21. Vecoli, *People of New Jersey*, 183–84; U.S. Immigration Commission, *Reports*, 11:37–38, 42.

22. See Masini, *Storia degli anarchici italiani nell'epoca degli attentati*; Pernicone, *Italian Anarchism*; Turcato, "Italian Anarchism."

23. Firmino Felice Gallo file, box 2256, CPC.

24. Bessone, *Uomini tempi*, 180; Rigazio, "Alberto Guabello," 166–67; Serafino Grandi file, box 2504, CPC.

25. Calculated from Giulietti, *Dizionario biografico*.

26. Rigazio, "Alberto Guabello," 181–82, 185; Turcato, *Making Sense of Anarchism*, 114–22; Malato, *Joyeusetés de l'exil*, 109–36; *QS*, April 29, 1899; Adele Guabello, Alberto Augusto Guabello, and Paolo Guabello files, box 2548, CPC.

27. Jennifer Guglielmo, *Living the Revolution*, 139, 156–57; Cesare Roda-Balzarini file, box 4368, CPC.

28. Galzerano, *Gaetano Bresci*; *AdR*, December 19, 1936; Antonioli et al., *Dizionario biografico*, s.v. Baracchi, Giovanni Matteo.

29. Antonio Cravello file and Ernestina Cravello file, box 1524, CPC.

30. Avrich, *Anarchist Voices*, 155.

31. *GdO*, June 18, 1892; Altarelli, "History and Present Conditions," 6; "Story of an Anarchist Group."

32. File 61-4625, OG.

33. Casanovas i Codina, "Pedro Esteve"; Jennifer Guglielmo, *Living the Revolution*, 158–59; Nichols, "Anarchists in America," 863.

34. *QS*, January 13, 1900; B. o G. B. Cominetti file, box 1428, CPC.

35. Maserati, *Anarchici a Trieste*, 33–34, 43–45.

36. Jennifer Guglielmo, *Living the Revolution*, 145.

37. Perrier, "Union républicaine," 317, 320; Avrich, *Anarchist Portraits*, 26–27.

38. Rigola, *Rinaldo Rigola*, 131–32, 97; Altarelli, "History and Present Conditions," 2–3.

39. Goyens, *Beer and Revolution*, 33–34, 135, 151.

40. *GdO*, October 1, 1892; *QS*, April 13, 1901.

41. *FAS*, June 23, 1893, December 8, 1899, March 4, 1905; *ME*, February 1908; *EN*, October 16, 1915; file 61-4625, OG.

42. Caminita, *Free Country!*, 8, 29.

43. *QS*, July 15, 1897; *EN*, July 8, 1916.

44. Jennifer Guglielmo, *Living the Revolution*; *NYT*, November 11, 1900; *NYH*, July 31, 1900.

45. Turcato, "Italian Anarchism," 425.

46. *EN*, July 17, 1915; Carey, "'Questione Sociale,'" 291–92; Lord, Trenor, and Barrows, *Italian in America*, 246.

47. *EN*, July 17, 1915.

48. Kelly, "Roll Back the Years," 18:4; *EN*, July 17, 1915.

49. Turcato, *Making Sense of Anarchism*, 79–81.

50. Pernicone, *Italian Anarchism*, 239–43; Turcato, "European Anarchism"; *QS*, September 2, 1899.

51. *QS*, April 15, 1897.

52. Fedeli, *Giuseppe Ciancabilla*; Antonioli et al., *Dizionario biografico*, s.v. Ciancabilla, Giuseppe.

53. *QS*, January 28, 1899.

54. Turcato, *Making Sense of Anarchism*, 84, 90–99, 177–80, 189; *QS*, September 2, 1899.

55. *QS*, September 2, 1899.

56. Ibid., September 30, October 14, 1899, January 26, April 27, 1901; Turcato, *Making Sense of Anarchism*, 110.

57. *QS*, October 7, 1899.

58. *L'Aurora*, June 29, 1901.

59. Pernicone, *Italian Anarchism*, 239–43; Turcato, "European Anarchism."

60. *L'Aurora*, September 16, 1899 (quote); Masini, *Storia degli anarchici italiani da Bakunin a Malatesta*, 227; Schmidt and van der Walt, *Black Flame*, 20.

61. *Man!*, March 1933; Berti, *Errico Malatesta*, 287.

62. Levy, "Anarchist Assassin"; Richard Bach Jensen, *Battle against Anarchist Terrorism*.

63. Bresci quoted in Carey, "Vessel, the Deed, and the Idea," 50.

64. *NYT*, July 31, 1900; *NYH*, July 31, 1900; Richard Bach Jensen, *Battle against Anarchist Terrorism*, 195–97.

65. *QS*, July 20, 1900. The Right to Existence Group denied that "Carbone" was even an anarchist, but L. Bianchi appears among the names of donors to *La Questione Sociale* in the January 31, 1897, issue.

66. Galzerano, *Gaetano Bresci*, 347–89.

67. Carey, "Vessel, the Deed, and the Idea"; Levy, "Anarchist Assassin"; Galzerano, *Gaetano Bresci*; Richard Bach Jensen, *Battle against Anarchist Terrorism*, 195–97. Cf. Gremmo, *Anarchici*.

68. *QS*, August 4, 1900.

69. Ibid., October 12, 1901.

70. *QS*, November 18, December 23, 1899, September 27, 1902; *La Protesta Umana*, May 31, 1903.

71. *NYH*, July 31, 1900; *NYT*, August 3, 1900; Jennifer Guglielmo, *Living the Revolution*, 143.

72. *NYH*, July 31, 1900.

73. Nelson, *Beyond the Martyrs*, 149.

74. Bessone, *Uomini tempi*, 61–67.

75. Gremmo, *Anarchici*, 39; Sione, "Industrial Work, Militancy, and Migrations," 169.

76. Giovanni Tamaroglio file, box 5013, CPC.

77. *NYT*, August 1, 1900; file 8000-385063, OG.

78. File 289493, OG; U.S. Congress, House, Committee on Immigration and Naturalization, *Communist Labor Party Deportation Cases*, 38.

79. Avrich, *Anarchist Voices*, 155.

80. *GdO*, November 30, 1894. See also Vecoli, "'Primo Maggio'"; Bencivenni, *Italian Immigrant Radical Culture*, 59–62.

81. *QS*, August 15, 1895; Bencivenni, *Italian Immigrant Radical Culture*, 101.

82. See, for example, *NYT*, August 1, 3, 1900; Bencivenni, *Italian Immigrant Radical Culture*, 65; Flynn, *Rebel Girl*, 245; Avrich, *Anarchist Voices*, 110, 132. It is likely that anarchist women wore red instead of black because Italian Catholic women's traditional attire was black.

83. Rigazio, "Alberto Guabello," 178–79; *QS*, October 21, 1899.

84. Altarelli, "History and Present Conditions," 3–4.

85. Carnevale, *New Language*; Altarelli, "History and Present Conditions," 2–3 (quote).

86. Carnevale, *New Language*, 137; Choate, *Emigrant Nation*, chap. 4.

87. *QS*, December 9, 1899, February 7, 1903.

88. Bencivenni, *Italian Immigrant Radical Culture*, 56–59; Gorman, "Anarchists in Education"; *QS*, August 10, 1901, March 14, 1903.

89. *EN*, September 25, October 16, December 25, 1915, February 12, December 23, 1916, February 3, 1917; *Il Bollettino de L'Era Nuova*, March 1, 1919; *Nuovi Tempi*, March 1918.

90. Iannarelli, *Sciopero dei tessitori*, 17; *EN*, February 3, 1917.

91. Aquilano, *Ordine figli d'Italia*, 69, 73; Biagi, *Purple Aster*, 214; Mason, "Industrial War in Paterson," 287.

92. Ostuni, *Diaspora politica*, 28; *NYT*, August 1, 1900; *QS*, September 1, 1900.

93. File 289493, OG.

94. *QS*, May 12, 1906; U.S. Congress, House, Committee on Immigration and Naturalization, *Communist Labor Party Deportation Cases*, 40.

95. Altarelli, "History and Present Conditions," 20; *QS*, February 11, 1899.

96. *GdO*, April 4, 1894; Falk, Pateman, and Moran, *Emma Goldman*, 1:206; "Story of an Anarchist Group."

97. Ernestina Cravello file and Vittorio Cravello file, box 1524, CPC; Jennifer Guglielmo, *Living the Revolution*, 161.

98. *NYT*, August 16, 1894.

99. Goldman and Berkman, *Nowhere at Home*, 185; *L'Aurora*, December 16, 1899.

100. Jennifer Guglielmo, *Living the Revolution*, 24; Herman, *Anarchist Bastard*, 78–80; *NYT*, August 3, 1900.

101. Dodyk, "Women's Work," 17; *QS*, August 31, 1907.

102. Jennifer Guglielmo, *Living the Revolution*, 151.

103. Ibid., 228; Ersilia Cavedagni file, box 1205, CPC; Antonioli et al., *Dizionario biografico*, s.v. Cavedagni, Ersilia. Cavedagni had previously been married and was therefore also known as Ersilia Grandi.

104. *GdO*, December 9, 1893; *QS*, August 24, 1901.

105. Bessone, *Uomini tempi*, chap. 19; Jennifer Guglielmo, *Living the Revolution*, 159–60; *QS*, September 15, 1897.

106. Bencivenni, *Italian Immigrant Radical Culture*, 107–8; Jennifer Guglielmo, *Living the Revolution*, 172–74.

107. Merithew, "Anarchist Motherhood."

108. *EN*, June 6, 1913.

109. *NYH*, July 31, 1900; Gremmo, *Anarchici*, 36.

110. File 315825, OG.

111. *GdO*, June 5, 1892.

112. Avrich, *Anarchist Voices*, 153–54.

113. *NYT*, August 5, 1900; Ernestina Cravello file and Vittorio Cravello file, box 1524, Gaspare Paolo Ferro file, box 2045, CPC; Avrich, *Anarchist Voices*, 154.

114. *QS*, March 15, 1896, June 30, 1897.

115. *L'Aurora*, October 28, 1899; *QS*, September 7, 1901; Merithew, "Anarchist Motherhood"; Jennifer Guglielmo, *Living the Revolution*, 166–68.

116. *QS*, July 1895.

117. *NYH*, July 31, 1900.

118. *QS*, September 20, 1902.

119. Ibid., July 7, 1900.

120. Ibid., July 1895.

121. *NYT*, July 31, 1900.

122. See, for example, Caminita, *Free Country!*; Vecoli, "'Free Country.'"

123. *EN*, June 13, July 11, 1908.

124. *CS*, July 6, 1907.

125. *EN*, February 20, 1909. See also Salerno, *"Delitti della Razza Bianca."*

126. Perry, "Hubert Harrison and Paterson."

127. Jacobson, *Whiteness of a Different Color*; Jennifer Guglielmo and Salerno, *Are Italians White?*; Thomas A. Guglielmo, *White on Arrival*; Roediger, *Working toward Whiteness*; *CS*, August 28, 1916.

128. Higham, *Strangers in the Land*, 90–91, 169, 184–85, 264.

129. *EN*, February 6, 1915.

130. *QS*, September 23, 1899.

131. Quoted in Ramella, "Across the Ocean," 109.

132. Starr, *Italians of New Jersey*, 23–24; Vecoli, *People of New Jersey*, 163; Altarelli, "History and Present Conditions," 23.

133. *GdO*, October 24, 1892; file 289493, OG.

134. *NYT*, April 8, 1917; file 289493, OG.

135. *NYT*, August 3, 1900; U.S. Immigration Commission, *Reports*, 26:235–36.

136. Gli Anarchici di Phillipsburg and Newark, N.J., "Agl'Intelligenti," [1907], folder 3374, Nettlau Papers.

137. *EN*, January 13, 1914.

138. *NYH*, July 31, 1900; *GdO*, June 30, 1892.

139. *The Rebel*, October 20, 1895.

140. *QS*, November 25, 1899.

141. *La Jacquerie*, May 21, 1919, copy in file 61-4625, OG.

142. *QS*, September 9, 1899.

143. *L'Aurora*, September 22, 1900; *QS*, September 15, 1895, September 30, 1899.

144. *GdO*, June 30, July 14, 1892.

145. Ostuni, *Diaspora politica*, 28; Panofsky, "View of Two Major Centers ," 273–74; Tresca, *Autobiography*, 143–44.

146. Gori, *Scienza e religione*, 13.

147. Caminita, *Che cose è la religione*; Ludovico Caminita file, box 973, CPC.

148. Vecoli, "Prelates and Peasants"; Tomasi, *Piety and Power*.

149. Bessone, *Uomini tempi*, chap. 10; Elwood, "Roots and Results," chap. 3; Altarelli, "History and Present Conditions," 21–22; "Story of an Anarchist Group."

150. Sione, "Industrial Work, Militancy, and Migrations," 271, 212–14.

151. *GdO*, June 5, 1892; Sione, "Industrial Work, Militancy, and Migrations," 214–16; Wood, "History of Labor," 156–59.

152. *QS*, February 28, May 1, March 30, August 15, December 15, 1897, February 4, 1899.

153. Galzerano, *Gaetano Bresci*, 578; *QS*, March 9, 23, May 18, 25, August 24, 31, 1901.

154. *QS*, September 15, 1895, January 12, June 29, 1901.

155. *NYT*, June 25, 1902, February 3, 2002.

156. *NYT*, April 23, 24, 1902; *QS*, December 30, 1899, April 26, 1902; Rigazio, "Alberto Guabello," 157.

157. Wood, "History of Labor," 179–83; *NYT*, June 27, 1902.

158. Ostuni, *Diaspora politica*, 163; *AdR*, September 23, 1933; *QS*, April 19, 1902.

159. *QS*, May 31, June 14, 1902.

160. Ibid., June 21, 1902; *NYT*, June 19, 1902; Ghio, *Anarchisme aux États-Unis*, 139–43.

161. Wood, "History of Labor," 184–90; *NYT*, June 19, 1902.

162. On MacQueen, see "*Free Commune* and Billy MacQueen." In Europe, Grossman adopted the name Pierre Ramus and became a prominent anarcho-syndicalist.

163. *CS*, May 18, 1907.

164. *QS*, August 23, September 6, 1902, February 28, 1903.

165. Altarelli, "History and Present Conditions," 10.

166. *QS*, July 19, 1902; *Boycottage et sabottage*; *QS*, October 6, 1900.

167. Salerno, *Red November, Black November*, 137; Salerno, "Introduction," 5–6.

168. *QS*, February 7, 1903; Wood, "History of Labor," 195.

169. *QS*, April 29, June 24, 1905.

170. Ibid., July 15, 1905. Andrà and Corna identified the other anarchist delegates as Jay Fox, Robert C. Goodwin, Julie Mechanic, Joseph Peukert, Lucy Parsons, and A. Wrink of Chicago; Andrew Klemencic of Pueblo, Colorado; John Riordan of Phoenix, British Colombia; Albert Ryan of Jerome, Arizona; and M. E. White of Denver, Colorado. (I have corrected spelling errors by cross-referencing their list with the official convention proceedings.) Corna and Andrà also mention but do not identify "several others": they included Spanish anarchist Florencia Bazora and, according to Salvatore Salerno, Thomas J. Hagerty (Salerno, *Red November, Black November*, chap. 3).

171. *QS*, August 5, 1905; Industrial Workers of the World, *Founding Convention*, 247.

172. *QS*, August 19, 1905, February 24, March 3, June 6, 1906; *IW*, May 1906; Iannarelli, *Sciopero dei tessitori*, 21; *IUB*, September 14, 1907.

173. *IUB*, March 23, April 6, 1907; Thompson and Bekken, *I.W.W.*, 27.

174. *IUB*, March 23, April 6, 13, 1907; Wood, "History of Labor," 201.

175. Shor, "'Virile Syndicalism'"; Topp, *Those without a Country*; Hewitt, "'Voice of Virile Labor.'"

176. *IUB*, April 13, June 29, October 12, 1907.

177. Ludovico Caminita file and Michele Caminita file, box 973, CPC; Caminita, "Twenty Years," 3–7; U.S. Congress, House, Committee on Immigration and Naturalization, *Communist Labor Party Deportation Cases*, 32.

178. *IUB*, April 20, April 27, June 15, 1907; *EN*, July 17, 1915; Industrial Workers of the World, "Third Annual Convention," 140.

179. *IUB*, May 9, 16, 1908.

180. Fenton, *Immigrants and Labor Unions*, 164; Wilcox, "These We Will Not Compromise." On the syndicalist Federazione Socialista Italiana, see Topp, *Those without a Country*.

181. Industrial Workers of the World, *Proceedings of the Second Annual Convention*, 190, 246.

182. L. Duvicu [Ludovico Caminita], "La Convenzione dell I.W.W.," *QS*, September 21-October 5, 1907; Industrial Workers of the World, "Third Annual Convention," 109–10, 134–37, 140–49, 459, 485.

183. Tripp, *I.W.W. and the Paterson Silk Strike*, 40–41; *IUB*, November 7, 1908, February 20, 1909; Wilcox, "These We Will Not Compromise," 34–37.

184. *NYT*, March 25, 1907; Carey, "Vessel, the Deed, and the Idea," 56.

185. Robert J. Goldstein, "Anarchist Scare."

186. *NYT*, March 29, April 3, 4, 10, 1908; *ME*, June 1908.

187. *NYT*, June 14, 1908; Caminita, "Twenty Years," 33–40; file 61-115, OG.

188. *EN*, September 26, 1908; *Nihil*, March 10, 1909.

189. File 61-4625, OG; Avrich, *Anarchist Voices*, 82; Pernicone, *Carlo Tresca*, 64–65.

190. U.S. Commission on Industrial Relations, *Industrial Relations*, 3:2593.

191. *IW*, April 2, 1910.

192. Iannarelli, *Sciopero dei tessitori*; Wilcox, "These We Will Not Compromise," 47–61; Tripp, *I.W.W. and the Paterson Silk Strike*, 45–60.

193. *Il Proletario*, June 1, July 13, 1912.

194. *IW*, March 14, 1912; Flynn, "Truth about the Paterson Strike," 216.

195. U.S. Commission on Industrial Relations, *Industrial Relations*, 11:2453.

196. Ibid., 2593; Fitch, "I.W.W.," 362; *Pageant of the Paterson Strike*, 22.

197. U.S. Commission on Industrial Relations, *Industrial Relations*, 11:2457, 2603; Most, "Modest Place."

198. U.S. Commission on Industrial Relations, *Industrial Relations*, 11:2455; Flynn, *Rebel Girl*, 155.

199. *TN*, September 6, 1913; Sanger, "Paterson Strike," 47.

200. *EN*, March 8, April 26, 1913.

201. Tripp, *I.W.W. and the Paterson Silk Strike*, 65–66; Golin, *Fragile Bridge*, 40–41; Mason, "Industrial War in Paterson," 284, 287.

202. U.S. Commission on Industrial Relations, *Industrial Relations*, 11:2448–49, 2593.

203. *EN*, March 29, 1913; Avrich, *Anarchist Voices*, 155; U.S. Commission on Industrial Relations, *Industrial Relations*, 11:2463, 2525.

204. *EN*, May 10, July 5, 1913; file 61-4625, OG.

205. Osborne, "Italian Immigrants," 22; *EN*, June 21, July 5, 12, 1913.

206. U.S. Commission on Industrial Relations, *Industrial Relations*, 11:2543, 2550–51.

207. Mason, "Industrial War in Paterson," 287; Golin, *Fragile Bridge*, 28, 49; *EN*, March 22, 1913.

208. Wisotsky, "Such a Life," 67–68.

209. "Pageant of the Paterson Strike," 428; Bird, Georgakas, and Shaffer, *Solidarity Forever*, 62.

210. Golin, *Fragile Bridge*, 81–82; Tripp, *I.W.W. and the Paterson Silk Strike*, 76.

211. *EN*, March 22, 1913.

212. *Pageant of the Paterson Strike*, 16–18; Tripp, *I.W.W. and the Paterson Silk Strike*, 145.

213. *EN*, August 3, 1913; Golin, *Fragile Bridge*, 192.

214. U.S. Commission on Industrial Relations, *Industrial Relations*, 11:2465, 2598–99; Wood, "History of Labor," 265, 270; Golin, *Fragile Bridge*, 196; David J. Goldberg, *Tale of Three Cities*, 35–37; *EN*, September 11, 1915.

215. *EN*, January 3, 17, 1914; *NYT*, January 21, 1916; Flynn, *Rebel Girl*, 171–73.

216. *EN*, November 29, 1913; Golin, *Fragile Bridge*, 194–96; Bird, Georgakas, and Shaffer, *Solidarity Forever*, 68.

217. *EN*, March 17, 1917; *ME*, May 1915.

Chapter 3. "All Flags Look Alike to Us"

1. Issel and Cherney, *San Francisco*, 24, 54.

2. *San Francisco Call*, March 6, 1908.

3. Levy, "Social Histories of Anarchism," 21; Ramnath, *Decolonizing Anarchism*, 78.

4. Issel and Cherney, *San Francisco*, 56; Rosenbaum, *Cosmopolitans*, chap. 7; Kazin, *Barons of Labor*, 20.

5. Cross, *History of the Labor Movement*, 89; Perrier, "Union républicaine," 313.

6. Cross, *History of the Labor Movement*, chap. 10; Avrich, *Haymarket Tragedy*, 68–70.

7. *NYT*, December 17, 1885; Saxton, *Indispensable Enemy*, chap. 9–10.

8. Cross, *History of the Labor Movement*, 159, 161–62; Ralph Edward Shaffer, "Radicalism in California," 62.

9. Creagh, *Anarchisme*, 996; Hill, *Men, Mobs, and Law*, 107.

10. Saxton, *Indispensable Enemy*, 221–23; Schwartz, *Brotherhood of the Sea*, 7.

11. *TN*, supplément littéraire, nos. 30–31, 1900.

12. *The Beacon*, August 8, 1891; Rosenbaum, *Cosmopolitans*.

13. *Egoism*, May 1890, September 1891.

14. Cesare Crespi file, box 1530, CPC; Lucarini, "Cesare Crespi"; Travaglio interview; Avrich, *Anarchist Voices*, 161.

15. Avrich, *Anarchist Voices*, 164; Lucarini, "Cesare Crespi."

16. *ME*, March 1915; *Secolo Nuovo* quoted in *QS*, August 4, 1900; *Newspaper Directory and Advertisers' Manual*, 19. I have located only two surviving issues of *Secolo Nuovo*, both from 1903 and preserved on microfilm at the Immigration History Research Center, University of Minnesota, Minneapolis.

17. Cordillot, *Sociale en Amérique*, s.v. Klemincic, A; *Discontent*, May 25, 1898.

18. *Solidarity*, March 15, 1898.

19. *San Francisco Call*, March 13, 1896; L'Alleanza Socialista Anarchica, "Dichiarazione di principii," [1896], folder 3374, Nettlau Papers.

20. *San Francisco Call*, March 16, April 3, 1896; *QS*, January 28, 1899.

21. *Discontent*, May 18, 1898; *Solidarity*, March 15, 1898; *QS*, August 2, 1899.

22. *Free Society*, May 17, 1903.

23. Avrich, *Anarchist Voices*, 161; *L'Aurora*, March 2, 1901; Enrico Travaglio file, box 5198, CPC; Fine, "Anarchism and the Assassination," 781–86; *L'Aurora*, October 2, 1901.

24. Avrich, *Anarchist Voices*, 164.

25. *L'Effort*, December 1904.

26. *CS*, April 1, 1905.

27. Cinel, *From Italy to San Francisco*, 106–8; Issel and Cherney, *San Francisco*, 74.

28. *CS*, March 16, 1907.

29. Fichera, *Italy on the Pacific*, 48–49, 53–57; Cinel, *From Italy to San Francisco*, 150, 214–26 (quote on 222).

30. Giovinco, "'Success in the Sun?'"; *Emigrazione e colonie*, 247–48.

31. Quoted in Cinel, *From Italy to San Francisco*, 222.

32. Knight, *Industrial Relations*, 174–75; *IUB*, June 6, 1908.

33. *CS*, October 27, 1906; *Emancipator*, May 1907; López and Cortés, *Partido Liberal Mexicano*, 184–85.

34. *Cogito, Ergo Sum*, September 15, October 15, November 15, 1908.

35. Carlo Guglielmo Dalboni file, box 1577, CPC.

36. Antonioli et al., *Dizionario biografico*, s.v. Antonelli, Adolfo; Di Paola, *Knights Errant of Anarchy*, 102–5, 108–11.

37. *Nihil*, June 20, 1908, May 22, 1909.

38. Bieito Alonso Fernández, *Obreiros*, 106; *CS*, May 30, 1914, March 27, 1915.

39. Albro, *To Die on Your Feet*, 72, 103.

40. *IW*, May 23, 1912; Street, *Beasts of the Field*, 854 n. 60; *IUB*, March 16, 1907. Mixed locals consisted of workers in trades that lacked enough IWW members to form separate industrial union locals.

41. Knight, *Industrial Relations*, 46; Sensi-Isolani, "Italian Radicals," 194.

42. *IUB*, May 18, June 8, 1907.

43. Ibid., September 14, 1907, April 25, 1908; *IW*, May 28, 1910; Weintraub, "I.W.W. in California," 22.

44. *The Agitator*, September 15, 1911; *Il Proletario*, May 12, June 2, September 29, 1911.

45. Cordillot, *Sociale en Amérique*, s.vv. Casas, Laurent and Saffores, B.; Duff, *Silent Defenders*, 53; *IW*, July 6, 1911. Laurent Casas (real name Humbert Rullière) later became a Socialist and editor of San Francisco's *L'Écho de l'Ouest*.

46. *IW*, July 6, 1911, January 11, May 30, 1912.

47. Luigi Parenti file, box 3732, CPC; Hughes, "Lest This Be Lost," n.p.

48. *Il Proletario*, June 22, 1912; *IW*, January 30, 1913; Hughes, "Lest This Be Lost," n.p; Luigi Parenti file, box 3732, CPC.

49. Sensi-Isolani, "Italian Radicals," 198–99.

50. *IW*, January 2, 1913.

51. Knight, *Industrial Relations*, 268–70; Monaco, "San Francisco Shoe Workers' Strike."

52. Hughes, "Lest This Be Lost," n.p.

53. Cordillot, *Sociale en Amérique*, s.v. Saffores B.

54. Weintraub, "I.W.W. in California," 90–91; Knight, *Industrial Relations*, 343–44.

55. *IUB*, April 25, 1908; Shor, "'Virile Syndicalism.'"

56. *Il Proletario*, August 25, 1911.

57. *IW*, August 31, 1911; *Revolt*, August 19, 1911; *SFC*, August 14, 1911; *Il Proletario*, September 1, 29, 1911.

58. Weintraub, "I.W.W. in California," 33; *IW*, August 24, 31, September 28, 1911.

59. Quoted in Ralph Edward Shaffer, "Radicalism in California," 251.

60. *IW*, February 1, 8, March 8, 14, 1912; Weintraub, "I.W.W. in California," 34–36.

61. *Il Proletario*, February 2, 1912, February 1, 1913.

62. Hughes, "Lest This Be Lost," n.p.

63. Michele Centrone file, box 1243, CPC; Gianfrate and Zimmer, *Michele Centrone*.

64. *Il Proletario*, September 29, December 15, 1911.

65. *CS*, January 29, 1916; Avrich, *Anarchist Voices*, 163; *The Blast*, April 1, 1916.

66. File 321621, OG.

67. Hughes, "Lest This Be Lost," n.p.

68. *Il Lavoratore Industriale/Le Travailleur Industriel*, May 1, 1912.

69. Hughes, "Lest This Be Lost," n.p.

70. Ibid.

71. David Koven, "Giovanni 'John' Vattuone, 1899–1994," 1994, file 131, David Koven Papers, IISH; Travaglio interview.

72. *The Blast*, April 1, July 1, 1916.

73. Ibid., March 15, April 1, 15, 1916.

74. Saxton, *Indispensable Enemy*.

75. Daniels, *Politics of Prejudice*, 27–28; Knight, *Industrial Relations*, 213.

76. Daniels, *Politics of Prejudice*, 30, 32–44.

77. *IUB*, April 11, 1908.

78. For anti-Asian sentiments, see *Egoism*, November 1890, April 1891; *The Demonstrator*, August 22, 1906; and the ambivalent statements in *The Agitator*, March 1, 1912. For

pro-Asian arguments, see *Egoism*, May, November 1891; *The Demonstrator*, June 24, 1903; *Free Society*, August 14, 1898; *The Syndicalist*, December 1, 1911.

79. *La Terra*, June 28, 1907; *Cogito, Ergo Sum*, September 15, October 15, 1908.

80. Industrial Workers of the World, *Founding Convention*, 298.

81. "Minutes of the General Executive Board of the Industrial Workers of the World, October 4, 1906-September 15, 1911," folder 1, box 7, Industrial Workers of the World Collection, Archives of Labor and Urban Affairs, Wayne State University, Detroit. See also *IUB*, May 4, 1907, June 27, 1908; *IW*, April 8, 22, 1909, March 30, 1911.

82. Chang, *Pacific Connections*, chap. 4; U.S. Commission on Industrial Relations, *Industrial Relations*, 5:4947; Roediger, "Gaining a Hearing."

83. *TN*, supplément littéraire, no. 25, 1900; Konishi, *Anarchist Modernity*, 211; Crump, *Origins of Socialist Thought*, 182, 190; Notehelfer, *Kōtoku Shūsui*, 61–62, 123; *ME*, August 1911; Henry, "Albert Johnson."

84. Avrich, *Anarchist Voices*, 164; Lang, *Tomorrow Is Beautiful*, 41.

85. Notehelfer, *Kōtoku Shūsui*, 124–27; Konishi, *Anarchist Modernity*, 231; Crump, *Origins of Socialist Thought*, 195, 200.

86. Crump, *Origins of Socialist Thought*, 199–206; Ichioka, *Issei*, 105–6.

87. *SFC*, December 30, 1906; *IUB*, March 9, 1907.

88. *Emancipator*, May 1907.

89. Falk, Pateman, and Moran, *Emma Goldman*, 2:229.

90. Ichioka, *Issei*, 110–13; Industrial Workers of the World, "Third Annual Convention," 274; Street, *Beasts of the Field*, 488–89.

91. Hall, *Harvest Wobblies*, 58; Street, *Beasts of the Field*, chap. 17; Industrial Workers of the World, "Third Annual Convention," 403–4; *IUB*, June 20, 1908.

92. *ME*, April 1910.

93. *IW*, June 4, 1910; Hall, *Harvest Wobblies*, 159.

94. Joan M. Jensen, *Passage from India*, chap. 2.

95. *The Beacon*, April 4, 1891; *Nihil*, March 10, 1909.

96. Ramnath, *Decolonizing Anarchism*, 92; Brown, *Har Dayal*, 112–14; Frost, *Mooney Case*, 48.

97. Ramnath, *Haj to Utopia*, 64; Brown, *Har Dayal*, 110–11, 132.

98. *Regeneración*, February 14, 1914; Brown, *Har Dayal*, 115–16.

99. Saxton, *Indispensable Enemy*, 268–69; Schwartz, *From West to East*, 169–70, 175.

100. *Land and Liberty*, May 1, 30, 1914.

101. Brown, *Har Dayal*, 138–40; Ramnath, *Haj to Utopia*, 32, 37, 44; Joan M. Jensen, *Passage from India*, 183, 186.

102. *Land and Liberty*, October 1914.

103. Ramnath, *Haj to Utopia*, 46, 64–69; Chang, *Pacific Connections*, 117; Bird, Georgakas, and Shaffer, *Solidarity Forever*, 51–52. On the Wheatland Strike, see Weintraub, "I.W.W. in California," 68–78; Hall, *Harvest Wobblies*, chap. 2.

104. Frost, *Mooney Case*, 113; Lang, *Tomorrow Is Beautiful*, 42.

105. Lang, *Tomorrow Is Beautiful*, 41–42.

106. *ME*, August 1907; Zaks, *Geshikhte fun Arbayter Ring*, 2:xxxiv.

107. Lang, *Tomorrow Is Beautiful*, 84.

108. Prpić, *South Slavic Immigration*, 192; *San Francisco Call*, August 25, 1909.

109. Kazin, *Barons of Labor*, 204–8; Avrich and Avrich, *Sasha and Emma*, 240–49. After his release, Caplan traveled to Soviet Russia and then escaped to Paris, where he reportedly committed suicide (Lang, *Tomorrow Is Beautiful*, 270–71; Wisotsky, "Such a Life," 150).

110. *The Blast*, June 1, 1917.

111. Ibid., July 15, 1916.

112. Ibid., July 1, 1916; *SFC*, July 25, 1916.

113. *The Blast*, May 1, July 1, 1916.

114. Avrich, *Anarchist Voices*, 30.

115. *SFC*, July 25, 1916; Ralph Edward Shaffer, "Radicalism in California," 284.

116. Berkman, *Bolshevik Myth*, 54.

117. Files 313343, 337716, OG.

118. *IW*, January 9, 1913.

119. Luigi Parenti file, box 3732, CPC; file 8000-2050, OG.

120. *San Francisco Examiner*, September 19, 1916.

121. The United States of America vs. William D. Haywood, et al., no. 6125, 157, folder 2, box 103, Industrial Workers of the World Collection, Archives of Labor and Urban Affairs, Wayne State University, Detroit.

Chapter 4. "The Whole World Is Our Country"

1. Catanuto and Schirone, *Canto anarchico*, 111. The original Italian reads, "Nostra patria è il mondo intero / nostra legge è la libertà / ed un pensiero / ribelle in cor ci sta."

2. Masini, *Storia degli anarchici italiani nell'epoca degli attentati*, chap. 5; Antonioli et al., *Dizionario biografico*, s.v. Gori, Pietro.

3. *I Congressi socialisti internazionali*, 5; Kelly, "Roll Back the Years," 33:1.

4. Nettlau, *Anarchisten und Sozialrevolutionäre*, chaps. 10–11.

5. Pernicone, *Italian Anarchism*, 194; Avrich, *Haymarket Tragedy*, 55–58, 68–78.

6. Yanovsky, *Ershte yorn*, 159–70.

7. Antonioli et al., *Dizionario biografico*, s.v. Gori, Pietro; Turcato, "1896 London Congress."

8. Esteve, *A los anarquistas*, 22, 72.

9. *Free Society*, October 28, 1900; *FAS*, October 12, 1900. According to Goldman's report in *Free Society*, there were five American delegates. She may have included in her count Hippolyte Havel, who had not yet migrated to the United States but was a proxy delegate representing a Czech-American anarchist group.

10. *TN*, supplément littéraire, nos. 23–32, 1900.

11. *QS*, October 6, 1900.

12. *International Anarchist Congress*; Nomad, "Anarchist Tradition," 86.

13. Falk, Pateman, and Moran, *Emma Goldman*, 2:556.

14. *Bulletin du congrès anarchiste international*, May, July 1914. My thanks to Constance Bantman for sharing her notes on this source with me.

15. Bantman, "Internationalism without an International?," 963.

16. Frank, "Anarkho-sotsialistishe ideyen"; Biagini, *Nati altrove*; Davidson, *Sewing Freedom*.

17. Rocker, *London Years*, 7; *Road to Freedom*, December 1926.

18. Shtupler, "Tsvey pionern," 52; Rocker, *London Years*, 7, 97–98; Avrich, *Russian Anarchists*, 39–40; *Anarquistas de Bialystok*, 25, 127.

19. Goldman, *Living*, 829.

20. Shtupler, "Tsvey pionern," 48–49; Avrich, *Anarchist Voices*, 328; *Anarquistas de Bialystok*, 22–23, 86, 74.

21. Avrich, *Anarchist Voices*, 359–60; Avrich, *Russian Anarchists*, 46–54.

22. Avrich, *Russian Anarchists*, 68–69 n. 120; Confino, "Organization as Ideology," 183; Richard Bach Jensen, *Battle against Anarchist Terrorism*, 36.

23. *FAS*, January 28, February 4, 1905.

24. Goldman, *Living*, 364; Avrich and Avrich, *Sasha and Emma*, 175; *ME*, November 1907.

25. *Anarquistas de Bialystok*, 131.

26. File 8000-385063, OG; Avrich, *Anarchist Voices*, 330.

27. Avrich, *Anarchist Voices*, 74, 364–65.

28. File 325570, BS.

29. New York, Legislature, Joint Legislative Committee to Investigate Seditious Activities, *Revolutionary Radicalism*, 1:861, 2:1448.

30. On Novomirskii, see Avrich, *Russian Anarchists*, 61–62, 124; Strypyansky, "Non-Conformists," 32; Joseph J. Cohen, *Yidish-anarkhistishe bavegung*, 188, 189. Avrich incorrectly states that Novomirskii remained in Siberia until the 1917 revolution.

31. Ralph Edward Shaffer, "Radicalism in California," 324 n. 72; *SFC*, September 12, 13, 15, 1915.

32. *SFC*, May 27, June 5, 1916.

33. Yelensky, *Struggle for Equality*; Avrich, *Anarchist Voices*, 377.

34. Weintraub, "I.W.W. in California," 299; *The Blast*, June 1, 1916.

35. Avrich, *Anarchist Voices*, 389.

36. Turcato, "Italian Anarchism," 419.

37. Bessone, *Uomini tempi*, 217–18, 325; Ostuni, *Diaspora politica*, 208.

38. Turcato, "Italian Anarchism," 427–28, 434.

39. *Trentennio di attività anarchica*, 25; U.S. Congress, House, Committee on Immigration and Naturalization, *Communist Labor Party Deportation Cases*, 40.

40. My calculations from Antonioli et al., *Dizionario biografico*.

41. Bettini, *Bibliografia*; Antonioli et al., *Dizionario biografico*; Turcato, "Italian Anarchism."

42. Quoted in Ostuni, *Diaspora politica*, 179.

43. *Revolt*, January 22, 1916.

44. Notehelfer, *Kōtoku Shūsui*, chaps. 7–8.

45. Crump, *Origins of Socialist Thought*, 203, 206; Tsuzuki, "Anarchism in Japan," 504.

46. *ME*, April 1910; *The Agitator*, March 1, 1911; Crump, *Origins of Socialist Thought*, 211 n. 121, 197.

47. Dirlik, *Anarchism in the Chinese Revolution*.

48. Dirlik, "Anarchism and the Question of Place"; Hwang, "Korean Anarchism."

49. Ramnath, *Haj to Utopia*, 157–62; Marshall, *Demanding the Impossible*, 422–27.

50. Anderson, "Preface," xvii. See also Anderson, *Under Three Flags*; Ramnath, *Decolonizing Anarchism*.

51. Cahm, "Bakunin," 35.

52. Berti, *Errico Malatesta*, 53, 99, 256.

53. Kropotkin, "Finland," 527–28; Kropotkin, "Letter to Maria Isidine Goldsmith," 138.

54. Sigal, *Kropotkin-zamlbukh*, 208–20; Graur, "Anarcho-Nationalism," 5–7.

55. *QS*, April 15, 1896; Gli Anarchici Residenti nel Nord America, "Al popolo italiano," [1895], folder 3378, Nettlau Papers.

56. *QS*, November 30, 1895, June 30, 1897.

57. Poyo, "Anarchist Challenge"; Kirwin R. Shaffer, "Cuba Para Todos"; Frank Fernández, *Cuban Anarchism*, 31–32.

58. Kelly, "Roll Back the Years," 8:1.

59. Esteve, *A los anarquistas*, 73–84; Casanovas i Codina, "Pedro Esteve," 68–70.

60. *QS*, November 30, 1895.

61. Anderson, *Under Three Flags*, 189–95; *QS*, August 15, 1897; *NYT*, August 1, 1900; *Germinal*, October 1, 1899; Falk, Pateman, and Moran, *Emma Goldman*, 1:277.

62. *TN*, June 4, 1898; Berti, *Errico Malatesta*, 288–89.

63. Falk, Pateman, and Moran, *Emma Goldman*, 1:386; *FAS*, October 6, 1899; Jacobson, *Special Sorrows*, chaps. 4–5.

64. *Discontent*, June 6, 1898; *Free Society*, September 25, 1898; *Germinal*, December 30, 1899; *TN*, September 23, 1898, September 9, 1899; *L'Effort*, December 1904; Kirwin R. Shaffer, *Black Flag Boricuas*, 149–58; Vega, *Memoirs*, 83.

65. *ME*, September 1906; Goldman, *Living*, 427–29; Avrich and Avrich, *Sasha and Emma*, 198.

66. *ME*, May 1909, March 1911.

67. Miller, *President and the Assassin*, 286.

68. *Free Society*, April 22, 1900.

69. *Regeneración*, April 6, 1912; *ME*, October 1912; *EN*, February 22, 1913, May 9, 1915.

70. Weintraub, "I.W.W. in California," 23; Weber, "Keeping Community," 218–20.

71. *Industrial Worker*, June 4, 1910; *SFC*, August 14, 1911; Street, *Beasts of the Field*, 604–15.

72. Vittorio Cravello file, box 1524, CPC; Caminita, "Twenty Years," 37–44; Struthers, "World in a City," 169–82; *Regeneración*, May 27, 1911.

73. Struthers, "World in a City," 198; Blaisdell, *Desert Revolution*, 39–40; Turner, *Revolution in Baja California*, 4–6.

74. *Regeneración*, April 29, 1911.

75. Turner, *Revolution in Baja California*, 23; Blaisdell, *Desert Revolution*, 74–77; Weintraub, "I.W.W. in California," 173; Adler, *Man Who Never Died*, 173.

76. Horne, *Black and Brown*, especially 135; Blaisdell, *Desert Revolution*, 74.

77. *Regeneración*, April 3, 1911.

78. Adler, *Man Who Never Died*, 171.

79. *Regeneración*, sezione italiana, August 12, September 2, 9, 1911.

80. *Fraye Gezelshaft*, February 1911.

81. *Industrial Worker*, May 25, 1911.

82. Ramnath, *Haj to Utopia*, 67.

83. *EN*, October 6, 1913.

84. Casanovas i Codina, "Pedro Esteve," 74.

85. Bartoli, "Adventurers"; Blaisdell, *Desert Revolution*, 110–11.

86. *EN*, June 24, 1911; *Regeneración*, May 20, 1911; *Industrial Worker*, June 8, 1911.

87. Blaisdell, *Desert Revolution*, 193; *CS*, September 11, 1911; *Regeneración*, February 24, 1912; Michele Presutto to the author, July 19, 2013.

88. Adler, *Man Who Never Died*, 140, 176–77; Bartoli, "Adventurers."

89. *CS*, September 11, 16, 1911; *Regeneración*, February 24, 1912.

90. Blaisdell, *Desert Revolution*, 146–51; *EN*, June 24, 1911.

91. Turner, *Revolution in Baja California*, 63–64; Blaisdell, *Desert Revolution*, 180–81; Adler, *Man Who Never Died*, 177–78.

92. *CS*, June 17, 1911.

93. Ibid., June 17, August 19, September 2, 1911, January 6, 1912.

94. Ibid., August 19, September 2, 1911, January 6, 1912; *Regeneración*, February 17, 1912.

95. *CS*, August 19, October 28, 1911; *TN*, September 30, 1911.

96. *Regeneración*, September 23, 1911.

97. *EN*, July 1, 1911; Esteve, *Reflexiones*, chap. 5.

98. *Regeneración*, November 11, December 9, 1911; *CS*, January 6, 1912; *Regeneración*, February 3, 1912.

99. *Regeneración*, July 26, 1913.

100. Ibid., July 8, 1911.

101. *TN*, April 27, 1912; *EN*, May 11, 1912.

102. *ME*, December 1911, January, February 1912; *FAS*, February 10, 1912.

103. *ME*, December 1913, February 1914. The arrested men received life sentences; two died in prison and several escaped before the rest were pardoned in 1926.

104. *Land and Liberty*, September 1914.

105. *Regeneración*, June 13, 1914.

106. *EN*, July 4, 1914.

107. *ME*, December 1914.

108. Goldman, *Living*, 564.

109. Cahm, "Kropotkin," 57, 60–61; *ME*, November 1914.

110. Day, "Seize (Le Manifeste des)."

111. *Revolt*, January 29, 1916; *ME*, October 1914; Harry Kelly to John Nicholas Beffel, October 27, 1947, folder 3, box 6, John Nicholas Beffel Collection, Archives of Labor and Urban Affairs, Wayne State University, Detroit.

112. *Land and Liberty*, November, December 1914.

113. Ibid., February 1915; Schwartz, *From West to East*, 181–83.

114. Whitaker, *Anarchist-Individualist Origins*, 39–49 (quote on 43); Fedeli, "Anarchici e la guerra: 2," 685–86; *Novatore*, November 1910.

115. Fedeli, "Anarchici e la guerra: 1," 624, 627; Luparini, *Anarchici di Mussolini*, chap. 1; Antonioli et al., *Dizionario biografico*, s.v. Agresti, Antonio.

116. Whitaker, *Anarchist-Individualist Origins*, 71; Masini, "Gli anarchici italiani."

117. Bertrand, "Italian Revolutionary Syndicalism"; Tinchino, *Edmondo Rossoni*; Topp, *Those without a Country*, 128–30, 135, 149–50, 167.

118. De Ciampis, "Storia del movimento socialista," 151; Salvemini, *Italian Fascist Activities*, 36–37.

119. Sterba, *Good Americans*, 60–67; Gordin, *Sh. Yanovsky*, 322–28; *FAS*, October 24, November 28, 1914.

120. *FAS*, October 31, November 21, December 12, 1914.

121. Joan M. Jensen, *Passage from India*, chap. 9; Brown, *Har Dayal*, 179–82; Puri, *Ghadar Movement*, 102–13; Ramnath, *Haj to Utopia*, 72–94.

122. Tunney, *Throttled!*, 247–50.

123. Joan M. Jensen, *Passage from India*, 190–93; Brown, *Har Dayal*, 194–206; Puri, *Ghadar Movement*, 230–42.

124. Avrich and Avrich, *Sasha and Emma*, 237–38; *ME*, May 1915.

125. *EN*, April 3, August 15, 1915.

126. Ibid., December 12, 1914, January 2, 9, 15, 1915.

127. Ibid., June 26, July 31, August 7, 1915.

128. *CS*, September 11, 1915.

129. *EN*, February 12, 1916; see also August 15, 1914, January 22, June 26, October 2, 1915, January 22, May 6, June 24, September 9, 1916, January 27, 1917.

130. Ibid., September 30, 1916, May 8, July 31, 1915.

131. Ibid., January 30, 1915.

132. Ibid., February 27, 1915.

133. *Land and Liberty*, October 1914, April 1915.

134. *EN*, November 7, 1914.

135. *The Blast*, June 1, 1917.

Chapter 5. Revolution and Repression

1. Murray, *Red Scare*; Preston, *Aliens and Dissenters*; Avrich, *Sacco and Vanzetti*.

2. Richard Bach Jensen, *Battle against Anarchist Terrorism*, 359.

3. *SFC*, July 31, 1916; Frost, *Mooney Case*, 113; Hughes, "Lest This Be Lost," n.p.

4. Frost, *Mooney Case*, 39, 44–45. Frost incorrectly claims that Weinberg "had never been a radical" (75).

5. *The Blast*, August 15, October 15, 1916; *SFC*, August 5, 1916; *San Francisco Examiner*, September 19, 1916; *EN*, October 21, 1916.

6. *Trentennio di attività anarchica*, 134.

7. *The Blast*, August 15, 1916; Frost, *Mooney Case*.

8. Avrich, *Sacco and Vanzetti*, 138; McCormick, *Hopeless Cases*, 25.

9. Avrich and Avrich, *Sasha and Emma*, 265.

10. Avrich, *Anarchist Voices*, 375; Frost, *Mooney Case*, 283–85; Reed, *Ten Days*, 234; Avrich and Avrich, *Sasha and Emma*, 262–65.

11. Ganz, *Rebels*, 268–69.

12. *EN*, May 19, 1917; *NYT*, April 8, 1917.

13. *NYT*, May 19, June 5, 1917; *ME*, June 1917.

14. *CS*, May 26, 1917.

15. U.S. Congress, House, Committee on Immigration and Naturalization, *Communist Labor Party Deportation Cases*, 40; file 61-4625, OG; *EN*, July 6, 1917.

16. *EN*, June 17, 1916; *Land and Liberty*, February 1915; file 8000-2050, OG; *San Francisco Examiner*, September 14, 1917.

17. *SFC*, June 28, 1935; *Il Martello*, December 21, 1929; Ralph Edward Shaffer, "Radicalism in California," 276–77.

18. Weintraub, "I.W.W. in California," 138.

19. Polenberg, *Fighting Faiths*, 48, 63; *ME*, July 1917.

20. Marcus Graham, "Autobiographical Note," vii–xii.

21. La Botz, "American 'Slackers.'"

22. *Trentennio di attività anarchica*, 135–36; Avrich, *Sacco and Vanzetti*, 60–65.

23. File 8000-385063, OG; *Il Bollettino de L'Era Nuova*, March 29, 1919; Avrich, *Anarchist Voices*, 156.

24. *NYT*, June 5, 1977.

25. File 110181, OG.

26. Grosser, *Alcatraz*.

27. *ME*, July 1917.

28. *EN*, July 6, 1917.

29. U.S. Congress, House, Committee on Immigration and Naturalization, *Communist Labor Party Deportation Cases*, 14.

30. Fedeli, *Luigi Galleani*, 102–3; file 315825, OG.

31. Szajkowski, *Jews, Wars, and Communism*, 1:181–82; Jaffe, *Crusade against Radicalism*, 63.

32. Gordin, *Sh. Yanovsky*, 329–32; file 170108, OG; *FAS*, January 12, 1918.

33. Szajkowski, *Jews, Wars, and Communism*, chap. 9; Sterba, *Good Americans*, 132, 163–72.

34. File 250619, OG.

35. Polenberg, *Fighting Faiths*, 22; file 8000-252583, OG.

36. Marcus Graham, "Autobiographical Note," xii.

37. Brown, *Har Dayal*, 218–19; Puri, *Ghadar Movement*, 114–15.

38. Files 313343, 337716, OG.

39. United States vs. Haywood, et al., August 14, 1918, 11757, folder 6, box 117, Industrial Workers of the World Collection, Archives of Labor and Urban Affairs, Wayne State University, Detroit; Files 289493, 200813, OG.

40. Kohn, *American Political Prisoners*, 122.

41. *ME*, May 1917; *EN*, March 24, 1917.

42. Szajkowski, *Jews, Wars, and Communism*, 1:292; Tunney, *Throttled!*, 269; Epstein, *Jew and Communism*, 24.

43. New York, Legislature, Joint Legislative Committee to Investigate Seditious Activities, *Revolutionary Radicalism*, 1:628–29; Boehm, *U.S. Military Intelligence Reports*, reel 1, 190–206.

44. Joseph J. Cohen, *Yidish-anarkhistishe bavegung*, 336.

45. Copp, "Role of the Anarchists," 54–56.

46. Quoted in Shuldiner, *Of Moses and Marx*, 64.

47. Minor, "Russia"; Avrich, *Anarchist Voices*, 374.

48. Copp, "Role of the Anarchists," 110–11, 172; Avrich, *Russian Anarchists*, 173–74 n. 7.

49. Avrich, *Anarchists in the Russian Revolution*, 71; Serge, *Memoirs*, 213.

50. Avrich, *Russian Anarchists*, 125, 146–47, 167 n. 60; Copp, "Role of the Anarchists," 64–65, 70–76; Yelensky, *In sotsialn shturem*, 14–54; "Synopsis of Minutes of Meeting of General Executive Board, Held June 29th–July 6th, 1917," folder 3, box 7, Industrial Workers of the World Collection, Archives of Labor and Urban Affairs, Wayne State University, Detroit.

51. Wade, *Red Guards*, 113–14, 121, 182–83, 286; Von Hagen, *Soldiers*, 42 n. 61, 89; Radkey, *Unknown Civil War*, 64, 111, 130; Podshivalov, *Siberian Makhnovshchina*.

52. Archibald, "Many Lives"; Yelensky, *In sotsialn shturem*, 85.

53. Copp, "Role of the Anarchists," 59.

54. Lenin, *State and Revolution*, 64.

55. Avrich, *Anarchist Voices*, 311; Avrich, *Modern School*, 150; *FAS*, January 19, 1918; *Freedom* (New Brunswick), October–November 1919.

56. Wade, *Red Guards*, 182; Avrich, *Russian Anarchists*, 133–35.

57. Avrich, *Russian Anarchists*, 196–200.

58. Harold Joel Goldberg, "Anarchists View the Bolshevik Regime," 255 n. 1.

59. Serge, *Memoirs*, 120, 155; Harold Joel Goldberg, "Anarchists View the Bolshevik Regime," 62; Kosta *Balkan Firebrand*, 206.

60. Harold Joel Goldberg, "Anarchists View the Bolshevik Regime," 136–49; *NYT*, March 9, 1930; Avrich, *Anarchist Voices*, 290.

61. Victor Serge suggested that Raevsky, whose real name was L. Fishelev, was the same Fishelev arrested in the mid-1920s for printing a Trotskyist platform. However, that individual was Michael Fishelev, a Socialist who had worked with Trotsky in New York before the revolution (Serge, *Memoirs*, 223; *Bulletin of the Relief Fund of the International Working Men's Association for Anarchists and Anarcho-Syndicalists Imprisoned or Exiled in Russia*, March 1928).

62. *Nuovi Tempi*, March 1918; *CS*, May 20, 1918; *Il Martello*, February 1, May 20, 1919.

63. Files 381751, 8000-385063, 289493, OG.

64. Ralph Edward Shaffer, "Radicalism in California," 306.

65. Avrich, *Modern School*, 251; New York, Legislature, Joint Legislative Committee to Investigate Seditious Activities, *Revolutionary Radicalism*, 1:846–47; *Nuovi Tempi*, March 1918.

66. Hughes, "Lest This Be Lost," n.p.

67. Joseph J. Cohen, *Yidish-anarkhistishe bavegung*, 240; Lang, *Tomorrow Is Beautiful*, 112.

68. *FAS*, January 26, 1918; New York, Legislature, Joint Legislative Committee to Investigate Seditious Activities, *Revolutionary Radicalism*, 2:2004.

69. Joseph J. Cohen, *Yidish-anarkhistishe bavegung*, 340–47.

70. Polenberg, *Fighting Faiths*.

71. *SFC*, January 10, 1918; *CS*, February 2, 1918; Whitten, "Criminal Syndicalism," 19–20.

72. *SFC*, February 14, 1918; Duff, *Silent Defenders*, 24.

73. Whitten, "Criminal Syndicalism," 20; Duff, *Silent Defenders*.

74. Weintraub, "I.W.W. in California," 153; *SFC*, August 17, 1919; file 216806, OG; *San Francisco Examiner*, December 19, 1919.

75. Sakovich, "Angel Island," 139.

76. Murray, *Red Scare*, 14.

77. Clark, *Deportation of Aliens*, 215–31.

78. Berkman and Goldman, *Deportation*, 21.

79. File 321621, OG; Sakovich, "When the 'Enemy' Landed."

80. Sakovich, "Angel Island," 140, 146–47.

81. File 289493, OG.

82. *NYT*, September 9, 1920; *Trentennio di attività anarchica*, 142; file 289493, OG.

83. Berkman and Goldman, *Deportation*, 10.

84. Sakovich, "Angel Island," 139; Dowell, *History of Criminal Syndicalism Legislation*; Weintraub, "I.W.W. in California," 165–66; Whitten, "Criminal Syndicalism," 28, 31, 52–53.

85. Weintraub, "I.W.W. in California," 183; Schwartz, *From West to East*, 190.

86. Polenberg, *Fighting Faiths*, 178–81; file 359916, OG; *Anarchist Soviet Bulletin*, April 1919.

87. File 359916, OG; Marcus Graham, "Autobiographical Note," vii–xii.

88. File 359916, OG; *NYT*, November 29, 1919.

89. Polenberg, *Fighting Faiths*, 184–85.

90. Avrich, *Sacco and Vanzetti*; McCormick, *Hopeless Cases*.

91. Avrich, *Sacco and Vanzetti*, 81.

92. Murray, *Red Scare*, 196–97; Jaffe, *Crusade against Radicalism*, 85, 179; *Anarchist Soviet Bulletin*, April 1920.

93. Robert J. Goldstein, *Political Repression*, 68, 147.

94. Avrich, *Anarchist Voices*, 364–65; Robert J. Goldstein, *Political Repression*, 155.

95. *Free Society*, May 1921.

96. Polenberg, *Fighting Faiths*; Avrich, *Anarchist Portraits*, 214–26.

97. Avrich, *Sacco and Vanzetti*, 205–7; Gage, *Day Wall Street Exploded*.

98. Murray, *Red Scare*, 257; Jaffe, *Crusade against Radicalism*, 225–27.

99. File 211793-0, BS; file 381751, OG.

100. File 289493, OG; Caminita, *Nell'isola*, 21–22. William Young and David E. Kaiser incorrectly surmised that the bureau's undercover agent within the L'Era Nuova Group was Eugenio Ravarini, an informant who briefly spent time in Paterson (*Postmortem*, 20). Subsequent historians have repeated this error. My thanks to Salvatore Salerno for alerting me to Joseph Define's role.

101. *NYT*, February 16, 1920; Caminita, *Nell'isola*, 11, 28, 30.

102. *NYT*, March 4, 1920; Caminita, *Nell'isola*, 33.

103. Files 61-4185, 61-4625, OG.

104. Caminita, *Nell'isola*, 24; file 61-115, OG.

105. File 54861/181, Records of the Immigration and Naturalization Service, Record Group 85, National Archives and Records Administration, College Park, Maryland; U.S. Congress, House, Committee on Immigration and Naturalization, *Communist Labor Party Deportation Cases*, 37; Caminita, *Nell'isola*, 109–10.

106. *NYT*, February 15, 1920; Caminita, *Nell'isola*, 24, 96–97.

107. Ibid., 109; file 360086, BS.

108. File 61-115, OG; Caminita, *Nell'isola*, 119.

109. File 61-115, OG; Caminita, "Twenty Years"; Caminita, *Nell'isola*, 131.

110. Files 61-115, 202600-143, OG; *AdR*, June 30, July 30, 1922.

111. File 61-115, OG; Caminita, "Twenty Years," 52, 54.

112. Avrich, *Sacco and Vanzetti*, chaps. 13–14; McCormick, *Hopeless Cases*, 55–60.

113. See J. Edgar Hoover to William J. Flynn, March 8, 1920, file 360086, BS: "I did not inform [Caminita] that we had learned [of] the print shop where the circular was put up. . . . It was Mazzotta who first stated that if anyone printed 'Plain Words' in New York it was Roberto Elia."

114. Clark, *Deportation of Aliens*, chap. 8–12.

115. Post, *Deportations Delirium*.

116. Clark, *Deportation of Aliens*, 220–21; Claghorn, *Immigrant's Day in Court*, 453–60.

117. Weil, *Sovereign Citizen*, 74–75.

118. Clark, *Deportation of Aliens*, 227–28; Pernicone, *Carlo Tresca*, 100–101.

119. Weil, *Sovereign Citizen*, chap. 4.

120. Files 359916, 203991, OG.

121. *Rising Youth*, December 1929; Marcus Graham, *Anthology of Revolutionary Poetry*, 42–43; Marcus Graham, "Autobiographical Note," xii–xvi.

122. Marcus Graham, "Autobiographical Note," xiv; *NYT*, February 27, 1921; Marcus Graham, *Anthology of Revolutionary Poetry*, 197.

123. File 203991, OG; Clark, *Deportation of Aliens*, 224–25, 407–8; Marcus Graham, "Autobiographical Note," xiii.

124. Avrich, *Anarchist Voices*, 208; Avrich, *Modern School*, 337–38.

125. Filippo Perrone file, box 3875, CPC; *Trentennio di attività anarchica*, 150.

126. Michele Centrone file, box 1243, CPC.

127. File 211793-0, BS; Avrich, *Sacco and Vanzetti*, 157, 197; U.S. Congress, House, Committee on Rules, *Attorney General A. Mitchell Palmer*, 36.

128. Murray, *Red Scare*, 257; Jaffe, *Crusade against Radicalism*, 225–27; Joseph J. Cohen to Max Nettlau, December 12, 1921, folder 303, Nettlau Papers.

129. Sorenson, *Life and Death*; Brinton, *Bolsheviks and Workers' Control*; Shkliarevsky, *Labor in the Russian Revolution*.

130. Avrich, *Russian Anarchists*, chap. 8; Arshinov, *History*; Palij, *Anarchism of Nestor Makhno*; Skirda, *Nestor Makhno*.

131. Avrich, *Russian Anarchists*, 184–85, 205–6, 215; Berkman, *Bolshevik Myth*, chap. 24; Goldman, *My Disillusionment*, 109–110; Palij, *Anarchism of Nestor Makhno*, 260; Arshinov, *History*, 212, 231; Archibald, "Many Lives"; Azarov, *Kontrrazvedka*.

132. Avrich, *Anarchist Portraits*, 122–23; *Freedom* (London), April 1922. Elias Tcherikower's investigation of Ukrainian pogroms found no evidence implicating Makhno, though "the average Jew in the Ukraine considered red Makhno a *pogromshchik*, and the fear of Makhno among the Jews was very great" (Voline, *Unknown Revolution*, 699; Tcherikower, *Ukrainer pogromen*, 300–302, 347–48).

133. Avrich, *Anarchist Voices*, 383; Mark Mrachnyi correspondence with Petr Arshinov, folders 1 and 4, Mark Mrachnyi Papers, Labadie Collection.

134. *Freedom* (London), November 1934.

135. *Free Society*, March 1921; Goldman, *My Disillusionment*, 189–92; Avrich, *Russian Anarchists*, 227.

136. Goldman, *My Disillusionment*; Berkman, *Bolshevik Myth*; Avrich, *Kronstadt*.

137. Avrich, *Russian Anarchists*, 230–32; Polenberg, *Fighting Faiths*, 356–63.

138. *Behind the Bars*, January 1924; *Bulletin of the Joint Committee for the Defense of Revolutionists Imprisoned in Russia*, October–November 1924; Voline, "Le vittime del potere comunista," *AdR*, July 21-October 13, 1923; Yelensky, *Struggle for Equality*, 36.

139. Kelly, "Roll Back the Years," 27:2.

140. *Freedom* (New York), January 15, 1919; *Il Bollettino de l'Era Nuova*, March 1, April 1, 1919.

141. *Freedom* (New York), February 15, 1919; New York, Legislature, Joint Legislative Committee to Investigate Seditious Activities, *Revolutionary Radicalism*, 1:652–53.

142. *Il Bollettino de L'Era Nuova*, May 10, 1919; Fred S. Graham, *Anarchism and the World Revolution*, 13, 15.

143. *Anarchist Soviet Bulletin*, April, August 1919.

144. *Il Martello*, supplement, February 16, 1919.

145. R. Rocker, "Raten-sistem oder diktatur?," *FAS*, May 15–29, 1920; Luigi Galleani, "Lenin," *CS* (Turin), June 12-July 10, 1920, reprinted in Fedeli, *Luigi Galleani*, 166.

146. "Kropotkin's S.O.S. for Russia," *Freedom* (New Brunswick), October–November 1919; "Peter Kropotkin's Last Message," *Free Society*, March 1921.

147. Berkman, *Russian Tragedy*; Berkman, *Der kronshtater oyfshtand*; Berkman, *Bolshevik Myth*; Goldman, *Crushing*; Goldman, *My Disillusionment*; International Committee for Political Prisoners, *Letters*.

148. Michael A. Cohn to Alexander Berkman, May 18, [1922], folder 14, Berkman Papers.

149. Zimmer, "Premature Anti-Communists," 56–57; Minor, "I Change My Mind a Little."

150. Fred S. Graham, *Anarchism and the World Revolution*; *Free Society*, January 1921.

151. Anarchist Communist Groups, Federation of Russian Anarchist Communist Groups, and Ukrainian Anarchist Communist Groups, *Manifesto*, 4.

152. Berkman, *Now and After*, 168; Goldman, *My Disillusionment*, 250–51; Goldman, *Crushing*, 7; Berkman, *Russian Tragedy*, 20.

153. Avrich, *Anarchists in the Russian Revolution*, 124; Avrich, *Russian Anarchists*, 193–95; Berkman, *Russian Tragedy*, 27, 54.

154. *The Clarion*, February–March 1934.

155. *AdR*, April 15, 1922.

156. Levy, *Gramsci and the Anarchists*; Di Lembo, *Guerra di classe*.

157. Paolo Schicchi to Joe Russo [translated], May 23, 1921, File 202600-2159, BS.

158. Delzell, *Mussolini's Enemies*, 40; Levy, *Gramsci and the Anarchists*, 223.

159. Fedeli, *Luigi Galleani*, 111–15; *Trentennio di attività anarchica*, 141; Antonioli et al., *Dizionario biografico*, s.v. Bacchini, Ruggero.

160. Tinchino, *Edmondo Rossoni*; Whitaker, *Anarchist-Individualist Origins*; Luparini, *Anarchici di Mussolini*.

161. Levy, *Gramsci and the Anarchists*, 228.

162. Luigi Parenti file, box 3732, CPC; Hughes, "Lest This Be Lost," n.p. A September

1942 obituary in *L'Adunata dei Refrattari* for anarchist Luigi Parenti, who died in Paterson, refers to a different individual; the Luigi Parenti discussed here died in Italy in 1961 without returning to the United States and is buried in Calcinaia (Thomas Lang to the author, November 5, 2013).

163. Luconi, "Ethnic Allegiance," 132; De Ciampis, "Storia del movimento socialista," 161; Salvemini, *Italian Fascist Activities*, 36–37; Cannistraro, *Blackshirts*, 16–17; Luconi, "From Left to Right."

164. *Social War Bulletin*, May 1918.

165. Ngai, *Impossible Subjects*, chap. 1; Roediger, *Working toward Whiteness*, 139–45.

Chapter 6. "No Right to Exist Anywhere on This Earth"

1. Anna L. Sosnovsky to Mollie Steimer, January 12, 1925, folder 29, Senya Fléchine Papers, IISH; *Freedom* (New York), March 18, 1933; Boehm, *U.S. Military Intelligence Reports*, reel 24, 0972; Conference Committee for Anarchist Propaganda in English to Joseph J. Cohen, May 1, 1939, "Anarchism—Cohen, Joseph J.," Subject Vertical File, Labadie Collection.

2. Iacovetta and Stradiotti, "Betrayal," 92–93; Antonioli et al., *Dizionario biografico*, s.vv. Schiavina, Raffaele and Volpin, Ottavio; David Koven, "Giovanni 'John' Vattuone, 1899–1994," 1994, file 131, David Koven Papers, IISH.

3. Arrigoni, *Freedom*, 210–14; Wilson, "Brand," 12.

4. Tomchuk, "Transnational Radicals"; Avrich, *Anarchist Voices*, 143; Camp, *Iron in Her Soul*, 137.

5. Grigorii Petrovich Maksimov to Mark Mrachnyi, June 22, 1925, February 1, 1927, folder 26, Mark Mrachnyi Papers, Labadie Collection.

6. Lee, *At America's Gates*; Chang, *Pacific Connections*; Tomchuk, "Transnational Radicals," 9.

7. Grigorii Petrovich Maksimov to Mark Mrachnyi, March 7, 1927, Mark Mrachnyi Papers, Labadie Collection; Arrigoni, *Freedom*, 180–91.

8. Lee, *At America's Gates*; Ngai, *Impossible Subjects*; Garland, "Not-Quite-Closed Gates."

9. Joseph J. Cohen, *Yidish-anarkhistishe bavegung*, 528.

10. Hill, *Men, Mobs, and Law*, chap. 4.

11. Zimmer, "Premature Anti-Communists," 60–61.

12. On Feinberg, see Epstein, *Yisroel Faynberg*.

13. Gordin, *Sh. Yanovsky*, 339–43, 552–69; Levine, *Women's Garment Workers*, 494.

14. Levine, *Women's Garment Workers*, 352–59; Stolberg, *Tailor's Progress*, 116.

15. Levine, *Women's Garment Workers*, 357.

16. Pesotta, *Bread upon the Water*, 99–100; Leeder, *Gentle General*, 26–30, 33; Wisotsky, "Such a Life," 237.

17. *Gerekhtikayt*, June 9, 1925, quoted in Gordin, *Sh. Yanovsky*, 374.

18. *Der Yunyon Arbayter*, February 22, March 8, 15, 29, 1926.

19. Ibid., December 4, 1925, January 11, 1926.

20. *New Unionist*, July 30, 1927; *Road to Freedom*, August 1925; Avrich, *Anarchist Voices*, 348.

21. Jennifer Guglielmo, *Living the Revolution*, 213–15; Pernicone, *Carlo Tresca*, 177; Zappia, "Unionism and the Italian American Worker," 220–21, 276.

22. Avrich, *Anarchist Voices*, 457; Anonymous male no. 2 interview.

23. Epstein, *Jewish Labor*, 2:140–41.

24. Epstein, *Yisroel Faynberg*, 66–67; Gordin, *Sh. Yanovsky*, 375.

25. Epstein, *Jew and Communism*, 141.

26. Epstein, *Jewish Labor*, 2:140–41, 147–48; Stolberg, *Tailor's Progress*, chap. 7; Parmet, *Master of Seventh Avenue*, 39, 58–59.

27. Daniel Katz, *All Together Different*, 113, 118; Dubinsky and Raskin, *David Dubinsky*, 105–6; *Vanguard*, April 1935.

28. Kessler-Harris, "Problems of Coalition Building"; Daniel Katz, *All Together Different*, 88.

29. Joseph J. Cohen, *Yidish-anarkhistishe bavegung*, 420; Liebman, *Jews and the Left*, 59.

30. Kessner, *Golden Door*, 109–10, 117, 155; Gurock, *When Harlem Was Jewish*, 145–46; Pritchett, *Brownsville, Brooklyn*, 14–28; Moore, *At Home in America*, 19.

31. *N. W. Ayer and Son's American Newspaper Annual and Directory*, 1923, 1924, 1925; Thorne interview.

32. *Freedom* (London), April 1922; *Man!*, September–October 1934; Naye Gezelshaft Grupe, David Edelshtadt Grupe, and *Amerikanskye Izvestia*, "Un oyfrukh tsu ale anarkhistn un simpatayzer!," 1923, folder 59.10, Territorial Collection—United States, YIVO, Institute for Jewish Research, New York.

33. Voltairine de Cleyre to Joseph J. Cohen, October 30, 1911, file 4, box 1, Papers of Voltairine de Cleyre and Joseph Cohen, YIVO Institute for Jewish Research, New York; Joseph J. Cohen, *Yidish-anarkhistishe bavegung*, 343–47; Frank, "Anarchism and the Jews," 282.

34. Avrich, *Anarchist Voices*, 350; Solomon, *Memoir*, 5.

35. Harry Kelly to Alexander Berkman, October 10, 1924, folder 43, Berkman Papers.

36. *Free Society*, October 1921; F. S. Graham [Shmuel Marcus] to Max Nettlau, June 28, 1922, folder 502, Nettlau Papers.

37. *Freedom* (London), January 1923.

38. Joseph J. Cohen to Max Nettlau, February 26, 1922, folder 303, Nettlau Papers; Avrich, *Anarchist Voices*, 344; Joseph J. Cohen, *Yidish-anarkhistishe bavegung*, 454.

39. Joseph J. Cohen, *Yidish-anarkhistishe bavegung*, 373; Harry Kelly to Max Nettlau, January 2, 1922, folder 701, Nettlau Papers; *Freedom* (London), March, April 1922; *Free Society*, January–February 1922.

40. Thorpe, *"The Workers Themselves."* In 1934, IWW members passed a referendum in favor of affiliation with the International Working Men's Association, but a subsequent referendum reversed this decision. The IWW's Marine Transport Workers Industrial Union affiliated independently of its parent organization in 1935.

41. Hippolyte Havel to Dear Comrade, November 13, 1925, folder 6, Fraye Arbayter Shtime Archive, IISH; *Road to Freedom*, March 1927. Ironically, *Road to Freedom* editor W. S. Van Valkenburgh complained that the paper was "not considered by the Jewish Federation nor by the Freie Arbiter Stimme [*sic*] outfit as being of any importance in the field of Anarchist propaganda" (W. S. Van Valkenburgh to Alexander Berkman, June 14, 1929, folder 62, Berkman Papers).

42. Avrich, *Anarchist Voices*, 423, 432; Agnes Inglis to Marcus Graham, August 14, 1933, box 4, Agnes Inglis Papers, Labadie Collection.

43. Joseph J. Cohen, *Yidish-anarkhistishe bavegung*, 393.

44. McGirr, "Passion of Sacco and Vanzetti."

45. Cohn, *Two Worlds*; Cohn, *Some Questions and an Appeal*; Bartolomeo Vanzetti to Michael Cohn, July 17, 1927, box 1, Michael A. Cohen Collection, YIVO Institute for Jewish Research, New York.

46. *Road to Freedom*, April 1928; "Minutes of the Road to Freedom Conference Held in New York, Oct. 12th to 14th, 1928," folder 1032, Nettlau Papers.

47. *Freedom* (New York), January 23, 1933; Harry Kelly to Max Nettlau, January 14, 1935, folder 704, Nettlau Papers.

48. Salvemini, *Italian Fascist Activities*; Cannistraro, *Blackshirts*; Cannistraro, "Duce and the Prominenti"; Vecoli, "Making and Un-Making"; Luconi, "Ethnic Allegiance"; Diggins, *Mussolini and Fascism*, especially 116.

49. Cannistraro, *Blackshirts*, 70; Pernicone, *Carlo Tresca*, 128, chap. 13.

50. Pernicone, *Carlo Tresca*, chap. 15; *Il Martello*, September 14, 1934.

51. *AdR*, April 15, 1922, March 24, 1923, January 2, 1926.

52. Meyer, "Italian Americans."

53. Diggins, *Mussolini and Fascism*, chap. 6; Pernicone, "Murder under the 'El'"; Pernicone, *Carlo Tresca*.

54. Galzerano, "Attentati anarcici"; Levy, "Anarchist Assassin," 208–9; Giulietti, *Movimento anarchico italiano*, 121; Bernabei, "London Plot"; Amedeo Fulvi file, box 2196, Alberto Guabello file, box 2548, Paolo Blotto file, box 677, Andrea Sardi file, box 4607, CPC.

55. Giulietti, *Movimento anarchico italiano*, 169–76; Galzerano, *Michele Schirru*; *Trentennio di attività anarchica*, 156; Di Lembo, *Guerra di classe*, 181–82.

56. *Umanità Nova*, November 1, 1924.

57. De Maria, "Anarchici italiani," 13; Alberto Guabello file, box 2548, Firmino Felice Gallo file, box 2256, CPC; *La Scopa*, October 1926.

58. Caminita, *Nell'isola*, 20; Bencivenni, *Italian Immigrant Radical Culture*, 151–52.

59. De Maria, "Anarchici italiani," 15; Wood, "History of Labor," 337–42; David J. Goldberg, *Tale of Three Cities*, 202–4.

60. *La Scopa*, September 24, 1927; Lowell, "Thousands in America."

61. Wood, "History of Labor," 345–47, 353.

62. Starr, *Italians of New Jersey*, 46; Salvemini, *Italian Fascist Activities*, 101.

63. *La Scopa*, October 16, 1926, May 28, December 17, 1927; Avrich, *Anarchist Voices*, 153, 156.

64. *AdR*, May 29, 1926; Alberto Guabello file, box 2548, Vittorio Paolo Blotto file, box 677, CPC.

65. Firmino Gallo to Errico Malatesta, February 26, 1928, in Firmino Felice Gallo file, box 2256, CPC; De Maria, "Anarchici italiani," 13–15. On the Mazzini Society, see Tirabassi, "Mazzini Society"; Pernicone, *Carlo Tresca*, 261–67.

66. File 61-115, OG; *La Difesa*, February 10, 1923; Ludovico Caminita file, box 973, CPC.

67. Marazzi, "Lacrime e libertà," 116–17.

68. Caminita, *Obici*, 10, 225, 109–10, 113, 214, 217–18.

69. Kazin, *Barons of Labor*, 95–99, 256; Fichera, *Italy on the Pacific*, 75.

70. Luconi, "Mussolini's Italian-American Sympathizers"; Fichera, *Italy on the Pacific*, 134–36, 154.

71. Martocchia and Lamantia interview; Hughes, "Lest This Be Lost," n.p.

72. *L'Emancipazione*, August 15, 1929; Vincenzo Ferrero file, box 2034, Adolfo Antonelli file, box 154, Luigi Chiesa file, box 1302, Gilberto Moni file, box 3354, CPC.

73. *Communist Dictatorship Expose* [*sic*], March 1928. On communism in North Beach, see Schwartz, *From West to East*, 245.

74. *SFC*, July 31, August 1, December 20, 1927; *San Francisco Examiner*, July 31, 1927; Avrich, *Anarchist Voices*, 504 n. 309; *L'Emancipazione*, January 1928.

75. On Dorr, see *SFC*, November 6, 2005. It has also been alleged that the two men who carried out a string of bombings at Saints Peter and Paul Catholic Church in 1926 and 1927 were anarchists or IWW members (see, for example, Fichera, *Italy on the Pacific*, 121). However, no reliable evidence of an anarchist connection exists, and one of the men involved, Celsten Eklund, was in fact a Protestant "fanatic" who was carrying a Bible when he was shot rather than an antireligious radical. See *Oakland Tribune*, March 7, 8, 9, 1927.

76. *AdR*, June 11, 1927; *L'Emancipazione*, September 1927, March 1931.

77. *L'Emancipazione*, December 1927.

78. David Koven, "An Anarchist Life: Domenic Sallitto, 1902–1991," 1992, 1–2, "Sallitto, Domenic," Subject Vertical File, Labadie Collection; Sallitto interview.

79. Luparini, *Anarchici di Mussolini*, 55–56 n. 145; Raffaele De Rango file, box 1739, CPC.

80. *Il Martello*, December 21, 1929; Vincenzo Ferrero file, box 2034, CPC.

81. Hughes, "Lest This Be Lost," n.p; Sallitto interview.

82. *L'Emancipazione*, July–August 1931.

83. Zaks, *Geshikhte fun Arbayter Ring*, 2:xxxiv.

84. *Road to Freedom*, June 1926.

85. *L'Emancipazione*, September 1927; *Road to Freedom*, October 1927.

86. Shuyao, "History of Meizhou Gongyi Tongmeng Zonghui," 25–26; Lai, "Anarchism," 58–59.

87. Lai, "Anarchism," 59–60, 173 n. 33; Avrich, *Anarchist Voices*, 409–10.

88. *L'Emancipazione*, November 1927; *Man!*, August–September 1933; Wong, "Pingshe"; Avrich, *Anarchist Voices*, 409.

89. *L'Emancipazione*, September, November, 1927.

90. Ibid., December 1927, January 1928.

91. *Man!*, March, April 1933.

92. Avrich, *Anarchist Voices*, 410.

93. Avrich, *Anarchist Voices*, 165–67; *L'Emancipazione*, September 1927, June 15, 1932.

94. Avrich, *Anarchist Voices*, 163; *Man!*, July 1933.

95. Avrich, *Anarchist Voices*, 167.

96. *L'Emancipazione*, April, May 1928; *Man!*, August–September 1933; Lai, "Anarchism," 60, 172 n. 33; Avrich, *Anarchist Voices*, 165.

97. On "paper sons," see Lee, *At America's Gates*, 194–207.

98. Among the vast literature on the period, see especially Lizabeth Cohen, *Making a New Deal*; Denning, *Cultural Front*; Ottanelli, *Communist Party of the United States*.

99. *Man!*, January 1934.

100. *Free Society Bulletin*, October 18, 1932; Frank Heiner to Alexander Berkman, February 16, 1935, folder 41, Berkman Papers; Joseph J. Cohen, *Yidish-anarkhistishe bavegung*, 506; Harry Kelly to Max Nettlau, February 1, 1937, folder 704, Nettlau Papers.

101. Hughes, "Lest This Be Lost," n.p; Goodfriend interview.

102. Michael A. Cohn to Max Nettlau, December 11, 1930, folder 306, Nettlau Papers; Avrich, *Anarchist Voices*, 41.

103. B. Axler to Alexander Berkman, August 21, 1930, folder 8, Berkman Papers; Michael A. Cohn to Alexander Berkman, August 31, 1931, folder 16, Berkman Papers.

104. Joseph J. Cohen, *Yidish-anarkhistishe bavegung*, 482–96; Joseph J. Cohen, *In Quest of Heaven*.

105. Michael A. Cohn to Alexander Berkman, December 29, 1930, folder 14, Berkman Papers; Michael A. Cohn to Rudolf Rocker and Milly Witcop, March 23, 1933, Michael A. Cohn to Rudolf Rocker, July 12, 1933, folder 78, Rudolf Rocker Papers, IISH; Michael A. Cohn to Max Nettlau, February 4, 8, 1935, folder 307, Nettlau Papers.

106. Abe Coleman [Bluestein] to Alexander Berkman, February 1, 1934, folder 62, Berkman Papers.

107. *Rising Youth*, December 1929; Avrich, *Anarchist Voices*, 433, 441.

108. Ibid., 448, 457, 460; Solomon, *Memoir*, 7; Goodfriend interview; Vanguard Group, "Bulletin No. 1," September 28, 1938, "Anarchism—Vanguard," Subject Vertical File, Labadie Collection.

109. "Biographies (Oral) Abe Bluestein," n.d., C26, box 2, Abe Bluestein Papers, Labadie Collection.

110. *Vanguard*, April 1932, February 1933; Avrich, *Anarchist Voices*, 451.

111. Avrich, *Anarchist Voices*, 460.

112. Abe Coleman [Bluestein] to Alexander Berkman, February 1, 1934, folder 62, Berkman Papers; *Il Martello*, September 14, 1934, March 1935.

113. Avrich, *Anarchist Voices*, 450.

114. *L'Emancipazione*, October 1932.

115. "Marcus Graham Tour, 1931–1932," scrapbook, "Anarchism—Marcus, Shmuel," Subject Vertical File, Labadie Collection; *Man!*, March 1934.

116. Marcus Graham to Agnes Inglis, December 30, 1935, box 4, Agnes Inglis Papers, Labadie Collection.

117. *Man!*, January 1934. In fact, Pesotta was quite skeptical of the National Recovery Act; see Daniel Katz, *All Together Different*, 194.

118. Pesotta, *Bread upon the Water*, 71–74; Wong, "Pingshe," 142, 145–46.

119. *Man!*, August 1934.

120. Ibid., May 1935, January 1939.

121. Ibid., April 1933, August 1934, June 1939.

122. Ibid., October, November, December 1933, February 1934.

123. Ibid., May 1934, April 1935; *Freedom of Thought Arraigned*, 3–4; *Fight against Deportation*, 5.

124. *Fight against Deportation*, 11.

125. For details see Zimmer, "Positively Stateless."

126. Domenico Sallitto file, box 4537, CPC.

127. *AdR*, December 7, 1935; Avrich, *Anarchist Voices*, 148.

128. *Los Angeles Times*, March 11, 1938.

129. U.S. Congress, *H.R. 8631*, 32, 35.

130. *Oakland Tribune*, October 20, 1939; Finzi, "Ricordando John."

131. *Freedom of Thought Arraigned*, 3, 9; *Man!*, August–September 1936, October 1937; Marcus Graham, "Autobiographical Note," xxi; Marcus Graham to Dear Friend, October 20, 1937, box 4, Agnes Inglis Papers, Labadie Collection.

132. *Man!*, June 1935; D. Alonso to Marcus Graham, n.d., Marcus Graham Papers, Labadie Collection; *Pour la liberté de pensée violée*; American Civil Liberties Union, *Eternal Vigilance!*, 15.

133. *Los Angeles Times*, January 14, 1938; *United States v. Parson*, 22 F. Supp. 149 (S.D. Cal 1938); *Oakland Tribune*, January 15, 1938.

134. *Los Angeles Times*, June 27, 1939; *Oakland Tribune*, June 27, 1939.

135. *Graham v. United States*, 112 F.2d 907 (9th Cir. 1940); *SFC*, June 7, 23, 1940.

136. *Man!*, May 1934.

137. Frank, "Anarkho-sotsialistishe ideyen," 269 n. 8; Horrox, *Living Revolution*; *FAS*, August 29, 1930; *Man!*, April 1938.

138. Joseph J. Cohen, *Yidish-anarkhistishe bavegung*, 428.

139. *Vanguard*, August–September 1936; Boulouque, "Anarchists, Zionism, and the Birth," 17.

140. Gordin, *Draysik yor*; Nedava, "Abba Gordin"; Goldman and Berkman, *Nowhere at Home*, 29; Harold Joel Goldberg, "Anarchists View the Bolshevik Regime," 201–7.

141. *The Clarion*, October, September 1932.

142. Gordin's works in this vein include *Oysbreyterungen fun di printsipn un tsveknderklerung fun der Yidish-etishe kultur-gezelshaft* (New York: n.p., 1936); *Grunt-printsipn fun idishkayt* (New York: Kooperativ farlag fun der yidish etisher kultur gezelshaft, 1938); *Idishe etik* (New York: Kooperativ farlag fun der yidish etisher kultur gezelshaft, 1937); *Idisher velt-banem* (New York: Kooperativ farlag fun der yidish etisher kultur gezelshaft, 1939); *Moral in idishn lebn* (New York: Kooperativ farlag fun der yidish etisher kultur gezelshaft, 1940); *Sotsiale obergloyberay un kritik* (New York: Yiddish-Etisher Gezelshaft, 1941).

143. Avrich, *Anarchist Voices*, 425.

144. Rocker, *London Years*; Fishman, *Jewish Radicals*, chap. 10; Graur, *Anarchist "Rabbi."*

145. Rocker, *London Years*, chap. 33; Graur, *Anarchist "Rabbi,"* 138–39, 144–67.

146. Michael A. Cohn to Rudolf Rocker and Milly Witcop, March 23, 1933, folder 78, Rudolf Rocker Papers, IISH; Leeder, *Gentle General*, 80; Coughlin, "History of a Book," 19.

147. Rocker, *Nationalism and Culture*, 200–201. Cf. Hobsbawm, *Nations and Nationalism*, 10, 78.

148. Rocker, *Nationalism and Culture*, 276–97, 435.

149. Ibid., 298–339 (quote on 338).

150. *Road to Freedom*, September 1931.

151. There is an abundant scholarship on Spanish anarchism in this period; see especially Ackelsberg, *Free Women of Spain*; Casanova, *Anarchism*; Christie, *We, the Anarchists!*; Ealham, *Anarchism and the City*.

152. Mintz, *Anarchism and Workers' Self-Management*; Pagès i Blanch, *War and Revolution*.

153. *Vanguard*, February–March 1937; *AdR*, December 18, 1937.

154. Solomon, *Memoir*, 8.

155. Casanova, *Anarchism*, 136–42; Rüdiger quoted in Alexander, *Anarchists*, 2:1140.

156. Sam Dolgoff, *Fragments*, 19.

157. *Cultura Proletaria*, August 15, October 17, 1936, August 14, October 30, 1937; *AdR*, September 5, October 17, November 14, 21, 28, December 5, 1936.

158. Calculated from financial reports published in *AdR* and *Spanish Revolution* as well as Yelensky, "25 Years of 'Free Society,'" 93; *Cultura Proletaria*, November 5, 1937.

159. See folder 63B, CNT (España) Archives, Archivo del Comité Nacional CNT, IISH.

160. Bruno Bonturi file, box 743, CPC; Solomon, *Memoir*, 8; Avrich, *Anarchist Voices*, 450.

161. Gallagher, *All the Right Enemies*, 159; *Cultura Proletaria*, January 23, 1937.

162. My estimate based on Giulietti, *Movimento anarchico italiano*, 243–64; Baumann, *Voluntarios latinoamericanos*; Berry, "French Anarchists"; Nelles, "Deutsche Anarchosyndikalisten und Freiwillige."

163. *AdR*, November 7, 1936; *Trentennio di attività anarchica*, 171. See also Ottanelli, "Anti-Fascism."

164. Vigna Antonio Pietro Casassa file, box 1138, Domenico Rosati file, box 25538, CPC; "Vercellesi, biellesi, e valsesiani volontari," s.vv. Albertini, Enrico and Cerruti, Pietro.

165. Anna Sosnovsky to Rose Pesotta, n.d., folder 62, box 3, Rose Pesotta Papers, YIVO Institute for Jewish Research, New York.

166. Berry, "French Anarchists," 430; Avrich, *Anarchist Voices*, 458.

167. Esther Dolgoff interview.

168. *AdR*, September 12, 1936; Gianfrate and Zimmer, *Michele Centrone*, 43–49.

169. *AdR*, September 19, 1936.

170. David Koven, "On Hanging In," 1986, folder 131, David Koven Papers, IISH; Nash, *Defying Male Civilization*, 151–53.

171. S. Freedman to Emma Goldman, March 10, 1937, folder 1, Fraye Arbayter Shtime Archive, IISH; "Biographies (Oral) Abe Bluestein," n.d., box 2, Abe Bluestein Papers, Labadie Collection; Bluestein, introduction, 1–2; Abe Bluestein to Mark Mrachnyi, September 27, 1937, folder 8, Mark Mrachnyi Papers, Labadie Collection.

172. Arrigoni, *Freedom*, 231–33; *Cultura Proletaria*, January 30, 1937.

173. Wilson, "Brand," 5; Arrigoni, *Freedom*, 330.

174. Graur, *Anarchist "Rabbi,"* 219; Leeder, *Gentle General*, 113–14; Pernicone, *Carlo Tresca*, 226.

175. Emma Goldman to Samuel Friedman, March 2, 1937, folder 18, Mark Mrachnyi Papers, Labadie Collection.

176. On the CNT-FAI's travails, see Alexander, *Anarchists*; Casanova, *Anarchism*; Christie, *We, the Anarchists!*; Peirats, *CNT in the Spanish Revolution*.

177. *Spanish Revolution*, January 8, 1937; *Man!* December 1936-January 1937; "Emma Goldman and the Alliance Proposals."

178. Rocker, *Tragedy of Spain*, 35. A similar interpretation of Soviet motives is offered in Cattell, *Communism*.

179. *AdR*, November 7, December 5, 1936.

180. Anna Sosnovsky to Rose Pesotta, n.d., folder 62, box 3, Rose Pesotta Papers, YIVO Institute for Jewish Research, New York.

181. Among the best studies of the May Days are Cattell, *Communism*, 133–48; Helen Graham, "'Against the State.'"

182. "Biographies (Oral) Abe Bluestein," n.d., C16–23, D29, box 2, Abe Bluestein Papers, Labadie Collection.

183. *Cultura Proletaria*, June 12, 1937.

184. Helen Graham, "'Against the State.'"

185. *Man!*, July–August 1937; *AdR*, July 10, 1937.

186. Arrigoni, *Freedom*, 343–80; Wilson, "Brand," 5.

187. *Il Martello*, May 28, 1937.

188. *Cultura Proletaria*, January 15, 1938.

189. *Man!* June 1937; *AdR*, April 30, 1938.

190. *Spanish Revolution*, July 19, 1937; *Il Martello*, September 14, 1940.

191. *Challenge*, June 4, 18, 1938.

192. *AdR*, September 4, 25, 1937; *Cultura Proletaria*, October 2, 1937; W. S. Van Valkenburgh to Carlo Tresca, August 14, 24, 1937, box 2, Warren Van Valkenburgh Papers, Labadie Collection; Sam Dolgoff, *Fragments*, 19.

193. Sam Dolgoff, *Fragments*, 55–56; Avrich, *Anarchist Voices*, 438.

194. Avrich, *Anarchist Voices*, 424, 442, 445; Sam Dolgoff, *Fragments*, 23; W. S. Van Valkenburgh to Maximiliano Olay, September 23, 1937, W. S. Van Valkenburgh to Mark Schmidt, September 16, 1937, box 2, Warren Van Valkenburgh Papers, Labadie Collection.

195. Peirats, *CNT in the Spanish Revolution*, 1:181.

196. *Cultura Proletaria*, July 24, 1937; *One Big Union Monthly*, September 1937.

197. Marcus Graham to Dear Friend, [1940], box 4, Agnes Inglis Papers, Labadie Collection.

198. Avrich, *Anarchist Voices*, 384.

199. Woodcock, *Anarchism*, 474.

200. Ottanelli, "Anti-Fascism," 22, 30 n. 60; Bruno Bonturi file, box 743, CPC.

201. Tomchuk, "Transnational Radicals," 290–99.

202. *Trentennio di attività anarchica*, 172–73.

Conclusion

1. Torpey, *Invention of the Passport*.

2. Goldman and Berkman, *Nowhere at Home*, 272–73; Goldman, *Living*, 981.

3. Luconi, "Mussolini's Italian-American Sympathizers," 129–30.

4. Hobsbawm, *Nations and Nationalism*, 146–50; Buhle, "Antifascism."

5. Joseph J. Cohen, *Yidish-anarkhistishe bavegung*, 522–23; Graur, *Anarchist "Rabbi,"* 223–24; Marcus Graham, *Issues in the Present War*.

6. See folder 61, box 3, Rose Pesotta Papers, YIVO Institute for Jewish Research, New York; Pesotta, *Bread upon the Waters*, chap. 34.

7. Cornell, "'For a World without Oppressors,'" 322–27.

8. Hughes, "Lest This Be Lost," n.p.; Martocchia and Lamantia interview.

9. Rose Pesotta, "Trip to Lodz," August 6, [1946], folder 7, box 11, John Nicholas Beffel Collection, Archives of Labor and Urban Affairs, Wayne State University, Detroit.

10. Frank, "Anarchism and the Jews," 287–89.

11. Graur, Anarchist "Rabbi," 204; Avrich, Modern School, 376.

12. Boulouque, "Anarchists, Zionism, and the Birth"; Horrox, Living Revolution.

13. Goncharok, "Stampa anarchica"; Nedava, "Abba Gordin"; Sam Dolgoff, Fragments, 157.

14. Arendt, Origins of Totalitarianism, 277–79.

15. Avrich, Anarchist Voices, 423; Epstein, Jewish Labor, 1:xlii.

16. Frank Fernández, Cuban Anarchism, 93.

17. Zimmer, "Premature Anti-Communists."

18. Lang, Tomorrow Is Beautiful, 28.

19. Emma Goldman to Dorothy Giessecke, March 21, 1938, folder 1, Fraye Arbayter Shtime Archive, IISH.

20. NYT, November 29, 1977; Goncharok, "Stampa anarchica."

21. Wisotsky, "Such a Life," 332.

22. Cornell, "'For a World without Oppressors,'" 428–36.

23. U.S. Commission on Industrial Relations, Industrial Relations, 11:2426.

24. Elwood, "Roots and Results"; Salerno, "Delitti della Razza Bianca," 112–14; Jennifer Guglielmo, Living the Revolution, 266–67.

25. Avrich, Anarchist Voices, 166.

26. Cornell, "'For a World without Oppressors,'" 375–91, 396–99.

27. SFC, June 8, 2003.

BIBLIOGRAPHY

Archival Material

American Labor Museum, Haledon, New Jersey

Archives of Labor and Urban Affairs, Wayne State University, Detroit: John Nicholas Beffel Collection; Industrial Workers of the World Collection

Archivio Centrale dello Stato, Rome: Casellario Politico Centrale

Immigration History Research Center, Elmer L. Anderson Library, University of Minnesota, Minneapolis: Italian American Periodicals Collection

Institute of International Studies, University of California, Berkeley: Emma Goldman Papers

International Institute of Social History, Amsterdam: Alexander Berkman Papers; CNT (España) Archives, Archivo del Comité Nacional CNT ; Senya Fléchine Papers; Fraye Arbayter Shtime Archive; David Koven Papers; Max Nettlau Papers; Rudolf Rocker Papers

Joseph A. Labadie Collection, Special Collections Library, University of Michigan, Ann Arbor: Abe Bluestein Papers; Marcus Graham Papers; Agnes Inglis Papers; Mark Mrachnyi Papers; Miscellaneous Manuscripts; Subject Vertical Files; Warren Van Valkenburgh Papers

National Archives and Records Administration, College Park, Maryland: Records of the Federal Bureau of Investigation, Record Group 65, Bureau Section Files and Old German Files; Records of the Immigration and Naturalization Service, Record Group 85

Kate Sharpley Library, Grass Valley, California

Robert F. Wagner Labor Archives, New York University, New York: Oral History of the American Left

YIVO Institute for Jewish Research, New York: Michael A. Cohen Collection, Record Group 313; Papers of Voltairine de Cleyre and Joseph Cohen, Record Group 1485; Rose Pesotta Papers, Record Group 1469; Territorial Collection—United States, Record Group 117

Interviews

Anonymous male no. 2. Interview by David Gurowsky, November 24, 1974. Tape 123B, International Ladies' Garment Workers' Union. Oral History of the American Left, Robert F. Wagner Labor Archives, New York University, New York.

Dolgoff, Esther. Interview by B. Lemisch, January 7, 1982. Tape 67A, Box 1. Oral History of the American Left, Robert F. Wagner Labor Archives, New York University, New York.

Goodfriend, Audrey. Interview by Kenyon Zimmer, July 11, 2011.

Keyser, Dora Stoller. Interview by Lynn Fonfa, 1974. Reformers and Radicals, Women's History, Virtual Oral/Aural History Archive, California State University Long Beach Digital Repository. http://symposia.library.csulb.edu/iii/cpro/DigitalItemViewPage .external;jsessionid=06EDBAA4589E46D41C879265C3AB8739?lang=eng&sp= 1001740&sp=T&sp=1&suite=def.

Martocchia, Anthony, and Philip Lamantia. Interview by Paul Buhle, October 31, 1982. Transcript. Oral History of the American Left, Robert F. Wagner Labor Archives, New York University, New York.

Sallitto, Aurora. Interview by David Koven, January 1992. Cassette tape. International Institute of Social History, Amsterdam.

Thorne, Ahrne. Interview by Paul Buhle, December 15, 1982. Tape 265, Box 2. Oral History of the American Left, Robert F. Wagner Labor Archives, New York University, New York.

Travaglio, Esther. Interview, October 30, 1982. Tape 257A, Box 1. Oral History of the American Left, Robert F. Wagner Labor Archives, New York University, New York.

Anarchist and Syndicalist Periodicals

L'Adunata dei Refrattari. New York, 1922–71.

The Agitator. Home, WA, 1910–12.

Anarchist Soviet Bulletin. New York, 1919–20.

L'Aurora. West Hoboken, NJ; Yohoghany, PA; Spring Valley, IL, 1899–1901.

The Beacon. Dallas; San Diego; San Francisco, 1888–91.

Behind the Bars. New York, 1924.

The Blast. San Francisco; New York, 1916–17.

Il Bollettino de L'Era Nuova. Paterson, 1919.

Bulletin of the Joint Committee for the Defense of Revolutionists Imprisoned in Russia. Berlin, 1923–26.

Bulletin of the Relief Fund of the International Working Men's Association for Anarchists and Anarcho-Syndicalists Imprisoned or Exiled in Russia. Paris and Berlin, 1926–31.

Challenge. New York, 1938–39.

The Clarion. New York, 1932–34.

Cogito, Ergo Sum. San Francisco, 1908.

Communist Dictatorship Expose. San Francisco, 1928.

Cronaca Sovversiva. Barre, VT; Lynn, 1903–19.

Cultura Proletaria. New York, 1927–53.

The Demonstrator. Home, WA, 1903–8.

La Difesa. New York, 1923–24.

Discontent. Home, WA, 1898–1902.

L'Effort. San Francisco, 1904.

Egoism. Oakland, 1890–98.

Emancipator. San Francisco, 1906–7.

L'Emancipazione. San Francisco, 1927–32.

L'Era Nuova. Paterson, 1908–17.

Fraye Arbeter Shtime. New York, 1890–94, 1899–1977.

Fraye Gezelshaft. New York, 1895–1900.

Fraye Gezelshaft. New York, 1910–11.

Free Society. San Francisco; Chicago; New York, 1897–1904.

Free Society. New York, 1920–22.

Free Society Bulletin. Chicago, 1932.

Freedom. London, 1886–1928.

Freedom. New York; New Brunswick, 1919.

Freedom. New York, 1933–34.

Germinal. Paterson, 1899–1902.

Il Grido degli Oppressi. New York; Chicago, 1892–94.

Industrial Union Bulletin. Chicago, 1907–9.

Industrial Worker. Joliet, 1906–7.

Industrial Worker. Spokane, Washington; Chicago, 1907–31.

La Jacquerie. Paterson, 1919.

Land and Liberty. Hayward, CA; San Francisco, 1914–15.

Il Lavoratore Industriale/Le Travailleur Industriel. San Francisco, 1912.

Liberty. Boston; New York, 1881–1908.

Man! San Francisco; Los Angeles; New York, 1933–40.

Il Martello. New York, 1916–46.

Mother Earth. New York, 1906–17.

Der Nayer Gayst. New York, 1897–98.

New Unionist. Los Angeles, 1927–31.

Nihil. San Francisco, 1908–9.

Novatore. New York, 1910–11.

Nuovi Tempi. Paterson, 1918.

One Big Union Monthly. Chicago, 1919–38.

Il Proletario. New York, 1905–18, 1919–42.

La Protesta Umana. San Francisco; Chicago, 1900–1905.

La Questione Sociale. Paterson, 1895–1908.

The Rebel. Boston, 1895–96.

Regeneración. Los Angeles, 1910–19.

Revolt. San Francisco, 1911–12.

Revolt. New York, 1916.

Rising Youth. New York, 1928–29.

La Rivolta degli Angeli. New York, 1924.

Road to Freedom. Stelton, NJ; New York, 1924–32.

La Scopa. Paterson, 1925–28.
Secolo Nuovo. San Francisco, 1894–1906.
Social War Bulletin. New York, 1918.
Solidarity. New York, 1892–98.
Spanish Revolution. New York, 1936–38.
The Syndicalist. Chicago, 1913.
Les Temps Nouveaux. Paris, 1895–1914.
La Terra. Stockton, California, 1906–10.
Umanità Nova. New York, 1924–25.
Vanguard. New York, 1932–39.
Varhayt. New York, 1889.
Why? New York, 1942–47.
Der Yunyon Arbayter. New York, 1925–27.

Other Periodicals

Los Angeles Times. Los Angeles, 1881-.
N. *W. Ayer and Son's American Newspaper Annual and Directory*. Philadelphia, 1910–29.
New York Herald. New York, 1835–1924.
New York Times. New York, 1861-
Oakland Tribune. Oakland, 1874-.
San Francisco Call. San Francisco, 1895–1913.
San Francisco Chronicle. San Francisco, 1865-.
San Francisco Examiner. San Francisco, 1865-.

Published Sources

Ackelsberg, Martha A. *Free Women of Spain: Anarchism and the Struggle for the Emancipa-tion of Women*. Rev. ed. Oakland: AK, 2005.
Adler, William M. *The Man Who Never Died: The Life, Times, and Legacy of Joe Hill, American Labor Icon*. New York: Bloomsbury, 2011.
Albro, Ward S. *To Die on Your Feet: The Life, Times, and Writings of Práxedis G. Guerrero*. Fort Worth: Texas Christian University Press, 1996.
Alexander, Robert J. *The Anarchists in the Spanish Civil War*. 2 vols. London: Janus, 1998.
American Civil Liberties Union. *Eternal Vigilance! The Story of Civil Liberty, 1937–1938*. New York: American Civil Liberties Union, 1938.
Anarchist Communist Groups of U.S. and Canada, Federation of Russian Anarchist Com-munist Groups of U.S. and Canada, and Ukrainian Anarchist Communist Groups of U.S. and Canada. *Manifesto on the Russian Revolution*. N.p., 1922.
Anarquistas de Bialystok, 1903–1908. 2nd ed. Barcelona: Furia Apátrida and Ediciones Anomia, 2011.
Anderson, Benedict. *Imagined Communities: Reflections on the Origin and Spread of Na-tionalism*. Rev. ed. New York: Verso, 1991.
———. Preface to *Anarchism and Syndicalism in the Colonial and Postcolonial World, 1879–*

1940: The Praxis of National Liberation, Internationalism, and Social Revolution, edited by Steven Hirsch and Lucien van der Walt, xiii–xxix. Boston: Brill, 2010.

———. *Under Three Flags: Anarchism and the Anti-Colonial Imagination*. London: Verso, 2005.

Antonioli, Maurizio, Giampietro Berti, Santi Fedele, and Pasquale Iuso, eds. *Dizionario biografico degli anarchici italiani*. 2 vols. Pisa: Biblioteca Franco Serantini, 2003–4.

Aquilano, Baldo. *L'Ordine figli d'Italia in America*. New York: Società Tipografica Italiana, 1925.

Archibald, Malcolm. "The Many Lives of Max Chernyak." *Bulletin of the Kate Sharpley Library* 66 (April 2011): 1–3.

Arendt, Hannah. *The Origins of Totalitarianism*. Rev. ed. New York: Harcourt, 1968.

Arrigoni, Enrico. *Freedom: My Dream*. 2nd ed. Berkeley: Ardent, 2012.

Arshinov, Peter. *History of the Makhnovist Movement (1918–1921)*. Translated by Lorraine Perlman and Fredy Perlman. Detroit: Red and Black, 1974.

Avrich, Paul. *An American Anarchist: The Life of Voltairine de Cleyre*. Princeton: Princeton University Press, 1978.

———. *Anarchist Portraits*. Princeton: Princeton University Press, 1990.

———. *Anarchist Voices: An Oral History of Anarchism in America*. Princeton: Princeton University Press, 1995.

———, ed. *The Anarchists in the Russian Revolution*. Ithaca: Cornell University Press, 1973.

———. *The Haymarket Tragedy*. Princeton: Princeton University Press, 1984.

———. *Kronstadt, 1921*. Princeton: Princeton University Press, 1970.

———. *The Modern School Movement: Anarchism and Education in the United States*. Princeton: Princeton University Press, 1980.

———. *The Russian Anarchists*. Princeton: Princeton University Press, 1967.

———. *Sacco and Vanzetti: The Anarchist Background*. Princeton: Princeton University Press, 1991.

Avrich, Paul, and Karen Avrich. *Sasha and Emma: The Anarchist Odyssey of Alexander Berkman and Emma Goldman*. Cambridge: Harvard University Press, 2012.

Azarov, Vyacheslav. *Kontrrazvedka: The Story of the Makhnovist Intelligence Service*. Edmonton, Alberta: Black Cat, 2008.

Baily, Samuel. *Immigrants in the Lands of Promise: Italians in Buenos Aires and New York City, 1870–1914*. Ithaca: Cornell University Press, 1999.

Bakunin, Mikhail. *The Basic Bakunin: Writings 1869–1871*. Edited by Robert M. Cutler. Amherst, MA: Prometheus, 1992.

———. *The Political Philosophy of Bakunin: Scientific Anarchism*. Edited by G. P. Maximoff. New York: Free Press, 1953.

Bantman, Constance. "Internationalism without an International? Cross-Channel Anarchist Networks, 1880–1914." *Revue Belge e Philologie et d'Histoire/Belgisch Tijdschrift voor Filologie en Geschiedenis* 84, no. 4 (2006): 961–81.

Baron, Salo W. *The Russian Jew under Tsars and Soviets*. 2nd ed. New York: Schocken, 1987.

Barondes, Joseph. "Zikhroynes fun amol." In *M. Katts Zamelbukh*, edited by A. Frumkin and Khaym Faynman, 34–38. Philadelphia: Merts, 1925.

Bartoli, James. "Adventurers, Bandits, Soldiers of Fortune, Spies and Revolutionaries: Recalling the Baja California Insurrection of 1911 One Hundred Years Later." *Journal of San Diego History* 58, no. 1 (2011): 71–102.

Baumann, Gerold Gino. *Los voluntarios latinoamericanos en la Guerra Civil Española en las brigadas internacionales, las milicias, la retaguardia y el Ejército Popular*. San José: Guayacán, 1997.

Bencivenni, Marcella. "'Fired by the Ideal': Italian Anarchists in New York City, 1885–1972." In *Radical Gotham: The Anarchist Tradition in New York City, 1870–2011*, edited by Tom Goyens. Urbana: University of Illinois Press, forthcoming.

———. *Italian Immigrant Radical Culture: The Idealism of the Sovversivi in the United States, 1890–1940*. New York: New York University Press, 2011.

Benequit, I. A. *Durkhgelebt un durkhgetrakht*. Vol. 2. New York: Kultur Federatsie, 1934.

Bercovici, Konrad. It's the Gypsy in Me: The Autobiography of Konrad Bercovici. New York: Prentice Hall, 1941.

Berkman, Alexander. *The Bolshevik Myth (Diary 1920–1922)*. New York: Boni and Liveright, 1925.

———. *Der kronshtater oyfshtand*. N.p., 1924.

———. *Now and After: The ABC of Communist Anarchism*. New York: Jewish Anarchist Federation, 1929.

———. *Prison Memoirs of an Anarchist*. 1912; Pittsburgh: Frontier Press, 1970.

———. *The Russian Tragedy*. Edited by William G. Nowlin. Sanday, Orkney, UK: Cienfuegos, 1976.

Berkman, Alexander, Henry Bauer, and Carl Nold. *Prison Blossoms: Anarchist Voices from the American Past*. Edited by Miriam Brody and Bonnie Buettner. Cambridge: Belknap Press of Harvard University Press, 2011.

Berkman, Alexander, and Emma Goldman. *Deportation: Its Meaning and Menace*. New York: n.p., 1919.

Bernabei, Alfio. "The London Plot to Kill Mussolini." *History Today* 49, no. 4 (April 1999): 2.

Bernstein, Samuel. *The First International in America*. New York: Kelley, 1965.

Berry, David. "French Anarchists in Spain, 1936–1939." *French History* 3, no. 4 (December 1989): 427–65.

Berta, Giuseppe. "La formazione del movimento operaio regionale: il caso dei tessili (1860–1900)." In *Storia del movimento operaio del socialismo e delle lotte sociali in Piemonte*, edited by Aldo Agosti and Gian Mario Bravo, 1:297–327. Bari, Italy: De Donato, 1979.

Berti, Giampietro. *Errico Malatesta e il movimento anarchico italiano e internazionale, 1872–1932*. Milan: Franco Angeli, 2003.

Bertrand, Charles L. "Italian Revolutionary Syndicalism and the Crisis of Intervention: August–December, 1914." *Canadian Journal of History* 10, no. 3 (December 1975): 349–67.

Bessone, Angelo Stefano. *Uomini tempi e ambienti operai che hanno preparato Oreste Fontanella*. Biella, Italy: Unione Biellese, 1985.

Bettini, Leonardo. *Bibliografia dell'anarchismo*. 2 vols. Florence: Crescita Politica, 1972.

Biagi, Ernest L. The Purple Aster: A History of the Order Sons of Italy in America. N.p.: Veritas, 1961.

Biagini, Furio. *Nati altrove: Il movimento anarchico ebraico tra Mosca e New York*. Pisa: Biblioteca Franco Serantini, 1998.

Bialostotsky, B. J., ed. *David Edelshtat gedenk-bukh: Tsum zekhtsikstn yortsayt, 1892–1952.* New York: Dovid Edelshtat Komitetn, 1953.

Bird, Stewart, George Georgakas, and Deborah Shaffer, eds. *Solidarity Forever: An Oral History of the IWW.* Chicago: Lake View, 1985.

Blaisdell, Lowell L. *The Desert Revolution: Baja California, 1911.* Madison: University of Wisconsin Press, 1962.

Bluestein, Abe. Introduction to Augustin Souchy, *With the Peasants of Aragon: Libertarian Communism in the Liberated Areas,* 1–2. Translated by Abe Bluestein. Sanday, Orkney, UK: Cienfuegos, 1982.

Blumenson, S. L. "Culture on Rutgers Square: The Fervent Days on East Broadway." *Commentary* 10 (July 1950): 65–74.

Boehm, Randolph. U.*S. Military Intelligence Reports: Surveillance of Radicals in the United States, 1917–1941.* Frederick, MD: University Publications of America, 1984.

Bordo-Rivkin, Mina, ed. *B. Rivkin: Lebn un shafn.* New York: Shtayn, 1953.

Borochov, Ber. "Two Currents in Poale Zion." In *Class Struggle and the Jewish Nation: Selected Essays in Marxist Zionism,* edited by Mitchell Cohen, 151–54. New Brunswick: Transaction, 1984.

Boulouque, Sylvain. "The Anarchists, Zionism, and the Birth of the State of Israel." Translated by Jesse Cohn. *Social Anarchism* 36 (Spring 2004): 15–21.

Boycottage et sabottage: Rapport de la Commission du Boycottage au Congrès Corporatif tenu à Toulouse en septembre 1897. Paris: Favier, 1897.

Brinton, Maurice. *The Bolsheviks and Workers' Control, 1917–1921: The State and Counterrevolution.* Montreal: Black Rose, 1975.

Brodkin, Karen. *How Jews Became White Folks, and What That Says about Race in America.* New Brunswick: Rutgers University Press, 1998.

Brown, Emily C. *Har Dayal: Hindu Revolutionary and Rationalist.* Tucson: University of Arizona Press, 1975.

Buhle, Paul. "Antifascism." In *Encyclopedia of the American Left,* edited by Mari Jo Buhle, Paul Buhle, and Dan Georgakas, 46–48. New York: Garland, 1990.

Bull, Ana Cento. "The Lombard Silk Spinners in the 19th Century: An Industrial Workforce in a Rural Setting." *The Italianist* 7 (1987): 99–121.

Burgin, Hertz. Di geshikhte fun der idisher arbayter bevegung in Amerika, Rusland, un England. New York: Fareynigte Idishe Geverkshaften, 1915.

Cahm, Jean Caroline. "Bakunin." In *Socialism and Nationalism,* edited by Eric Cahm and Vladimir Claude Fišera, 1:33–49. Nottingham, England: Spokesman, 1978.

———. "Kropotkin and the Anarchist Movement." In *Socialism and Nationalism,* edited by Eric Cahm and Vladimir Claude Fišera, 1:50–68. Nottingham, England: Spokesman, 1978.

Caminita, Ludovico. *Che cose è la religione.* 2nd ed. Chieti, Italy: di Sciullo, 1906.

———. *Free Country!* [Paterson]: n.p., n.d.

———. *Nell'isola delle lagrime: Ellis Island.* New York: Stabilimento Tipografico Italia, 1924.

———. *Obici: Biografia.* New York: Scarlino, 1943.

Camp, Helen C. *Iron in Her Soul: Elizabeth Gurley Flynn and the American Left.* Pullman: Washington State University Press, 1995.

Cannistraro, Philip V. Blackshirts in Little Italy: Italian Americans and Fascism, 1921–1929. West Lafayette, IN: Bordighera, 1999.

———. "The Duce and the Prominenti: Fascism and the Crisis of Italian American Leadership." *Altreitalie* 31 (December 2005): 76–86.

Carey, George W. "'La Questione Sociale': An Anarchist Newspaper in Paterson, N.J. (1895–1908)." In *Italian Americans: New Perspectives in Italian Immigration and Ethnicity*, edited by Lydio F. Tomasi, 289–98. New York: American Italian Historical Association, 1985.

———. "The Vessel, the Deed, and the Idea: Anarchists in Paterson, 1895–1908." *Antipode* 10–11 (1979): 46–58.

Carlson, Andrew R. *Anarchism in Germany: The Early Movement*. Metuchen: Scarecrow, 1972.

Carnevale, Nancy C. *A New Language, A New World: Italian Immigrants in the United States, 1890–1945*. Urbana: University of Illinois Press, 2009.

Casanova, Julián. *Anarchism, the Republic, and Civil War in Spain, 1931–1939*. Edited by Paul Preston. Translated by Andrew Dowling and Graham Pollok. London: Routledge, 2005.

Casanovas i Codina, Joan. "Pedro Esteve (Barcelona 1865–Weehauken [*sic*], N.J. 1925): A Catalan Anarchist in the United States." *Catalan Review* 5, no. 3 (July 1995): 57–77.

Cassedy, Steven, ed. *Building the Future: Jewish Immigrant Intellectuals and the Making of Tsukunft*. New York: Holmes and Meier, 1999.

———. *To the Other Shore: The Russian Jewish Intellectuals Who Came to America*. Princeton: Princeton University Press, 1997.

Catanuto, Santo, and Franco Schirone. *Il canto anarchico in Italia nell'Ottocento e nel Novecento*. Milan: Zero in Condotta, 2009.

Cattell, David T. *Communism and the Spanish Civil War*. Berkeley: University of California Press, 1955.

Cerrito, Gino. "Sull'emigrazione anarchica italiana negli Stati Uniti d'America." *Volontà* 22, no. 4 (August 1969): 269–76.

Chang, Kornel. *Pacific Connections: The Making of the U.S.-Canadian Borderlands*. Berkeley: University of California Press, 2012.

Cheah, Pheng, and Bruce Robbins, eds. *Cosmopolitics: Thinking and Feeling beyond the Nation*. Minneapolis: University of Minnesota Press, 1998.

Choate, Mark I. *Emigrant Nation: The Making of Italy Abroad*. Cambridge: Harvard University Press, 2008.

Christie, Stuart. *We, the Anarchists!: A Study of the Iberian Anarchist Federation (FAI), 1927–1937*. Hastings, East Sussex, UK: Meltzer, 2000.

Cinel, Dino. *From Italy to San Francisco: The Immigrant Experience*. Stanford: Stanford University Press, 1982.

Claghorn, Kate Holladay. *The Immigrant's Day in Court*. New York: Harper, 1923.

Clark, Jane Perry. *Deportation of Aliens from the United States to Europe*. New York: Columbia University Press, 1931.

Cohen, Joseph J. *In Quest of Heaven: The Story of the Sunrise Co-Operative Farm Community*. New York: Sunrise History Publishing Committee, 1957.

———. *Di yidish-anarkhistishe bavegung in Amerike: Historisher iberblik un perzenlekhe iberlebungen*. Philadelphia: Radical Library, Branch 273 Arbeter Ring, 1945.

Cohen, Lizabeth. *Making a New Deal: Industrial Workers in Chicago, 1919–1939*. New York: Cambridge University Press, 1990.

Cohn, Michael A. "In Neters keler." In *David Edelshtat gedenk-bukh: Tsum zekhtsikstn yortsayt, 1892–1952*, edited by B. J. Bialostotsky, 183–85. New York: Dovid Edelshtat Komitetn, 1953.

———. *Some Questions and an Appeal*. New York: Independent Sacco-Vanzetti Committee, 1927.

———. *Two Worlds: An Imaginary Speech Delivered by Bartolomeo Vanzetti before Judge Webster Thayer*. New York: Independent Sacco-Vanzetti Committee, 1927.

Collomp, Catherine, and Marianne Debouzy. "European Migrants and the U.S. Labor Movement, 1880s–1920s." In *Roots of the Transplanted*, edited by Dirk Hoerder, Horst Rössler, and Inge Blank, 2:339–81. Boulder: East European Monographs, 1994.

Confino, Michael. "Organization as Ideology: Dilemmas of the Russian Anarchists (1903–1914)." *Russian History* 37, no. 3 (2010): 179–207.

I Congressi socialisti internazionali. Paterson: Tipografia della Questione Sociale, 1900.

Cordillot, Michel, ed. *La sociale en Amérique: Dictionnaire biographique du mouvement social francophone aux États-Unis (1848–1922)*. Paris: Les Éditions de l'Atelier, 2002.

Coughlin, Mike. "History of a Book." *The Dandelion*, Summer 1980.

Creagh, Ronald. *L'Anarchisme aux Etats-Unis*. 2 vols. Paris: Didier Érudition, 1986.

Cross, Ira B. *A History of the Labor Movement in California*. Berkeley: University of California Press, 1935.

Crump, John. *The Origins of Socialist Thought in Japan*. New York: St. Martin's, 1983.

Damiani, Gigi. *Razzismo e anarchismo*. Newark: Biblioteca L'Adunata dei Refrattari, 1938.

Daniels, Roger. *The Politics of Prejudice: The Anti-Japanese Movement in California and the Struggle for Japanese Exclusion*. Berkeley: University of California Press, 1962.

D'Attilio, Robert. "L'Adunata dei Refrattari." In *Encyclopedia of the American Left*, edited by Mari Jo Buhle, Paul Buhle, and Dan Georgakas, 4–5. New York: Garland, 1990.

Davidson, Jared. *Sewing Freedom: Philip Josephs, Transnationalism, and Early New Zealand Anarchism*. Oakland: AK, 2013.

Davis, John A. "Socialism and the Working Classes in Italy before 1914." In *Labour and Socialist Movements in Europe before 1914*, edited by Dick Geary, 182–230. New York: Berg, 1989.

Day, Hem. "Seize (Le Manifeste des)." In *Encyclopédie anarchiste*, edited by Sebastien Faure, 4:2541–53. Paris: La Librairie Internationale, 1934.

De Ciampis, M. "Storia del movimento socialista rivoluzionario italiano." *La Parola del Popolo* 9, no. 37 (December 1958–January 1959): 136–63.

Delzell, Charles F. *Mussolini's Enemies: The Italian Anti-Fascist Resistance*. 1961; New York: Fertig, 1974.

De Maria, Carlo. "Anarchici italiani negli Stati Uniti: Le biografie parellele di Mattia Giurelli e Alberto Guabello." *Diacronie: Studi di Storia Contemporanea*, no. 5 (January 2011). http://www.studistorici.com/wp-content/uploads/2011/01/DEMARIA_Anarchici-italiani-negli-Stati-Uniti.pdf.

Denning, Michael. *The Cultural Front: The Laboring of American Culture in the Twentieth Century*. New York: Verso, 1996.

Diggins, John P. *Mussolini and Fascism: The View from America*. Princeton: Princeton University Press, 1972.

Di Lembo, Luigi. *Guerra di classe e lotta umana: L'Anarchismo in Italia dal biennio rosso alla Guerra di Spagna (1919–1939)*. Pisa: Biblioteca Franco Serantini, 2001.

Dinnerstein, Leonard. *Antisemitism in America*. New York: Oxford University Press, 1995.

Di Paola, Pietro. *Knights Errant of Anarchy: London and Diaspora of Italian Anarchists (1880–1917)*. Liverpool: Liverpool University Press, 2013.

Dirlik, Arif. "Anarchism and the Question of Place: Thoughts from the Chinese Experience." In *Anarchism and Syndicalism in the Colonial and Postcolonial World, 1879–1940: The Praxis of National Liberation, Internationalism, and Social Revolution*, edited by Steven Hirsch and Lucien van der Walt, 131–46. Boston: Brill, 2010.

———. *Anarchism in the Chinese Revolution*. Berkeley: University of California Press, 1991.

Dodyk, Delight W. "Women's Work in the Paterson Silk Mills: A Study in Women's Industrial Experience in the Early Twentieth Century." In *Women in New Jersey History: Papers Presented at the Thirteenth Annual New Jersey History Symposium*, 10–28. Trenton: New Jersey Historical Commission, 1985.

Dolgoff, Sam. *Fragments: A Memoir*. Cambridge, UK: Refract, 1986.

Domsky-Abrams, Mary. "My Reminiscences of the Triangle Fire." *Remembering the 1911 Triangle Factory Fire*. http://www.ilr.cornell.edu/trianglefire/primary/survivorInterviews/MaryDomskyAbrams.html.

Dowell, Eldridge Foster. *A History of Criminal Syndicalism Legislation in the United States*. Baltimore: Johns Hopkins Press, 1939.

Dubinsky, David, and Abraham Henry Raskin. *David Dubinsky: A Life with Labor*. New York: Simon and Schuster, 1977.

Duff, Harvey. *The Silent Defenders, Courts, and Capitalism in California*. Chicago: Industrial Workers of the World, n.d.

Ealham, Chris. *Anarchism and the City: Revolution and Counter-Revolution in Barcelona, 1898–1937*. Oakland: AK, 2010.

Emigrazione e colonie: Raccolta di rapporti dei rr. agenti diplomatici e consolari. Vol. 3. Rome: Cooperativa Tipografica Manuzio, 1908.

"Emma Goldman and the Alliance Proposals." *Spain and the World*, March 4, 1938.

Epstein, Melech. *The Jew and Communism: The Story of Early Communist Victories and Ultimate Defeats in the Jewish Community, U.S.A., 1919–1941*. New York: Trade Union Sponsoring Committee, 1959.

———. *Jewish Labor in U.S.A.: An Industrial, Political, and Cultural History of the Jewish Labor Movement*. New ed. 2 vols. [New York]: Ktav, 1969.

———. *Yisroel Faynberg: Kemfer far frayhayt un sotsyaler gerekhtikayt*. New York: Lerman, 1948.

Esteve, Pedro. *A los anarquistas de España y Cuba: Memoria de la Conferencia anarquista Internacional celebrada en Chicago en septiembre de 1893*. Paterson: Despertar, 1900.

———. *Reflexiones sobre el movimiento revolucionario de México*. 1911. http://www.antorcha.net/biblioteca_virtual/politica/reflexiones/indice.html.

Ewen, Elizabeth. *Immigrant Women in the Land of Dollars: Life and Culture on the Lower East Side, 1890–1925*. New York: Monthly Review Press, 1985.

Eyges, Thomas B. *Beyond the Horizon: The Story of a Radical Emigrant*. Boston: Group Free Society, 1944.

Falk, Candace, Barry Pateman, and Jessica M. Moran, eds. *Emma Goldman: A Documentary History of the American Years.* 3 vols. to date. Berkeley: University of California Press, 2003-.

Fedeli, Ugo. "Gli anarchici e la guerra: 1." *Volontà* 4, no. 10 (April 15, 1950): 622–28.

———. "Gli anarchici e la guerra: 2." *Volontà* 4, no. 11 (May 15, 1950): 684–90.

———. *Giuseppe Ciancabilla.* Cesena, Italy: Antistato, 1965.

———. *Luigi Galleani: Quarant'anni di lotte rivoluzionarie (1891–1931).* New ed. Catania, Italy: Centrolibri, 1984.

Fenton, Edwin. *Immigrants and Labor Unions, a Case Study: Italians and American Labor, 1870–1920.* New York: Arno, 1975.

Ferguson, Kathy E. *Emma Goldman: Political Thinking in the Streets.* Lanham, MD: Rowman and Littlefield, 2011.

Fernández, Bieito Alonso. *Obreiros alén mar: Mariñeiros, fogoneiros, e anarquistas galegos en New York (1900–1930).* Santo Tirso, Portugal: A Nosa Terra, 2006.

Fernández, Frank. *Cuban Anarchism: The History of a Movement.* Translated by Chaz Bufe. Tucson: See Sharp, 2001.

Fichera, Sebastian. *Italy on the Pacific: San Francisco's Italian Americans.* New York: Palgrave Macmillan, 2011.

Fight against Deportation: Free Ferrero and Sallitto. New York: Ferrero-Sallitto Defense Conference, 1936.

Fine, Sidney. "Anarchism and the Assassination of McKinley." *American Historical Review* 60, no. 4 (July 1955): 777–99.

Finzi, Paolo. "Ricordando John, cioè Vincenzo." *Bollettino Archivio G. Pinelli*, no. 32 (December 2008): 38–39.

Fischler, Steven, and Joel Sucher. *Free Voice of Labor: The Jewish Anarchists.* Videocassette. Pacific Street Films, 1980.

Fishman, William J. Jewish Radicals: From Czarist Stetl to London Ghetto. New York: Pantheon, 1974.

Fitch, John. "The I.W.W., an Outlaw Organization." *Survey*, June 7, 1913.

Fleming, Marie. *The Geography of Freedom: The Odyssey of Elisée Reclus.* Montreal: Black Rose, 1989.

Flynn, Elizabeth Gurley. *The Rebel Girl: An Autobiography.* New York: International, 1973.

———. "The Truth about the Paterson Strike." In *Rebel Voices: An I.W.W. Anthology*, edited by Joyce L. Kornbluh, 215–26. Ann Arbor: University of Michigan Press, 1968.

Forman, Michael. *Nationalism and the International Labor Movement: The Idea of the Nation in Socialist and Anarchist Theory.* University Park: Pennsylvania State University Press, 1998.

Frank, Herman. "Anarchism and the Jews." In *Struggle for Tomorrow: Modern Political Ideologies of the Jewish People*, edited by Basil J. Vlavianos and Feliks Gross, 276–90. New York: Arts, 1953.

———. "Anarkho-sotsialistishe ideyan un bavengungen bay yidn." In *Geklibene shriftn*, 255–306. New York: Dr. Herman Frank Bukh-Komitet/Bialistoker Historishe Gezelshaft, 1954.

"Free Commune and Billy MacQueen." Bulletin of the Kate Sharpley Library 70–71 (July 2012): 1–2.

Freedom of Thought Arraigned: Four Year Persecution of "MAN!" Los Angeles: Marcus Graham Freedom of the Press Committee, 1939.

Frost, Richard H. *The Mooney Case.* Stanford: Stanford University Press, 1968.

Frumkin, A. *In friling fun idishn sotsializm: Zikhroynes fun a zshurnalist.* New York: A. Frumkin Yubiley Komitet, 1940.

Gabaccia, Donna. *Militants and Migrants: Rural Sicilians Become American Workers.* New Brunswick: Rutgers University Press, 1988.

Gage, Beverly. *The Day Wall Street Exploded: A Story of America in Its First Age of Terror.* Oxford: Oxford University Press, 2009.

Gallagher, Dorothy. *All the Right Enemies: The Life and Murder of Carlo Tresca.* New Brunswick: Rutgers University Press, 1988.

Galzerano, Giuseppe. "Attentati anarchici a Mussolini." In *Atti della giornata di studi su l'antifascismo rivoluzionario: Tra passato e presente,* 77–98. Pisa: Biblioteca Franco Serantini, 1993.

———. Gaetano Bresci: Vita, attentato, processo, carcere e morte dell'anarchico che "giustiziò" Umberto I. 2nd ed. Salerno, Italy: Galzerano/Atti e Memoire del Popolo, 2001.

———. Michele Schirru: Vita, viaggi, arresto, carcere, processo, e morte dell'anarchico italo-americano fucilato per l'"intenzione" di uccidere Mussolini. Salerno, Italy: Galzerano/Atti e Memoire del Popolo, 2006.

Ganz, Marie. *Rebels: Into Anarchy—and Out Again.* New York: Dodd, Mead, 1919.

Garland, Libby. "Not-Quite-Closed Gates: Jewish Alien Smuggling in the Post-Quota Years." *American Jewish History* 94, no. 3 (September 2008): 197–224.

Ghio, Paul. *L'anarchisme aux États-Unis.* Paris: Colin, 1903.

Gianfrate, Mario, and Kenyon Zimmer. *Michele Centrone, tra vecchio e nuovo mondo: Anarchici pugliesi in difesa della libertà spagnola.* Sammichele di Bari, Italy: SUMA, 2012.

Giovinco, Joseph. "'Success in the Sun?': California's Italians during the Progressive Era." In *Struggle and Success: An Anthology of the Italian Immigrant Experience in California,* edited by Paola A. Sensi-Isolani and Phylis Cancilla Martinelli, 20–37. New York: Center for Migration Studies, 1993.

Giulietti, Fabrizio. *Dizionario biografico degli anarchici piemontesi.* Salerno, Italy: Galzerano/Atti e Memoire del Popolo, 2013.

———. Il movimento anarchico italiano nella lotta contro il fascismo, 1927–1945. Rome: Piero Lacaita, 2003.

Glenn, Susan A. Daughters of the Shtetl: Life and Labor in the Immigrant Generation. Ithaca, NY: Cornell University Press, 1990.

Goldberg, David J. *A Tale of Three Cities: Labor Organization and Protest in Paterson, Passaic, and Lawrence, 1916–21.* New Brunswick: Rutgers University Press, 1989.

Goldberg, N. "Pionire der frayhayt." In *Geshikhte fun der yidisher arbeter-bavengung in di Faraynikte Shtatn,* edited by E. Tcherikower, 2:297–318. New York: YIVO, 1945.

Goldman, Emma. *The Crushing of the Russian Revolution.* London: Freedom, 1922.

———. *Living My Life.* 1931; Salt Lake City: Peregrine and Gibbs M. Smith, 1982.

———. *My Disillusionment in Russia.* London: Daniel, 1925.

Goldman, Emma, and Alexander Berkman. *Nowhere at Home: Letters from Exile of Emma Goldman and Alexander Berkman.* Edited by Richard Drinnon and Anna Maria Drinnon. New York: Schocken, 1975.

Goldstein, Eric L. *The Price of Whiteness: Jews, Race, and American Identity*. Princeton: Princeton University Press, 2006.

Goldstein, Robert J. "The Anarchist Scare of 1908: A Sign of Tensions in the Progressive Era." *American Studies* 15, no. 2 (Fall 1974): 55–78.

———. *Political Repression in Modern America from 1870 to 1976*. Urbana: University of Illinois Press, 2001.

Golin, Steve. *The Fragile Bridge: Paterson Silk Strike, 1913*. Philadelphia: Temple University Press, 1988.

Goncharok, Moshe. "La stampa anarchica yiddish in Israele." *Bollettino Archivio G. Pinelli*, no. 15 (April 2000): 42–43.

Goodwin, George Sands. "What Anarchy Is—A View in Detail." *The Era*, December 1902.

Gordin, Abba. *Draysik yor in Lite un Poyln (oytobiografie)*. Buenos Aires: Yidisher Ratsionalistisher Gezelshaft, 1958.

———. *Sh. Yanovsky: zayn lebn, kemfn un shafn, 1864–1939*. Los Angeles: Sh. Yanovsky Odenk Komitet, 1957.

Gori, Pietro. *Scienza e religione: Conferenza tenuta il 14 luglio 1896 a Paterson N.J. negli Stati Uniti d'America*. Rome and Florence: Serantoni, 1905.

Gorman, Anthony. "Anarchists in Education: The Free Popular University in Egypt (1901)." *Middle Eastern Studies* 41, no. 3 (May 2005): 303–20.

Goyens, Tom. *Beer and Revolution: The German Anarchist Movement in New York City, 1880–1914*. Urbana: University of Illinois Press, 2007.

Graham, Fred S. [Shmuel Marcus]. *Anarchism and the World Revolution: An Answer to Robert Minor*. 2nd ed. N.p., 1921.

Graham, Helen. "'Against the State': A Genealogy of the Barcelona May Days (1937)." *European History Quarterly* 29, no. 4 (1999): 485–542.

Graham, Marcus [Shmuel Marcus], ed. *An Anthology of Revolutionary Poetry*. New York: Active, 1929.

———. "Autobiographical Note." In *MAN! An Anthology of Anarchist Ideas, Essays, Poetry, and Commentaries*, edited by Marcus Graham, viii–xxi. London: Cienfuegos, 1974.

———. *The Issues in the Present War*. London: Freedom, 1943.

Graur, Mina. *An Anarchist "Rabbi": The Life and Teachings of Rudolf Rocker*. New York: St. Martin's, 1997.

———. "Anarcho-Nationalism: Anarchist Attitudes towards Jewish Nationalism and Zionism." *Modern Judaism* 14, no. 1 (February 1994): 1–19.

Grave, Jean. *Moribund Society and Anarchy*. Translated by Voltairine de Cleyre. San Francisco: Isaak, 1899.

Green, James R. *Death in the Haymarket: A Story of Chicago, the First Labor Movement, and the Bombing That Divided Gilded Age America*. New York: Pantheon, 2006.

Green, Nancy L. "Women and Immigrants in the Sweatshop: Categories of Labor Segmentation Revisited." *Comparative Studies in Society and History* 38, no. 3 (July 1996): 411–33.

Gremmo, Roberto. *Gli anarchici che uccisero Umberto I°: Gaetano Bresci, il "Biondino" e i tessitori biellesi di Paterson*. Biella, Italy: Storia Ribelle, 2000.

Grosser, Philip. *Alcatraz, Uncle Sam's Devil's Island: Experiences of a Conscientious Objector in America during the First World War. 1933*; London: Sharpley, 2007.

Guglielmo, Jennifer. *Living the Revolution: Italian Women's Resistance and Radicalism in New York City, 1880–1945.* Chapel Hill: University of North Carolina Press, 2010.

Guglielmo, Jennifer, and Salvatore Salerno, eds. *Are Italians White? How Race Is Made in America.* New York: Routledge, 2003.

Guglielmo, Thomas A. *White on Arrival: Italians, Race, Color, and Power in Chicago, 1890–1945.* New York: Oxford University Press, 2003.

Gurock, Jeffrey S. *When Harlem Was Jewish, 1870–1930.* New York: Columbia University Press, 1979.

Gutman, Herbert, and Ira Berlin. "Class Composition and the Development of the American Working Class, 1840–1890." In *Power and Culture: Essays on the American Working Class,* edited by Ira Berlin, 380–94. New York: Pantheon, 1987.

Haberer, Erich. *Jews and Revolution in Nineteenth-Century Russia.* New York: Cambridge University Press, 1995.

Hadda, Janet. *Yankev Glatshteyn.* Boston: Twayne, 1980.

Hall, Greg. *Harvest Wobblies: The Industrial Workers of the World and Agricultural Laborers in the American West, 1905–1930.* Corvallis: Oregon State University Press, 2001.

Hapgood, Hutchins. *The Spirit of the Ghetto: Studies of the Jewish Quarter of New York.* New ed. New York: Schocken, 1966.

Henry, Josephine K. "Albert Johnson: Philosopher, Individualist, Atheist, Materialist, Humanitarian." *Blue-Grass Blade,* October 4, 1908.

Herman, Joanna Clapps. *The Anarchist Bastard: Growing Up Italian in America.* Albany: Excelsior/State University of New York Press, 2011.

Hewitt, Nancy A. "'The Voice of Virile Labor': Labor Militancy, Community Solidarity, and Gender Identity among Tampa's Latin Workers." In *Work Engendered: Toward a New Understanding of Men, Women, and Work,* edited by Ava Baron, 142–67. Ithaca: Cornell University Press, 1991.

Higham, John. *Strangers in the Land: Patterns of American Nativism, 1860–1925.* New Brunswick: Rutgers University Press, 1955.

Hill, Rebecca N. *Men, Mobs, and Law: Anti-Lynching and Labor Defense in U.S. Radical History.* Durham: Duke University Press, 2008.

Hillquit, Morris. *History of Socialism in the United States.* New York: Funk and Wagnalls, 1906.

Hirsch, Steven, and Lucien van der Walt, eds. *Anarchism and Syndicalism in the Colonial and Postcolonial World, 1870–1940: The Praxis of National Liberation, Internationalism, and Social Revolution.* Boston: Brill, 2010.

Hobsbawm, Eric J. *The Age of Extremes: A History of the World, 1914–1991.* New York: Vintage, 2000.

———. *Nations and Nationalism since 1780: Programme, Myth, Reality.* 2nd ed. New York: Cambridge University Press, 1990.

Hollinger, David A. *Postethnic America: Beyond Multiculturalism.* New York: Basic Books, 1995.

Hong, Nathaniel. "The Origin of American Legislation to Exclude and Deport Aliens for Their Political Beliefs, and Its Initial Review by the Courts." *Journal of Ethnic Studies* 18, no. 2 (Summer 1990): 1–36.

Horne, Gerald. *Black and Brown: African Americans and the Mexican Revolution, 1910–1920.* New York: New York University Press, 2005.

Horrox, James. *A Living Revolution: Anarchism in the Kibbutz Movement*. Oakland: AK, 2009.

Howe, Irving. *World of Our Fathers*. New York: Simon and Schuster, 1976.

Hwang, Dongyoun. "Korean Anarchism before 1945: A Regional and Transnational Approach." In *Anarchism and Syndicalism in the Colonial and Postcolonial World, 1879-1940: The Praxis of National Liberation, Internationalism, and Social Revolution*, edited by Steven Hirsch and Lucien van der Walt, 95-129. Boston: Brill, 2010.

Iacovetta, Franca, and Lorenza Stradiotti. "Betrayal, Vengeance, and the Anarchist Ideal: Virgilia D'Andrea's Radical Antifascism in (American) Exile, 1928-1933." *Journal of Women's History* 25, no. 1 (Spring 2013): 85-110.

Iannarelli, Giuseppe. *Lo sciopero dei tessitori di seta di Paterson New Jersey*. New York: Nicoletti, 1916.

Ichioka, Yuji. *The Issei: The World of the First Generation Japanese Immigrants, 1885-1924*. New York: Free Press, 1988.

Industrial Workers of the World. *The Founding Convention of the IWW: Proceedings*. 1905; New York: Merit, 1969.

———. *Proceedings of the Second Annual Convention of the Industrial Workers of the World*. Chicago: Industrial Workers of the World, 1906.

———. "Proceedings of Third Annual Convention Industrial Workers of the World: Official Report." 1907. http://www.slp.org/pdf/slphist/iww_conv_1907.pdf.

The International Anarchist Congress Held at Plancius Hall, Amsterdam, on August 26th-31st, 1907. London: Freedom, 1907.

International Committee for Political Prisoners. *Letters from Russian Prisons*. New York: Boni, 1925.

Issel, William, and Robert W. Cherney. *San Francisco, 1865-1932: Politics, Power, and Urban Development*. Berkeley: University of California Press, 1986.

Jacobson, Matthew Frye. *Special Sorrows: The Diasporic Imagination of Irish, Polish, and Jewish Immigrants in the United States*. Cambridge: Harvard University Press, 1995.

———. *Whiteness of a Different Color: European Immigrants and the Alchemy of Race*. Cambridge: Harvard University Press, 1998.

Jaffe, Julian F. *Crusade against Radicalism: New York during the Red Scare, 1914-1924*. Port Washington, NY: Kennikat, 1972.

Jensen, Joan M. *Passage from India: Asian Indian Immigrants in North America*. New Haven: Yale University Press, 1988.

Jensen, Richard Bach. *The Battle against Anarchist Terrorism: An International History, 1878-1934*. New York: Cambridge University Press, 2014.

———. "The United States, International Policing, and the War against Anarchist Terrorism, 1900-1914." *Terrorism and Political Violence* 13, no. 1 (Spring 2001): 15-46.

Joseph, Samuel. *Jewish Immigration to the United States from 1881 to 1910*. 1914; New York: Arno, 1969.

Katts, M. "Zayn geshtalt." In *David Edelshtat gedenk-bukh: tsum zekhtsikstn yortsayt, 1892-1952*, edited by B. J. Bialostotsky, 178-180. New York: Dovid Edelshtat Komitetn, 1953.

Katz, Daniel. *All Together Different: Yiddish Socialists, Garment Workers, and the Labor Roots of Multiculturalism*. New York: New York University Press, 2011.

Katz, Dovid. "Alexander Harkavy and His Trilingual Dictionary." In Alexander Harkavy,

Yiddish-English-Hebrew Dictionary, 2nd ed., vi–xxiii. New Haven, CT: Yale University Press, 2006.

Kazin, Michael. *Barons of Labor: The San Francisco Building Trades and Union Power in the Progressive Era*. Urbana: University of Illinois Press, 1987.

Kelley, Robin D. G. *Hammer and Hoe: Alabama Communists during the Great Depression*. Chapel Hill: University of North Carolina Press, 1990.

Kessler-Harris, Alice. "Problems of Coalition Building: Women and Trade Unions in the 1920s." In *Gendering Labor History*, 52–70. Urbana: University of Illinois Press, 2007.

Kessner, Thomas. *The Golden Door: Italian and Jewish Immigrant Mobility in New York City, 1880–1915*. New York: Oxford University Press, 1977.

Khuri-Makdisi, Ilham. *The Eastern Mediterranean and the Making of Global Radicalism*. Berkeley: University of California Press, 2010.

Kissman, Joseph. "The Immigration of Rumanian Jews up to 1914." *YIVO Annual of Jewish Social Science* 2–3 (1947–48): 160–79.

Kitz, Ori. *The Poetics of Anarchy: David Edelshtat's Revolutionary Poetry*. New York: Lang, 1997.

Kliger, Hannah, ed. *Jewish Hometown Associations and Family Circles in New York: The WPA Yiddish Writers' Group Study*. Bloomington: Indiana University Press, 1992.

Knight, Robert Edward Lee. *Industrial Relations in the San Francisco Bay Area, 1900–1918*. Berkeley: University of California Press, 1960.

Knowles, Rob. *Political Economy from Below: Economic Thought in Communitarian Anarchism, 1840–1914*. New York: Routledge, 2004.

Kobrin, Rebecca. *Jewish Bialystok and Its Diaspora*. Bloomington: Indiana University Press, 2010.

Koettgen, Ewald. "Making Silk." *International Socialist Review*, March 14, 1914.

Kohn, Stephen M. *American Political Prisoners: Prosecutions under the Espionage and Sedition Acts*. Westport, CT: Praeger, 1994.

Konishi, Sho. *Anarchist Modernity: Cooperatism and Japanese-Russian Intellectual Relations in Modern Japan*. Cambridge: Harvard University Asia Center, 2013.

Kopeloff, I. *Amol in Amerike: Zikhroynes fun dem yidishn lebn in Amerike in di yorn 1883–1904*. Warsaw: Bzshoza, 1928.

———. "M. Katts's tetigkayt in der anarkhistisher un sots. revolutsionerer bevegung." In *M. Katts zamelbukh*, edited by A. Frumkin and Hayim Fineman, 21–29. Philadelphia: Merts, 1925.

Kosak, Hadassa. *Cultures of Opposition: Jewish Immigrant Workers, New York City, 1881–1905*. Albany: State University of New York Press, 2000.

Kosta, Todorov. *Balkan Firebrand: The Autobiography of a Rebel Soldier and Statesman*. Chicago: Ziff-Davis, 1943.

Kropotkin, Peter. "Finland: A Rising Nationality." *Nineteenth Century*, March 1885.

———. "Letter to Maria Isidine Goldsmith." In *Direct Struggle against Capital: A Peter Kropotkin Anthology*, edited by Iain McKay, 137–48. Oakland: AK, 2014.

Kuznets, Simon. "Immigration of Russian Jews to the United States: Background and Structure." *Perspectives in American History* 9 (1975): 33–124.

La Botz, Dan. "American 'Slackers' in the Mexican Revolution: International Proletarian Politics in the Midst of a National Revolution." *The Americas* 62, no. 4 (April 2006): 563–90.

Lai, Him Mark. "Anarchism, Communism, and China's Nationalist Revolution." In *Chinese American Transnational Politics*, 53–76. Urbana: University of Illinois Press, 2010.

Lang, Lucy Robins. *Tomorrow Is Beautiful*. New York: Macmillan, 1948.

Lederhendler, Eli. *Jewish Immigrants and American Capitalism, 1880–1920: From Caste to Class*. New York: Cambridge University Press, 2009.

Lee, Erika. *At America's Gates: Chinese Immigration during the Exclusion Era, 1882–1943*. Chapel Hill: University of North Carolina Press, 2003.

Leeder, Elaine J. *The Gentle General: Rose Pesotta, Anarchist and Labor Organizer*. Albany: State University of New York Press, 1993.

Lenin, V. I. *The State and Revolution*. 1919; Beijing: Foreign Language Press, 1976.

Levine, Louis. *The Women's Garment Workers: A History of the International Ladies' Garment Workers' Union*. New York: Huebsch, 1924.

Levy, Carl. "Anarchism and Cosmopolitanism." *Journal of Political Ideologies* 16, no. 3 (October 2011): 265–78.

———. "The Anarchist Assassin and Italian History, 1870s to 1930s." In *Assassinations and Murder in Modern Italy: Transformations in Society and Culture*, edited by Stephen Gundle and Lucia Rinaldi, 207–21. New York: Palgrave Macmillan, 2007.

———. *Gramsci and the Anarchists*. New York: Berg, 1999.

———. "Social Histories of Anarchism." *Journal for the Study of Radicalism* 4, no. 2 (Spring 2010): 1–44.

Liber, Benzion. *A Doctor's Apprenticeship (Autobiographical Sketches)*. New York: Rational Living, 1956.

Liebman, Arthur. *Jews and the Left*. New York: Wiley, 1979.

López, Chantal, and Omar Cortés, eds. *El Partido Liberal Mexicano (1906–1908)*. Mexico City: Ediciones Antorcha, 1986.

Lord, Eliot, J. D. Trenor, and Samuel J. Barrows. *The Italian in America*. New York: Buck, 1905.

Lowell, Esther. "Thousands in America Renounce Mussolini's Italy." *New Leader*, March 27, 1926.

Lucarini, Umberto. "Cesare Crespi." *La Parola del Popolo* 9, no. 37 (December 1958–January 1959): 286–87.

Luconi, Stefano. "Ethnic Allegiance and Class Consciousness among Italian-American Workers, 1900–1941." *Socialism and Democracy* 22, no. 3 (2008): 123–42.

———. "From Left to Right: The Not So Strange Career of Filippo Bocchini and Other Italian American Radicals." *Italian American Review* 6 (Autumn 1997–Winter 1998): 59–79.

———. "Mussolini's Italian-American Sympathizers in the West: Mayor Angelo J. Rossi and Fascism." In *Italian Immigrants Go West: The Impact of Locale on Ethnicity*, edited by Janet E. Worrall, Carol Bonomo Albright, and Elvira G. Di Fabio, 124–33. Cambridge, MA: American Italian Historical Association, 2003.

Luparini, Alessandro. *Anarchici di Mussolini: Dalla sinistra al fascismo, tra rivoluzione e revisionismo*. Montespertoli: M. I. R., 2001.

Mahler, Raphael. "The Economic Background of Galician Jewish Emigration to the United States." *YIVO Annual of Jewish Social Science* 7 (1952): 255–67.

Malatesta, Errico. *The Method of Freedom: An Errico Malatesta Reader*. Edited by Davide Turcato. Translated by Paul Sharkey. Oakland: AK, 2014.

Malato, Charles. *Les joyeusetés de l'exil*. 2nd ed. 1897; Mauléon, France: Acratie, 1985.

Marazzi, Martino. "Lacrime e libertà: Profilo di Ludovico Michele Caminita." *Nuova prosa* 50 (2009): 105–28.

Margolis, Rebecca E. "A Tempest in Three Teapots: Yom Kippur Balls in London, New York, and Montreal." In *The Canadian Jewish Studies Reader*, edited by Richard Menkis and Norman Ravvin, 141–63. Calgary, Alberta, Canada: Red Deer, 2004.

Marmor, Kalmon. *Yosef Bovshover*. New York: Kalmon Marmor yubiley-komitet, 1952.

Marsh, Margaret S. *Anarchist Women, 1870–1920*. Philadelphia: Temple University Press, 1981.

Marshall, Peter. *Demanding the Impossible: A History of Anarchism*. London: HarperCollins, 1992.

Maryson, J. A. "Der ershter period fun der anarkhistisher bavegung." In *M. Katts Zamelbukh*, edited by A. Frumkin and Khaym Faynman, 30–33. Philadelphia: Merts, 1925.

———. *Di teorie un praktik fun anarkhizm*. New York: Naye Gezelshaft un Ferrer Senter Brentches fun Arbayter Ring, 1927.

Maserati, Ennio. *Gli anarchici a Trieste durante il dominio Asburgico*. Milan: Giuffrè, 1977.

Masini, Pier Carlo. "Gli anarchici italiani tra 'interventismo' e 'disfattismo rivoluzionario.'" *Rivista Storica del Socialismo*, no. 5 (1959): 208–211.

———. *Storia degli anarchici italiani da Bakunin a Malatesta (1862–1892)*. Milan: Rizzoli Editore, 1969.

———. Storia degli anarchici italiani nell'epoca degli attentati. Milan: Rizzoli Editore, 1981.

Mason, Gregory. "Industrial War in Paterson." *The Outlook*, June 7, 1913.

McCormick, Charles H. *Hopeless Cases: The Hunt for the Red Scare Terrorist Bombers*. Lanham: University Press of America, 2005.

McGirr, Lisa. "The Passion of Sacco and Vanzetti: A Global History." *Journal of American History* 93, no. 4 (March 2007): 1085–1115.

Mendelsohn, Ezra. *Class Struggle in the Pale: The Formative Years of the Jewish Workers' Movement in Tsarist Russia*. Cambridge: Cambridge University Press, 1970.

———. "The Russian Roots of the American Jewish Labor Movement." *YIVO Annual of Jewish Social Science* 16 (1976): 150–77.

Menes, Abraham. "The *Am Oylom* Movement." *YIVO Annual of Jewish Social Science* 4 (1949): 9–33.

Merithew, Caroline Waldron. "Anarchist Motherhood: Toward the Making of a Revolutionary Proletariat in Illinois Coal Towns." In *Women, Gender, and Transnational Lives: Italian Workers of the World*, edited by Donna R. Gabaccia and Franca Iacovetta, 217–46. Toronto: University of Toronto Press, 2002.

Messer-Kruse, Timothy. *The Haymarket Conspiracy: Transatlantic Anarchist Networks*. Urbana: University of Illinois Press, 2012.

Meyer, Gerald. "Italian Americans and the American Communist Party." In *The Lost World of Italian American Radicalism: Politics, Labor, and Culture*, edited by Philip V. Cannistraro and Gerald Meyer, 205–27. Westport, CT: Praeger, 2003.

Michels, Tony. *A Fire in Their Hearts: Yiddish Socialists in New York*. Cambridge: Harvard University Press, 2005.

Miller, Scott. *The President and the Assassin: McKinley, Terror, and Empire at the Dawn of the American Century*. New York: Random House, 2011.

Minor, Robert. "I Change My Mind a Little." *The Liberator*, October 1920.

———. "Russia—The World's Greatest Labor Case." *New York Call*, September 14, 1919.

Mintz, Frank. *Anarchism and Workers' Self-Management in Revolutionary Spain*. Translated by Paul Sharkey. Oakland: AK, 2013.

Moisseiff, Leon. "M. Katts—Der faraynigender element in der bavegung." In *M. Katts Zamelbukh*, edited by A. Frumkin and Khaym Faynman, 39–42. Philadelphia: Merts, 1925.

Monaco, F. "San Francisco Shoe Workers' Strike." *International Socialist Review*, May 1913.

Moore, Deborah Dash. *At Home in America: Second Generation New York Jews*. New York: Columbia University Press, 1981.

Morton, James F., Jr. *The Curse of Race Prejudice*. New York: the Author, 1906.

Most, Mel. "A Modest Place in History." *Bergen Sunday Record*, September 1, 1973.

Murray, Robert K. *Red Scare: A Study in National Hysteria, 1919–1920*. Minneapolis: University of Minnesota Press, 1955.

Nadell, Pamela S. "From Shtetl to Border: East European Jewish Emigrants and the 'Agents' System, 1868–1914." In *Studies in the American Jewish Experience*, edited by Jacob R. Marcus and Abraham J. Peck, 2:49–77. Lanham, MD: University Press of America, 1984.

Nascimbene, Adalberto. *Il movimento operaio lombardo tra spontaneità e organizzazione (1860–1890)*. Milan: SugarCo, 1976.

Nash, Mary. *Defying Male Civilization: Women in the Spanish Civil War*. Denver: Arden, 1995.

Nathans, Benjamin. *Beyond the Pale: The Jewish Encounter with Late Imperial Russia*. Berkeley: University of California Press, 2004.

Nedava, Joseph. "Abba Gordin: Portrait of a Jewish Anarchist." *Soviet Jewish Affairs* 4, no. 2 (1974): 73–79.

Nelles, Dieter. "Deutsche Anarchosyndikalisten und Freiwillige in anarchistischen Milizen im Spanischen Bürgerkrieg." *Internationale wissenschaftliche Korrespondenz zur Geschichte der deutschen Arbeiterbewegung* 33, no. 4 (1997): 500–519.

Nelson, Bruce C. *Beyond the Martyrs: A Social History of Chicago's Anarchists, 1870–1900*. New Brunswick: Rutgers University Press, 1988.

Nettlau, Max. *Anarchisten und Sozialrevolutionäre: Die historische Entwicklung des Anarchismus in den Jahren 1880–1886*. 1931; Vaduz, Liechtenstein: Tropos, 1981.

New York. Legislature. Joint Legislative Committee to Investigate Seditious Activities. *Revolutionary Radicalism: Its History, Purpose, and Tactics with an Exposition and Discussion of the Steps Being Taken and Required to Curb It*. 4 vols. Albany, NY: Lyon, 1920.

Newspaper Directory and Advertisers' Manual. Detroit: Savage, 1907.

Ngai, Mae M. *Impossible Subjects: Illegal Aliens and the Making of Modern America*. Princeton: Princeton University Press, 2004.

Nichols, Francis H. "The Anarchists in America." *The Outlook*, August 10, 1901.

Nomad, Max. "The Anarchist Tradition." In *The Revolutionary Internationals, 1864–1943*, edited by Milorad M. Drachkovitch, 57–92. Stanford: Stanford University Press, 1966.

———. *Dreamers, Dynamiters, and Demagogues: Reminiscences*. New York: Waldon, 1964.

Notehelfer, F. G. *Kōtoku Shūsui: Portrait of a Japanese Radical*. Cambridge: Cambridge University Press, 1971.

Osborne, James D. "Italian Immigrants and the Working Class in Paterson: The Strike of 1913 in Ethnic Perspective." In *New Jersey's Ethnic Heritage: Papers Presented at the Eighth*

Annual New Jersey History Symposium, edited by Paul A. Stellhorn, 10–34. Trenton: New Jersey Historical Commission, 1978.

Ostergaard, Geoffrey. "Resisting the Nation-State: The Pacifist and Anarchist Traditions." In *The Nation-State: The Formation of Modern Politics*, edited by Leonard Tivey, 171–96. New York: St. Martin's, 1981.

Ostuni, Maria Rosaria. *La diaspora politica dal biellese*. Milan: Electa, 1995.

Ottanelli, Fraser. "Anti-Fascism and the Shaping of National and Ethnic Identity: Italian American Volunteers in the Spanish Civil War." *Journal of American Ethnic History* 27, no. 1 (Fall 2007): 9–31.

———. *The Communist Party of the United States: From the Depression to World War II*. New Brunswick: Rutgers University Press, 1991.

The Pageant of the Paterson Strike. New York: [Industrial Workers of the World], 1913.

"Pageant of the Paterson Strike." *The Survey*, June 28, 1913.

Pagès i Blanch, Pelai. *War and Revolution in Catalonia, 1936–1939*. Translated by Patrick L. Gallagher. Leiden, Holland: Brill, 2013.

Palij, Michael. *The Anarchism of Nestor Makhno, 1918–1921: An Aspect of the Ukrainian Revolution*. Seattle: University of Washington Press, 1976.

Panofsky, Gianna S. "A View of Two Major Centers of Italian Anarchism in the United States: Spring Valley and Chicago, Illinois." In *Italian Ethnics: Their Languages, Literature, and Lives*, edited by Dominic Candeloro, Fred L. Gardaphé, and Paolo A. Giordano, 271–96. Staten Island: American Italian Historical Association, 1990.

Park, Robert E. *The Immigrant Press and Its Control*. New York: Harper, 1922.

Parmet, Robert D. *The Master of Seventh Avenue: David Dubinsky and the American Labor Movement*. New York: New York University Press, 2005.

Peirats, José. *The CNT in the Spanish Revolution*. Edited by Chris Ealham. Translated by Paul Sharkey and Chris Ealham. 3 vols. Hastings, East Sussex, UK: Meltzer Press/ ChristieBooks, 2001–6.

Pernicone, Nunzio. *Carlo Tresca: Portrait of a Rebel*. Rev. ed. Oakland: AK, 2010.

———. *Italian Anarchism, 1864–1892*. Princeton: Princeton University Press, 1993.

———. "Murder under the 'El': The Greco-Carillo Case and the Fascist League of North America." *Italian American Review* 6, no. 2 (Autumn 1997–Winter 1998): 20–45.

Perrier, Hubert. "L'Union républicaine de langue française et les sections françaises de l'Association Internationale des Travailleurs aux États-Unis (1868–1876)." In *Les Français des Etats-Unis: D'hier à aujourd'hui*, edited by Ronald Creagh, 297–332. Montpellier, France: Espaces 34, 1994.

Perry, Jeffrey B. *Hubert Harrison: The Voice of Harlem Radicalism, 1883–1918*. New York: Columbia University Press, 2009.

Pesotta, Rose. *Bread upon the Waters*. Edited by John Nicholas Beffel. New ed. New York: ILR, 1987.

Podshivalov, Igor. *Siberian Makhnovshchina: Siberian Anarchists in the Russian Civil War (1918–1924)*. Translated by Malcolm Archibald. Edmonton, Alberta: Black Cat, 2012.

Polenberg, Richard. *Fighting Faiths: The Abrams Case, the Supreme Court, and Free Speech*. New York: Penguin, 1987.

Polland, Annie. "'May a Freethinker Help a Pious Man?': The Shared World of the 'Religious' and the 'Secular' among Eastern European Jewish Immigrants to America." *American Jewish History* 93, no. 4 (December 2007): 375–407.

Post, Louis F. *The Deportations Delirium of Nineteen-Twenty: A Personal Narrative of an Historic Official Experience.* Chicago: Kerr, 1923.

Pour la liberté de pensée violée. n.p.: Marcus Graham Freedom of the Press Committee, Section Française, 1939.

Poyo, Gerald E. "The Anarchist Challenge to the Cuban Independence Movement, 1885–1890." *Cuban Studies* 15, no. 1 (Winter 1985): 29–42.

Pratt, Norma Fain. "Culture and Radical Politics: Yiddish Women Writers, 1890–1940." *American Jewish History* 70 (September 1980): 68–90.

Preston, William, Jr. *Aliens and Dissenters: Federal Suppression of Radicals, 1903–1933.* New York: Harper and Row, 1963.

Pritchett, Wendell E. *Brownsville, Brooklyn: Blacks, Jews, and the Changing Face of the Ghetto.* Chicago: University of Chicago Press, 2003.

Prpić, George J. *South Slavic Immigration in America.* Boston: Twayne, 1978.

Puri, Harish K. *Ghadar Movement: Ideology Organization and Strategy.* 2nd ed. Amritsar, India: Guru Nanak Dev University, 1993.

Radkey, Oliver H. *The Unknown Civil War in Soviet Russia: A Study of the Green Movement in the Tambov Region, 1920–1921.* Stanford, CA: Hoover Institution Press, 1976.

Ramella, Franco. "Across the Ocean or over the Border: Expectations and Experiences of Italians from Piedmont in New Jersey and Southern France." In *Distant Magnets: Expectations and Realities in the Immigrant Experience, 1840–1930*, edited by Dirk Hoerder and Horst Rössler, 105–25. New York: Holmes and Meier, 1993.

———. *Terra e telai: Sistemi di parentela e manifattura nel Biellese dell'Ottocento.* Turin, Italy: Einaudi, 1984.

Ramnath, Maia. *Decolonizing Anarchism: An Antiauthoritarian History of India's Liberation Struggle.* Oakland: AK, 2012.

———. *Haj to Utopia: How the Ghadar Movement Charted Global Radicalism and Attempted to Overthrow the British Empire.* Berkeley: University of California Press, 2011.

Ravage, M. E. *An American in the Making: The Life Story of an Immigrant.* Edited by Steven G. Kellman. New Brunswick: Rutgers University Press, 2009.

Reed, John. *Ten Days That Shook the World.* New York: Boni and Liveright, 1922.

Reisen, Zalman. *Leksikon fun der yidisher literatur, prese, un filologye.* 4 vols. Vilnius, Lithuania: Kletskin, 1926.

Rigazio, Francesco. "Alberto Guabello, Firmino Gallo, e altri anarchici di Mongrando nella catena migratori dal biellese a Paterson N.J." *Archivi e storia* 23–24 (2004): 143–258.

Rigola, Rinaldo. *Rinaldo Rigola e il movimento operaio nel Biellese: Autobiografia.* Bari, Italy: Gius. Laterza & Figli, 1930.

Rischin, Moses. *The Promised City: New York's Jews, 1870–1914.* Cambridge: Harvard University Press, 1962.

Rivkin, B. "The Distinguishing Characteristics of Yiddish Literature." Translated by Sam Schwartz. *Direction* 1, no. 3 (February 1937): 91–105.

———. *Grunt-tendentsn fun der yidisher literatur in Amerike*. Edited by Mina Bordo-Rivkin. New York: Ikuf, 1948.

Rocker, Rudolf. *The London Years*. Translated by Joseph Leftwich. 1956; Oakland: AK, 2005.

———. *Nationalism and Culture*. Translated by Ray E. Chase. Los Angeles: Rocker Publications Committee, 1937.

———. *The Tragedy of Spain*. New York: Freie Arbeiter Stimme, 1937.

Roediger, David R. "Gaining a Hearing for Black-White Unity: Covington Hall and the Complexities of Race, Gender, and Class." In *Towards the Abolition of Whiteness: Essays on Race, Politics, and Working Class History*, 127–76. New York: Verso, 1994.

———. *Working toward Whiteness: How America's Immigrants Became White*. New York: Basic Books, 2005.

Rosenbaum, Fred. *Cosmopolitans: A Social and Cultural History of the Jews of the San Francisco Bay Area*. Berkeley: University of California Press, 2009.

Rosenberg, Abraham. *Di klokmakher un zeyere yunyons: Erinerungen*. New York: Klok Opereytors Yunyon Lokal 1, 1920.

Rosenberg, Karen. "The Cult of Self-Sacrifice in Yiddish Anarchism and Saul Yanovsky's *The First Years of Jewish Libertarian Socialism*." In *Yiddish and the Left*, edited by Gennady Estraikh and Mikhail Krutikov, 178–94. Oxford: Oxford University Press, 2001.

Sakovich, Maria. "When the 'Enemy' Landed at Angel Island." *Prologue*, Summer 2009. http://www.archives.gov/publications/prologue/2009/summer/angel.html.

Salerno, Salvatore. "*I Delitti della Razza Bianca* (Crimes of the White Race): Italian Anarchists' Racial Discourse as Crime." In *Are Italians White? How Race Is Made in America*, edited by Jennifer Guglielmo and Salvatore Salerno, 111–23. New York: Routledge, 2003.

———. Introduction to *Direct Action and Sabotage: Three Classic IWW Pamphlets from the 1910s*, edited by Salvatore Salerno, 1–18. Chicago: Kerr, 1997.

———. *Red November, Black November: Culture and Community in the Industrial Workers of the World*. New York: State University of New York Press, 1989.

Salvemini, Gaetano. *Italian Fascist Activities in the United States*. Edited by Philip V. Cannistraro. New York: Center for Migration Studies, 1977.

Sanders, Ronald. *The Downtown Jews: Portraits of an Immigrant Generation*. New York: Harper and Row, 1969.

Sanger, Margaret R. "The Paterson Strike." In *The Revolutionary Almanac: 1914*, edited by Hippolyte Havel, 47–49. New York: Rabelais, 1914.

Saxton, Alexander. *The Indispensable Enemy: Labor and the Anti-Chinese Movement in California*. Berkeley: University of California Press, 1971.

Schappes, Morris U. "The Political Origins of the United Hebrew Trades, 1888." *Journal of Ethnic Studies* 5, no. 1 (Spring 1977): 13–44.

Schmidt, Michael, and Lucien van der Walt. *Black Flame: The Revolutionary Class Politics of Anarchism and Syndicalism*. Oakland: AK, 2009.

Schneiderman, Rose, and Lucy Goldthwaite. *All for One*. New York: Eriksson, 1967.

Schulman, Elias. "Di 'Varhayt.'" In *Zamlbukh likhvoyd dem tsvey hundert un fuftsiksn yoyvl fun der yidisher prese, 1686–1936*, edited by Jacob Shatsky, 197–211. New York: Amopteyl fun YIVO, 1936.

Schwartz, Stephen. *Brotherhood of the Sea: A History of the Sailors' Union of the Pacific, 1885–1985*. New Brunswick, NJ: Transaction, 1986.

———. From West to East: California and the Making of the American Mind. New York: Free Press, 1998.

Scott, James C. *The Art of Not Being Governed: An Anarchist History of Upland South Asia*. New York: Yale University Press, 2009.

Scranton, Philip B. "An Exceedingly Irregular Business: Structure and Process in the Paterson Silk Industry, 1885–1910." In *Silk City: Studies on the Paterson Silk Industry, 1860–1940*, edited by Philip B. Scranton, 35–72. Newark: New Jersey Historical Society, 1985.

Seller, Maxine. "The Uprising of the Twenty Thousand: Sex, Class, and Ethnicity in the Shirtwaist Makers' Strike of 1909." In *"Struggle a Hard Battle": Essays on Working Class Immigrants*, edited by Dirk Hoerder, 280–303. DeKalb: Northern Illinois University Press, 1986.

Sensi-Isolani, Paola A. "Italian Radicals and Union Activists in San Francisco, 1900–1920." In *The Lost World of Italian American Radicalism: Politics, Labor, and Culture*, edited by Philip V. Cannistraro and Gerald Meyer, 189–203. Westport, CT: Praeger, 2003.

Serge, Victor. *Memoirs of a Revolutionary*. Translated by Peter Sedgwick. 1963; Iowa City: University of Iowa Press, 2002.

Shaffer, Kirwin R. *Black Flag Boricuas: Anarchism, Antiauthoritarianism, and the Left in Puerto Rico, 1897–1921*. Urbana: University of Illinois Press, 2013.

———. "Cuba Para Todos: Anarchist Internationalism and the Cultural Politics of Cuban Independence, 1898–1925." *Cuban Studies* 31 (2000): 45–75.

Shannon, Deric, Anthony J. Nocella, and John Asimakopoulos, eds. *The Accumulation of Freedom: Writings on Anarchist Economics*. Oakland: AK, 2012.

Shkliarevsky, Gennady. *Labor in the Russian Revolution: Factory Committees and Trade Unions, 1917–1918*. New York: St. Martin's, 1993.

Shor, Francis. "'Virile Syndicalism' in Comparative Perspective: A Gender Analysis of the IWW in the United States and Australia." *International Labor and Working-Class History* 56 (Fall 1999): 65–77.

Shtupler, Benyamin. "Tsvey pionern fun der revolutsionerer arbeter-bavegung in Bialistok." In *Natsyonale un politishe bavegung bay yidn in Byalistok (materyal tsu der geshikhte)*, edited by Herman Frank, D. Klementinowski, and Zeydl Khabatski, 47–55. New York: Gezelshaft far geshikhte fun Byalistok, 1951.

Shuldiner, David P. *Of Moses and Marx: Folk Ideology and Folk History in the Jewish Labor Movement*. Westport, CT: Bergin and Garvey, 1999.

Shuyao. "History of Meizhou Gongyi Tongmeng Zonghui (Unionist Guild of America)." Translated by Him Mark Lai. *Chinese America: History and Perspectives*, January 1, 2008.

Sigal, Jacob, ed. *Kropotkin-zamlbukh*. Buenos Aires: Grupe Dovid Edelshtat, 1947.

Skirda, Alexandre. *Nestor Makhno, Anarchy's Cossack: The Struggle for Free Soviets in the Ukraine, 1917–1921*. Translated by Paul Sharkey. Oakland: AK, 2004.

Skowronek, Stephen. *Building a New American State: The Expansion of National Administrative Capacities, 1877–1920*. New York: Cambridge University Press, 1982.

Solomon, Clara Freedman. *A Memoir: Some Anarchist Activities in New York in the 'Thirties and 'Forties*. [Los Angeles]: Clara Freedman Solomon Memorial Gathering, 2001.

Solotaroff, Hillel. *Geklibene shriften.* Edited by Joel Entin. 3 vols. New York: Dr. H. Solotaroff Publication Committee, 1924.

Sorenson, Jay B. *The Life and Death of Soviet Trade Unionism, 1917–1928.* New York: Atherton, 1969.

Sorin, Gerald. *The Prophetic Minority: American Jewish Immigrant Radicals, 1880–1920.* Bloomington: Indiana University Press, 1985.

Soyer, Daniel. "Cockroach Capitalists: Jewish Contractors at the Turn of the Twentieth Century." In *A Coat of Many Colors: Immigration, Globalism, and Reform in the New York City Garment Industry,* edited by Daniel Soyer, 91–113. New York: Fordham University Press, 2005.

———. *Jewish Immigrant Associations and American Identity in New York, 1880–1939.* Cambridge: Harvard University Press, 1997.

Spivak, Joseph. "Der lebnsveg fun Yankev Eybrams." In *Y. Eybrams-bukh (dos lebn un shafn fun an eygnartike perzenlekhkeyt),* 9–19. Mexico City: Yidishn kultur-tsenter, 1956.

Starr, Dennis J. *The Italians of New Jersey: A Historical Introduction and Bibliography.* Newark: New Jersey Historical Society, 1985.

Sterba, Christopher M. *Good Americans: Italian and Jewish Immigrants during the First World War.* Oxford: Oxford University Press, 2003.

St. John, Rachel. *Line in the Sand: A History of the Western U.S.-Mexico Border.* Princeton: Princeton University Press, 2012.

Stolberg, Benjamin. *Tailor's Progress: The Story of a Famous Union and the Men Who Made It.* Garden City, NY: Doubleday, Doran, 1944.

"Story of an Anarchist Group." *New York Sun,* December 9, 1906.

Stowe, Harriet Beecher. *Onkel Tom's kebin; oder, Di shvartse shklaven in Amerika.* Translated by J. Jaffa. New York: Hibru Publishing Kompany, 1911.

Street, Richard Steven. *Beasts of the Field: A Narrative History of California Farmworkers, 1769–1913.* Stanford: Stanford University Press, 2004.

Strypyansky, Max. "Non-Conformists of the Russian Revolution." *Soviet Russia,* July 1921.

Szajkowski, Zosa. *Jews, Wars, and Communism.* 2 vols. New York: Ktav, 1972.

Sznaider, Natan. *Jewish Memory and the Cosmopolitan Order.* Cambridge, UK: Polity, 2011.

Tcherikower, Elias. *The Early Jewish Labor Movement in the United States.* Translated by Aaron Antonovsky. New York: YIVO, 1961.

———. *Di ukrainer pogromen in yor 1919.* New York: YIVO, 1965.

Thompson, Fred, and Jon Bekken. *The I.W.W.: Its First One Hundred Years, 1905–2005.* Cincinnati: Industrial Workers of the World, 2006.

Thorpe, Wayne. *"The Workers Themselves": Revolutionary Syndicalism and International Labour, 1913–1923.* Boston: Kluwer Academic, 1989.

Tinchino, John J. *Edmondo Rossoni: From Revolutionary Syndicalism to Fascism.* New York: Lang, 1991.

Tirabassi, Maddalena. "La Mazzini Society (1940–1946): Un'associazione degli antifascisti italiani negli Stati Uniti." In *Italia e America dalla grande guerra a oggi,* edited by G. Spini, G. G. Migone, and M. Teodori, 141–58. Venice: Marsilio, 1976.

Tomasi, Silvano M. *Piety and Power: The Role of the Italian Parishes in the New York Metropolitan Area, 1880–1930.* New York: Center for Migration Studies, 1975.

Topp, Michael Miller. *Those without a Country: The Political Culture of Italian American Syndicalists*. Minneapolis: University of Minnesota Press, 2001.

Torpey, John. *The Invention of the Passport: Surveillance, Citizenship, and the State*. Cambridge: Cambridge University Press, 2000.

Un trentennio di attività anarchica (1915–1945). Cesena, Italy: L'Antistato, 1953.

Tresca, Carlo. *The Autobiography of Carlo Tresca*. Edited by Nunzio Pernicone. New York: Calandra Italian American Institute, 2003.

Tripp, Anne Huber. *The I.W.W. and the Paterson Silk Strike of 1913*. Chicago: University of Chicago Press, 1987.

Tsuzuki, Chushichi. "Anarchism in Japan." *Government and Opposition* 5, no. 4 (Autumn 1970): 501–22.

Tunney, Thomas J. *Throttled! The Detection of the German and Anarchist Bomb Plotters*. New York: Small, Maynard, 1919.

Turcato, Davide. "The 1896 London Congress: Epilogue or Prologue?" In *New Perspectives on Anarchism, Labour, and Syndicalism: The Individual, the National, and the Transnational*, edited by David Berry and Constance Bantman, 110–25. Newcastle upon Tyne, England: Cambridge Scholars, 2010.

———. "European Anarchism in the 1890s: Why Labor Matters in Categorizing Anarchism." *Working USA* 12, no. 3 (September 2009): 451–66.

———. "Italian Anarchism as a Transnational Movement, 1885–1915." *International Review of Social History* 52 (2007): 407–45.

———. *Making Sense of Anarchism: Errico Malatesta's Experiments with Revolution, 1889–1900*. New York: Palgrave Macmillan, 2012.

Turner, Ethel Duffy. *Revolution in Baja California: Ricardo Flores Magón's High Noon*. Edited by Rey Devis. Detroit: Ethridge, 1981.

Urofsky, Melvin I. *American Zionism from Herzl to the Holocaust*. Garden City, NY: Doubleday, 1975.

U.S. Commission on Industrial Relations. *Industrial Relations: Final Report and Testimony Submitted to Congress by the Commission on Industrial Relations*. 11 vols. Washington, DC: U.S. Government Printing Office, 1916.

U.S. Congress. *H.R. 8631: A Bill for the Relief of Vincenzo Ferrero*. 75th Cong., 2nd sess., 1938. In *Unpublished U.S. House of Representatives Committee Hearings*, 75 HIm-T.107 and 75 HIm-T.108. Bethesda, MD: Congressional Information Service, 1988.

U.S. Congress. House. Committee on Immigration and Naturalization. *Communist Labor Party Deportation Cases*. Washington, DC: U.S. Government Printing Office, 1920.

U.S. Congress. House. Committee on Rules. Attorney General A. Mitchell Palmer on Charges Made against Department of Justice by Louis F. Post and Others: Hearings before the Committee on Rules, 66th Congress, 3rd Session. Washington, DC: U.S. Government Printing Office, 1920.

U.S. Immigration Commission. *Reports of the Immigration Commission*. 41 vols. Washington, DC: U.S. Government Printing Office, 1911.

Vecoli, Rudolph J. "'Free Country': The American Republic Viewed by the Italian Left, 1880–1920." In *In the Shadow of the Statue of Liberty: Immigrants, Workers, and Citi-*

zens in the American Republic, 1880–1920, edited by Marianne Dobouzy, 23–44. Urbana: University of Illinois Press, 1992.

———. "The Making and Un-Making of the Italian American Working Class." In *The Lost World of Italian American Radicalism: Politics, Labor, and Culture*, edited by Philip V. Cannistraro and Gerald Meyer, 51–75. Westport, CT: Praeger, 2003.

———. *The People of New Jersey*. Princeton, NJ: Van Nostrand, 1965.

———. "Prelates and Peasants: Italian Immigrants and the Catholic Church." *Journal of Social History* 2, no. 3 (Spring 1969): 217–68.

———. "'Primo Maggio' in the United States: An Invented Tradition of the Italian Anarchists." In *May Day Celebration*, edited by Andrea Panaccione, 55–83. Venice: Marsilio, 1988.

Vega, Bernardo. *Memoirs of Bernardo Vega: A Contribution to the History of the Puerto Rican Community in New York*. Edited by César Andreu Iglesias. Translated by Juan Flores. New York: Monthly Review Press, 1984.

Venturi, Franco. *Roots of Revolution: A History of the Populist and Socialist Movements in Nineteenth Century Russia*. Translated by Francis Haskell. New York: Grosset and Dunlap, 1960.

"Vercellesi, biellesi, e valsesiani volontari antifascisti in Spagna: Biografie." *Istituto per la storia della Resistenza e della società contemporanea nelle province di Biella e Vercelli*, n.d. http://www.storia900bivc.it/pagine/spagna/biospagna.html.

Voline [V. M. Eikhenbaum]. *The Unknown Revolution, 1917–1921*. Edited by Holley Cantine and Fredy Perlman. Montreal: Black Rose, 1990.

Von Hagen, Mark. *Soldiers in the Proletarian Dictatorship: The Red Army and the Soviet Socialist State, 1917–1930*. Ithaca, NY: Cornell University Press, 1990.

Wade, Rex A. *Red Guards and Workers' Militias in the Russian Revolution*. Stanford: Stanford University Press, 1984.

Weber, Devra. "Keeping Community, Challenging Boundaries: Indigenous Migrants, Internationalist Workers, and Mexican Revolutionaries, 1900–1920." In *Mexico and Mexicans in the Making of the United States*, edited by John Tutino, 208–35. Austin: University of Texas Press, 2012.

Weil, Patrick. *The Sovereign Citizen: Denaturalization and the Origins of the American Republic*. Philadelphia: University of Pennsylvania Press, 2012.

Weinberg, Chaim. *Forty Years in the Struggle: The Memoirs of a Jewish Anarchist*. Edited by Robert P. Helms. Translated by Naomi Cohen. Duluth, MN: Litwin, 2008.

Whitaker, Stephen B. *The Anarchist-Individualist Origins of Italian Fascism*. New York: Lang, 2002.

Whitten, Woodrow C. "Criminal Syndicalism and the Law in California: 1919–1927." *Transactions of the American Philosophical Society* 59, no. 2 (1969): 3–73.

Wong, Jane Mee. "Pingshe: Retrieving an Asian American Anarchist Tradition." *Amerasia Journal* 34, no. 1 (2008): 133–51.

Woodcock, George. *Anarchism: A History of Libertarian Ideas and Movements*. New York: Meridian, 1962.

Yanovsky, Saul. *Ershte yorn fun yidishn frayhaytlekhn sotsializm*. New York: Fraye Arbeter Shtime, 1948.

———. "Genose H. Zolotarov der frayhayts-pioner in der idisher arbeter bavegung in Amerika." In Hillel Solotaroff, *Geklibene shriftn*, edited by Joel Entin, 1:27–32. New York: Dr. H. Solotaroff Publication Committee, 1924.

———. *Der olef beys fun anarkhizmus*. New York: Radikal Riding Rum, 1902.

Yelensky, Boris. "25 Years of 'Free Society' Activity in Chicago." In *The World Scene from the Libertarian Point of View*, 90–94. Chicago: Free Society Group of Chicago, 1951.

———. *In sotsialn shturem: Zikhroynes fun der rusisher revolutsie*. Buenos Aires: Yidisher Ratsionalistisher Gezelshaft, 1967.

———. *In the Struggle for Equality: The Story of the Anarchist Red Cross*. Chicago: Alexander Berkman Aid Fund, 1958.

Yevzerov, Katherina. *Di froy in der gezelshaft*. New York: Grupe Zsherminal, 1907.

Young, William, and David E. Kaiser. *Postmortem: New Evidence in the Case of Sacco and Vanzetti*. Boston: University of Massachusetts Press, 1985.

Zaks, A. S. *Di geshikhte fun Arbayter Ring, 1892–1925*. 2 vols. New York: Natsionale Ekzekutiv Komite fun Arbeyter Ring, 1925.

Zhitlowsky, Kh. "Dr. Hillel Zolotarov un zayn natsionalistisher anarkhizm." In Hillel Solotaroff, *Geklibene shriftn*, edited by Joel Entin, 1:9–25. New York: Dr. H. Solotaroff Publication Committee, 1924.

Zimmer, Kenyon. "American Anarchist Periodicals Circulation Data, 1880–1940." 2014. https://www.academia.edu/7715169/American_Anarchist_Periodical_Circulation_Data_1880-1940.

———. "Positively Stateless: Marcus Graham, the Ferrero-Sallitto Case, and Anarchist Challenges to Race and Deportation." In *The Rising Tide of Color: Race, State Violence, and Radical Movements across the Pacific*, edited by Moon-Ho Jung, 128–58. Seattle: University of Washington Press, 2014.

———. "Premature Anti-Communists? American Anarchism, the Russian Revolution, and Left-Wing Libertarian Anti-Communism, 1917–1939." *Labor: Studies in Working-Class History of the Americas* 6, no. 2 (2009): 45–71.

Unpublished Sources

Altarelli, Carlo C. "History and Present Conditions of the Italian Colony of Paterson, N.J." Master's thesis, Columbia University, 1911.

Caminita, Ludovico. "Twenty Years of Experience in the Radical Movement." Unpublished manuscript, 1922. File 61–115, Old German Files, Records of the Federal Bureau of Investigation, Record Group 65, National Archives and Records Administration, College Park, Maryland.

Copp, John W. "The Role of the Anarchists in the Russian Revolution and Civil War, 1917–1921: A Case Study in Conspiratorial Party Behavior during Revolution." Ph.D. diss., Columbia University, 1992.

Cornell, Andrew. "'For a World without Oppressors': U.S. Anarchism from the Palmer Raids to the Sixties." Ph.D. diss., New York University, 2011.

Elwood, Sophie L. "The Roots and Results of Radicalism among Piedmontese Silk Workers, 1848–1913." Certificate of Advanced Study, Wesleyan University, 1988.

Goldberg, Harold Joel. "The Anarchists View the Bolshevik Regime, 1918–1922." Ph.D. diss., University of Wisconsin, 1973.

Hughes, Russia. "Lest This Be Lost." Unpublished manuscript, 1980. Copy in author's possession.

Kelly, Harry. "Roll Back the Years: Odyssey of a Libertarian." Unpublished manuscript, n.d. Emma Goldman Papers, Institute of International Studies, University of California, Berkeley.

Koenig, Brigitte Anne. "American Anarchism: The Politics of Gender, Culture, and Community from Haymarket to the First World War." Ph.D. diss., University of California, Berkeley, 2000.

Perry, Jeffrey B. "Hubert Harrison and Paterson: The Paterson Strike, the 'New Negro Movement,' the KKK, and Community Ties." Paper presented at the Paterson Silk Strike Centennial Conference. William Paterson University, 2013.

Sakovich, Maria. "Angel Island Immigration Station Reconsidered: Non-Asian Encounters with the Immigration Laws, 1910–1940." Master's thesis, Sonoma State University, 2002.

Shaffer, Ralph Edward. "Radicalism in California, 1860–1929." Ph.D. diss., University of California, Berkeley, 1962.

Sione, Patrizia. "Industrial Work, Militancy, and Migrations of Northern Italian Workers in Europe and in Paterson, New Jersey, 1880–1913." Ph.D. diss., State University of New York at Binghamton, 1992.

Struthers, Dave. "The World in a City: Transnational and Inter-Racial Organizing in Los Angeles, 1900–1930." Ph.D. diss., Carnegie Mellon University, 2010.

Tomchuk, Travis. "Transnational Radicals: Italian Anarchist Networks in Southern Ontario and the Northeastern United States, 1915–1940." Ph.D. diss., Queen's University, 2010.

Weintraub, Hyman. "The I.W.W. in California: 1905–1931." Master's thesis, University of California, Los Angeles, 1947.

Wilcox, Peter M. "These We Will Not Compromise: The 'Detroit' Industrial Workers of the World, 1908–1927." Master's thesis, San Diego State University, 1995.

Wilson, Peter Lamborn. "Brand: An Italian Anarchist and His Dream." Unpublished manuscript, 2003. Copy in author's possession.

Wisotsky, Isidore. "Such a Life." Unpublished manuscript, n.d. Joseph A. Labadie Collection, Special Collections Library, University of Michigan, Ann Arbor.

Wood, James Earl. "History of Labor in the Broad-Silk Industry of Paterson, New Jersey, 1872–1940." Ph.D. diss., University of California, Berkeley, 1941.

Zappia, Charles Anthony. "Unionism and the Italian American Worker: A History of the New York City 'Italian Locals' in the International Ladies' Garment Workers' Union, 1900–1934." Ph.D. diss., University of California, Berkeley, 1994.

Clay Frick, 31–32, 34, 55–56; imprisoned, 31, 35; and Lexington Avenue bomb, 42; on Mexican Revolution, 129; and Mooney-Billings case, 36, 137–38; and *Nationalism and Culture*, 195; and Joseph Peukert, 31; prison break attempt, 36, 108, 113; and Russian Revolution, 143, 160–62; in San Francisco, 88, 107–8; suicide of, 195, 201; and unemployed demonstrations, 41; on Universalists, 193; and World War I, 133, 135, 137, 139–40; and Yiddish, 22

Berlin India Committee, 133

Berner Street Club, 113

Bernshtayn, L., 218n31

Bernstein, Ethel, 150, 151, 152, 160

Bernstein, Rose, 142

Bertone, B., 85, 127

Bialystok, 115, 116, 208

Bianchi, Luigi, 61, 224n65

Biella (Italian province): anarchists in, 51, 53, 62, 72; labor movement in, 50–54, 55, 68, 118

Biennio Rosso, 12, 163, 198

Billings, Warren, 36, 99, 137–38

birth control, 44, 101, 108

Black International, 112–13

Blackwell, Alice Stone, 191

Blast, 101, 108–9, 137, 212; banned, 140–41; and World War I, 133, 135

Blecher, Abraham, 170

Bleikhman, I. S., 145

Blotto, Vittorio, 178

Bluestein, Abe, 185, 186, 199–200, 202, 203

Bluestein, Esther, 185

Bluestein, Mendel (Max), 168, 172, 185

Bobba, Romolo, 167, 212

Bocchini, Filippo, 165

Bollettino de L'Era Nuova, Il, 141, 160

Bollettino della Sera, Il, 178

Bolsheviks: anarchist critiques of, 146–47, 160–63, 180; and Russian anarchists, 145–46, 158–60, 193; and World War I, 130

bombings: Barcelona, 32, 34; Haymarket Affair, 3, 10, 20–21, 31; Lexington Avenue, 42; *Los Angeles Times*, 107; of 1919, 150–52, 158; Paterson, 82, 85; Russia, 115; Sacramento, 147; San Francisco, 136–37, 180, 246n75; Union Square, 41, 82; Wall Street, 152

Bombino, Michele, 137

Bonturi, Bruno, 198, 205

Borba, 115

Borghi, Armando, 166, 167, 180, 183, 184

Borochov, Ber, 40

Bovshover, Joseph, 21, 22, 31, 36

Braslavsky, Abba, 23–24

Braut, Bessie, 46

Brazil, 119

Bresci, Gaetano, 54, 60–61, 65, 66, 93

Bresci Circle, 40

Brodkin, Karen, 15

Brooklyn, 18, 22, 172, 186

Brown, John, 42

Brownsville (Brooklyn), 22, 32, 35, 42

Broyt un Frayhayt Group, 143, 220n95

Bruch, Giordano, 210

Buda, Mario, 152

Buford, 152, 156, 169

Bureau of Immigration, 151, 157. *See also* INS

Bureau of Investigation: and First Red Scare, 151–58; founded, 10; and *Man!*, 190; and Paterson anarchists, 146, 240n100; and San Francisco anarchists, 99, 110, 142; and Saul Yanovsky, 141

Butte Daily Bulletin, 161

Buwalda, William, 123–24

Caci, Filippo, 155, 158

Caffodio, Dominick, 180

Cahan, Abraham, 32

Cai Xian (Liu Zhongshi/Jonesie), 182, 183, 184

Caminita, Lucifero (Ludwig, Jr.), 74, 155

Caminita, Ludovico (Michele), 80–83; accused of spying, 155–56, 241n113; arrested, 83, 124, 153–54; and Joseph Define, 153; deportation threatened, 155; and *The Emancipator*, 94; and fascism, 178–79; and *La Jacquerie*, 154; and Mexican Revolution, 124–29; and *Il Minatore*, 179; and religion, 74; returns to Paterson, 129; and Carlo Tresca, 154–56; and Saul Yanovsky, 56

Canada: anarchists flee to, 77, 139–40, 158, 191; illegal immigration from, 157, 167, 205; Emma Goldman in, 207; Yiddish anarchists in, 114, 115

Canova, Amalia, 82–83, 154

Cánovas del Castillo, Antonio, 70, 122

Caplan, David, 107, 233n109

Cappiali, A., 97

Capuana, Vincenzo, 176

Carbone, Sperandio. *See* Bianchi, Luigi

Carnot, Marie François Sadi, 70

Caron, Arthur, 42

Carrington, Glenn (George Creighton), 186

Casas, Laurent, 94, 96, 231n5

Casassa, Vigna Antonio, 198
Castranova (Fascist), 178
Catholicism, 74–75
Cavedagni, Ersilia, 67, 69, 93, 226n103
Celler, Emanuel, 190
Centrone, Michele, 99; arrested, 99,
    137, 147–49; deported, 149, 158; and
    L'Emancipazione, 181; and Spanish Civil
    War, 199
Cerruti, Pietro, 198
Challenge, 203, 204
Chandra, Ram, 108, 142
Chavez, Marie, 42
Cheka, 159, 193
Chen Shuyao, 182, 183
Chernoe Znamia, 115, 117, 144
Chernyak, Maxim, 144, 159
Chernyshevsky, Nikolay, 19
Chesalkin, Gregory (George Nelson), 117
Chicago: anarchist newspapers in, 88, 92–93;
    International Anarchist Congress, 113; Ital-
    ian anarchists in, 50, 68, 178, 181; IWPA in,
    3; IWW in, 78, 80, 142; Yiddish anarchists
    in, 24, 107, 144
Chinese anarchists, 120, 182, 183
Chinese Exclusion Act, 10, 101
Chinese immigrants, 89, 101–3, 124, 125, 182
Chun, David, 183
Ciancabilla, Giuseppe, 58; arrested, 67, 92–93;
    and *L'Aurora*, 59, 70; death of, 93; in San
    Francisco, 88; on tactics, 58–61, 77
Cini, Francesco, 58
Circolo Comunista Anarchico Carlo Cafiero,
    49–50
Circolo di Coltura Operaia, 65, 87
Circolo Educativo Sociale, 177, 178
Circolo Instruzione e Diletto Edmondo De
    Amicis, 65, 87
Circolo Sociale e Filodrammatico, 64
citizenship: anarchist critiques of, 10–11, 28,
    72, 135, 191; attained by anarchists, 157, 166,
    167, 184; denaturalization, 148, 157, 194, 207
City Lights Bookstore, 212
Clarion, 193
Club Avanti, 40
CNT, 196–205, 249n176
CNT-FAI, 196–205, 249n176
Cogito, Ergo Sum, 94–95, 102
Cohen, Ida, 173
Cohen, Joseph J., 19; and Cold War, 209;
    and *Fraye Arbeter Shtime*, 162, 173, 183,
    185; on Haymarket Affair, 21; on interwar

anarchism, 167; on Shmuel Marcus, 174;
    and Max Nettlau, 158; and Radical Library
    Group, 34; and World War I, 133; on Saul
    Yanovsky, 32–33; on Yiddish anarchism, 47;
    on Yom Kippur balls, 26; on Zionism, 208
Cohen, Sam, 183
Cohen, Selma, 199, 202, 203
Cohen, Sophie, 86, 87
Cohn, Michael A., 21, 22; and Alexander Berk-
    man, 161, 195; and Communsim, 147, 161;
    death of, 208; and *Fraye Arbeter Shtime*,
    185; and *Free Society*, 91; and Great Depres-
    sion, 185; and International Revolutionary
    Congress, 113; on Pioneers of Liberty, 28;
    and Rudolf Rocker and Milly Witcop, 194;
    and Sacco-Vanzetti case, 174; and World
    War I, 133
Cold War, 206–7, 209–10
Colton, James, 206–7
Columbus, Christopher, 74
Cominetti, Battista, 55
Comintern, 1, 145, 161
Comité de Defensa y de Auxilio al Pueblo Es-
    pañol, 198
Commission on Industrial Relations, 102, 211
Committee for the Relief of Political Prisoners
    in Russia, 180
Communism, anarchist critiques of, 146–47,
    160–63, 176, 203, 210
Communist International (Comintern), 1, 145,
    161
Communist Party of Spain, 196, 201, 202
Communist Party USA: and AFANA, 176;
    anarchist members, 146; eclipses anarchist
    movement, 167; former anarchist members,
    161–62, 172; and Great Depression, 184; and
    ILGWU, 169–71; and IWW, 168; repres-
    sion of, 210; in San Francisco, 183, 189; and
    Spanish Civil War, 203–4
Como, Italy, 50, 51, 53
Confederación Nacional del Trabajo (CNT),
    196–205, 249n176
Congress of Industrial Organizations, 184, 186
conscription, 138–40, 207
Cook, Cassius V., 90
cooperatives, 33, 63
Corna, Joe, 78–79, 228n170
Corriere Biellese, 118
Corriere d'America, Il, 178
Corriere del Popolo, Il, 180
Cortese, Roberto, 82
cosmopolitanism: and antiracism, 71, 101–3;

and the Cold War, 207; and citizenship, 191; critiques of, 38–39, 131, 208; definition of, 7–8; in practice, 8–9, 86, 109, 193, 210–13; and Spanish Civil War, 199; and transnationalism, 111–12, 199; and World War I, 130, 135, 140, 183; and *yidishkayt*, 15–16, 27–28, 40–43, 48

Costa, Carlo, 42

Cravello, Antonio, 54

Cravello, Ernesta (Ernestina), 54, 66, 68, 69, 70, 73

Cravello, Vittorio: and Lega di Resistenza fra i Tessitori Italiani, 75; and Paterson Silk Strike of 1902, 77; and PLM, 125, 126, 128, 130; on silk dyers, 52

Crespi, Cesare, 90, 94

Criminal Syndicalism Law, 149

Cronaca Sovversiva: banned, 140–41, 164; and Michele Caminita, 80; and Michele Centrone, 99; founded, 78; and Mexican Revolution, 126, 128–29; on racialization of Italians, 71; and Russian Revolution, 146, 161; in Turin, 161; and World War I, 133, 134, 139

Cronache Rosse, 141

Cuba, 59, 167, 198, 210

Cuban anarchists, 40, 113, 121–22, 210

Cuban War of Independence, 121–22, 130, 134

Cullen, Countee, 188, 190, 191

Cultura Obrera, 126, 129

Cultura Proletaria, 197, 200, 202, 204

Current Events Club, 108

Czech anarchists, 3, 131, 233n9

Czolgosz, Leon, 10, 34, 67, 124

Dalboni, Carlo, 94–95

Damiani, Gigi, 7, 9

D'Andrea, Virgilia, 166, 180

Danielewicz, Sigismund, 89–90, 91, 105

Daughters of the American Revolution, 190

Dayal, Har, 105–6, 108, 120, 133, 142

de Cleyre, Voltairine, 173

Define, Joseph, 152–54, 240n100

De Leon, Daniel, 75, 81, 82

Delesalle, Paul, 78

Della Barile, Giovanni, 59

Dellinger, David, 211, 212

Demonstrator, 94

Department of Justice, 142, 154, 156–57

Department of Labor, 156–57. *See also* Perkin, Frances

deportation of anarchists: before 1919, 10; during First Red Scare, 148–49, 151–52, 156–58,

166, 169; during Second Red Scare, 210; from Soviet Union, 160

De Rango, Raffaele, 181

Despertar, El, 55, 122

Dewey, John, 190

Di Nardo, Giovanni, 76, 79

Di Prima, Diane, 212

Díaz, Porfirio, 94, 95, 124, 126

Dickstein, Ruth, 186, 201, 203

Dickstein, Zina, 186, 201, 203

Difesa, La, 179

Diritto, Il, 141

Doherty, Henry Jr., 85

Dolgoff, Esther, 199, 209

Dolgoff, Sam, 186, 204, 209

Domsky, Mary, 46–47, 142, 152, 160

Dorr, Jessey, 180

Dover Club, 178, 207

Dressmakers Trade Union Circle, 171–72

Dreyfus Affair, 38, 221n106

Dropkin, Celia, 44

Dubinsky, David, 171, 194, 201

Du Bois, W. E. B., 42, 190

Dumas, Michel, 77, 80, 84, 122–23

Dunbar, Paul Laurence, 188

Dundee Lake (Elmwood Park), 65

Durruti, Buenaventura, 198

Eastman, Max, 190

L'Écho de l'Ouest, 231n45

Edelman, John H., 41

Edelsohn, Rebecca, 43

Edelstadt, David: on African Americans, 42; and *Fraye Arbeter Shtime*, 24, 30; laborer, 18, 22, 29; poetry of, 23, 25; on tenement houses, 18; tuberculosis of, 18, 30, 31; on United States, 19, 20–21; on women, 43; and Yiddish, 22, 48

Edelstadt, Sarah, 43

L'Effort, 93, 123

Egoism, 90

Egypt, 65, 114, 119, 120

Eight Hour League, 83, 84

Eklund, Celsten, 246n75

Elia, Roberto, 156, 241n113

Elisabeth of Austria, 70

Ellis Island, 12, 150, 154, 155, 158

Emancipator, 94, 104

L'Emancipazione, 181–82, 183, 184, 187, 189

L'Enfant Terrible, 90

England: anarchists deported from, 95, 194; anarchists return to, 77, 131, 166, 173, 175;

general strike threatened, 157; Italian anarchists in, 119; Jewish immigrants in, 16, 20. *See also* London

English language: and Italian immigrants, 72–73; and Jewish immigrants, 27, 48; as a lingua franca, 8

English-language activism: deficiencies of, 9, 173, 175; growth of, 166; Italian anarchists and, 72–73; in San Francisco, 90, 108–9, 135, 187, 212; Vanguard Group and, 186–87; Yiddish anarchists and, 22, 41–43, 48, 114

Epstein, Melech, 209

L'Era Nuova: and anticolonialism, 130; antiracism of, 71–72; banned, 140–41; founded, 83; Emma Goldman on, 87; and international events, 112; and IWW, 83–85; and *La Jacquerie*, 154; Mexican Revolution, 126, 128–29; on nationalism, 73–74; and Paterson Silk Strike of 1913, 86; raided, 138; and Russian Revolution, 143; and World War I, 133–34, 139

L'Era Nuova Group, 83, 141, 152–56, 158, 240n100. *See also* Right to Existence Group

Espionage Act, 140–41, 147, 149, 158

Esteve, Pedro: and antifascism, 176–77; and Ludovico Caminita, 80; and Cuban War of Independence, 122, 126, 134; and *Cultura Obrera*, 126; and International Anarchist Congress (Chicago), 113; and Errico Malatesta, 59; and *Il Martello*, 177; and Mexican Revolution, 126, 129; and *La Questione Sociale*, 55, 57, 62, 78; and Maria Roda, 55, 69; in Tampa, 80, 126; and World War I, 134

Ethiopia, 121

Eyges, Thomas, 24

Eyntsiker, Der, 140, 142

Eyre, Eleanor, 183

factory committee movement (Russia), 144, 158–59, 162

FAI, 196–205, 249n176

Faiddi, Giovanni, 178

Faltsblat (anarchist), 218n31

Farber, Simon, 168, 170, 171

Farber, Sonia, 46

Farbiash, Isidore, 170

fascism: and Italian-Americans, 175, 178, 179, 207; in Italy, 163–64; in Spain, 168, 196; and World War II, 206. *See also* antifascism; Nazis

Fascist League of North America, 165

Federación Anarquista Ibérica (FAI), 196–205, 249n176

Federación Obrera Regional Argentina, 111

Federazione Socialista-Anarchica dei Lavoratori Italiani nel Nord-America, 57, 113

Federazione Socialista Italiana, 80, 96, 132, 165

Feinberg, Israel, 168, 171

Feinberg, Leon, 35

Ferdinand, Franz, 130

Ferlinghetti, Lawrence, 212

Ferrer i Guàrdia, Francisco, 33

Ferrero, Vincenzo: arrested, 137, 139, 181, 189–90; on Sam Cohen, 183; and *L'Emancipazione*, 181; goes underground, 191, 211; on International Group of San Francisco, 183; and Shmuel Marcus, 187; testifies before Congress, 190–91

Ferro, Gaspare, 69

filodrammatici, 63–64, 67, 68

Firebrand, 91

First International, 1; anarchists in, 6, 111, 112; Italian Federation, 49; in Paterson, 55; in San Francisco, 89

First Red Scare, 10, 12, 136; anarchists arrested in, 139–42, 147–51, 153–54; and Ludovico Caminita, 154–56; and decline of anarchism, 168, 172, 179, 182; deportations of, 151–52, 156–58

Fishelev, Michael, 239n61

Fleischmann, Leopold, 103

Fleshin, Senya, 160

Flores Magón, Ricardo, 126, 127–28

Flynn, Bina, 167, 212

Flynn, Elizabeth Gurley, 84, 156, 167

Flynn, William J., 155, 241n113

Folla, La, 154–55

Forverts, 33, 35, 36; and First Red Scare, 141; and ILGWU, 171; and Philippine-American War, 123; and Socialist Party of America, 47

Foster, William Z., 41

Fox, Jay, 41, 228n170

Fox, Lucy. *See* Lang, Lucy Robins

Frager, Jack, 186

France: Alexander Berkman in, 195; Italian anarchists in, 119, 164, 166, 176; Italian immigrants in, 50, 53, 55; syndicalism in, 78, 81; Vichy government, 205; and World War I, 131, 132; Yiddish anarchists in, 114, 115. *See also* Paris

Francis, David, 138

Francisco Ferrer Association (New York), 146

love, 45; and unemployed demonstrations, 41, 43; and World War I, 138
Garibaldi, Giuseppe, 129
Garibaldi Battalion, 198
garment workers: African American, 42–43; Chinese, 182, 187–88; Italian, 40; Jewish, 18–19, 29–30, 46–47, 168–72. *See also* ILGWU
Garside, Thomas Hamilton, 29–30
General Jewish Labor Bund, 115
Gentlemen's Agreement, 102, 104
Gerboth, Louise, 183
Gerekhtikayt, 168–69, 171
German anarchists: and Anarchist Federation of New York, 41; decline of, 4; and IWPA, 3; and Johann Most, 20, 31; in Paterson, 55–56, 75; in San Francisco, 89; and *Solidarity*, 40; women in, 43; and Yiddish anarchists, 20, 22
German immigrants, 20, 52, 576–77, 80, 89
Germany: Rudolf Rocker in, 194; and Spanish Civil War, 196; and World War I, 131, 132, 133, 142; and World War II, 205; Yiddish anarchists in, 114. *See also* Nazis
Germinal (Chicago), 178
Germinal (Paterson), 55, 77, 80, 122–23
Germinal Group (Paterson), 113
Germinal Group (San Francisco), 93, 94, 95
Ghadar, 106
Ghadar Party, 106, 108–9, 120; and Communism, 182; Hindu Conspiracy Trials, 142; and Mexican Revolution 126; and World War I, 133
Girdzshansky, Max, 21, 30–31
Glanz-Leyeless, A., 35, 44
Glatstein, Jacob, 35, 44
Globus, J., 185, 188
Gold, Mike (Itzok Granich), 140, 146, 172
Goldberg, Nathan, 24
Goldman, Emma, 2, 21, 22, 74; and Alexander Berkman, 31; arrested, 101, 140; and Enrico Arrigoni, 203; and Cánovas del Castillo, 122; citizenship of, 157, 206–7; and cloak makers' strikes, 29, 30; and Leon Czolgosz, 34; death, 208; deported, 152, 156; on Dreyfus Affair, 38; on First Red Scare, 148, 149; and free love, 45; and International Anarchist Congress (Amsterdam), 114, 116; and International Revolutionary Congress, 113, 233n9; on Italian and Spanish anarchists, 66; on Japanese anarchists, 104; on Jewishness, 7; and Shusui Kotoku,

119; and Johann Most, 22, 31–32, 43; and *Mother Earth*, 35, 41; in Paterson, 87; and Joseph Peukert, 31; on Philippine-American War, 123; and Pioneers of Liberty, 218n32; in Russia, 115, 160; and Russian Revolution, 145, 160, 161, 162; and Russian Revolution of 1905, 116; in San Francisco, 91, 107, 123; on Second Boer War, 124; and Spanish Civil War, 201; and World War I, 131, 133, 139, 140; and Yiddish, 22; on Yiddish anarchists, 43, 48, 210–11
Goldstein, David, 20
Golos Truda, 117, 143, 144, 146, 160
Goodfriend, Audrey, 45, 185, 186
Goodfriend, Gussie, 186
Goodfriend, Morris, 186
Goodman, Elizabeth, 185–86
Goodman, Joseph, 159
Goodman, Max, 56
Goodman, Paul, 211, 212
Goodman, Sara, 185–86
Goodwin, Robert C., 228n170
Gordin, Abba, 163, 192–93, 209, 248n142
Gordin, Jacob, 36
Gordin, Velvel, 192–93
Gori, Pietro, 57, 73, 111; on general strike, 75–76; on religion, 74; in San Francisco, 91, 94; and Second International, 113
Graham, Marcus. *See* Marcus, Shmuel
Granberg, Morris, 138
Grandi, Serafino, 53, 85, 146, 149, 153
Granich, Itzok. *See* Gold, Mike
Granotti, Luigi, 61
Grave, Jean, 8–9, 129, 131
Great Depression, 12, 179, 184
Greek immigrants, 94, 172
Grido degli Oppressi, Il, 50, 54, 56; on Christopher Columbus, 74; and free love, 68, 69; on Italian nationalism, 73; and Maria Roda-Balzarini, 66
Grido della Stirpe, Il, 165
Grosner, Abe, 185
Grosser, Philip, 140
Grossman, Rudolf, 77, 227n162
Groupe Socialiste-Révolutionnaire, 55, 112
Group Louise Michel, 101
Grupe Frayhayt (Paterson), 56
Grupe Frayhayt (San Francisco), 107, 108, 118
gruppi femminili, 68, 101
Gruppo Anarchico Volontà. *See* Volontà Group
Gruppo Augusto Spies, 54

Gruppo Diritto all'Esistenza. *See* Right to Existence Group

Gruppo Emancipazione della Donna, 62, 68–70

Gruppo Iconoclasti, 99

Gruppo i Risorti, 62

Gruppo Libertario, 197

Gruppo Propaganda Femminile, 62

Gruppo Socialista Anarchico "Pensiero ed Azione," 62

Gruppo Socialista-Anarchico-Rivoluzionario Italiano "Carlo Cafiero," 49

Gruppo Veritá, 62

Guabello, Adalgisa, 54, 67, 177

Guabello, Adele, 53

Guabello, Alberto, 51, 73; and antifascism, 177, 178; arrested, 53, 149, 153; and *L'Aurora*, 59; and Ludovico Caminita, 83; and *L'Era Nuova*, 83; and Adalgisa Guabello, 67, 177; and IWW, 79, 80, 84; migrations of, 53, 55; and *La Questione Sociale*, 57, 59; and syndicalism, 76

Guabello, Paolo, 53, 84–85, 153, 154, 177

Guabello, Spartaco, 54, 140

Guerrero, Práxedis, 95

Guglielmo, Jennifer, 67

Gutman, Joseph, 159

Gutman, Leah, 159

Hagerty, Thomas J., 228n170

Haledon, 77, 177, 178

Hanson, Carl, 42

Hapgood, Hutchins, 32, 45

Harkavy, Alexander, 27–28, 48, 195

Harlem, 33, 35, 37, 42, 141

Harrison, Hubert, 43, 71, 87

Hartz, Esther, 101

Haskalah, 17, 22, 24, 26

Haskell, Burnette, 89

Havel, Hippolyte, 119, 150, 165, 175, 233n9

Hawaii, 90, 92, 123

Haymarket Affair, 3, 10, 20–21, 31

Hays, Arthur Garfield, 190

Haywood, William (Big Bill), 84

Hicks, Granville, 190

Hill, Joe, 125

Hitler, Adolf, 188

Holocaust, 206, 208

Hoover, J. Edgar, 152, 153, 155, 241n113

Horr, Alexander, 107, 139, 182

Hourwich, Isaac, 24

House Committee on Immigration and Naturalization, 190–91

Hovevei Tsion, 27

Howe, Irving, 15, 42

Hughes, Langston, 188, 190

Hughes, Russia: on Aurora Alleva, 181; on anarchist culture, 99, 100–101; and Mark Lucca, 180; named for Russian Revolution, 146; and New Deal, 185; and World War II, 207–8

Hurwitz, Rachel, 159

ILGWU (International Ladies' Garment Workers' Union): anarchists in, 46–47, 118, 168–72; and antifascism, 176; Communists in, 169–72; Current Events Committee, 169; and Ferrero-Sallitto case, 190; founded, 46; legacy, 212; in San Francisco, 188; shop delegate leagues, 169; Socialists in, 46, 169–71; and Vanguard Group, 186; women in, 46–47, 172; Workers' Council, 169; and World War II, 207, 208

illegal aliens, 10, 148, 184, 190

illegal immigration, of anarchists, 157, 158, 166–67, 191, 205

immigration: and American working class, 2; and anarchism, 1–2, 13, 165; historiography of, 13

Immigration Act of 1924, 11–12, 165

Immigration and Naturalization Service (INS), 190–92

Independent Social Club, 178

India, 105, 120, 133

Indian immigrants, 101, 105–7. *See also* Ghadar Party

individualist anarchism, 58, 90, 95, 99, 132

Industrial Worker, 126–27

Industrial Workers of the World. *See* IWW

Inglis, Agnes, 174, 187

INS, 190–92. *See also* Bureau of Immigration

Insorti, Gli, 155, 158

International Anarchist Communist Federation, 41

International Anarchist Congress: Amsterdam, 114, 116, 233n9; Berlin, 173–74; Chicago, 113

International Anarchist Group of San Francisco, 135. *See also* International Group of San Francisco

"International Anarchist Manifesto on the War," 133

International Brigades, 198, 199. *See also* Abraham Lincoln Brigade

International Committee of the Mexican Liberal Junta, 125

International Federation of Chicago, 114
International Group of New York (1900s), 37, 220n95
International Group of New York (1920s), 174–75, 181, 187–88, 197
International Group of San Francisco, 183–84, 187–88, 197
International Ladies' Garment Workers' Union. *See* ILGWU
International Libertaire Club, 91
International Libertarian Committee against Fascism, 197–98
International Radical Club, 105
International Revolutionary Congress (Paris), 113–14
International Social Revolutionary Conference (London), 112
International Working Men's Association. *See* First International
International Working Men's Association (anarchist; Black International), 112–13
International Working Men's Association (Syndicalist International), 174, 194, 244n40
International Working People's Association. *See* IWPA
International Workmen's Association (IWA), 89–90
internationalism: and anticolonialism, 106, 112; and cosmopolitanism, 7; critiques of, 38; informal, 114; Italian anarchists and, 86, 91, 132; and World War I, 131, 132
L'Internazionale, 82
In Zikh, 35
Isaacson, Jack, 158
Isaak, Abe, 91, 92
Isaak, Mary, 91, 92
Israel, 40, 208–9
L'Italia, 179, 181
Italian Anarchist Club, 91
Italian anarchists, 2, 4–5, 12–13, 40, 62, 83, 119, 179; and African Americans, 70, 71; and antifascism, 163–67, 175–81, 197; and Associated Silk Workers, 177–78; atheism of, 68, 74–75, 98, 100; chain migration of, 53–54; cosmopolitanism of, 9, 73–74, 86; counterculture of, 62–65, 99; and Cuban War of Independence, 121–22; and ILGWU, 170–71; and *italianità*, 72–73; and IWW, 79, 80–81, 83–87, 96; and labor unions, 75–80, 96; and Mexican Revolution, 124–30; and mutual aid societies, 65–66; in New York City, 40, 41, 49, 56; return to Italy, 53, 163; and Sons

of Italy, 65, 85–86; and Spanish Civil War, 198–99, 202; transnationalism of, 2, 65, 118–19; on the United States, 70–72; women, 66–70, 91, 100–101, 181, 225n82; and World War I, 132–35, 140. *See also individual cities and groups*
Italian Communists, 176, 177–78, 180
Italian immigrants, 2; and Asian immigrants, 102; and Catholicism, 75; and English language, 72–73; and fascism, 175, 178–79, 207; gender roles, 51, 66–67; and Italian language, 64; and labor unions, 75–80, 96; as "Latins," 93–94; mutual aid societies of, 51, 65–66; national identity of, 64; naturalization of, 72; in New York City, 40; northern vs. southern, 51–52, 64, 78, 93; in Paterson, 49–53, 64–66, 75, 211; prejudice against, 71, 93–94, 102, 132; restriction of, 165; in San Francisco, 89, 93–94, 179–80; and whiteness, 11, 71, 93; and World War II, 207. *See also* Italian anarchists; silk workers
Italian Socialist Party, 53, 163
Italy: anarchism in, 49, 51, 53, 56–58, 163–64; anarchist critiques of, 73–74, 99–100, 134; fascism in, 163–64; invasion of Abyssinia, 121; invasion of Libya, 124, 132; and Spanish Civil War, 196; and World War I, 132, 134
IWA, 89–90
IWPA (International Working People's Association), 3; and Germans, 20; and Haymarket Affair, 3–4; and Black International, 113; and Italians, 49; in San Francisco, 89–90; and Yiddish anarchists, 21
IWW (Industrial Workers of the World): anarchists in, 79–81, 94, 102, 228n170; and Asians, 101–5, 120; and Communist Party, 168, 204; conventions, 79–82, 102; "Detroit IWW," 82, 83; free-speech fights, 87, 97–99, 124–25; in Fresno, 98, 104, 124–25; and Har Dayal, 105–6; and International Working Men's Assoc., 174, 244n40; Marine Transport Workers' Union, 197, 244n40; and Mexican Revolution, 124–28; and Mexicans, 124; mixed locals, 230n40; in New York, 47, 86; 1924 split, 168; in Paterson, 79–80, 83–87, 142, 152, 156; preamble of, 79–82; repression of, 142, 147–48; and Russian Revolution, 144; in San Francisco, 95–98, 107, 109, 125, 139–40; and SLP, 80–82; syndicalism of, 78; and ULO, 197; and UORW, 116–18; and Vanguard Group, 186; and "vir-

ile syndicalism," 79–80, 97, 102–3; women in, 79–80, 97; and World War I, 132, 139

Jacquerie, La, 74, 141
Jaffa, Joseph, 23, 42
Jagendorf, Moritz, 175
Japanese American internment, 206, 207–8
Japanese anarchists, 103–5, 119–20
Japanese and Korean Exclusion League, 101, 105
Jewish Anarchist Federation of America and Canada, 173; and Great Depression, 185; and *Road to Freedom*, 244n41; in San Francisco, 182, 183; and Spanish Civil War, 201; and ULO, 197
Jewish anarchists. *See* Yiddish anarchists
Jewish diasporism, 16, 27–28. See also *yidish-kayt*
Jewish Ethical Culture Society, 193
Jewish immigrants, 2, 15–19; culture of, 36–37; gender roles, 18, 43; and Judaism, 25–26; leave Lower East Side, 172; in Paterson, 56; in San Francisco, 89, 90, 107; and UORW, 117; and whiteness, 11, 42; women, 17, 18, 23, 41; and World War I, 132–33. *See also* garment workers: Jewish; Yiddish anarchists
Jewish Self-Education Group, 220n95
Jewish socialists. *See* Yiddish socialists
Jewish Times, 24
Jones, Red. *See* Cai Xian
Johnson, Albert (anarchist), 103
Johnson, Albert (congressman), 149
Johnson, Fenton, 188
Johnson, Georgia Douglas, 188
Johnson, James Weldon, 188
Joseph, Jacob, 25
Josephs, Philip, 114–15
Justice, 168–69

Kaganovich, Shleme, 115
Kaiser, David E., 240n100
Kakumei, 103–4
Kamf, Der, 115
Kantorovitch, Haim, 147
Kaplansky, H., 218n31
Kats, Mosheh, 147
Katts, Moyshe, and *Fraye Arbeter Shtime*, 24; on Jewishness, 26–27; and labor unions, 29; and Pioneers of Liberty, 21; playwright, 36; and Saul Yanovsky, 34; and Zionism, 38, 40
Katzes, Arthur, 150, 152
Keller, Elena, 159

Kelley, Robin D. G., 2
Kelly, Harry: and anarchist congresses, 112, 173; on Joseph J. Cohen, 173; and Cuban War of Independence, 122; and *Freedom*, 175; on Pietro Gori, 57; and Rachel Krimont, 41; and New Deal, 184–85; in Paterson, 87; and Russian Revolution, 160; and World War I, 131, 133
Kershner, Jacob, 157
Keyser, Dora, 43, 44, 45
Kirtzman, Nicholas, 168
Kishinev Pogrom, 38, 121
Klemencic, Andrew (Al), 91, 92, 102, 123, 228n170
Klotz, Harry, 152
Knights of Labor, 29, 75
Knights of Liberty, 20, 21, 24
Kobrin, Leon, 20
Kontrrazvedka, 159
Kopeloff, Isidore, 17, 21, 26, 38, 217n10
Korean anarchists, 120
Kotoku, Shusui, 103–5, 119–20
Koven, David, 101, 199
Kramer, Louis, 140
Krimont, Mary, 41
Krimont, Rachel, 41
Kronstadt, 160, 161, 193, 203
Kropotkin, Peter, 19; and anticolonialism, 120–21, 131, 134; and *antiorganizzatori*, 60; antiracism of, 7–8; death of, 159–60; on Dreyfus Affair, 38; and Emma Goldman, 104; and Shusui Kotoku, 103, 120; on Mexican Revolution, 129; on Russian Revolution, 159, 161; and World War I, 131, 134, 135; and Zionism, 121
Kropotkin Literary Society, 36
Ku Klux Klan, 71
Kushnarev, Theodore, 169

Lachowsky, Hyman, 147, 152
Land and Liberty, 106, 130, 131, 139
landsmanshaft, 37
Lanfranco, C. F., 85
Lang, Lucy Robins, 45, 107, 210
Larsen, Clara, 168
Lassalle, Ferdinand, 28–29
Latin anarchists, 88, 94–98, 119
Latvian anarchists, 41–42
Lavrov, Peter, 19
Leib, Mani, 35
Lenin, Vladimir, 145, 146–47, 161
Leopold II of Belgium, 60

Levy, Louis, 168
Lewis, Sinclair, 190
Libertarian Circle, 212
Libertarian League, 211
libertarian socialism, 1, 216n1
Liberty Group, 91
Libreria Sociologica, 63, 67, 118, 124, 146, 156
Libreria Sovversiva Italo-Spagnuola, 95
Lieb, Bertha, 45
Lipman, Samuel, 147, 152, 160
Little, Frank, 125
Liu Zhongshi. *See* Cai Xian
Lodz Ghetto, 208
London: anarchist congresses in, 112–14; Har
    Dayal in, 105; Italian anarchists in, 57–59,
    76, 111; Jewish immigrants in, 20; Yiddish
    anarchists in, 20, 32, 114–15, 168, 193–94
London, Ephraim, 23
London, Meyer, 23, 168
Los Angeles, 107, 124–25, 127, 140, 191
Los Angeles Times, 107
Lovestone, Jay, 172
Lower East Side: German immigrants in, 20;
    Jewish immigrants in, 15, 18, 21, 42, 172. *See*
    also New York City
Luca, Angelo, 180
Luca, Mark, 180, 207–8
Ludlow Massacre, 41–42
Luis, Roman, 21, 24, 29, 30
lynchings, 42, 71

Macario, Joseph, 101
MacQueen, William, 77
Madero, Francisco I., 128
Madrid, 196, 201, 203
Maisel, Max M., 36
Makhno, Nestor, 159, 173, 241n132
Maksimov, Grigorii Petrovich, 160, 167
Malatesta, Errico: on anarchism, 50, 212; and
    anticolonialism, 120; and Gaetano Bresci,
    60–61; and cosmopolitanism, 74; in Cuba,
    59, 123; and Pedro Esteve, 59; and Luigi
    Galleani, 76–77; on organization, 57–60; in
    Paterson, 59–60, 62; on propaganda by the
    deed, 62; and *La Questione Sociale*, 59, 74;
    on syndicalism, 114; on the United States, 72
Malato, Charles, 51
Malaysia, 120
Mallozzi, Domenico, 212
Malta, 119
Man!, 187–91, 204, 212; and International

Group of San Francisco, 183, 187; and Pal-
    estine, 192; and Spanish Civil War, 197, 201,
    203–4
"Manifesto of the Sixteen," 131
Marchese, Giuseppe, 138, 139
Marcus, Shmuel (Robert Parsons/Marcus Gra-
    ham), 174, 187; and *Anarchist Soviet Bulle-
    tin*, 150, 157, 173; *Anthology of Revolutionary
    Poetry*, 188, 191; arrested, 150; and deporta-
    tion, 157–58, 191–92, 212; on *Fraye Arbeter
    Shtime*, 173; and *Free Society*, 162, 173; and
    Man!, 187–89, 204; on Robert Minor, 162;
    on Russian Revolution, 162; on violence,
    174, 188–89; and World War II, 207
Margarita, Ilario, 205
Margolin, Ana, 35, 44
marriage. *See* free love
Martello, Il, 141; and Ludovico Caminita,
    154–56; and Pedro Esteve, 177; and Luigi
    Parenti, 164; in Paterson, 177; and Russian
    Revolution, 146, 161; in San Francisco, 180;
    and Spanish Civil War, 197; and Vanguard
    Group, 186; and World War II, 207
Martí, José, 121–22
Martin, Peter, 212
Martorelli, Giuseppe, 139
Marx, Karl, 6, 23
Marxism, 19, 60, 89, 128–29, 145
Maryson, Jacob, 34–36, 40; and the *Fraye Ar-
    beter Shtime*, 24, 147; and *Varhayt*, 27; and
    Katherina Yevzerov, 21
Maryson, Katherina. *See* Yevzerov, Katherina
May Day, 56, 63, 182, 212
May Days (Barcelona), 202–3, 204, 250n181
Mazzinianism, 6, 51, 75
Mazzini Society, 178
Mazzotta, Beniamino, 72, 153–54, 156–57, 177,
    241n113
McCarthyism, 210
McDevitt, William, 107
McKay, Claude, 188
McKinley, William: assassination, 10, 34, 56,
    62, 92; and wars, 122–24
Mechanic, Julie, 228n170
Meizhou Gongyi Tongmeng Zonghui, 182
Mello, Gemma, 68, 141
Menicucci, Umberto, 165
Merlino, Francesco Saverio, 40, 68
Messaggero, Il, 90
Mexicali, 125–26, 128
Mexican Americans, 124, 125

Mexican anarchists, 4, 9, 94, 112, 183. *See also* Partido Liberal Mexicano

Mexican immigrants, 93, 95, 104, 124

Mexican Revolution, 12, 13, 124–30, 167

Mexico, 94, 124–30, 140, 160, 167

Milan, 53, 60, 61

Milano, Edoardo, 57, 63

Militant Anarchist Youth, 186

Military Intelligence Division, 152, 166

Millay, Edna St. Vincent, 191

Minatore, Il, 179

Minkin, Helene, 41

Minor, Robert, 108, 143, 161–62

Mintz, Samuel, 93

Mirsky, Rose, 168

Modern Schools, 33–34, 42, 56, 65

Moisseiff, Leon, 19, 172

Mongrando, Italy, 51, 53

Mooney, Rena, 137

Mooney, Tom, 36, 99, 108, 137–38

Montreal, 40

Monza, 60, 61

Morgan, Henry Lewis, 44

Morgenshtern, Der, 23

Morton, Eric B., 108, 113, 116

Morton, James F., Jr., 9

Mosby, Jack, 127, 128

Moscow Soviet, 193

Most, Helene. *See* Minkin, Helene

Most, Johann, 20, 28–29, 31; arrested, 34; and Emma Goldman, 22; and Helene Minkin, 41; and propaganda by the deed, 31, 55; on women, 43

Mother Earth: and Anarchist Federation of New York, 41; banned, 140–41; and Alexander Berkman, 108; and Ludovico Caminita, 124; and Ram Chandra, 108; on citizenship, 10–11; English audience of, 41; and Mexican Revolution, 126, 129; on Philippine-American War, 123; and Rebekah Raney, 101; in Russia, 115; on territorialism, 39; and World War I, 130, 133; and Yiddish anarchists, 35

Mother Earth Bulletin, 141

Mozzoni, Anna Maria, 69

Mratchny, Mark, 159, 167, 185, 199, 204–5

Mujeres Libres, 196

Mussolini, Benito, 143, 163–64, 175–76, 178, 181

Nabat Confederation of Anarchist Organizations, 159, 167

Nadelman, Morris, 37, 143

Nathan-Ganz, Edward, 112

National Association for the Advancement of Colored People, 42

nationalism: American, 207; anarchist critiques of, 6–7, 73–74, 99–100, 134, 192–95; and anticolonialism, 120–21, 130; Indian, 106; and internationalism, 106; Italian, 132, 164–65. *See also* anticolonialism; cosmopolitanism; fascism; territorialism; Zionism

Nationalism and Culture (Rocker), 194–95

national liberation struggles. *See* anticolonialism

National Recovery Act, 187, 247n117

Naturalization Act of 1906, 10–11

Nayer Gayst, Der, 27

Nazis, 188–89, 194, 205, 206, 207

Negro, Bartolomeo Bertoldo, 63

Netter, A. Jacob, 21

Netter, Anna, 21, 29, 43

Nettlau, Max, 158, 184

New Deal, 184–85, 187, 190

New Economic Policy, 145, 163

New Jersey, politics of, 72

New Left, 211, 212

New Orleans, 158, 167

New York City: African Americans in, 42; Italian immigrants in, 40, 49–50, 56, 175–76, 178; Jewish immigrants in, 17, 37; raids on UORW, 151; Russian immigrants in, 116, 143; Spanish immigrants in, 55, 56. *See also* Brooklyn; Brownsville; Harlem; Lower East Side

New York Evening World, 161

New York Herald, 56, 62, 68, 178

New York Sun, 75

New York Times, 66, 77, 209

New York World, 66, 178

Nicholas II of Russia, 126, 132, 141, 143

Nihil, 95, 99, 105

Nineteenth Century, 120–21

No-Conscription League, 139

Nolan, Edward, 137

Nomad, Max, 47

North Beach (San Francisco): anarchists in, 93–101, 105, 110; fascism in, 179; IWW in, 96–99; population of, 93, 102. *See also* San Francisco

Norwood, E., 106

Novatore, 132

Novomirskii, Daniil (Iakov Kirillovskii), 117, 145–46, 160, 234n30

Novorossiysk, 144
Nuovi Tempi, 141

Oakland, Calif.: Italian anarchists in, 93, 107,
181, 189; IWW in, 98, 103, 105, 139, 149; Ser-
bian anarchists in, 107
Oakland World, 98
Obici, Amedeo, 179
Occupy Wall Street, 212
Olay, Anna, 198
Olay, Maximiliano, 198
olef beys fun anarkhizmus, Der (Yanovksy),
34, 115
Order of the Sons of Italy in America, 65,
85–86, 178
organizzatori, 57–59, 61, 80, 93, 178
Origins of Totalitarianism, The (Arendt), 209
Osokin, Vladimir (Philip Ward), 117, 118
Ostergaard, Geoffrey, 5
Ostroff, Israel, 47, 168
Ottoman Empire, 114, 120, 124
Outlook, 49
Owen, William C., 106, 130, 131

Pacific Branch of the International Workmen's
Association, 89
Pacific Coast Hindi Association. *See* Ghadar
Party
Pagani, Ambrogio, 85
Palestine, 16, 27, 39, 141, 192
Palmer, A. Mitchell, 149, 151
Panunzio, Constantino, 180
Parenti, Elpidio, 100, 146
Parenti, Luigi: arrested, 97, 137, 139; and Mi-
chele Centrone, 99; cosmopolitanism of,
109–10; death of, 242–43n162; and fascism,
164; and IWW, 96–97, 142; and Elpidio
Parenti, 100; "voluntary repatriation" of,
142
Paris: anarchists in, 58, 113, 117, 193, 208; exiles
in, 160, 164, 199, 233n109; International
Revolutionary Congress, 113–14; as radical
hub, 89, 95, 116, 120
Park, Robert E., 35–36
Parker, Dorothy, 190
Parsons, Lucy, 228n170
Partido Liberal Mexicano (PLM), 94, 98, 106,
124–30, 131
Partido Obrero de Unificación Marxista
(POUM), 202–3
Paterson, N.J.: antifascism in, 176–78; Catho-
lic Church of, 75; fire and flood of 1902,

76; and First Red Scare, 142, 150, 152–56;
French anarchists in, 55; German anarchists
in, 55–56; Italian anarchists in, 9, 49–54, 62,
87, 118, 211; Italian population of, 50, 56, 65;
IWW in, 79–80, 83–87, 142, 152, 156; mayor
of, 82; 1919 bombing, 152, 158; silk industry
in, 49, 50–53, 76; Sons of Italy in, 65; and
Umberto I, 61–62; and World War I, 138–39,
149; Yiddish anarchists in, 24, 56. *See also*
Italian anarchists; Italian immigrants; silk
workers
Paterson Philosophical Society, 71, 87
Paterson Silk Strikes: of 1902, 49, 76–77; of
1913, 13, 49, 83–87, 127
Paterson Strike Pageant, 86
Pazzaglia, Domenico, 60
Perkins, Frances, 190
Pernicone, Nunzio, 113
Perrone, Filippo, 98, 128–29, 158
Peru, 119
Pesotta, Rose: anti-Communism of, 169; and
ILGWU, 168–69, 171; and International
Group of New York, 174; and National Re-
covery Act, 187, 247n117; relationships of,
45; and Rudolf Rocker and Milly Witcop,
194; in San Francisco, 187–88; and Spanish
Civil War, 201; and UORW, 118; and World
War II, 207, 208
Pessina, Giuseppe, 61, 75
Petrel, 93
Petrograd, 138, 144, 146, 159
Petrograd Soviet, 145
Peukert, Joseph, 31, 228n170
Philadelphia: Ludovico Caminita in, 82; Yid-
dish anarchists in, 20, 24, 34, 139, 150
Philippine-American War, 123–24
Piccinini, Carinda (Cari), 97, 99, 100–101, 207
Piccinini, Mario, 99, 100–101, 137, 180, 207
Piccinini, Russia. *See* Hughes, Russia
Piedmont Club, 64
Pingdeng, 182, 184, 187
Pingshe, 182, 187–88
Pioneers of Liberty, 21–26, 27, 28–30, 41,
218n31
Pirani, Alberico, 140, 167
Pironi, Nicola, 72
Pirozzi, Nicola, 65
Pitea, Antonio, 65–66
Pitea, Francesco, 65–66, 177
Pitea, Jacques, 65–66
Pittsburgh, 3, 82, 89, 141, 143
PLM, 94, 98, 106, 124–30, 131

Plunkett, Charles, 41, 42
Poale Zion, 40
pogroms, 16, 17, 38, 121, 159, 241n132. *See also* anti-Semitism
Poland, 7, 16
Polish anarchists, 183
Ponderano, Vittorio, 85
Popular Front: in Spain, 196, 198, 201, 203; in United States, 184, 204
Port Sudan, 119
Portugal, 196, 204
Post, Louis F., 156–57
Post Office, 82, 108, 140–41, 158, 173
Pouget, Émile, 78
POUM, 202–3
Poylisher Yidl, Der, 20
Pravda, 144
Prenner, Isidore, 21, 22, 30
Preparedness Day bombing, 136–37, 180
Problemot/Problemen, 209, 211
Progressive Union of Silk Workers, 75
Progressive Women's Society, 56
Proletario, Il, 164
prominenti, 75, 175, 179
propaganda by the deed: and International Social Revolutionary Conference, 112; Italian anarchists and, 57, 58, 60–62, 95; Japanese anarchists and, 103, 119; Yiddish anarchists and, 28, 31–32, 34, 103
Protagoras, 187
Protesta Humana, La, 91, 92, 93, 99
Proudhon, Pierre-Joseph, 27, 90
Puerto Rican anarchists, 40, 123

Quazza, Emma, 61
Questione Sociale, La, 55, 56–57, 76, 82; on African Americans, 70, 71; on anarchist congresses, 112; and anticolonialism, 121–22; and Ludovico Caminita, 56, 80, 82; and Giuseppe Ciancabilla, 58–59; and Pedro Esteve, 55, 57, 62, 78; and Luigi Galleani, 65, 76–78; and Pietro Gori, 57, 111; and Italian identity, 64, 72–75; on Italian nationalism, 73–74; and IWW, 78–80; and Lega di Resistenza, 75; and Errico Malatesta, 50, 59; on mutual aid societies, 65, 66; and Philippine-American War, 123; on propaganda by the deed, 61–62, 122; on syndicalism, 75–76, 78–80; on United States, 70–72; and Franz Widmar, 62; women and, 67, 69–70
Quintavalle, Nicola, 61, 66

racism, anarchist critiques of, 8–9; Italian, 70–72, 134–35; Rudolf Rocker's, 195; in San Francisco, 101–6, 188; Yiddish, 42
Radical Library Group, 34, 150
Radinowsky, Isaac, 197
Raevsky, Maksim (L. Fishelev), 117, 146, 239n61
Ramella, Tony, 63
Ramnath, Maia, 7
Raney, Rebekah (Reb), 101
Ravage, Marcus, 19, 25, 43
Ravarini, Eugenio, 240n100
Raveggi, Luigi, 92
Rebel Youth, 186
Recchioni, Emidio, 176, 178
Reclus, Élisée, 8, 90
Red Army, 144, 159, 205
Red Guards, 138, 144, 146
Red International of Labor Unions, 169
Red Scare. *See* First Red Scare; McCarthyism
Reed, John, 138
Refrattario, Il, 141
Regeneración: banned, 140–41; and Ludovico Caminita, 124, 129; and Mexican Revolution, 125–26, 128; and William C. Owen, 106
Resettlement Administration, 185
Resistance Group, 211
Revolt, 119
Rexroth, Kenneth, 212
Rey y García, Manuel (Louis Raymond), 175
Ricco, Matteo, 177
Right to Existence Group, 54, 55, 70, 83; and Luigi Bianchi, 224n65; and Ludovico Caminita, 83; and education, 65; and *L'Era Nuova*, 83; and IWW, 79; and *La Questione Sociale*, 56, 58, 59; and syndicalism, 78; and Umberto I, 61. *See also* L'Era Nuova Group
Rigola, Rinaldo, 51, 55
Riordan, John, 228n170
Rising Youth, 185
Rising Youth Group, 185–86
Rivkin, B. (Barukh Weinrebe), 28, 36, 37, 118, 186
Rivkind, Victor, 116
Rivolta degli Angeli, La, 74
Riz, Camillo Rosazza, 83
Road to Freedom, 174–75, 244n41
Robins, Bob, 107
Robins, Lucy. *See* Lang, Lucy Robins
Rocca, Massimo (Libero Tancredi), 132, 134, 164
Rockefeller, John D., 42

Rocker, Rudolf: and *Arbayter Fraynd*, 115; cosmopolitanism of, 193–94; *Nationalism and Culture*, 192, 194–95; and Russian Revolution, 161; and Spanish Civil War, 201; and World War II, 207; and Zionism, 208
Roda-Balzarini, Cesare, 51, 53–54
Roda-Balzarini, Maria (Maria Roda): in Como, 51; and Pedro Esteve, 55, 59, 69; and Gruppo Emancipazione della Donna, 68; in Milan, 53–54; in Paterson, 66; in Tampa, 56
Rodo, 104
Rodriguez, Armando, 205
Romania, 16–17, 19, 150
Rome, 118, 164, 176
Romero Palacios, Rafael, 56
Roosevelt, Eleanor, 194
Roosevelt, Franklin, 206
Roosevelt, Theodore, 10, 82, 123
Rosati, Domenico, 198, 205
Rosenfeld, Morris, 23
Rossi, Angelo, 179
Rossoni, Edmondo, 132, 164
Rothman, Sara, 168
Rovaldi, Fred, 98, 127
Rubino, Antonio, 65
Rüdiger, Helmut, 197
Russia, 16–17, 19, 114–16, 132–34. *See also* Soviet Union
Russian anarchists, 4, 19; and Mooney-Billings case, 138; in New York, 41; and Russian Revolution, 138, 143–46, 159–60; in San Francisco, 107–8, 182–83; and Yiddish anarchists, 114–18. *See also* UORW
Russian Federation of Anarchist Communists of the United States and Canada, 173
Russian Federation of the Socialist Party, 143
Russian Progressive Union, 19, 21
Russian provisional government, 143, 145, 162
Russian Revolution (1917): anarchist critiques of, 160–63; anarchists in, 138, 143–46; and First Red Scare, 136, 147; and *Fraye Arbeter Shtime*, 141, 146–47; initial anarchist views of, 143, 146–47
Russian Revolution of 1905, 12, 13, 93, 115–16, 192
Russian Social Democratic Labor Party, 115. *See also* Bolsheviks
Russo, Joe, 163
Russo-Japanese War, 103
Ryan, Albert, 228n170
Rygier, Maria, 132, 134

sabotage, 78
Sacco, Nicola, 2, 140
Sacco-Vanzetti case: and anarchist movement, 99, 168, 174, 180–81; and Ludovico Caminita, 156; and Wall Street bombing, 152
Sachs's Café, 36
Sacramento, 147–48
Saffores, Basil, 96, 97, 147–48
Saints Peter and Paul Catholic Church, 98, 246n75
Sakutaro, Iwasa, 119
Salerno, Salvatore, 228n170, 240n100
Sallitto, Domenico, 181, 183, 189–91, 211
Salsedo, Andrea, 156
Salvemini, Gaetano, 180
Salvino, Lora, 77
San Diego, Calif., 90, 127
Sanfanshi Gongyi Tongmeng Zonghui, 182
San Francisco: African Americans in, 188; anarchist groups in, 91–93, 107–9, 179–80, 182, 211–12; anarchist newspapers in, 88; anarchist population of, 88–89, 179; fascism in, 211; First Red Scare in, 137–39, 147, 149, 179; free-speech fight of 1911, 97–100; Great Depression in, 179; immigrant population of, 88–89; IWW in, 95–96; UORW in, 117. *See also* North Beach (San Francisco)
San Francisco Chronicle, 98
San Francisco Earthquake (1906), 94, 103
San Francisco Examiner, 110
San Francisco Freethought Society, 91, 103
San Francisco General Strike, 188
San Francisco Labor College, 189
San Francisco Labor Council, 94, 101
Sanger, Margaret, 84, 87
Scali, Giuseppe, 137, 149
Schiavina, Raffaele (Max Sartin), 166–67, 184, 188
Schicchi, Paolo, 163
Schirru, Michele, 176
Schmidt, Mark, 186, 204
Schmidt, Matthew, 107
Schmuckler's Café, 36–37
Schneider, Joseph, 168
Schneiderman, Rose, 46
Schwartz, Jacob, 147
Scopa, La, 177, 178
Scott, James C., 7
Scottsboro Boys, 188
Scranton, 179
Scuola Moderna Francesco Ferrer (Paterson), 56, 65, 87, 154, 156

Syndicat des Ouvriers Blanchisseurs Français de San Francisco, 97

Takahashi, T., 104
Tamaroglio, Giovanni, 62–63
Tampa, 56, 80, 126
Tancredi, Libero. *See* Rocca, Massimo
Tannenbaum, Frank, 41
Tarbell, Ida B., 190
Tcherikower, Elias, 241n132
Teatro Sociale, 68
Tefilah zakah, 25
Tel Aviv, 209
Temps Nouveaux, Le, 113–14, 123, 129
tenement houses, 18–19
Termini, Joseph. *See* Define, Joseph
Terra, La, 94
territorialism, 39–40
Tetsugoro, Takeuchi, 104
Third International (Comintern), 1, 145, 161
Thomas, Norman, 190
Thorne, Ahrne, 28
Tijuana, 98, 126–28, 129, 140
Toilers of the World, 97
Tokyo, 103, 120
Tori, Louis, 137, 140, 148
Toronto, 140, 142, 208
Trade Union Educational League, 169
Transvaal Republic, 124
Trautmann, William E., 79
Travaglio, Enrico (Eugene): and China, 90, 120; on Chinese immigrants, 102; and Giuseppe Ciancabilla, 92–93; Esther Hartz on, 101; and *Secolo Nuovo*, 90–91; and *La Terra*, 94
Travaglio, Sylvia, 90
Tresca, Carlo: and antifascism, 175–76; and *L'Avvenire*, 82; and Ludovico Caminita, 154–56; citizenship of, 157; and ILGWU, 170–71; and *Il Martello*, 141; and Peter Martin, 212; and Paterson Silk Strike of 1913, 84; and Spanish Civil War, 198, 201, 203–4; and unemployed demonstrations, 41; and Vanguard Group, 186; and World War I, 141; and World War II, 207
Triangle Shirtwaist Company Factory, 47
Trieste, Italy, 55, 91, 95
Troiani, Gaetano, 139
Trombetta, Domenico, 132, 165
Trotsky, Leon, 143, 145, 146, 239n61
Tua, Camillo, 63
Tucker, Benjamin, 90

Tunisia, 59, 76, 119
Turcato, Davide, 118
Turin, 51, 65, 163, 166
Turkestan-Siberia Railway, 146

UHT, 29–30
Ukraine, 116, 144, 159
ULO, 197, 203–4
Umanità Nova (Rome), 118, 164, 177
Umanità Nova (New York), 176–77
Umberto I of Italy: assassination of, 49, 60, 63, 75, 113; attempted assassination of, 61; memorial service for, 65
Uncle Tom's Cabin (Stowe), 42
Unemployed Councils, 184
unemployed demonstrations, 41, 43
Unione fra Tessitori e Tessitrici di Lingua Italiana, 78, 79
Unione Sindicale Italiana, 164
Union of Anarcho-Syndicalist Propaganda, 144
Union of Russian Toilers, 172, 197. *See also* UORW
Union of Russian Workers of the United States and Canada. *See* UORW
Union of Soviet Socialist Republics (USSR). *See* Soviet Union
Union of the Oppressed Five, 193
United Brotherhood of Carpenters, 99
United Dyers, Helpers, and Finishers of America, 76, 79
United Front, 176, 177, 184
United Garment Workers Union, 30
United Hat and Cap Makers' Union, 46
United Hebrew Trades, 29–30
United Libertarian Organizations, 197, 203–4
United Mine Workers, 78–79
United Silk Workers of America, 76, 77
United Silk Workers of Hudson County, 75
United States government. *See* U.S. government
United Trade Unions of New York and Vicinity, 30
United Workingmen's Organizations of America, 29
UNITE-HERE, 212
Universalists (Russian anarchist group), 193
Università Popolare, 65
UORW (Union of Russian Workers of the United States and Canada), 116–17, 172; and *Anarchist Soviet Bulletin*, 150; Jews in, 117; government suppression of, 151–52; and

Yartchuk, Khaym (Efim), 117, 145, 160
Yelensky, Boris, 118, 144, 160, 208
Yevzerov, Katherina, 21, 35, 36, 43, 44
Yiddish anarchists, 4–5, 15, 114; and AFL, 30; decline of, 172–73, 210–11; and Dreyfus Affair, 38; and education, 33–35; and German anarchists, 8, 20; and Great Depression, 185; and ILGWU, 46–47, 168–72; *intelegentn*, 21–22, 36; and IWW, 47, 86; on Jewishness, 24, 26–28, 42; and Judaism of, 16, 24–26, 193; and Kishinev Pogrom, 38–39; on labor unions, 28–29, 33; in London, 20, 32, 114–15, 168, 193–94; and Nestor Makhno, 159; and Johann Most, 31–32; newspapers of, 4–5, 43, 210; and non-Jewish radicals, 40–43; in Palestine, 192; in Paterson, 56; in Philadelphia, 20, 24, 34, 139, 150; return to Russia, 138, 143, 147, 159; "rooted cosmopolitans," 9, 16; and Russian anarchists, 114–18; and Russian Revolution (1917), 144–46; and Russian Revolution of 1905, 115–16; in San Francisco, 89–90, 107, 182–83; and territorialism, 38–40; women, 43–46, 172, 199; and World War I, 132–33, 141–42; and World War II, 207–8; and Yiddish culture, 35–37; and Yiddish language, 16, 22–23, 210; and *yidishkayt*, 15–16; and Zionism, 16, 38, 167, 172, 192, 208–9

Yiddish language, 15–16, 20, 22–23, 27, 208; and second-generation immigrants, 172, 186
Yiddish socialists, 23–24, 29–30, 46, 47, 169–72
Yiddish Writers' Club, 36
yidishkayt, 15–16, 28, 40, 48, 210
Yom Kippur balls, 24–25
Young, William, 240n100
Yudelevitsh, M., 218n31
Yugoslav League of Independent Socialists, 107
Yunge, Di, 35
Yunge Odler, Di, 186
Yunyon Arbayter, Der, 169–70
Yunyon Tsaytung, Di, 30
Yuster, Rose, 41

Zapata, Emiliano, 128, 129
Zhitlowsky, Chaim, 39, 40
Zionism, 12, 13, 16, 40, 167; anarchist critiques of, 38, 121, 192, 208–10; and Balfour Declaration, 141, 172. *See also* territorialism
Zsherminal Group, 44, 220n95

KENYON ZIMMER is an assistant professor of history at the University of Texas at Arlington.

The University of Illinois Press
is a founding member of the
Association of American University Presses.

Composed in 11/13 Bulmer
with Solano Gothic display
by Jim Proefrock
at the University of Illinois Press
Manufactured by Sheridan Books, Inc.

University of Illinois Press
1325 South Oak Street
Champaign, IL 61820-6903
www.press.uillinois.edu